Deuteronomy

Moses' last Discourses

Peter Russell-Yarde

DEDICATION

To my dear wife of 59 years (married 30.12.1961) who has been
deprived of my company for many hours.

To the Lord God of Israel who provided all the inspiration.

PETER RUSSELL-YARDE

BOOKS PUBLISHED BY PETER
Kindle & Paperback Formats

Biblical Comment:
The Origin of Life : God's Relationship with Man in Genesis
God Rescues His People : Birth of Nation According to Exodus
The Wilderness Training School : Powerful Lessons in Numbers
Seeing Into the Future : Understanding the Revelation of John

Matters of Faith:
Are There Demons? & Other Matters of Faith
Letters to the Seven Churches in Revelation
Lost Souls : The danger of losing sight of God
Covenant & Testament : God's rules for God's people to obey
Belief and Faith : Understanding the Essentials
Ordinary People : Extra-ordinary faith
So You Think You Know About Faith : Learning to Trust God
The Path of Wisdom : A Study of Proverbs Chapters 1 to 4
A Fresh Look at Easter
You Will Receive Power
Assuredly God IS!
Christ IS King : A Guide for Doubters
Law & Grace (Lessons from the Kings of Judah & Israel)
Hosea
Truth & Doubt : A Study of Matthew 11

Autobiographical:
A Tale of Three Men (Provides background information about how these books came to be written and distributed)

What our faith is all about
The Tent of the Meeting : Illustrating God's Plan of Salvation

Except we study the Bible
With a receptive, prayerful mind,
We will never be able to find God,
We will never understand God,
Nor know the heart of God.

Except we are prepared
To open our hearts to God,
Receive Him fully into our lives,
And love Him completely,
We will never know God personally.

Except we tell Him we regret our sinfulness,
Repent of all our sins, asking for His forgiveness,
And commit ourselves and our lives to Him,
We will never know His peace,
Or be made alive spiritually.

Except the Holy Spirit enters into our hearts and lives,
We will have no contact with the Father,
Be unable to understand the word of God
Or be transformed by the
Renewing of our minds.

PREFACE

This book was commissioned by my dear friend Derek, a Jew who has taught me a great deal, and who in turn has been blessed by studying most of my growing library of books.

However daunting a task it may have at first appeared to be, I am indebted to him for 'encouraging me to get started on this book'. Deuteronomy is foundational to scripture as it is referenced throughout the First Testament and by Paul in his letters to the churches and studying it for this project has been an enormous blessing. Truth to say I have learned far more about the scriptures in general than I might otherwise have done, which is especially encouraging because the writer inevitably gains a very great spiritual understanding from the text because of the intensity of the preparatory study that writing a book such as this requires.

Certainly it is my hope that you, the reader, will gain a better grasp of the teaching contained in Deuteronomy than by merely reading the Biblical narrative and you will be encouraged to study it in depth.

The prayerful research that has gone into writing this book, has for me opened up the greatest Aladdin's cave of priceless, glittering Divinely inspired treasures that one could ever hope to find. I am so thankful to God for all the inspiration He has given to me, and the excitement in my spirit as I have delved ever deeper into the meaning of the Biblical text.

This is not a study of Deuteronomy in isolation! Rather it is a study of the text in relation to the complete Bible, because it seems that during my research studies God has pointed out to me that studying Deuteronomy in isolation would deprive the book of a considerable amount of valuable spiritual teaching.

Questions must be asked such as, "Why did God say that?" or "Why did God require that of His chosen people?" and for those questions to be to be answered to the satisfaction of the reader.

It has taken many hours of study and just as many hours of writing, reading through and rewriting.

As no editing, proof reading or any other checks have been done by others due to financial constraints, any mistakes in grammar and spelling that escaped scrutiny are all mine, therefore any sentence or paragraph that does not quite make sense, I own that error too.

However, with a treasure trove of spiritual knowledge contained within this book I hope that in generally terms its contents will be as much a blessing to you the reader as it has been to both me and Derek.

CONTENTS

ACKNOWLEDGMENTS

Derek, who first 'encouraged' me to write this book, and has been a continuing source of encouragement.

Caroline Oliveira for her very helpful advice

PETER RUSSELL-YARDE

INTRODUCTION

Deuteronomy is undoubtedly *the* most important book in the Old Testament as it is the foundational document for the relationship between the Israelites and their God. As the Messiah Yeshua said publicly that He had come to fulfil the law not abolish it, these discourses of Moses are essential reading material for all who call upon the name of the Lord God of Israel.

Unless we study this book carefully in order to understand the principles by which man in general must order his life to live in communion with God, then we will not, even in this 21st century be able to fully integrate with God as much as we would want to do.

Deuteronomy is therefore not to be ignored and by studying it we will be better able to understand the ups and downs of the lives of the people of Israel and Judah[1], and the church.

God by Revelation

There is one matter of pressing importance that needs to be established before proceeding with this study and that concerns *the* main character that dominates the pages of the Bible. The person of God.

---

[1] See my book Law & Grace and Hosea, because it is made very clear in those books that it was because of their negligence in studying the teaching in Deuteronomy that resulted in God withdrawing His protection and blessing from them.

The choice Adam was given was between the instructions of God and the miss-information whispered by the rebellious angel Lucifer, otherwise known as Satan or the Devil, who is the author of lies, doubt and chaos. Of all the many trees in God's garden only one was forbidden, and alongside it was a tree that would have transformed his life and that of his wife Eve. God told Adam that the day he ate of the fruit of the forbidden tree he would surely die. But that death was not physical but spiritual, and as it is through the spirit that man communicates with God a great chasm opened up between man and Go because God cannot look upon sinful man.

The one thing that can be said about the God of the Bible is that as the One God, solely responsible for the whole of creation, He is the God of truth. What He says happens. He spoke and it was done.

> *And God said, "Let there be light"; and there was light. God saw that the light was good and He both affirmed and sustained it; and God separated the light from the darkness.*

God told Adam not to eat the fruit of the forbidden tree, he did and was evicted from God's Garden, although not before God had provided the pair with clothing. There has been that separation of man from God in that one-to-one physical/spiritual intimacy ever since.

In the case of Noah, God told him to build a sea going vessel because He told him that He was going to flood the earth, and He did. Through Noah's obedience God did not have to start with a new Adam, but was able to regenerated mankind through a family, with the sign of the rainbow as the mark of His covenant with Noah never to flood the whole earth again.

In so many ways the Hebrew writers unanimously agree that God's first and predominant revelation of Himself is always in conduct, with His purity and strict sense of law and order being preeminent. There is also a very clear statement throughout scripture that there is nothing of which He is ignorant.

> *I am the Lord, that is My Name;*
> *My glory I will not give to another,*
> *Nor My praise to carved idols.*
> *Indeed, the former things have come to pass,*

Now I declare new things;
Before they spring forth
I proclaim them to you."
(Is. 42:8, 9)

What is more we have only to look into Isaiah 43 and realize that His activities do not go unnoticed, for so many of His miraculous actions are on very international public display and often involve another nation. After all the plagues, in which Pharaoh played a prominent role, were played out on the world stage and the effect of them reverberated around the whole of that area, putting terror into the heart of the people in the city of Jericho and beyond.

Because we are here dealing with both God and demonic powers that inhabit the effigies of gods (witches have demonic spiritual powers), we have to be aware that we are talking about the spiritual world that God created alongside the physical world that man cannot normally see. Satan is a spiritual not a physical being which means that he can chose whether or not to reveal himself and can even appear as an angel of light.

Through Isaiah God challenged the Gentile nations that trust in idols and are spiritually blind even though they have physical sight, and are spiritually deaf even though they have functioning ears, as to who could predict that Judah would return from their captivity in Babylonian, even though no other nation was able to return to their possessions and re-establish themselves as a sovereign nation.

What soothsayer or magician or chiromancer has prophetic powers of insight into spiritual things and is able to confirm that any one of their idols has been able to foretell such things as to what is going to happen in the future.

Bring out the people who are blind, even though they have eyes,
And the deaf, even though they have ears.
Gather the nations together
Assemble the peoples of the world.
Which of their idols can correctly predict
what will happen tomorrow?
Where are the witnesses to such remarkable events?

Because as true believers in the Lord Jesus Christ Gentiles enter into the fold of Israel, what Isaiah is stating here is of paramount concern for us also. If we do not have proof within ourselves of the reality of God through revelation of all that He has done not only for the Israelites throughout their history, but also in our own search for faith in the living God through the ministry of God's Son and in our own lives and experiences, then our faith is tissue thin, and has no substance.

> *"You are My witnesses*
> *O people of Israel," declares the Lord,*
> *"And My servant whom I have chosen,*
> *That you may know and believe Me*
> *And understand that I am He.*
> *Before Me there was no god formed,*

As creator He alone existed: gods only came into being through those that had abandoned God their creator, such as Cain who was at the mercy of Satan and his angelic followers. Effigies of gods are the invention of man.

> *And there will be none after Me.*

Where there is no reality of personal experience of God in an individual's heart and mind, and no real substance in their personal relationship with almighty God, there can be no resulting faith.
God had the overwhelming right to declare:

> *I alone am the Lord,*
> *And there is no Saviour besides Me.*

Surely through all their experiences in their journey through the wilderness, God's love for them is so clearly illustrated through His guidance and provisions, because they never wanted for any necessity.

> *I have declared future events*
> *and saved the nation and through those events;*
> *I have proclaimed that I am God,*

> *proving that there was no strange*
> *or alien god among you;*
> *Therefore you [the people of Israel] are My witnesses*
> *among the pagan nations," declares the Lord,*
> *"That I am God.*
> *Even from eternity I am He,*
> *And there is no one who can rescue from My hand;*
> *I act, and who can change it?"*
> *(Is. 43:8 – 13)*

God has not lost His ability to talk to individuals, and many of us are proof of that. God spoke to Abram, just one man amongst a pagan people. He heard and followed Him.

If for any reason we doubt the truth of God then this book is of no practical use.

The Foundational Document

As Deuteronomy is the most comprehensive book of the law, it is most probably this book that was found in the temple by Hilkiah the high priest of the time and sent to King Josiah of Judah who, on reading it, was horrified by how far the nation had deviated from the worship and service of God (2 Kgs. 22:8 – 20)

This is what I wrote in Law & Grace:

> The discovery of the book of the law governing worship was enthusiastically received, providing a clear structure for services for the priests with a heart for God. This had not always been the case, indeed the falling away of the priests from ministering to God to ministering to pagan images was to cause the destruction of the Temple of the Lord along with the collapse of the whole Temple worship system, ending up with most of the population being exiled to Babylon.

In some ways it can also be thought of as the equivalent of the letters of Paul in particular, which have provided the church with the basis of the Christian doctrine, although Deuteronomy is direct from God through Moses and, as a result, far more comprehensive and was, in fact, the source of much of Paul's understanding and teaching.

Although there are five books of Moses that constitute the Torah (Pentateuch), it is this book that not only contains a summary of the other four but, more than any of others, is designed to bring the people into a right relationship with their remarkable and loving God and be the basis of their daily lives in the promised land.

What is particularly interesting is that it also contains information regarding why the Lord Jesus had to hang on a tree (wooden cross), and His body could not be left on the cross over night. It is, therefore, a very important book for modern day believers, whether they be Jews or Gentiles, to read and understand.

Also the Lord Jesus said that He had not come to abolish the law but to fulfil it, therefore an understanding of Deuteronomy is considerably advantageous, if not essential, for all believers in the Lord Jesus Christ.

The book of Deuteronomy, or Second Law, is a record of the final speeches of Moses at the end of the tortuous route the Israelites had taken from Egypt in order to prepare them for their entry into the promised land as a mature nation.

It contains Moses' final instruction to the people before his death, as God had forbidden him to enter the Promised land, and is therefore oratorical in nature.

The Bible is not just a history book of God's relationship with Israel. Rather it is the memoir of the life of Israel and its relationship with the God who created man, and who, therefore, can be referred to as the father of mankind.

The first five verses of chapter one provide an introduction to this remarkable and essential book which provides us with a record of Moses' final instructions to all Israel regarding their life under God.

The book was originally called Devarim which means [The] Words, echoing the initial sentence, *"These are **the words** which Moses spoke unto all Israel when they were camped to the east of the Jordan river."*

It is the fifth of the series of five books of Moses, called the Torah, that charts the history of the creation of the world by God, His intention for man when creating him, the fall of man, the development of man and the gradual development of Israel from its embryonic beginnings starting with the call of Abram, the experiences of Isaac, the selection of Jacob instead of Esau, the development of the nation of Israel in the furnace of Egypt, and their remarkable exodus under the leadership of Moses.

Moses was right to warn the people of the implications of not remaining faithful to the God who had called them to be His people in the world when they took over the promised land, because he had a great deal of experience of the fickleness of man.

Now, as the nation was being prepared to face the hostility of the nation's then living in Canaan, Moses needed to remind them of God's ability to save them even when they were in extreme danger. Indeed it is interesting that God saved them at the Red Sea before he instructed them on rules for life.

This study of Deuteronomy is as relevant for us today as it was to those who went into possess the land of promise. Perhaps more so for us because, with the knowledge of all that the Messiah taught and did, we have a far deeper understanding of God's relationship with man and the importance of the way man approaches and enters into a relationship with God.

Please note that due to restricted finance, no proofreading or editorial activity was undertaken on the text of this book, so please excuse any typographical and grammatical errors. HOWEVER, because it contains a great deal of God inspired spiritual Biblical teaching, please focus on the message within the text and always have an open study or reference bible with you and refer to is regularly.

MOSES FIRST DISCOURSE

PETER RUSSELL-YARDE

1 A RECAP OF EVENTS

With full confidence we are assured that God,
who has a deep and abiding love for us
ensures that all things work together for good
for those who love Him,
to those who are called
according to His plan and purpose.
(taken from Romans 8:28)

Deuteronomy is undoubtedly *the* most important book in the Old Testament being the foundational document of Judaic doctrine that establishes the relationship between the Israelites and their God. It is, therefore, not a book to be ignored, and by studying it in relation to the rest of the Hebrew scriptures along with the New Testament, as we will be doing in this book, we will, in the end, be better able to understand the ups and downs, successes and failures of Israel and Judah and, importantly, the spiritual state of the nation at the time of the Messiah's arrival.

Moses stands before the people

This was a poignant moment for Israel as the great man mounted a prominent point so that the whole of the congregation of Israel could see him.

It was a long time since he was first introduced secretly to the leaders of the Hebrews after his arrival from the wilderness where he had been shepherding his father-in-law's sheep.

The onetime prince of Egypt, no longer the energetic army commander he was when he escaped the wrath of the Pharaoh for killing the Egyptian, but a much quieter, mature and humble man in his eightieth year, and a man of upright stature who still commanded attention by his rugged weather-beaten features, with long unkempt hair and beard, with his skin tanned by the heat of the sun and weather-beaten by the severe cold and wind of the lonely wilderness nights.

Introduced by Aaron, who had been called by God to go out to meet his long lost brother even before Moses had accepted God's commission, Moses performed the miraculous signs God had shown him at the burning bush to prove to the leaders of Israel that he had been sent by God to lead the people out of slavery in answer to their prayers.

From that time he gradually recovered his old authority as the adopted son of Pharaoh's daughter. Standing before the latest supposed incarnation of the sun god Ra, Moses' stance and confidence got stronger, allowing him to demonstrate greater authority as each plague came and went, until in great boldness he announced God's finally judgement on the Egyptians that so dramatically proved to the Pharaoh that the God of the Hebrews was greater and far more powerful than he.

That last plague was the trigger that set the people off on their journey to freedom under his leadership.

Moses' trust in, and his ability to communicate with God, had also increased throughout the plagues so that by the time he was faced with the sea before him and Pharaoh's army fast approaching behind him, he was able to say to the people with great and assured boldness,

"Do not be afraid.
Stand still and see the salvation of the Lord
that He will accomplish for you today"

He then led them through the passage that had opened up through the sea to the other side and then witnessed the sea return to its natural state so fast that the Israelites were able to see the elite section of the Egyptian army, led by the Pharaoh himself, disappear under the water.

After celebrating such a miraculous event, and giving the glory to God, Moses then led the people into the wilderness with a great stabilizing strength.

Throughout their journey, even in times when there was great turmoil and unrest within the camp, it was Moses who, with humble and quiet authority, commanded respect in bringing peace into the camp, even when many thousands of the people had died during one of the incidents of rebellion.

At times of spiritual intimacy with God in a tent set up away from the camp, Moses face glowed so bright that the people found it difficult to look him in the eyes and so asked him to wear a veil until the glow diminished, fearful of the brightness of his countenance.

During their years of wandering through the wilderness he had been the trusted judge, deciding cases, often from early morning to late at night, until other judges were appointed. A leader the people learned to respect and not oppose, as some had done to their cost.

Now at the end of their journeying they had claimed their first territory from the two Amorite kings and had settled down to prepare themselves to enter the promised land to the west, across the river Jordan.

Imagine the scene and the feeling within the camp on the first day of Moses' giving his final instructions to the people, knowing that he would not lead them over the river. It was a time of great expectancy yet of great sadness, a change such long established strong leadership brings that will have caused some to be very nervous about the future.

The book of Deuteronomy looks both back to the time of their stay at the base of the holy mountain of Horeb and forwards to the time when they would enter into the promised land.

Moses first reminds Israel of their growing population and the reason why he had each tribe *Choose for yourselves wise, understanding, experienced, and respected men from your tribes, and I will appoint them as leaders over you. So made the chosen men of your tribes leaders over you, commanders of thousands, and hundreds, and fifties, and tens, and administrative officers for your tribes.*

And then, in preparation for their time in the promised land Moses *commanded their judges at that time, saying, 'Hear the matters between your fellow countrymen, and judge righteously and fairly between a man and his brother, or the stranger (non-Israelite) who is with him. You shall show no partiality in judgment; you shall pay careful attention to case be it minor or major. You shall not fear man, for the judgment is God's.*

He then reminded Israel about their departure from Horeb (Sinai) where they had met with the Lord their God. That meeting was crucial for them and us, because it was then that the engagement of God and the nation in an eternal union, was agreed and sealed with the verbal signing of the covenant, the agreement by both parties that was to underpin their relationship.

It is a covenant under which we as believers must also live, as modified by the new covenant in Christ's blood. For by accepting Christ as our Lord and Saviour we become part of spiritual Israel, which is the Church born out of physical Israel.

Israel separated unto God

It is very important at this juncture that we recognize the uniqueness of Israel and the special role God has assigned to it in His plan for mankind. That plan, which was written and sealed before ever anything was created, had within it a way for their salvation along with those that became part of Israel.

Sadly most Christians are completely unaware of this fact, indeed some have even believed that God abandoned His people at some point, and yet Paul clearly states (Ro. 11:1 – 5).

> *I say then, has God cast away His people? Certainly not! For I also am an Israelite, of the seed of Abraham, of the tribe of Benjamin.*
>
> *God has not cast away His people whom He foreknew. Or do you not know what the Scripture says of Elijah, how he pleads with God against Israel, saying,*
>
> *"Lord, they have killed Your prophets and torn down Your altars, and I alone am left, and they seek my life"?*
>
> *But what is the Divine response? "I have reserved for Myself seven thousand men who have not bowed the knee to Baal."*
>
> *Even so then, at this present time there is a remnant according to the election of grace.*

Also God is using the free access to the news of salvation He has given to the Gentiles to provoke the Jew's jealousy concerning their faith to seek Him afresh. This was clearly demonstrated by the reaction of some of the Jews in Jerusalem when they heard about the people in Cornelius' household receiving the baptism in the Holy Spirit

> *Now the apostles and brethren who were in Judea heard that the Gentiles had also received the word of God. And when Peter came up to Jerusalem, those of the circumcision contended with him, saying, "You went in to uncircumcised men and ate with them!" (Acts 11:1 – 3)*

But in the end they had to glorify God that the Gentiles were being included:

> *Then I, Peter, remembered how the Lord said, 'John indeed baptized with water, but you shall be baptized with the Holy Spirit.' If therefore God gave them the same gift as He gave us when we believed on the Lord Jesus Christ, who was I that I could withstand God?"*
>
> *When they heard these things they became silent; and they glorified God, saying, "Then God has also granted to the Gentiles repentance to life." (Acts 11:16 – 18)*

As Gentiles, therefore, it is important that this opportunity to receive the salvation on offer is not wasted, but utilized to the full by dedicating ourselves to the complete, rather than selective, study of His word so that we might live our lives in a way that conforms to His instructions and thereby serve Him according to His will and purpose for us. That can only be done by studying the First Testament enabling us to better understand the Second.

For this reason the study of Moses' book of Deuteronomy must not be done in isolation. Certainly Paul refers to it in his letters to teach believers truths about salvation and the importance of Israel's part in it as we have already seen.

For instance, the one thing that we cannot set aside from our studies is the fact that the union made at Sinai between God and Israel was/is an eternal spiritual union that is finally to be consummated at the marriage supper of the Lamb.

Therefore if we, as Gentiles, want to be part of what God is doing on the earth to save mankind, then we must get to know God by meditating on all the instructions God gave the Israelites regarding their relationship with Him, after all at that time there would have been many not born of Israel listening to Moses speak.

This is the reason why the study of Moses' final three discourses, as recorded in the book of Deuteronomy, is so vitally important to Gentile believers of today. Moses was speaking the words of God not just to Israel but to all that were prepared to listen, no matter that the what we read could well have been committed to paper years later. They are still the word Moses received through inspiration of the Holy Spirit who with the Father and the Son are ever the same.

In this book Moses lays, out for all who would hear, the way in which God wants created man to live that will enable him to live a life of blessing that God intended them to live when He designed man. After all God designed man to live in **Man + breath of God** spiritual union with Him for why else would he breath into Adam's nostrils the breath of spiritual life? Surely it was to make us in His image, that is to have his characteristics, and the most significant characteristic is that God is a Spirit, with no physical form, and there will come a time when we leave this earth that we will be with Him clothed in a spiritual body (1 Cor. 15 esp. 42 – 49).

Here we come to the problem of unbelief amongst so many, particularly those that died during their time in the wilderness through rebellion and others such as the sons of Eli and Samuel through unbelief. Fortunately, these do not represent the loyal core of Israel, which has remained dedicated to their God to this very day.

Previously Gentiles had to become proselytes to enjoy the means of salvation then available through the sacrifice of animals. But since the sacrifice of the Messiah, the Aaronic priesthood and the earthly temple in Jerusalem have been made redundant, because when Christ died and rose again from the dead He became not only the new eternal spiritual high priest in the heavenly temple, and our advocate before the Father, but also King of Israel.

The church that the Messiah founded has nothing to do with the western idea of 'church.' Paul, in speaking of Israel being a cultivated olive tree (Ro. 11:1 – 25), points out that all those that are born of Israel by physical birth that have fallen away because of unbelief are like branches that have been pruned from the Olive Tree that is Israel. Therefore we must not think like the Roman Catholic priest who announces at a baptism that Christianity is passed from parents to children, for this is spiritual language, for consider what Paul wrote to the Gentile believers in Ephesus regarding the 'church'.

> *... you are no longer strangers and foreigners, but fellow citizens with the saints and members of the household of God. Through your personal faith in Christ, when you were born again into the Spirit of God, you have been spiritually built on the foundation of both the apostles and the prophets, with Jesus Christ Himself being the chief cornerstone.*
>
> *It is in Him and through Him that the whole building, is being fitted together, for it to finally grow into a holy temple in the Lord. It is in that God designed and ordained structure in Christ as Saviour that you also are being built together, with all the other Jewish and Gentile believers, for a dwelling place of God in the Spirit. (see Eph. 2:19 – 21; cf. 1 Cor. 6:19, 20)*

Those Gentiles that come to faith in Christ are like branches from a wild olive tree (as opposed to the cultivated olive tree that is Israel) that have been grafted into Israel, although their position in the tree is dependent upon them retaining that faith. For it is just as possible for Gentile believers to have their branch removed and for repentant Jews to have their branch restored.

When considering the salvation God is providing for all mankind though the sacrifice of His Son Jesus, it is impossible to ignore the irrefutable importance of Israel. Therefore the focus of attention for all Gentiles that have come to faith in Christ, must be on understanding the instructions handed down to Israel through all the prophets and particularly Moses and what he told Israel during his recorded discourses, in the light of the new covenant in Christ Jesus.

Sinai covenant and Israel

The Sinai covenant still holds good and therefore must not be ignored. After all the first commandment clearly states that God requires all those that are called by His name to love Him with their whole being, along with the other commandments, laws and statutes. That is still relevant. In fact the Messiah Himself told the people that

He had come to fulfil the law and the prophets, not to do away with that which formed the foundation of Israel's relationship with their God all those years ago.

Let there be no doubt whatsoever that the covenant agree at Sinai has not gone away, therefore it is imperative that we understand, by studying Deuteronomy, how that Sinai covenant and the subsequent teachings and pronouncements of Moses affect us today.

What Deuteronomy tells us is how essential it is for us to focus our attention and daily lives on living according to the will of God. It is true we are no longer under the law but under grace, but we will learn more about what that means later in this study.

In this first discourse, after the introduction we read that *Moses began to explain this law, saying, "The Lord our God spoke to us ..."* What is so remarkable about this statement is that the very God that created all things in love, spoke directly to the children of Israel as they were gathered at the base of Mount Sinai sometime after He had, through His own mighty power, released them from slavery from one of the premier countries in that area, even to the destruction of the army of Egypt and the Pharaoh himself.

For them to be chosen of God was awesome, if only they realized just how awesome it was.

If we are not awed by the way God wanted direct involvement with this tiny embryonic nation, formed during its time of slavery in Egypt, then we have not fully grasped its significance, nor the consistency and loyalty of God towards those that love Him, just as Abraham had done.

Throughout scripture the accent must, therefore, be on *The Lord **our** God*, the unassailable creator of all things, because the whole of scripture is solely about man's relationship with his maker, and how that relationship can work when man applies himself to opening up his mind and heart and reaching up and out to almighty God and receiving His Spirit.

In fact, the phrase *"The Lord **our** God"* speaks of the intimacy so essential between believers and the God who wants to become an intimate part of their lives.

There are two other phrases that we do well to consider right from the start. The first was, as far as Israel was concerned, the promised land, *the land God has given you.* In other words the land was a gift from God to the people, and from their behaviour throughout their travels in the wilderness, it was totally undeserved.

The land was a gift originally promised to Abraham who had willingly given his life to God in complete surrender, and had shown an incredible trusting faith in God by his willingness to sacrifice his long awaited son Isaac, that God referred to him as being righteous.

Sadly the descendants of Abraham had not shown a willingness to surrender themselves to God in the same way. Yet God had honoured His promise to Abraham by rescuing his descendants from slavery in Egypt, and ensured they were the recipients of that gracious gift.

The second phrase is that the people had to *go in and possess the land*. Although the land was a gift from God it was necessary for them to go in and possess it, but only with His support, because not only was he prepared to go in ahead of them and subdue the opposition, it was essential that they were not able to boast that they had taken the land by their own strength. To succeed in the life that God has given to us, no one can do it on their own.

Just as salvation is a gift of God, the repentant sinner must receive it and make it their own for it to be effective. Surely this is a lesson of life, because a gift is of no use except the intended recipient of that gift accepts it and then uses it. If unaccepted the gift remains just that: a gift.

But let us consider this gift of land from the perspective of the people of Israel. It was an unknown land, apart from the report of the spies sent in by Moses. What they did know was that those already living in the land would not give it up without a fight, therefore it would require them to trust the Lord for His guidance and support to help the active members of the army to overcome them.

The inhabitants were a people God had rejected because they had completely rejected Him as their landlord and provider. They were thanking things that were made by Him for the harvests, their lives and provisions, when He alone was the provider; something many of the descendants of those who would go in and possess the land would emulate, resulting in their considerable grief.

Sadly so many of the leaders and people seemed to be unaware that God was their landlord and provider. The people of Israel only retained ownership of the land by recognizing God's authority over them and obeying His conditions of ownership.

During these discourses the Israelites were on the east side of the river Jordan. They had spent about a year camped in wild solitude in the region of Horeb in order to, in that settled state, lay the essential foundation of a new special settled community.

With the temple in the centre of the camp surrounded by the Levitical clans, and the twelve tribes surrounding them, the layout put God at the centre and enabled the social and political elements to develop within the religious character of the nation, which was so necessary for the cohesion of the people prior to their engagement with the hostile tribes in Canaan.

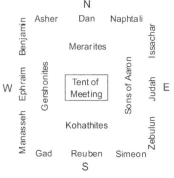

God told the people through Moses that He had set the land before them and His instructions were for them to go in and possess it; a land that God had sworn as an oath, that only He could honour, to the patriarchs — Abraham, Isaac and Jacob — to give to them, and their descendants after them. It was there, and God assured them it was accessible, providing they were at all times in tune with, and obedient to Him.

During their time camped in the quiet of the wilderness, they had time to build the necessary social/political structure within the nation in readiness for their future settled status. It was also a time of assessing the past in order to prepare themselves for the future.

Hindsight can provide some very important teaching. So Moses looks back, not to the moment of the exodus but to the time of camping around the base of Mount Sinai. It was the one moment in their history where God spoke directly to the nation from the top of the mountain and they received the ten commandments, with the nation committing itself to worshipping and serving God alone.

Moses starts his first discourse

3 In the fortieth year, on the first day of the eleventh month, Moses spoke to the children of Israel in accordance with all that the Lord had commanded him to say to them, after he had defeated Sihon the king of the Amorites, who lived in Heshbon, and Og the king of Bashan, who lived at Ashtaroth in Edrei. East of the Jordan in the land of Moab, Moses began to explain this law, saying,

Moses reserved the delivery of his most important exhortation, which contained both warnings and encouragements, for the final days of his life., in the same way as Jacob (Gen. 49), Joshua (Josh. 24), Samuel (1 Sam. 12) and David (1 Kgs 2).

There is no doubt that words spoken by an outstanding leader at the solemn time immediately prior to their departure from this life not only leaves a deep impression on the minds of their hearers, but they tend to be remembered and their teaching passed on to others, particularly the young.

Moses oratorical master classes are no exception because we in the 21st century are still benefitting from them; particularly as they focus the minds of hearers and readers alike on the Lord God of Israel and present to us the option of being able to walk in tune with God or to reject Him.

5 "The Lord our God spoke to us at Horeb, saying, 'You have stayed long enough on this mountain. Turn and resume your journey, and go to the hill country of the Amorites, and to all their neighbours in the Arabah, in the hill country and in the lowland (the Shephelah), in the Negev to the south and on the west coast of the Mediterranean Sea, the land of the Canaanites, and Lebanon, as far as the great river Euphrates.

What is clear right from the start is the essential nature of the guidance Israel received from their God, with the initial phrase *The Lord our God spoke to us at Horeb*. Moses made it very clear that it was God Himself who had been the true leader with him being the channel through whom God worked, and even now it was God who was guiding him regarding what he was to tell the people.

Not only that but the Lord was informing them that it was He who had set the land before them.

Look, I have set the land before you; go in and take possession of the land which the Lord swore (solemnly promised) to your

fathers, to Abraham, to Isaac, and to Jacob, to give to them and to their descendants after them.'
(*Deut. 1:3 – 8*)

There was no place for their opinion or assessment as there had been before. Here the Lord told them *"I have set the land before you; go in and take possession of the land"*

This was Moses finest speech in which he announces the end of the wilderness wanderings and identifies the moment God signalled when it was finally time for the people to go in and claim the land He had originally promised to Abraham.

Tribal Leaders Appointed
(Deut. 1:9 – 18; Ex. 18:13 – 26; Num. 11: 10 - 29)

I spoke to you at that time, saying, 'I am not able to bear the burden of you alone, because the Lord your God has multiplied you, so that, today you are as numerous as the stars of heaven.

How can I alone bear the weight and pressure and burden of you and your contentious and complaining ways alone? Choose wise, understanding, experienced, and respected men from your tribes, and I will appoint them as leaders over you.'
(*Deut. 1:9,10, 11 – 13*)

Moses is speaking to the children of those who had left Egypt and experienced the transformative nature of the changes made necessary because of the growth of the nation, which was about six hundred thousand souls. Not a small company of people.

It was Moses' father-in-Law, Jethro, witnessing the huge burden Moses was carrying by having to judge the whole nation, who suggested Moses delegate the workload to others. So leaders were appointed over thousands, hundreds, fifties and tens.

The severity of the case brought would determine whether it could be dealt with by the judge of ten people or the judge of a thousand or if it needed to be dealt with by Moses himself (Ex. 18).

This obviously drastically cut his workload, and made the administration of justice far more accessible to the ordinary people.

But there is another equally remarkable incident that needs to be included here and that is Moses' sense of uselessness when the whole camp rebelled, weeping throughout their families at the door of their tents (Num. 11:10).

> *Now Moses heard the families weeping in self-pity at the doorway of their tent; and the anger of the Lord blazed hotly, and Moses regarded their behaviour as evil.*

This incident illustrates two things: The first being the inability of a man to lead a nation by himself, and second God's ability to change a negative situation into a positive one, and perhaps a third, a challenge when the Lord said to Moses

> *"Is the Lord's arm (power) shortened (limited or inadequate)? Now you shall see whether or not My word will come to pass."* *(Num. 11:23)*

As was mentioned in the introduction that the God of Israel is the God of revelation. In other words we know He exists because of the way His reveals Himself, often in obscure ways, such as the times Sarah was saved from becoming member of a harem by God warning the King/Pharaoh that she was Abraham's wife, although she was also his sister although not by the same mother. Abraham's reason for the deception was to prevent him being killed.

Another occasion was God's appearance on the top of Mount Sinai and the fact that He spoke to the people.

In the incident mentioned above the people were pining for meat in their now practiced way of having an unreal, rosy remembrance of their life in Egypt, from which servitude they were then pleading with the Lord to rescue them.

Had they really thought about it, those were not the 'Good Old Days' that their make-believe minds had concocted. It is amazing how the cruelty and hardship of those far off days had mellowed in their minds.

Moses had come to realize that he was just one man amongst a nation of 600,000 able men and was fearful not only of an out of control population, but whether or not he had enough of a control over them to stop them attacking him.

Moses was desperate and cried out to God (Num. 11:11, 12)

"Why have You afflicted Your servant? And why have I not found favour in Your sight, that You have laid the burden of all these people on me? Was it I who conceived all these people? Was it I who brought them forth, that You should say to me, 'Carry them in your arms as a nurse carries the nursing infant, to the land which You swore to their fathers'?

This was not what he had signed up to at the burning bush. When he was fighting against the Pharaoh it came down to a fight between the two men with Moses knowing that the power of God was supporting him.

But this situation was something entirely different, requiring a completely different style of handling. How was he to pacify a nation almost in hysterics? Moses was in despair, unable to understand what he could do with so little resources, pleading with the Lord for help.

Elijah was also to experience despair as he was suddenly faced with the wrath of Queen Jezebel who was actually out of her depth in her fight against God. Had Elijah not seen God's power demonstrated mightily on Mount Carmel? Therefore what was the Queen capable of doing against such a God of revelatory power?

Where am I to get meat to give all these people? For they weep before me and say, 'Give us meat, so that we may eat.' I am not able to carry all these people alone, because the burden is too heavy for me.

The problem with being in a situation that has emotionally overwhelmed us is that it is very difficult to think rationally. What affected Moses so much was that this vast company of distressed people *weep before me and say, 'Give us meat, so that we may eat.* The ra emotion being expressed distressed him but from the point of view that practically he had no means of satisfying their need, nor any means of pacifying them.

Such public distress can be self-sustaining and there is the potential to get out of control. Such an unexpected turn of events floored Moses, hence his cry to God:

If this is the way You are going to deal with me, please kill me at once, if I have found favour in your sight, and do not let me see

24

my wretchedness." (or my inability to control this crisis.) (Num. 11:13 – 15)

It is easy for us to want to remind Moses of all the miraculous things that his revelatory God had done previously and that all Moses had to do was to call upon the name of the Lord, but having taken on being father to the nation he found himself emotionally involved and therefore, at such times, unable to think rationally.

It was then that the Lord took charge and instructed Moses to call upon seventy men known to be the elders of Israel, that is older men with the wisdom of years and leadership experience and therefore well qualified to bear the burden of shared leadership (cf. 1 Tim. 3).

Why seventy? Well the number seven represents perfection and the number ten represents completeness and God's law. Therefore, seventy symbolizes perfect spiritual order.

God would then come down and speak with them,

> *… and I will take away some of the Spirit who is upon you, and will put Him upon them; and they shall bear the burden of the people with you, so that you will not have to bear it all alone.*

Moses would still have a sufficient endowment of the Spirit of God for his role as ultimate national leader, but with the leadership dispersed in that way, a speedy resolution to any problem was now available. As it was God came down in a cloud and caused them to prophesy just that once to confirm their commissioning.

The whole nation was then instructed to *sanctify themselves* for meat that would appear. Afterwards a wind from the Lord brought them quail in vast numbers.

It is unknown, except to God, who started the rumour about the desire for meat but it obviously hit a nerve for it no grew in strength and spread throughout the camp so that it gained a power of its own to dominate the people's thinking.

It is possibly those starting the rumour because of their own desire for meat that when the quails came, such was their greed that they gorged themselves on the meat and, because their digestive system was not used to the strong meat, many became ill with some dying.

It was in remembring that moment when he experienced such terrifying inadequacy that had Moses reminiscing on the appointment of tribal leaders to help him control the growing numbers of sometimes excitable people, as well as the appointment of judges that helped prepare the nation for their settled lives in Canaan.

Disaster of the spies (Deut. 1:20 – 46; Num. 13)

God knows our minds and hearts, He also knows the future, in fact there is nothing that He does not know (Is. 42:9).

From Egypt, the Israelites could have reached Canaan in about eleven days going by the shortest route; but that was not the purpose of their journey. From the ragtag assembly of those born into one of the twelve tribes and those from other nations that had managed to escape with them in the confusion of the exodus, God was determined to weld them into a nation that stood a chance of not only overcoming the hostile tribes then inhabiting the promised land, but also a nation through which He could reach out to the world.

There had been many tests along the way, even when Moses was kept on the mountain for forty days and nights collecting the two stone tablets on which God had inscribed the ten commandments.

Whilst he was on the mountain, various rebel members of the nation decided that they had waited long enough for Moses and inveigled Aaron into making a golden calf that they then declared was the god that had led them out of Egypt.

Such a claim seems not just incredible, but totally nonsensical, until you get to know someone who is totally impervious to spiritual things. A friend of mine of many years completely rejects any thought of a God in spite of the turmoil and total lack of stability in many parts of the world (particularly in 2020 and early 2021) where increasingly dominant dictatorial leadership groups are seeking to gains repressive control on more and more territory and people.

When Moses came down and witness the depraved activity he called on all those loyal to God to take up arms and attack the rebels and all those that partied, slaughtering them wholesale. In fact throughout their wanderings in the wilderness many thousands were culled because of unbelief or rebelliousness.

This might seem draconian, but it is essential that we remember the purifying process God was putting them through to sort out the wheat from the chaff. This is right at the beginning of the formation and consolidation of Israel as a unique nation of God and by the time the people went into to possess the land they had to be God focused. This was because God was putting the nation at the heart of His plan of salvation for all mankind, including you and me.

We may be considering events right at the beginning of the formation of Israel as a sovereign nation in its own right, but it must not escape us all that even now God is separating the sheep from the goats. After all there is not one individual that has lived, is living, or will live in the future that will not stand before the great white throne and be judged. All those with a true heart for God will be separated with the sheep and all those who have no real interest in the almighty creator God that we are studying right now will be separated with the goats.

Let there be no doubt in your mind whatsoever, that only those who will have the seal of God on their forehead will enter into the place, the New Jerusalem, that Jesus has gone to prepare for those that truly love Him. All the others will suffer in that place where God is ever absent and will weep and wail for eternity.

Now is the day of salvation. Unless we reach out to God and grab this opportunity to commit ourselves to Him in love now, the opportunity will disappear and hell will become our place of everlasting misery.

It is true many of them were distracted and went the way of the world, but God retained for Himself a remnant that was for ever loyal and true to Him.

Sadly as we know the history of the Israelite nation is one of faithlessness and rebelliousness, causing God to punish them time and again.

The moment when twelve spies were selected and sent into the promised land became another major landmark in their history that brought about another time of culling the rebellious.

Then you all approached me and said, 'Let us send men to spy out the land before us, and bring back to us word regarding the way we should go, and the cities we should enter.' The plan pleased me and I took twelve of your men, one man from each tribe. They went up into the hill country, and spied out the Valley of Eshcol taking some of the fruit of the land in their hands and brought it down to

*us. They reported back and said, 'It is a good land which the Lord
our God is about to give us.'(Deut. 1:20 – 25)*

The sending out of the spies, as suggested by the people
themselves, and agreed by Moses and allowed by God, was another
test. By selecting a man from each of the twelve tribes the
responsibility for the report was spread over the whole nation, but it
also exposed a fear within them concerning such a task and their lack
of trust in God.

It should also be made clear that the men selected were likely to
be those who had been raise under slavery and experienced in being
under orders. Therefore they lacked the boldness and adventurism
required for such a mission.

The twelve men journeyed from south to north and back,
checking the whole of the land, even bringing back samples of the
produce grown there. And with that they started their report.

> *"We went into the land to which you sent us and it truly flows with
> milk and honey and this is just a sample of its fruit",*
> immediately adding, *"However, the people who dwell in the land
> are strong; the cities are fortified and very large; moreover we saw the
> descendants of Anak"* (people of giant stature).

Remember these were men brought up under the taskmaster's
whip, so they were not bold men even though they had fought a
number of battles and won. They were still not self-assured and
found it exceedingly difficult to visualize or accept that God had the
power to enable them to succeed in taking the land. Yet God was
giving it to them as a gift, so why would he make it impossible for
them to take it over? Surely He had demonstrated to them His power
from the Red Sea to that time.

Caleb did his best in trying to settle the people saying, *"Let us go up
at once and take possession, for we are well able to overcome it."* But ten of the
men who had gone up with him were insistent saying, *"We are not able
to go up against the people, for they are stronger than we."* And it was true. On
their own they were not strong enough, but it was also clear that they
were not able to appreciate the power of God, even though they had
witnessed that power numerous times, and should have included it in
their assessment.

This matter of the spies was a turning point for many. The faith of the majority of the spies was completely absent. Hearing what the spies had told them, it was obvious the people would not be willing to take the risk of going in to take possession of the land if the report of ten of the spies was so negative. After all they were their eyes and ears.

So it was back to murmuring in their tents *'Because the Lord hates us He has brought us from the land of Egypt to hand us over to the Amorites to destroy us.* If there was no one else to blame then blame the Lord. But how did they come to that conclusion? Caleb and Joshua were firmly for going in, having total faith in God being able to support them in their fight against even the giants, as happened later.

Moses did his best to encourage them saying,

> *'Do not be shocked, nor fear them. The Lord your God who goes before you will fight for you Himself, just as He did in Egypt before your eyes, and also in the wilderness where you saw how the Lord your God carried and protected you, just as a man carries his son, all along the way which you travelled until you arrived at this place.' (Deut. 1:26 – 40)*

but to no avail.

Such was their unreasonable and deep mistrust of God in spite of all that the Lord their God had done for them even to the extent of going before them *along the way, in fire by night and in a cloud by day, to seek a place for you to make camp and to show you the way in which you should go.* So what does this tell us? Perhaps it tells us to challenge ourselves to think about what we would do if we were to face a similar situation. How **real and strong** is our faith in our God? It is one thing reading about others, but if we transfer that situation to ourselves what would be our immediate reaction?

It is easy for us to condemn them for their decision as we read the scriptures in the safety of our own homes, although having said that some could well be reading this in more temporary and less secure conditions.

What we must ask ourselves, however, is "just how far would we trust God when faced with a very challenging situation as the Israelites then faced?" We do not know what is going to happen in the next minute, let alone an hour or day ahead. So if God asked you to trust Him knowing that to serve Him could potentially put you in a place of danger, would you submit to Him as the children of Israel were being asked to do? Never criticize except you are prepared to literally obey God no matter what.

It is not surprising that God had had enough of them and decided:

> *Not one of the men of this evil generation, shall see the good land which I solemnly promised to give to your fathers, except Caleb the son of Jephunneh; he shall see it, and to him and to his children I will give the land on which he has walked, because he has followed the Lord and remained true to Him.*

It has always been the same; a faithful remnant has kept the faith.

Where the people had apparently been concerned for their children, God had something to say about that:

> *Moreover, your little ones whom you said would become prey, and your sons, who today have no knowledge of good or evil, shall enter Canaan, and I will give it to them and **they shall** possess it.*

It was only after that rebuke that they thought twice about not going in and, in spite of God telling them that He would not support them, they went in and got soundly beaten.

Just as Moses was no longer able to stand the strain of leading the nation anymore, because he had got worn out leading such a difficult and fickle people, so these men were no good to God because they could not bring themselves to sufficiently trust Him to enable them to go in and possess the land whatever the obstacles and opposition they might face.

This meant that another thirty-eight years were added to their time of training in the wilderness to ensure all the doubters had died, either by natural causes or during the many times when God's anger flared up and caused the rebels to be killed, before a fresh attempt was made. In fact this first discourse of Moses was used to inform the new generation of what had happened in order to ensure they did not make the same mistake (Deut. 2:14).

God does not give us a second chance when He has specifically instructed us to do something and we fail to respond to His call as spectacularly as the Israelites did on this occasion.

The reason this study is so very important for believers today is that we must work out where the Israelites went wrong, given all the information He had given to them, and assess the degree of our own willingness and commitment to trust God no matter what we face, and be obedient to His guidance.

The whole of the First Testament is an amazing resource of information of how we should approach our relationship with God and what God requires of us.

Yet so much of Christendom is, for the most part, totally ignorant this resource, believing it to be old and out of date, hence the reason my preference to calling it the First Testament, because it is followed by the Second which is a fulfilment of all the promises of the First.

After all you would not build a house of just bedrooms without building the ground floor accommodation first. Nor would you read the last few chapters of a book and whilst totally ignore the first part.

Leave your relatives alone (Deut. 2:1 – 23)

> *Then we turned, and journeyed into the wilderness by the way of the Red Sea, as the Lord directed me; and **for many days** we journeyed around Mount Seir.*

That statement is remarkable because the phrase, ***for many days,*** represents 38 years, following the disastrous incident of the spies and their defeat at the hands of the Canaanites.

> *And the Lord spoke to me [Moses], saying, You have roamed around this mountain country long enough; now turn northward.*

That was the signal from God that they had served their time and the rebellious generation of freed slaves had died off by one means or another. Only then did God allow Moses to lead the nation back up north in preparation for the final assault on the nations then inhabiting the land God had promised to the descendants of Abraham, Isaac and Jacob.

During the journey to get to the point where they would launch their bid to take over the land, they would have to pass through the territory of the descendants of distant relatives.

It would be useful to remind ourselves of their significance rather than just quickly pass over this useful piece of recorded information.

Esau

Esau was older than his twin brother Jacob by the foot that he stuck out and then withdrew during birth, but in terms of character they could not have been more different.

We are told that Esau was a man of the outdoors, *of the field*, and *a skilful hunter*, whereas Jacob was a mild man; one given to thinking and learning, who preferred tent life. Jacob was the one most likely to learn from his father Isaac about his experiences of life and faith in the God of his grandfather Abraham, along with his own experiences of God's guidance.

Sin, that insidious virus that buries itself deep into the soul that can have such a devastating effect on the character of an individual, was a key influencer of Esau.

Purity was of paramount importance in the early development of this tribe that would ultimately become God's chosen people of Israel. Esau had no time for all those niceties. As a man of the world he was his own man and he decided to choose his own wives. So, contrary to the will of God and that of his parents, he went out and married two pagan Hittite women.

Prior to their birth Rebekah was greatly discomforted by the twins apparently fighting in her womb. So she cried out to God asking Him what was happening, and God told her that there were two nations in her womb. Of the two people that were to be born one was stronger than the other, but the older would serve the younger.

Remembering this, Rebekah was determined that Jacob would receive the blessing of their father for it was right that he should become the head of the tribe after the death of her husband.[2]

When Esau came to realize that he had lost his birth-right, even though it was through his own rebellious and completely selfish attitude, he initially hated Jacob and wanted to kill him, but with Jacob's sudden departure to find a wife (he was away for fourteen years), along with his success in building up a tribe of his own, he was sufficiently self-satisfied with his lot that he lost that hared.

However he had rebelled against God and set off, just like Cain, on a Godless path. Satan took over, as he always does in a spiritual

---

[2] In my book The Origin of Life, there is a full account of the tussle for the birth right.

vacuum[3]. And the descendants of Esau, Lot and Ishmael, even in this day and age, still seek to destroy God's chosen people.

There are two interesting references that it would be good to mention here:

> *Therefore, dear brothers and sisters, you have no obligation to do what your sinful nature urges you to do. For if you live by your natural sinful contaminated instincts, you will die (for the wages of sin is death). But if through the power of the Spirit you put to death the deeds of your sinful nature, you will live. This is because all who are led by the Spirit of God are children of God. (Ro. 8:12 – 14)*

And:

> *When Isaac married Rebekah, she gave birth to twins. But before they were born, before they had done anything good or bad, she received a message from God. (This message clearly demonstrates that God chooses people according to his own purposes; he calls people, but not according to their good or bad works.)*
> *Rebekah was told, "Your older son will serve your younger son." In the words of the Scriptures, "I loved Jacob, but I rejected Esau."*

From the text of Genesis we can understand why God did that. But what it also demonstrates is that God foreknew the type of people the two embryos would become.

Lot

Lot is a very interesting case because of his adoption by Abraham. It is true that Lot grew up enjoying the wealth of his uncle and in turn became wealthy himself. But something of Abraham's experiences in the spiritual field must surely have rubbed off on him and yet his life turned out to be a complete disaster.

Two wealthy tribes living within the same area was bound to cause problems, so it was inevitable that the two tribes would have to go their separate ways. Although he was the older and should therefore have made the decision, Abraham gave the choice of the land before them to his nephew Lot.

---

[3] See Lk. 11:24 – 26; Matt. 12:43 – 45

From their vantage point, Lot chose the lush valley of the river Jordan and settled near Sodom. But sometime after he settled there, Bera, the king of Sodom, who had been a vassal of Chedorlaomer, king of Elam, for twelve years, formed an alliance with four other kings to rebel against their overlord. Unfortunately Bera lost and as a consequence Lot was captured along with many others.

Is it not interesting that one of Lot's men was able to escape and reported everything to Abram the Hebrew, who was living near the oak grove belonging to Mamre, the Amorite. Mamre and his relatives, Eshcol and Aner, were Abram's allies.

As soon as he was informed about Lot's situation, Abraham and his friends went after the king of Elam and managed to free Lot and his family and the other captives along with their possessions. Surely God was in that rescue.

Sadly, however, that was not the end of Lots troubles. It was most unfortunate that he decided that a life of ease was for him, because although Abraham took the least desirable area, his relationship with God had ensured he remained in good hands.

Sodom had a reputation that is well known today. It was a place of severe corruption, so a morally strong man would have left long ago. Certainly homosexuality and other depraved activities abounded to the point where God was ready to take a hand and sent angels to destroy it, and the equally nefarious neighbouring city of Gomorrah.

Abraham again managed to save Lot but, the angels having warned the family not to look back, Lot's wife, who is not named, did and died, leaving just Lot and his two daughters.

Having lost their fiancés in the fire and brimstone that descended from heaven, the two daughters found themselves hiding in a cave with their father. In order to preserve the family line, they decided to have children by their father. Thus was born to Lot by his elder daughter a son who was to found the people of Moab, and the people of Ammon by his younger daughter. Both tribes were pagan.

From a position of opportunity in the care of God's chosen servant Abraham, Lot focused on the things of this world and had no moral standing. Finally he ended up a refugee, fathering children by his two daughters whose descendants ultimately disappeared as a definite entity.

Kingdom of Edom

First the Israelites had to negotiate the land of Edom, the territory of the descendants of Esau. Previously they had been refused permission to pass through the western part of the land (Num. 20:14 – 21) which was located between the Dead Sea and the Gulf of Aqaba. But this time they would be passing through the eastern part which was inhabited mostly by Bedouin that were related to the Israelites and thus more willing to allow them free passage.

God had made it possible, but the people were to be on their best behaviour when they passed through the territory of Edom. What is particularly interesting in all this is that God is the ruler of the whole world, therefore all nations are under His providential rule.

As we read the Hebrew scriptures it is made very clear that nations have the territories that are assigned to them. The rise and fall of nations was under God's providential control and no nation has been able to do precisely what it wants in God's world, not even Israel.

In this case Israel had to respect the right of the Edomites to live where they did, after all they were not yet a conquering nation, for their goal was the land of Canaan. Thus they were to pass through Edom peacefully, paying for whatever provisions they required because:

... the Lord your God has blessed you in everything to which you have put your hand. He has known your every step as you walked through this great wilderness. In fact in all these forty years the Lord your God has been with you, and you have lacked nothing.

One of the factors that becomes very clear in reading history is the rise and fall of empires. In fact the nations of the world have been in a state of flux ever since the beginning of time. Israel is one of the few that has been sustained ever since its formation, because God had a plan for it.

What is interesting are the nations mentioned in Deut. 2:10 – 12, such as the Horites, which no longer exist. The Philistines also disappeared as a nation.

Kingdom of Moab

The territory of Moab, the descendants of Lot through the son of his elder daughter, called Moab, was also to be travelled through peacefully. The Moabitess Ruth was to be in the line of king David having married Boaz.

There would be conflict between Moab and Israel much later in their history, but for the moment Israel had other nations to conquer.

Moses reminds us of the death of the rebellious Israelite men of war, which cost Moses not only the ability to set foot in the Promised land, but much anguish of soul throughout their much extended travels.

Kingdom of Ammon

Again Moses reminds us of the death of the rebellious Israelite men of war.

The territory of Ammon, the descendants of Lot through Ben-ammi the son of his younger daughter, was also to be travelled through peacefully. The map above shows that it was located just above the kingdom of Moab and occupied the northern Central Plateau from the latter part of the second millennium BC to at least the second century CE.

Conflict (Deut. 2:24 – 37; 3:1 – 11)

King Sihon of Heshbon

The Amorite kingdom referenced here is something of an unknown quantity. The Amorites are thought to have been armed herders who took land from others for their flocks as they needed it, but little is known of these people. In this case they lived between the river Jordan and the north eastern part of the Dead Sea and the Kingdom of Ammon.

The area being referred to here was ruled by king Sihon whose capital was Heshbon. It was the first acquisition of land made by the Israelites under Moses.

Moses tells us that he sent messengers when they were still travelling through the wilderness to the king asking for clear passage through his kingdom. It is interesting that we are told first that a dread and fear of the Israelites had percolated the minds and hearts of the Amorite people, just as would happen to the people of Jericho.

News travelled through the various caravan routes in that area, and like today, there is good accurate news and embellished news about small incidents made to appear so large that they are enough to frighten people of the unknown.

Also certain news stays in the memory of some people and it is brought up in conversation long after the event, such as the plagues in Egypt and the defeat of the Egyptian army in the Red Sea.

It is not known if this Amorite kingdom was on a main caravan route. If it wasn't then the news available to them could have been stale, and if perpetuated could easily loom large in the minds of the people especially if they are not strongly protected by topography or manmade defenses. Also if they had heard that the population of the Israelites greatly outnumbered their own, the people would rightly be afraid of them coming too close as suspicion would have loomed large.

Whatever the cause of their fear, the king would not have wanted such a large nomadic nation coming across his land, even had they passed peacefully through three other kingdoms. Especially as the Amorites had an underlying aggressive nature themselves.

All things considered, a frightened people would be an easy enemy for the Israelites to conquer, especially as God was with them.

With the king having a rebellious spirit, he decided to take matters into his own hands and led his fighting men out to meet with the Israelites at Jahaz, but he and his people were defeated and slaughtered.

It is worth repeating, particularly for those who cannot see why even children were killed. Solomon married foreign women worshipping pagan gods against God's instructions, and the influence of their religious beliefs caused even his devotion to God to diminish.

Thus it was imperative that all pagan people, who worshipped demonic gods and objects God had created, and whose descent into immorality through acts of worship had got to a point where God was willing to stand no more, were killed to prevent them contaminating God's chosen people.

Having killed the entire Amorite population under Sihon, the Israelites took over the cities, livestock and anything of value.

King Og of Bashan

It was a short distance further north to Bashan the capital of the Amorite king Og, where, even though there were fortified cities with high walls and barred gates, along with rural towns, they were all taken and the whole population slaughtered. Their livestock and valuable items were taken as the spoils of war.

Distribution of Land (Deut. 3:12 – 20)

The land they had acquired was divided between the tribes that were the descendants of Reuben, Gad and the half-tribe of Manasseh. Manasseh was one of the sons of Joseph.

It is worth pointing out here that there was no tribe of Joseph, rather the descendants of Manasseh, his elder son, and Ephraim the younger son, represented the tribe of Joseph, thus they were referred to as half-tribes.

In Genesis there was pattern of reversal in the lives of many children:

Isaac — supplants Ishmael,

Jacob — supplants Esau,

Rachel — was more beloved than her older sister Leah, although it was Leah who produced six sons for Jacob including Judah, the patriarch of the tribe of kings, and Levi the priestly clan of which Moses was an outstanding member.

Peretz — David's progenitor, followed Zerach out of the womb of Tamar as the result of Judah, her father-in-Law lying with her.[4]

Joseph — supplants 10 older brothers and one sister.

---

[4] For the full story see my book The Origin of Life

After Genesis, the Levite clan was chosen to serve as Temple officiants, thereby displacing the firstborn of each family, who initially had that role (Num. 3).

What is particularly intriguing is, when Joseph's two boys were presented to Jacob he blessed them, taking the two boys to be his own because of Joseph's role in saving the people of Israel. As God made Joseph the eldest of the brothers, because he was the only one who really loved God and served Him with distinction, he was blessed with a double portion with his two sons taking his place in the list of the tribes of Israel.

Although Joseph would have wanted his older son to be blessed with Jacob's right hand and thus preferred, which is why he positioned the boys before Jacob for him to just reach out his hands to place his hands on their heads; for some unaccountable reason, although virtually blind, Jacob, knowing what Joseph would have done purposely crossed his arms so that his right hand was on the head of Ephraim, thus Jacob made Ephraim the senior.

This was emphasized when Ephraim became the strongest tribe in Israel and was sometimes named in scripture in place of Israel, although after the split between the ten tribes and Judah with Benjamin, the land of Ephraim made up the bulk of Samaria.

The reason the Samaritans were hated by the Jews at the time of Jesus was because after the 10/2 split of the nation of Israel creating Israel and Judah, the first king of the ten tribes, Jeroboam, produced two golden calf statues for the people to worship which set that nation on a course away from their God. Because of their rebellion God left them to their own devices and on more than one occasion the Assyrians took some of the Israelite population into exile and replaced them with people from other nations thus corrupting the tribes that had taken ownership of that part of the promised land.

The condition for the tribes of Reuben, Gad and the half-tribe of Manasseh taking possession of the land of kings Sihon and Og, was the promise that the military men of those tribes would fight alongside the other tribes of Israel as they invaded and took over the Promised land.

2 CHANGE OF LEADERSHIP

(Deut. 3:21 – 29)

I commanded Joshua at that time, saying, 'Your eyes have seen everything that the Lord your God has done to these two kings [Sihon and Og]; so the Lord shall do the same to all the kingdoms into which you are about to cross. Do not fear them, for the Lord your God is fighting for you.'

Then I pleaded with the Lord at that time for His favour, saying, 'O Lord God, You have only begun to show Your servant Your greatness and Your mighty hand; for what god is there in heaven or on earth that can do such works and mighty acts as Yours? Please, let me go over and see the good land that is beyond the Jordan.'

But the Lord was angry with me because of you and your rebellion at Meribah, and would not listen to me; and the Lord said to me, 'Enough! Speak to Me no longer about this matter.

Go up to the top of Mount Pisgah, raise your eyes toward the west and north and south and east, and see it with your eyes, for you shall not cross this Jordan.

But command Joshua and encourage and strengthen him, for he shall go across and lead this people, and he will give them the land which you see as an inheritance.' So we stayed in the Valley opposite Beth-peor.

One has to feel some sympathy for Moses, who had weathered so many storms, being prevented from setting foot in the promised land, but he had caused a problem for God and needed to be retired as the leader given all that was to happen after the people had crossed over the river Jordan,

Y'hoshua

Joshua's original name was Hoshea (salvation) son of Nun, but Moses renamed him Yehoshua (Yahweh is salvation) which seems to be significant because it focused on God being the provider of salvation. Also that was the name given to the Messiah, being translated into English as Jesus.

Changing his name might also have been Moses' way of alerting his young disciple to rely on God and not on the people who, in his long experience of leading the nation, were a major headache continually.

> *Also at that time I gave this order to Y'hoshua: 'Your eyes have seen everything that the Lord your God has done to these two kings. He will do the same to all the kingdoms you encounter when you cross over. Don't be afraid of them, because the Lord your God will fight on your behalf.'*

Joshua was initially chosen to select some fighting men to go and do battle with the Amalekites that were threatening them (Ex. 17:8). With Moses on a high hill with his arms raised, God enabled Joshua to be victorious (Ex. 17:13). Then God instructed Moses to record the victory in a book and to acknowledge Joshua, thus confirming that Joshua was His chosen successor to Moses.

More information about the relationship between Moses and Joshua can be found in Numbers 11:28

> *While Israel was in the wilderness and with the Israelites continually complaining, Eldad and Medad began to prophesy in the camp of Israel. So Joshua, Moses assistant, presumably concerned with the purity of the camp and the purity of God's truth, asked Moses to stop them.*
> *But Moses rebuked Joshua saying, "Are you zealous for my sake?" adding, "O that all the Lord's people would be true and reliable prophets of God, with the Lord's Spirit upon them.*

It is interesting that in this text, we find a fascinating truth about Joshua and his relationship to Moses for it reveals that Joshua was a servant — minister — of Moses from his youth. suggesting an ongoing, persistent, durative relationship where Joshua served, cared for, ministered to, and aided Moses in any way he possibly could.

In Numbers 27 we learn that Moses called on the Lord to:

> *appoint a man who will guide them wherever they go and will lead them into battle, so the people of the Lord will not be like sheep without a shepherd.*

In reply:

> *The Lord instructed Moses to, "Take Joshua son of Nun, who has the Spirit in him, and lay your hands on him. Present him before the whole community to Eleazar the priest, and publicly commission him to lead the people. Transfer some of your authority to him so the whole community of Israel will obey him.*
>
> *When direction from the Lord is needed, Joshua will stand before Eleazar the priest, who will use the Urim — one of the sacred lots cast before the Lord — to determine his will. This is how Joshua and the rest of the community of Israel will determine everything they should do." (Nu. 27:18 – 21)*

So what are the attributes of Joshua, a man who spent 40 years quietly behind the scenes as the understudy to Moses by being his assistant, his aid, his minister, his confidant, before taking over the leadership of Israel.

Scripture shows that he has quite an amazingly profound characteristic of humility and service, because for all that time he was willing to be the unseen servant of Moses; so often seen but not heard because he loyally served Moses as the God chosen future leader of Israel.

We can therefore say that Joshua was a Spirit filled fearless leader, with the protective instincts of a shepherd. He was a deeply spiritual man with whom God could communicate, and as such the people had seen him being commissioned so that he was recognized by the people as a man appointed to lead. A man in authority, who was humble enough to be able to handle that authority wisely.

Quite a man.

Moses

So near and yet so far. Moses still wanted to at least set his foot on the promised land but God would have none of it. A new land meant a new start with a new leader. But what can we learn from this?
None of us are perfect, but leaders will be judged far more severely by God, as James writes:

> *Not many of you should become teachers, my brothers, since you know that we will be judged more severely. For we all stumble in many ways; (James 3:1, 2a)*

Sadly Moses made two mistakes that counted against him.

Firstly the way he handled the event with the spies, because he allowed the people too much freedom to decide what they should do having heard the report of the spies.

Instead of hearing that report himself and then passing on an appropriate assessment of the spies' report, they were given the freedom to report direct to the people, who were known to be of a fickle nature. The result of the people's decision on what to do about whether or not to go into the land was therefore inevitable.

Unfortunately, the people did not possess the necessary faith in God or determination to succeed, and thus were not in a fit state to tackle the opposition that they were likely to meet in Canaan to see the task of taking possession of the Promised land through to the end.

Secondly, at Kadesh Moses hit rather than spoke to the rock for it to give up its stored water, which had an adverse effect on what the Lord was trying to teach the people. What is made very clear in the account of the creation is that God only had to speak and it was done, and here God wanted the people to understand the power of His voice as spoken by Moses.

There is so much in this scripture that is important for our education in relation to the style of our faith in God, and how it must be demonstrated by the way we live. Faith and works must go hand in hand:

Who among you is wise and understanding? Let him demonstrate that wisdom by his good way of life, by actions done in the humility that grows out of wisdom.

Except we fully understand our position before God, pride in our position before others can so easily mar any ministry we might think we have. Putting God first in everything we do, and accepting His authority over us is essential.

Consider what the writer to the Hebrews says on this matter:

Therefore, as the Holy Spirit says,
"Today, if you hear God's voice, don't harden your hearts, as you did in the bitter quarrel on that day in the Wilderness when you put God to the test.

The time being referred to is the rock at Rephidim:

The people camped in Rephidim; but there was no water for the people to drink. Which prompted the people to contended with Moses, and say, "Give us water, that we may drink."

So Moses said to them, "Why do you contend with me? Why do you tempt the Lord?"

And the people thirsted there for water, and the people complained against Moses, and said, "Why is it you have brought us up out of Egypt, to kill us and our children and our livestock with thirst?" (Ex. 17:1 – 3)

This was not a peaceful protest, for the people were ready to throw stones at Moses, even after all that they had gone through together. This shows so clearly that there was still an element within the people that was devoid of any understanding of God's love and care for the nation; a harness of heart that was to prove disastrous in future years.

Notice how the people were always ready to complain, and sometimes violently so. When do we read about their thanks to God for all His provisions, and to Moses for his amazingly humble leadership? Had they ever been in real want? Not even their shoes wore out! So:

Yes, your fathers put Me to the test, challenging Me, and yet they saw My work for forty years! Therefore, I was disgusted with that generation — and I said, 'Their hearts are always going astray, they have not understood how I do things'; therefore in my anger, I swore that they would not enter my rest."

By simply hitting the rock, water poured out and the people were able to drink. But it was their continual questioning of the motive of God and Moses that irritated God the most. *"Why is it you have brought us up out of Egypt, to kill us and our children and our livestock with thirst?"*

They were only too happy to leave slavery behind, but they seemed to want everything presented to them on a plate. As we all know life is a struggle and living for God even harder with all the distractions and reverses around and within us.

As for Moses, God allowed him to see the promised land from a distance, from a high point looking out from the mountain, all points of the compass, but now was the time to encourage Joshua and prepare him for his new role as the leader of the people.

Remember it was Moses that appeared to the Messiah with Elijah on the mount of transfiguration.

Remembering Sinai (Deut. 4: 1 – 43)

In spite of the fact that the new generation of adults were young children at the time of the exodus, many of them would have been sufficiently aware of the events at Sinai and would most probably have had the exceptional events explained to them by their parents or relatives.

But now, at this momentous time prior to their entering the promised land, it was imperative that God, through His servant Moses, put before His people the conditions of His care and protection in the future.

Now, O Israel, listen and pay attention to the statutes and the judgments, [God's legal requirements that are to order your future lives] which I am teaching you to observe, so that you may live and go in and take possession of the land which the Lord, the God of your fathers, is giving you.

You shall not add to the word which I am commanding you, nor take away from it, so that you may keep the commandments of the Lord your God which I am commanding you.

In the free living and free thinking social atmosphere of the 21st century, people tend to question every law and rule. Even in churches the Holy Scriptures are debated and changed according to the social thinking of the time, with the people believing they have every right to do so. Yet in 'amending' them where they see fit, they do not realize that by doing so they are rebelling against God, just as the Israelites did.

In so doing they sadly lose their affiliation with the God of creation and of Israel. Without a knowledge of scripture they are unaware of a confirmation of the rule about not tampering with the word of God found in Revelation.

In the free living and free thinking social atmosphere of the 21st century, people tend to question every law and rule. Even in churches the Holy Scriptures are debated and changed according to the social thinking of the time, with the people believing they have every right to do so. Yet in 'amending' them where they see fit, they do not realize that by doing so they are rebelling against God, just as the Israelites did.

In so doing they sadly lose their affiliation with the God of creation and of Israel. Without a knowledge of scripture they are unaware of a confirmation of the rule about not tampering with the word of God found in Revelation.

I [John] testify and warn everyone who hears the words of the prophecy of this book, [all its instructions and teaching]: if anyone adds anything at all to them, God will add to him the plagues and calamities written in this book; and if anyone takes away from, or distorts in any way the words of the book of this prophecy, God will take away [from that person] his share from the tree of life and place in the holy city (the new Jerusalem which is our eternal; abode), which are written in this book (Rev. 22:18, 19).

Before we proceed any further let us all be of no doubt whatsoever that we are dealing with THE God of all creation. This is His earth and above are His heavens, and we also are an intricate part of His creation.

It is entirely up to us how we live our lives. We are not robots but free people. God wants to meet with us and relate to us as we are, all the while wanting to fashion us into people sensitive to the ministrations of His Holy Spirit. For consider the change that came over the disciples after the Holy Spirit came upon them and transformed them.

Consider the change that came over in Moses from the time he met with God at the burning bush and his relationship with God as he led the nation through the wilderness.

For us it depends on how we relate to God and are obedient to His rules for living as to how our relationship develops. What happens to us after our physical death will be His decision and it all rests on how we live according His instructions and rules in this life.

Let there be no doubt whatsoever in our minds or understanding, because God breathed into the nostrils of the first man the

Man + breath of God

(**BODY** \ **SOUL** \ **SPIRIT**)

Animals

(**BODY** \ **SOUL**)

breath of His Spirit, unlike the rest of all other living creatures therefore we are body soul and spirit. However after the body dies we live on after the death of our earthly body as soul and Spirit.

Man After Death

(**SOUL** \ **SPIRIT**)

That is an indisputable fact, no matter whether or not you want to believe it.

Thus accepting the purity of the word is essential if we are to fully understand what God requires of us because of the fact that we are not dealing with other human beings in this matter but with the sovereign creator God.

It was imperative that Moses reminded the people, not only of the transformation of the relationship between God and them as His people when they became betrothed at Sinai, but also of their personal; and collective responsibility as the people of Israel in keeping their promises made to God by their parents on their behalf, and on behalf of all future generations.

The betrothal on Mount Sinai is central to the relationship between God and the chosen people and confirmed by the Messiah for the marriage itself — which the Messiah referred to several times, calling Himself the bridegroom — would have to wait until the marriage supper of the Lamb in the new Jerusalem, when all true believers, both Jew and Gentile members of spiritual Israel, are gathered together in their spiritual bodies in the place of God's rest.

The extent of the environmental turbulence when God came down to the summit of Sinai and spoke to the nation, would have frightened not just the parents, who were direct witnesses of it, but also the children in the camp. And in those days memories were exceptionally good and long.

It was also important that Moses reminded the people of the disastrous consequences of defying God and disobeying His laws such as the incident at Baal-Peor when Moabite women invited the men of Israel to the worship of their gods, feasting and bowing down to those gods, thereby having spiritual intercourse with a demonic god and being joined spiritually to that god. No wonder God was angry with them.

An even greater insult was when a man brought into the camp a Midianite women in full view of Moses and many Israelites, and took her to his tent to lay with her. The priest Phinehas would have none of it and thrust a spear through both of them and killed them, thereby stopping the plague God had sent among them. Let us never arouse God's anger.

We are told that we cannot worship God and the world He had made at the same time; therefore the purity of our relationship with God must be of paramount importance in our minds and in our hearts, otherwise God will withdraw Himself from us and leave us to our own devices.

This was demonstrated by the fact that those who worshipped the Moabite god died, but those that remained loyal to God lived on. It was by these practical experiences that the ordinary people were taught that it was better to stay loyal to the God who had such power over life and death.

What Moses was pointing out was the importance of obedience. As in marriage, sanctity is everything because it breeds trust that results in the security and intimacy of that marriage; after all the man and the woman are still individuals with their own thoughts, feelings and desires which they both need to bring under control in order to focus on the needs of each other.

Moses the teacher

Look, I have taught you laws and rulings, just as the Lord my God commanded me, so that you can behave in accordance with them in the land where you are going in order to take possession of it. Therefore, observe and follow them; so that all peoples will see you as having wisdom and understanding. When they hear of all these laws, they will say, 'This great nation is surely a wise and understanding people.' (Duet. 4:5, 6)

It is interesting that Moses uses the past tense, I have taught you, because this is not the first time he had proclaimed the Divine announcements. In fact in this discourse Moses is recounting critical matters of the past. The reason why was *so that you can behave in accordance with them* (the Divine announcements) *in the land where you are going* because it was a condition of their task in the promised land, *in order* for you *to take possession of it.*

The final part is meant equally for us today as for the Israelites at that time because they were to be witnesses to what God could do in their lives, *so that all peoples will see you as having wisdom and understanding.* We have already discussed the revelatory nature of God as it was revealed I Egypt and during their journey in the wilderness.

Such must be the ultimate aim of all believers — witnesses to the truth and reality of God in order for unbelievers to see them as *having wisdom and understanding.*

The other important point Moses made was that all that he had taught them was *just as the Lord my God commanded me.* Unlike tribal leaders and kings of other nations at that time, Moses was passing on to the people instructions that he had received from their eternal God. Therefore it was essential that the people paid heed to what he passed on to them and live by them.

Consider further the expression, therefore, observe and follow them or apply them, because the whole purpose of teaching someone something is for the student to consider carefully what they were taught and apply that teaching to their lives. God does not give us pointless laws and instructions concerning how we need to live our lives. Rather He alone knows well what is best for us.

Moses asked the people,

"What other nation has such a God as the Lord God of Israel looking after them, being always within talking distance and available all the time?"

In so doing he was emphasizing the fact that throughout their time in the wilderness God had guided them, and supported all of them to that day. They needed water and they got water, they cried out for meat and they were provided with meat. And what about the righteous statutes and ordinances they had received from God that regulate their daily lives. Did they not bring order and purpose to their lives?

They had received an inheritance that is beyond price because they had been born into a nation that was chosen by God. Referring to that inheritance Moses reminds them of *the Lord, the God of your ancestors (4:1)* which means their fathers belonged to God, at least those that were still alive because they were found faithful, and they were born the people of God, but they could only continue to come under God's authority by consent if, for them, He became the Lord *my* God to each and every one of them.

John the Baptist warned the religious leaders of his day not to rely on tracing their family line back to Abraham, because without that personal, dynamic relationship with God He would have nothing to do with them.

How many believers today can give witness to God working in their lives? For those that have no clear evidence, there is a warning to rectify that situation and start seeking God's face, otherwise they will not be received into God's rest.

The Israelites had no excuse after 40 years of training and experiencing God working among them. But it was no good if they did not pass on all that they had learned through those experiences to the next generation. What better teaching could there be for a child than to hear practical examples of God at work in the lives of their parents and grandparents.

9 Only pay attention and be very conscious of the way you live your lives, and diligently follow this law in your daily lives all the days of your life, lest you forget what you have seen, and lose them from your heart.

How easy it is to *forget what you have seen, and lose them from your heart* (memory) in the general turbulence of everyday life. Unless they remembered that the basic principle of God's Law represents the spiritual purity of the God who gave them and His abhorrence of all idolatrous representations of Him or His creation because the intimacy He desires can only come when those that worship Him do so in spirit and in truth, without any distractions.

The birth of the true nation of Israel was established at Horeb (Sinai). It was a spectacular, if very frightening event. But one that could not easily be forgotten because it was there that God laid the foundation for their mutual relationship.

The first commandment concerned the love pact between God and the people; the command not to make any craven image elevated that relationship to a higher spiritual level that if neglected could easily put the relationship in jeopardy; which it frequently did.

It was the incredibly deep love of God for man, and his determination that His plan of salvation should never be defeated, that kept the plan of salvation alive and on course; from which we have so clearly benefitted.

And teach them to your children and your grandchildren, especially concerning the day you stood before the Lord your God in Horeb, wo that they might follow in your footsteps.

The other important matter was the transfer of the basics of their faith in God being passed to *your children and your grandchildren.* Such teaching from personal experience within the senior members of the family when a child is young, and with their memory clear of the accumulation of other things, can be exceptionally important in the later life of the child. It ensures the prosperity of the nation through future generations so that the nation does not descend into heathenism.

The continuing prosperity of the nation, depended on it because the nation's future, as can be seen from the recorded history of the nation, was indelibly tied up in their relationship with God. Good, loving memories passed on to children from parents and grandparents can have a profound effect on them.

Throughout Deuteronomy Moses was insistent that they did not neglect this transcendent duty, this sacred obligation of religious education that accented on the spirituality of their God to their children and grandchildren.

Now you might want to ask the question, "But I am not part of Israel so why should what I am reading affect me?" Let us look at Peter's first letter to the dispersion, that is Jewish believers, this included Gentile believers that had been brought into the fold of Israel, in Jesus as the Messiah. Believers that had scattered to other places due to persecution by the Jewish religious leaders and the zealots:

> *But you are a chosen race, a royal priesthood, a special people for God's own possession, so that you may proclaim the praises [that is all the wonderful deeds and virtues and perfections that each of us has experienced since we believed] of Him who called you out of darkness into His marvellous light.*

Now this second statement is particularly for all those that were not physically born of Israel,

> *Once you were not a people, but now you are God's people; once you had not received mercy, but now you have received mercy.*

So all we are studying was not, is not, just for Israel, for the simple reason God always intended for all that He spoke to Israel to also be passed on to the Gentiles, for He created Adam and therefore all mankind.

Yes Israel was chosen of God, but for the purpose of being an example of those living their lives according to God's Divine instructions; the single channel or mouthpiece for God's word to the nations.

That was Israel's primary task. To be the means of bringing light to the Gentiles, but it was a task in which, for much of their history, they signally failed. What was far worse was that they themselves failed to remember their nation's appointment with God at Sinai and suffered greatly as a result. How could they be a missionary nation if they themselves lost their belief and denied their commission from God?

Remember the fact that it was essential for the people pass on their personal experiences to their children and grandchildren of the never to be forgotten day, a mere thirty eight years previous

> *That day you stood before the Lord your God at Mount Sinai. The Lord instructed me to, 'Assemble the people and I will let them hear My words, so that they may learn to fear Me with awe-filled reverence and profound respect all the days they live on the land, and so that they may teach their children.*

What an awesome moment when they were gathered to hear the almighty creator God speak to them directly. They will have experienced nothing like it in Egypt at the pagan services that were performed on a regular basis.

> *At that time you came near and stood at the foot of the mountain, that burned with fire to the midst of heavens which were in darkness, with cloud and thick gloom. The Lord Himself spoke to you from the midst of the fire; and although you heard the sound of the words, you saw no form — just a voice.*

Surely reading this verse must have made a big impression on subsequent generations. The awesome experience of Almighty God Himself speaking to them out of this cacophony of environmental activity, when the people learned about the two-fold obligation to learn and live according to God's will and to pass on that learning to their offspring.

Not just the environmental violence, but the fact that the people *heard the sound of the words, BUT saw no form.* So why did Moses have to repeat the warning, *And beware that you do not raise your eyes toward heaven and see the sun and the moon and the stars, and all the host of heaven, and let yourselves be led astray to worship them and serve them, which the Lord your God has created and allotted to benefit all the peoples under the whole heaven?*

It was nonsensical.

> *So God declared to you His covenant which He commanded you to follow, the Ten Commandments; and He wrote them on two tablets of stone.*

Although the people heard the ten commandments concerning the regulation of their lives, during the forty days on the mountain God instructed the leader and teacher how to steer the nation through the years ahead; how to observe and live by the laws they were given.

> *14 The Lord commanded me at that time to teach you those statutes and judgments, so that you might do them in the land which you are going over to possess.*

The whole of the journey from Egypt to the promised land was a time of training in preparation for their new settled life in the land He was giving to them.

It is one thing hearing the rules, but quite another thing living a life in accordance with those rules, as we know today because our prisons are full of those who have broken the law of the land. In going back over old ground Moses was at pains to stress the importance not just of hearing the law and how it was delivered to the people living at the time, many of whom were naturally rebellious, but their need to put it into practice.

The one crucial factor was that the people did not at any time see God in physical form.

> *15 So pay attention and watch yourselves carefully — for you did not see any identifiable physical form of God on the day the Lord spoke to you at Horeb from the midst of the fire*

What the people of that time were unlikely to be aware of, or understand, was that God is Spirit and has no physical form. We read in Genesis, *In the beginning God,* which means that before there was anything physical, only God existed. If God was before anything physical existed, all that does exist must have been created by God, so why worship something He created when we can worship the one that created it?

The only way the people could even start to learn about God being without any physical form was for God to tell them not to make any carved or moulded image of Him in any way shape or form because they clearly had no idea what He looked like.

16 so that you do not act corruptly by making for yourselves a carved or sculpted image in the form of any figure, in the likeness of male or female, of any animal that is on the earth, or of any winged bird that flies in the sky, or of anything that crawls on the ground, or of any fish that is in the waters beneath the earth.

All that could be seen in the heavens and the earth were all evidence of His creative skills but had no power in themselves.

And beware that you do not raise your eyes toward heaven and see the sun and the moon and the stars, all the host of heaven, and let yourselves be led astray and worship them and serve them, for the Lord your God has allotted them to serve and benefit all the peoples under the whole heaven.

But what is there in our lives that we worship that is of any physical form? And with all the sophistication of our modern life can we in anyway grasp the fact that God has no physical form?

True the Lord Jesus Christ came to the earth in the form of a human being, but the Holy Spirit was with Him and part of Him. However, the people did not see the Holy Spirit, only evidence of His activity because when Jesus gave the command for the rough waters to become calm, the fact that they became calm was the action of the Holy Spirit. Indeed even today we can experience the presence of that same Spirit, but not see Him.

Having been used to seeing the statues of gods in Egypt it was just another hurdle for them to overcome, which is why Moses emphasized all that God had done for them, from bringing them out of the iron furnace of Egypt *to be a people for His own possession, as you are this day,* even though they could not see Him.

In admitting his mistake *at the waters of Meribah,* although he rightly put the blame on them because they were always a major problem for him, Moses was emphasizing that God punishes those that disobey Him.

23 So be on your guard and watch yourselves, so that you do not forget the covenant of the Lord your God which He has made with you, and make for yourselves a carved or sculpted image in the form of anything which the Lord your God has forbidden you. For the

Lord your God is a consuming fire; He is a jealous God [rightfully protective of their attention and worship of Him because as their creator it uniquely belonged to Him].

God was their benefactor and did not appreciate them worshipping something that He had created or a human had designed from his imagination and then constructed. An object that had no power or ability to function. It was dead. He alone was their creator, sustaining and supporting them. As Isaiah recorded, *I am the Lord, that is My Name; My glory I will not give to another, Nor My praise to carved idols.* Such activities were an insult to Him.

This matter of a jealous and zealous God that would not accept His chosen people worshipping any other gods or images, was a concept either unknown or not understood by other religions, either then or now. A Hindu work colleague was annoyed that Christians thought theirs was the only religion, but it was and is.

Sadly some 'Christians' also do not accept that the God of Israel is truly the only god.

But God's unwillingness to accept any lurking belief in magic, witchcraft, old customs [however apparently innocuous] or anything else that might interfere with a their intimate walk with Him, directly affects the ability of such people to enter into the essential spiritual unity with Him that would transform their lives.

Of His own choosing, God was in a loving covenant relationship with Israel and could never be a stand-off God. There were times when He would intervene purely on account of his great name and His need to keep His plan of salvation, that permeates the whole of the First Testament, on course.

The Hebrew *el kanna* means a zealous God because He was rightly full of zeal regarding His holiness and justice, thus the doings and dealings of the members of His chosen nation were not a matter of indifference to Him because they affected how He was perceived by those of other nations. This is a matter all Gentile believers in the Lord Jesus Christ must also take to heart because our task is to demonstrate in and through our lives the love and power of our God.

But this word was not just for them, because whatever they did was bound to influence succeeding generations:

25 When you become the father of children and grandchildren and have grown old in the land, then if you corrupt yourselves by making a carved or sculpted image in the form of anything to worship, and do evil in the sight of the Lord your God, provoking Him to anger, I call heaven and earth as witnesses against you today, that you will soon utterly perish from the land which you are crossing the Jordan to possess. You shall not live long on it, but will be utterly destroyed.

Nor was this an idle threat as we know from the Biblical accounts of the nation. In fact it was by going back to the books of Moses, and particularly this book of Deuteronomy, that later generations discovered why they had suffered so much; yes and even today.

27 The Lord will scatter and disperse you among the pagan nations, and you will be left few in number among the nations where the Lord drives you. And there you will serve their false gods, the work of human hands, images of wood and stone that have no life in them, which neither see nor hear nor eat nor smell the food offerings presented to them.

A good example of the uselessness of idols can be seen in the account of the capture of the Ark by the Philistines. The greatest insult to God was for the Ark containing the covenant agreement between Him and Israel being put at the feet of their god, Dagon.

On the first morning the image had fallen in front of the Ark so that the image did homage to the Ark. On the second morning the image was in pieces before the Ark (1 Sam.5).

It would be when their situation got to being desperate that they would be reminded of the better times that they had enjoyed:

*So from there you will seek the Lord your God, and you will find Him **if** you search for Him **with all your heart and all your soul.***

Rather like the prodigal son returning to his father, and God would respond in like manner.

30 When you are in distress and suffering tribulation and all
these things have come on you, in the latter days, you will return to
the Lord your God and listen to His voice. (cf. 1 Chron. 7:14;
Zech. 12:10)

Therefore this word was not just for those listening to Moses, but
also for future generations.

This next part is aimed at getting them to remember all those
times when they complained that God had only brought them out of
Egypt to kill them through thirst or starvation.

31 For the Lord your God is a merciful and compassionate God;
He will not fail you, nor destroy you, nor forget the covenant with
your fathers which He swore to them.

The death of the nation, their children or livestock did not happen
at any time. *For the Lord your God is a merciful and compassionate God.* So
how could those that rebelled, using distorted thinking, possibly
believe that God's intention had been to bring about their death. So
this is a command to them to:

32 ask now about the days that are past, the days that were
then before you, in fact ever since the day that God created man on
the earth, and ask from one end of the heavens to the other. Has
anything like this great thing happened, or has anything been heard
that was anything like it?

The meeting of the people with God at Sinai was outstanding in
its uniqueness, power and magnificence. It had never happened
before to any people living at that time, nor would it ever happen
again in the future.

It was unique, a one off that had happened only to them which
made them unique in the world. For God to come to them to speak
with them was a single event, an accolade that they must recognize as
outstanding for it emphasized God's particular love and desire for
them. What is more, of course, is that they lived to tell the tale.

33 Did any people ever hear the voice of God speaking out of
the midst of the fire to a nation, as you heard, and live? Or has any
image of a god ever tried to take for himself a nation from within

another nation by trials, by signs and wonders and by war and by a mighty hand and by an outstretched arm and by great terrors, as the Lord your God did for you in Egypt in your sight?

thinking?

Or has any image of a god ever tried to take for himself a nation from within another nation by trials, by signs and wonders and by war and by a mighty hand and by an outstretched arm and by great terrors, as the Lord your God did for you in Egypt in your sight?

This surely is the most insightful explanation of the comparison between the power of God and a carved image. Moses rightly asks the people this question, *has any image of a god ever tried to take for himself a nation from within another nation by trials?* as God had done by taking Israel out of Egypt?

The sheer scale of all the plagues performed in Egypt were off the scale with regard to power, extent and control. The whole of Egypt was impacted. And there was nothing the magicians and priests of any of the gods could do about it. This meant that none of the gods of Egypt, including the Pharaoh, who was supposed to be a reincarnation of the sun god Ra (but was really just another powerless human being whose life process was no different to that of any other human being), had any power whatsoever. After all the Pharaoh did not have the ability to stop the death of his eldest son and heir.

As it was God was able to display His power unopposed and thus rescue His people, even to the demise of the Egyptian army with the Pharaoh at its head in the Red Sea.

Even we today must be challenged by the words of Moses concerning the unique power and authority of God over the earth and mankind, for in spite of man's advance to such technological heights, he is still unable to control the environmental forces as God did in Egypt and through Israel since then.

We have only to look at the mess man has made of the earth's environment and the lack of peace on the earth to see that man is out of control.

35 It was shown to you so that you might personally know and comprehend that the Lord is God; that there is no other besides Him. Out of the heavens He let you hear His voice to discipline and admonish you; and on earth He let you see His great fire, and you heard His words from the midst of the fire.

Authority and power can be used for good or ill, particularly such as the unassailable power as is held by the Lord God of Israel. What clearly identifies the manner in which God uses His power and authority is in one word, love. But His is no ordinary love (1 Cor. 13), for it far exceeds the love of man.

> *37 And because He **loved** your fathers, He chose their descendants, and brought you from Egypt with His Presence, with His great and awesome power, dispossessing and driving out from before you nations, greater and mightier than you, to bring you to the place where He could give you their land as an inheritance, as it is this day.*

One factor that uniquely identifies our God is His omnipresence and unassailable power, *driving out from before you nations, greater and mightier than you*. A Spirit, yet a person in His own right and in whose image we are created.

We have a God created spirit within our body, as breathed into the nostrils of Adam, and brought back to life individually by the same Holy Spirit as we respond to the same call to which Abraham responded. And our soul and spirit have implanted into them the same characteristics as those of God. Is that not remarkable?

Although the place of His rest (Heb. 4:1 – 3) is outside creation, yet He is still, and will ever be until its demise, the omnipresent God of the physical creation, and able to percolate throughout all that He has created.

What has also been made clear in scripture is that there will come a time in the future when God will create another heaven and earth (Rev. 21:1), the new Jerusalem, that will appear at the right time for our spiritual selves to live in His presence for eternity.

For a moment we need to think about the fact that man is made in the image of God. That is because the answer greatly affects how we relate to God and what we can learn from what Moses announced to the people of Israel.

The evolutionists focus on the fact that man has evolved from apes, and there seems to be an abundance of evidence that man has developed over the millennia from some creature (depending how far you go back in history) to walk upright and to increase in intelligence. That proves that man is part of the animal kingdom.

But there is a problem with that view point, which is the repeated statement that man is made in the image or likeness of God (Gen. 1:26; 5:1 and 9:6) for in breathing spiritual life into man, not only did that give man Divine credentials, it also lifted him far above the animal kingdom. Which means death does not completely obliterate him.

Whereas all members of the animal kingdom are confined to the world meaning their life begins and ends on the earth. Notice that they have no spirit, just body and soul, which means that when the body dies the soul dies with it.

It is because of that input from God that allows scripture to put man on a much higher level than members of the animal kingdom from which researchers have surmised man has evolved.

It is true, scripture tells us that man alone was created in the likeness of the creator, but does not provide us with an explanation as to how it was accomplished or its full meaning and implication although the diagrams above enable us to have an idea. God is God and no one has the mind of God nor His creational ability.

To summarize, there is no purpose in arguing with the evolutionists concerning the gradual development of the first man because archaeological evidence suggests otherwise, and there is no reason why that should not be accepted because there is more that we can learn about the development of man and when in that process God was able to say that He created man, and no one can argue about that.

It is very clear that all animals, indeed all living things have singular characteristic that single out individual living things as having an individual character, best known as the soul. But man had the distinction of being transformed by that breath of God into an individual thinking, and rational being that could communicate with and enter into a full relationship with God. Something no other creature could do.

Now it is true that man could never be God because he is confined to the earth and is dependent upon the food and air supply on the earth, of which God has no need. However God was able, through His eternal life giving Spirit, to furnish man with similar personal characteristics to His own and become dependent not just on physical food, but more importantly spiritual food that only God could supply, being the spiritual source of the development of man.

We are now seeing a picture where God may have developed the body of the man over millennia, but then separately created within that body a completely independent human being with a body, soul and spirit that related to Him in a way beyond that of any other living creature.

What clarifies this matter further is the fact that having designed the man, God then replicated the man by taking a rib from him to create, with a minor alteration, a women. Also God had designed both the man and the woman in such a way that together they could reproduce. It was undoubtedly that clear fact that God produced woman from man and that in future man will be born of a woman, that separated human beings from the rest of His creation.

Also at some time in the evolutionary process, God put within man emotions and attitudes towards others, that were part of His character, such as Paul lists in his letter to the Galatians:

> *But the fruit of the Spirit is love, joy, peace, longsuffering, kindness, goodness, faithfulness, gentleness, self-control. Against such there is no law. And those who belong to Christ, that is they have committed themselves to Him according to the first commandment, have crucified the flesh with its passions and desires. Therefore, if we live in the Spirit, let us also walk in the Spirit.*

This must give us a clue for it is the *fruits of the Spirit* that give us a special identity, for the key seems to be that *we live in the Spirit of God,* in a way that no members of the animal kingdom are able to do.

The God breathed spirit gives **After man sinned** man eternal life, and it was by the spirit within a man being deprived of spiritual food, that is *every word*

that proceeds from the mouth of God (Matt. 4:4), that caused the spirit within an individual, to die of spiritual starvation. Such a situation allows Satan to take control.

Why else would the Messiah have told Nicodemus that he needed to be born again of the Spirit? Why else the need for the Holy Spirit to fall upon the disciples in the upper room prior to Peter's incredible oration on the day of Pentecost.

It would seem that it is the breath of the Spirit of God that was the basic ingredient that transformed man from that identified by the evolutionists, to the man with a character similar to that of God, who is blessed with intelligence, wisdom and understanding.

Although these are thoughts and ideas that would have been unknown to the people Moses was speaking to at that time; what it does reveal is why Moses, Joshua and Caleb in particular were so God focused, unlike the majority of the Israelites.

> *39 Therefore know and understand today, and take it to your heart, that the Lord is God in the heavens above and on the earth below; and there is no other like Him.*

Such was and still is the omnipresence of God that He was and still is *in the heavens above and on the earth below;* both at the same time *and* therefore *there is no other like Him,* for how else could He have displayed so much awesome power in Egypt unopposed by any of their gods? How many things do we prefer than relying totally on this same God.

Moses knew God! After all it was God who had called him to service, and God who had been his guide and protector all those years from floating on the Nile in a basket up to that day. Therefore Moses, led of God as he was, was anxious to impress upon the people their need to get close to God.

> *40 So you shall keep His statutes and His commandments which I am commanding you today, that it may go well with you and with your children after you, and so that you may live long on the land which the Lord your God is giving you for all time."*

Accidents are unavoidable so God wanted to ensure the individual who caused a death accidentally had somewhere to go where the bereaved could not wreak vengeance and be guilty of premeditated murder.

> *41 Then Moses set apart three refuge cities beyond the Jordan toward the rising of the sun in the East, so that someone who had committed manslaughter accidentally could flee there, to save his life: The three cities were: Bezer in the wilderness on the plateau for the Reubenites, Ramoth in Gilead for the Gadites, and Golan in Bashan for the Manassites.*

MOSES SECOND DISCOURSE

PETER RUSSELL-YARDE

3 FOUNDATIONS OF THE COVENANT

Deut. 4:45 – 5:22

> *The Lord our God made a covenant with us at Horeb. He did not make this covenant with our fathers, but with us, all of us who are alive here today.*
>
> *The Lord spoke with you face to face at the mountain from the midst of the fire.*
>
> *I was standing between the Lord and you at that time, to declare to you the word of the Lord; for you were afraid because of the fire and did not go up the mountain. (Deut. 5:2 – 5)*

Here Moses seeks to deal not only with the foundations of the covenant but the spirit in which the covenant is to be kept and the right motives of those who seek to obey it. Indeed the purpose is to define the relationship between God and Israel, emphasizing the basic *spiritual* demands such a relationship imposed on the people of Israel.

The covenant represented a considerable distinction for them, promoting them above all other nations of the earth if only they took time to think about it. The problem the people of the nation of Israel had was that they could not bring themselves to realize just how much of a distinction it was because they, like so many within the church today, could not lift their eyes up from the things of the earth and think about spiritual matters, with many of them not being aware of the distinction between the physical and spiritual. Even many of the priest had the same difficulty.

Remembering that some of the people Moses was addressing were not necessarily present at Mount Sinai, about 38 years previously when the commandments were given to these people, Moses repeats the Ten Commandments to them.

He proclaims the unity of God, together with the duty of each member of the nation to love Him with all their heart, soul and might. This relationship of love between God and His people, and its sustained intimacy through Spirit to spirit communion, had seen them not just released from Egypt, but saved from other more aggressive nations and supplied with all their physical needs in the way of food and drink. Such attention from God clearly demonstrated His total commitment to them and identified the uniqueness of the nation as being particularly special to Him.

Because it was to be an ongoing relationship that would come to fulfilment, not with the arrival of the Messiah, but in the place of God's rest, it was essential for it to be implanted in the minds and hearts of the successive generations to ensure the future of the nation.

What is particularly interesting is that His *love* should be at the centre of the relationship, because the first commandment states that all the people should love the Lord their God with all their heart, soul, mind and strength.

Let us consider each of these elements:

The **heart** was considered to be the centre of their being, both from a physical and spiritual perspective, because that is the source of evil as well as good, and love is at the heart of God. Therefore for them to love God with all their heart means that their love for Him was the foundation of a relationship deep within each person that cannot be changed.

Let us consider this in respect of an incident in which the Lord was involved (Matt. 15:1 – 20)

> *Then the scribes and Pharisees who were from Jerusalem came to Jesus, saying, "Why do Your disciples transgress the tradition of the elders? For they do not wash their hands when they eat bread."*

As the Pharisees were so concerned about following traditions, Jesus took them to task about how they flouted the commandments of God by following the verbal laws compiled by rabbis over centuries that, in many cases, were completely opposite to the commandments of God (vs. 3 – 7; cf. Ps. 78:36; Is. 29:13; Ez. 33:31).

These people draw near to Me with their mouth,
And honour Me with their lips,
But their heart is far from Me.
And they worship Me in vain,
Teaching as doctrines the commandments of men.

The Lord then explained to the crowd:

"Hear and understand: It is not what goes **into** *the mouth that defiles a man [makes him spiritually unclean]; but what* **comes out** *of the mouth, defiles a man."*

The disciples did not get what Jesus meant so they asked Him to explain:

Do you not yet understand that whatever enters the mouth goes into the stomach and is eliminated?

That is the passage the food takes, which is what the Pharisees were concerned about. The oral law was all about obeying physical laws that directed people's life style but had no relationship to their belief in God. But it was about spiritual (God to Man and man to God) matters that, as teachers of the commandments of God, they should have been more concerned about.

But those things which proceed out of the mouth come from the heart (the centre of the person's character, will and understanding), *and it is they that defile a man.*
For out of the heart proceed evil thoughts, murders, adulteries, fornications, thefts, false witness, blasphemies.
These are the things which defile a man, but to eat with unwashed hands does not defile a man." Rather it is a matter of hygiene, therefore it concerns the physical, it is not a moral or spiritual thing.

The **soul** is the person themselves, therefore it was not just the heart of a person but their whole being, their persona, that was involved in loving God. Therefore the soul can be considered as representing the principle of human life within a person, their feelings, thoughts, and actions.

Now all life has a soul, as was mentioned previously, because even animals have individual characters. What separates humans from all other creatures is the *spiritual* breath God breathed into Adam's nostrils, which not only allowed man to communicate with God, but caused man to be transformed into the image of God, that is having many of His attributes and thus removing man from the animal kingdom of which he was once a member.

It is that Spirit breath — spoken about to Nicodemus — that both makes us compatible with God and enables us to communicate with God and gives the soul of man eternal life.

The Lord Jesus is spoken about as being 'tented' amongst us, therefore the real us is not our bodies, which are perishable, being made from the dust of the ground and will ultimately decomposed and return to the ground, but that which is living within the body.

For the **mind** we will have to use our modern day understanding, which is connected to the brain, the hearing, seeing and thinking part of us because it is by using the mind that we search for and discover and seek to understand things. It is with the mind that we process the information we receive in whatever form, particularly those direct messages from God.

And lastly **strength** means that they had to give it their all. The obedience to the commandments of God had to be fulfilled with their whole selves and not give up.

Love is very powerful because it is of God who is its source. It brings people together and unites them. Love binds the new born infant to its mother and father and allows the child to grow up into a well-balanced adult. A lack of love, or hate, destroys. Surely this above all other evidence points to a God of love.

Knowing all about the people's many rebellions and times of questioning the Lord their God and His care of and love for them, it became very clear that it was not because of their own righteousness that they would soon successfully conquer the nations currently inhabiting the land, but for the oath God swore to their fathers, and for his great name's sake.

For He had purposed in His plan for the salvation of all mankind to use the nation of Israel to speak to the nations throught the example of their lives, and provide the ultimate sacrifice for sin. But first God had to prepare the ground that would be to us Gentiles and Jews alike an instruction book for our life in tune with God.

It is essential that not only Israel, but also all believers study and remember the many lessons learnt during the wilderness years, because they are very important to our spiritual wellbeing and growth. As it was the nation did forget time and again how they should relate to and approach their God. Although they did not perish, as did the nations they went into the land to disposes, they came very close to it.

> *Now this is the law Moses presented to the children of Israel. The testimonies, the statutes, and the judgments which Moses announced to the children of Israel after they came out of Egypt and whilst they were camped to the east of the Jordan river in what had once been foreign territory.*

At the beginning of their preparations for going into the promised land, it was essential for the people to know their conditions of service, because ultimately it was God's land that He was prepared to give them in order for them to purify it by their God fearing lives and service.

Deut. 4:45 is an elaboration of v 44. *The testimonies* — literally, attestations — to attest means to declare something is true — *the statutes, and the judgments which Moses announced to the children of Israel.* Moses had to ensure the people knew exactly what God expected of them as He told them about their new life in Him.

As it was so important for the people of Israel to know what was expected of them, should not the same principle be applied to those of us who have accepted Jesus Christ as our Lord and Saviour? Should we not know what God expects of us as we enter into a union with Him through Christ?

The Ten Commandments Repeated (Deut. 5)

This was the summary of religious life, the basic foundation for all human conduct not just for Israel but for all humanity.

1 Calling all Israel together Moses said to them: "Hear, O Israel, I am announcing the statutes and judgments to you today, for you to learn and be careful to observe them.

Moses announced the commandments one by one, as had been given to him by the Divine voice out of the fire and darkness and etched upon the tablets of stone. He reminded those old enough to have remembered that time at the base of the mountain when they *were afraid because of the fire* and he stood *between them and the Lord at that time to declare the word of the Lord* to them because they *did not go up the mountain.*

First Commandment

It was at that time at the base of the mountain that the people heard the voice of the Lord when He spoke with them face to face *out of the midst of the fire.*

What a remarkable occasion that must have been when they heard the voice of the Lord their rescuer from the horror of slavery by many miraculous events and then looked after them throughout their wanderings in the wilderness, even though many died through rebellion against the hand that fed them.

When the Lord spoke with them He declared who He was, *'I am the Lord your God who brought you out of slavery in the land. of Egypt.* He was and is the revelatory God. *I am the Lord (YHWH) the eternal power that guides the destinies of men and nations,* which is no idle boast. Indeed He has complete power over all that He has made, because He is the creator and sustainer of all things.

From the Israelites point of view, this situation could not have been better because the God that created all things was their God, and they were His chosen vessels through which He wanted to reach out to all mankind. How incredible was that?

The surrounding heathen nations may have had their deities, but they lacked any understanding of the far greater matter of the things of the spirit, dealing as they were with Satan, the god of chaos and confusion, of spiritual blindness and death.

Second Commandment

The Israelites had the considerable advantage that the one and only creator God had chosen them to be a nation to carry His name.

First God chose one dedicated man, Abraham, and the one offspring that He had promised, Isaac — Ishmael was the product of Sarai's impatience — then Jacob, one of Isaac's twin sons.

It was through Jacob searching for God in his heart on the mountain that He met with God before meeting with his brother Esau. At that meeting struggling with God, Jacob's name was changed to Israel, which means contending or wrestling with God for Jacob came face with God. What a time that must have been.

From his twelve sons came the twelve tribes but only after the family of Jacob was welded into the nation of Israel in the furnace of Egypt. No longer the patriarch in charge, with the eldest replacing him on his death.

The theme throughout the Bible is about man's fall from grace and the history of God's plan to provide individuals with the gift of salvation, culminating in God Himself coming down and being the eternal Passover sin offering replacing the animal sacrifices.

It is clear throughout that only a small remnant continually kept faith with God, possibly not realizing the crucial role they played in enabling God to reach out to all mankind.

We Gentiles would not have known what we have learned about the love and mercy of God from the beginning of time if it had not been for the records provided by Spirit filled prophets recording God's word to them and providing us with such an important source of knowledge.

How sad that from the start the majority of those who left Egypt with Moses, and their descendants never properly realized the awesome privilege it was for them to have been chosen by the God who, through His mighty and unlimited power, had created all things and sustains all things.

Then the amazing ceremony in which the people entered into that spiritual betrothal with God on Mount Sinai, uniting them in a loving relationship that would ultimately lead to the marriage supper of the Lamb, when the whole of the new spiritual Israel (both Jew and Gentile) will be accepted into His rest, and the full spiritual bonding of saved man with God can be celebrated. The consummation of spiritual intercourse. O the rejoicing that will be enjoyed by the faithful at that time.

Because God rescued them, openly defying all the gods of Egypt, including the Pharaoh, by so many miraculous events that no human could have achieved, it is reasonable that He should be the sole recipient of their devoted worship and praise.

You shall have no other gods before Me.

Because of their betrothal, their relationship with God had to be pure and faithful as with any betrothal; in other words He had to be *the* only God in their lives. The closeness between them and God depended solely on trust and loyalty. The provocation was to be all the greater because the gods they would worship over time were not even real gods, rather the images and other pagan paraphernalia were inhabited by demonic spirits and part of Satan's deception, therefore their insulting behaviour before God was all the greater.

It is interesting that Moses tells the people that the covenant declared in Horeb was not applicable to their fathers, because God knew that they would all have died before the nation entered the land of promise. Rather the covenant which survived the men with whom it was first made, was a binding force upon all future generations.

The announcement of the ten Hebraic words (the decalogue) here repeated, were not necessarily word for word as recorded in Exodus because they were part of Moses' discourse to the new generation and he wanted the freedom to expand and emphasize certain sections of it.

8 'You shall not make for yourself an idol as an object of worship, having any likeness to what is in heaven above or on the earth beneath or in the water under the earth.

There was no point in trying to make an image of God because as an eternal Spirit He has no shape or form. That is why God gave them (and us) the ability to talk to Him from spirit to Spirit.

The problem everyone has is that as soon as they create an image, that image itself has form and there is always the potential for people to worship that image not the One who created all things.

That happened to a family in Austria that accepted Christ as their Lord and Saviour, but there was no movement of the Holy Spirit within the family; so the church pastor and elders went to the family home and prayed. In the corner of the living room was a group of carvings representing the Holy family. As soon as they were removed and destroyed the Spirit fell on all those present. This is undoubtedly a commandment of which many churches need to take notice and remove all idols.

You shall not bow down to worship them or serve them;

It seems rather unfortunate that a human being should consider bowing down to, or praying to some carved or formed object of whatever material, be it wood, stone, silver or gold. What it indicates is just how Satan can convince a person that that object, whatever it is, has superhuman or magical powers, or is in any way a meaningful representation of the person or thing it represents. The commandment is very clear, *You shall not make for yourself an idol as an object of worship,* or indeed as a help in the act of worship.

The problem for the Israelites was that they were surrounded by peoples and nations that were held in fear by superstitions that caused their minds to be so obsessed with certain objects and ceremonies that they became less than human. That was not what God had intended man to be.

It is very important to understand the concept of a jealous God, because the word jealousy is a human concept. God cannot be jealous of a god as being a rival of equal standing with Himself, because there is no one equal to Him. What God sees is a human being made in his image degrading himself.

God's anger was always directed towards those in Israel who reneged on their covenant with Him and worshipped something that had no value. God rightly demands we worship Him because He is the only one who is of any standing in the heavens or the earth.

for I, the Lord your God, am a jealous (zealous) God justly demanding what is rightfully and uniquely mine because I am the creator of all things,

Unless we have fixed in our minds that God created each one of us and is the only one who has any real and sustained power over us, then we will be open to any suggestion by the evil one. For God alone is the guardian of our souls, and the only one who is able to guide and bless us and forgive us our sins.

visiting the iniquity of the fathers on the children, to the third and the fourth generations of those who hate Me,

The word iniquity means to be bent or crooked, therefore any child will more often than not take on the attitude and manner of their parents so that it is inevitable that the descendants of such a person will be a copy of that parent until the third or fourth generation when it is possible that some of the descendants will be either reformed or have the potential to be reformed.

but showing graciousness and lovingkindness to thousands of generations of those who love Me and keep My commandments.

The reverse of the above situation is where the parents are of a loving and obedient persuasion, in which case their descendants are far more likely to be of the same attitude.

The nation of Israel had something special, far beyond anything owned any other nation. They were to worship not something that had been created either by God or man, but the creator Himself. Surely that was so much more beneficial to them, particularly because of His power to assist and empower them.

Third Commandment

'You shall not use the name of the Lord your God, except with the greatest respect and honour because He is supreme above all human and spiritual powers and authorities. God is so awesome that it is impossible for the mind of man to conceive just how great He is.

There is always the danger in this 21st century for us to consider God as our friend in such a way that His true status as our supreme and exalted creator and saviour can so easily be minimized in our minds, thus bringing God down to a human level.

However, it is by being very sensitive to the covenant relationship Israel had with God that was to have the greatest control over how His name was held and used.

God is saying, *do not swear by My name which is above every other name that is named,* even when the oath is true, and certainly not when the oath is to declare a lie.

He has good reason to hold those who utter oaths in His name in contempt for doing such a thing, because they do not know the mind of God, nor His wishes. Such is His authority over all of creation that God Himself can swear by His name as there is no name under heaven that is higher. But that is His right.

There were a number of times when God saved Israel, not for their sake, but for His own name's sake, because He holds His name in such high esteem. Sometimes, it was to preserve the nation through which He would save mankind.

Consider Isaiah 48 (it is worth reading the whole of the chapter because it explains that there is no one like Him, for He knows all things.)

> *This is what the Lord your Redeemer,*
> *the Holy One of Israel says:*
> *"I am the Lord your God, who teaches*
> *you what is good for you*
> *and leads you along the paths you should follow.*
> *O, that you had listened and acted according to my commands!*
> *Then you would have enjoyed peace flowing like a gentle river*
> *and righteousness rolling over you like waves in the sea.*
> *Your descendants would have been like the sands along the seashore,*
> *far too many to count!*
> *There would have been no need for your destruction,*
> *or for cutting off your family name."*
> *(Is. 48:17 – 19)*

This was to be the key message Moses gave to the people. If you are obedient to the commandments and instructions of God, then all will be well with you because He is the perfect guide and will bless all those who live in accordance with His wishes. In other words, not only does He know what is best for you, but He is the only one who can ensure your safety and peace.

Wow! Is that not something we in this century should be willing to do, knowing all the trials and tribulations the people of Israel went through because of their rebelliousness?

God designed all His plans not just for the people of Israel, but for the whole of mankind; plans that were to be developed and worked out through that nation. It was therefore imperative that He maintained the existence of Israel, which He has done to this very day.

Because of that imperative, there were times when for His name's sake it was necessary for Him to preserve the nation in spite of their rebelliousness and obduracy.

Again consider these other words from Isaiah 48:

> *You have heard my prophetic announcements*
> *and seen them fulfilled,*
> *yet you refuse to admit it.*
> *So now I will tell you new things,*
> *secrets unknown to you.*
> *They are created now, not things from the past.*
> *So you cannot say, 'We knew about them all the time!'*
> *"Yes, I will tell you of things that are entirely new,*
> *things you had never heard of before.*
> *For I know so well what treacherous people you are.*
> *You have been rebels from birth.*
> *(Is. 48:6 – 8)*

Here God is telling the people in no uncertain terms just how bad they had been and that by rights He should have obliterated their name from the history of the earth, but He had chosen them for a purpose and therefore it was necessary for Him to sustain them in order for them to, however precariously, continue to serve Him as He had wanted them to.

> *Yet for my own sake and for the honour of my name,*
> *I will hold back my anger and not wipe you out.*
> *(Is. 48:9)*

God's will and purpose for the nation of Israel was uppermost in His mind, so He restrained Himself from doing what He wanted to do to these rebels, not forgetting that throughout their history there was always that remnant of totally loyal followers, just as there are today.

> *I have refined you, but not as silver is refined.*
> *Rather, I have refined you in the furnace of suffering.*
> *I will rescue you for my sake,*
> *yes, for my own sake!*

I will not let my reputation be tarnished,
(Is. 48:10, 11)

Here God is refusing to allow the rebellious people, who thought they were great and powerful to dictate terms to Him. Rather He was causing them to be punished for their attitude to Him making it very clear that He alone was almighty.

With the last line making the point that they can worship idols as much as they liked, but that would do them no good at all because He alone retained all the power over the earth and all that is in it. As they were associated with Him, He would deal with them accordingly because, *"I will not let my reputation be tarnished."*

and I will not share my glory with idols!
(Is. 48:6 – 11)

To put it as clearly as possible:

I alone am God, the First and the Last.
It was my hand that laid the foundations of the earth,
my right hand that spread out the heavens above.
When I call out to the stars, they all appear in order."
(Is. 48:12b, 13)

What is very clear from what Moses was telling the people, is that God cares about individuals, whatever their station and situation in life, but He will never allow anyone to damage His name or use it in a defamatory way.

Fourth Commandment

'Observe the Sabbath day, to keep it holy, as the Lord your God commanded you. Six days you shall labour and do all your work, but the seventh day is the Sabbath of the Lord your God. In it you shall do no work: you, nor your son, nor your daughter, nor your male servant, nor your female servant, nor your ox, nor your donkey, nor any of your cattle, nor your stranger who is within your gates, that your male servant and your female servant may rest as well as you.

Man is not an automaton, but a physical/spiritual being that God designed to need periods of body and mental rest and recuperation. The need to keep just one prescribed day holy meant that it was a time of setting aside the cares of this world and getting close to God.

The reason God made it a commandment was because He knew what man was like and the societal structure that would inevitably be created. The richer a person got, the richer they would want to get, and that would inevitably mean that, as there was no automation in those days, pressure would be put on servants and slaves and animals to work all the hours they could be made to work to increase profits.

There is a difference between the word **observe** used here – meaning to obey a law or rule with its requirement to refrain from things of every working day, and the word **remember** used in Exodus which is considered to refer to a general rule regarding behaviour, as to its sanctification through the use of wine, prayer and sabbath joy as it relates to the people's relationship with God.

The first is for the people's physical health and wellbeing and the second for the people's spiritual God focused wellbeing. God considered six days sufficient time do all that is necessary to provide an income, with the seventh set aside for the mind and body to be prepared ready for the next weeks toil.

The other reason for this day of rest being considered holy, was not so that it could be policed, but because it was a time of relaxation, recuperation and refreshment, of replenishment of the whole nation both spiritually and physically because the two elements are interdependent.

It was to be a time when busy-ness gave way to contemplation and thanking God for His mercy and goodness in regard to the bounty of the earth and the provision of life itself.

As the sabbath belonged to God, just as man belonged to God, it could be said that it was a time when all men, from the top to the bottom of society, had time to re-submit themselves to God.

It was a collective day of rest when *you shall do no work, nor your family, your servants, animals, nor the stranger who is within your gates, that all may rest as well as you.*

It is interesting that the commandment is all encompassing including the consideration of the servant/slave, because, as human beings they also were created in the image of God, and the livestock, because only a heartless person harms an innocent defenceless animal and God rejects such people.

What this commandment tells us is just how much God cares for the whole of His creation. By reminding the people, not only that they must not abuse others as they were abused when they were slaves in Egypt, but that it was the Lord their God who rescued them and cared for them through all their wanderings and gave them the land they were about to inhabit. Because of that it was only right that they should remember Him at least once a week and spend time bonding with Him. Surely that was a very important reason for dedicating that one day per week to such a merciful God.

Going back to the beginning, God worked on the creation over six periods, referred to as days, creating man last, and then. rested. So God knew from the beginning that a 'day' of rest was necessary for life.

Fifth Commandment

'Honour your father and your mother, as the Lord your God has commanded you, that your days may be long, and that it may be well with you in the land which the Lord your God is giving you.

The family is the true building block of any society and nation. The greater the respect within the family, the more stable the society. If an individual does not respect his parents then the family falls apart. Sadly some parents cannot be respected because they themselves are rebels and rejects, as I found as a prison visitor.

Remember Cain respected neither God nor his brother Abel and we know from Hosea how man without God becomes corrupted by the selfishness of the Satan dominated world.

It is only in Deuteronomy that the phrase *that it may be well with you in the land which the Lord your God is giving you* appears, because it stresses the truth that a sound national life can only result from a sound family life within a nation that is focused on observing the commandments of God.

Paul writing to the Ephesian church said:

Children, obey your parents in the Lord, for this is right. "Honour your father and mother," which is the first commandment with the promise:

"that it may be well with you
and you may live long on the earth."

And you, fathers, do not provoke your children to anger or
resentment, but bring them up in the training and admonition of the
Lord.

Moses told the people to do what God was telling him, yet it is
clear from Matthew 15 considered previously, that religious leaders
over the centuries had created alternative laws to those written down
in the word of God, thus *teaching as doctrines the precepts of men.* These
are lessons we in the 21st century AD need to take to heart in case
anyone of us is guilty of doing the same and thus alienating people
from God and the true church.

Sixth Commandment

'You shall not murder.' – Prior to Noah, man was a vegetarian. It was
only after the flood that animals could be slaughtered for food.

Every moving thing that lives shall be food for you; just as I gave
you the green plants and vegetables, so I give you every moving thing.

In commanding Noah and his descendants *not to eat meat along with*
its life, that is, its blood, God made very clear that blood was symbolic
of life. Therefore:

Whoever unlawfully sheds man's blood,
By the judicial government of man
shall his blood be shed,
For God made man in His image.

Because of the unique importance of blood, bringing about the
death of a fellow human being, created in the image of God, is a
crime against God Himself.

This commandment raises the stakes in two ways. Firstly it
emphasizes the sacredness of life, because we are all made in His
image, therefore an attack on a human being is an attack on God

Himself. Secondly by making blood central to the Judaic faith, the illegal shedding of blood is punishable by death.

Seventh Commandment

'*You shall not commit adultery*' – Marriage is a sacred covenant. In Genesis we have God's design of marriage:

> *For this reason a man shall leave his father and his mother, and shall be joined to his wife* (the woman He created as a helpmeet for man)*; and they shall become one flesh (Gen. 2:24)*

The phrase *and they shall become one flesh* not only refers to their physical state when their bodies are joined together. In fact there are three states, emotional, physical and spiritual. If any one of those three dominates, or is not fully shared by both individuals then the marriage is not a balanced marriage.

Hosea clearly illustrated the importance of the nation's relationship with God because of His betrothal (engagement) to Israel on the mountain by his marriage to Gomer. Sadly, over their history as a nation separated unto God, they were constantly playing the harlot, engaging in spiritual adultery so that on numerous occasions God threatened them with divorce[5]. Without the faithfulness of the remnant that could so easily have happened, except for God's plan of salvation, which was the determining factor in God sustaining a part of the nation.

We are not righteous but we are being made righteous, we are not saved, rather we are being saved because God is working in those that have dedicated their lives to Him to bring about holiness within them by the time they enter heaven.

In the centre of the Bible is the Song of Solomon, a love story, which is there to constantly remind us that God is the source of love because it was in love that God created all things, and it is His love that sustains the faithful.

In Mark's gospel we read this conversation between the Pharisees and Jesus:

> *Pharisees: Is it lawful for a man to divorce his wife?*

---

[5] Read my book Hosea

Jesus:	*What did Moses command you?*
Pharisees:	*Moses permitted a man to write a certificate of divorce, and to dismiss her*
Jesus:	*"Because of the hardness of your heart he wrote you this precept. But from the beginning of the creation, God 'made them male and female.' For this reason a man shall leave his father and mother and be joined to his wife, and the two shall become one flesh'; so then they are no longer two, but one flesh. Therefore what God has joined together, let not man separate."*

The coming together of a man and a woman wishing to commit themselves to each other is cemented in the act of sexual intercourse where the two bodies are physically joined together. But they are also spiritually joined together through the love that God imparted to man.

This is the fundamental law of God.

It was man who needed an amendment to that fundamental law to permit divorce. But notice that God says that through that one act of marriage the two *are no longer two, but one flesh.* If at some point after that coming together one or other is joined to someone outside the marriage, then they are an adulterer and sin greatly against God and is separated from Him.

Such was the case of the nation of Israel and particularly the ten tribes that separated to become Israel. The whole nation was spiritually bonded to Almighty God, yet went after other gods. As the record of Jesus speaking about divorce in the passage above makes clear, those Pharisees that challenged Him were not spiritually bonded to God as they should have been.

As in the physical, God's law of marriage also applies to the spiritual relationship of man with God. And Christian believers today must accept that it applies to them today, so that those who neglect God and go after other gods and pleasures will be rejected.

God's command is still the same, both in the physical and spiritual sense: *You shall not commit adultery!*

Eighth Commandment

We have been dealing with commandments that seek to stop the destructive elements of the nation in their tracks by re-emphasizing

God's instructions for living a good and secure life. Sadly succeeding generations were to ignore God's rules and adopt Satan's chaos.

Hosea in exasperation cried out:

> *There is only cursing, lying and murder, stealing and adultery;*
> *they break all bounds, and bloodshed follows bloodshed.*

We have the incredible advantage of all this recorded experiential evidence available to us, and yet so many are totally ignoring this treasury of spiritual knowledge and following in the same shameful ways of Israel. Those that are finally rejected by God have no excuse because they did no take advantage of such a valuable resource.

So to the eighth commandment: *'You shall not steal'* – which deals with honesty and righteousness. If we want to have a relationship with our creator then we must follow the path of righteousness.

In Proverbs we read,

> *ill-gotten treasures have no lasting value, but righteousness delivers from death*, and *the LORD detests lying lips, but he delights in trustworthy people.*

The emphasis is that if we are to maintain our relationship with our righteous God then righteousness must be our goal.

Stealing destroys trust and causes insecurity within a family and throughout society. It is one of a number of negative values. God is the God of the positive.

Consider what Paul wrote to the Corinthians:

> *Do you not know that the unrighteous will not inherit the kingdom of God or have any share in it? Do not be deceived; neither the sexually immoral, nor idolaters, adulterers, perversely effeminate, homosexuals, thieves, the greedy, drunkards, revilers [those who use words as weapons to abuse, insult, humiliate, intimidate, or slander], nor swindlers will inherit or have any share in the kingdom of God.*
>
> *And such were some of you before you believed. But you were washed by the atoning sacrifice of Christ, you were sanctified, set apart for God, and made holy, you were justified being declared free of guilt in the name of the Lord Jesus Christ and in the Spirit of*

our God who is the source of the believer's new life and changed behaviour].

Evil encourages evil. Only the righteous, looking to God for their help and inspiration, will enjoy God's rest.

Ninth Commandment

'You shall not bear false witness against your neighbour' – and the Lord's description of the good Samaritan fully describes who is our neighbour. By using a Samaritan as the main character in that parable, the Lord was also telling the arrogant, self-opinionated, religious Jews that they were not the only product of God's creation, but there were other sheep not of the Jewish fold that He had to bring into the fold of the new spiritual Israel.

With these commandments God illustrates how He wanted men to live whilst revealing His fore-knowledge of what man would become throughout their history which started with Adam being persuaded by his wife Eve to defy God and eat of the forbidden fruit with her, knowing full well what God had said to him about eating the fruit of the forbidden tree. They were quickly followed by Cain who committed the first killing. For mankind, it all went downhill from there until the golden thread of those chosen of God who remained faithful and lived according to God's commandments.

Here we are dealing with another dishonest aspect of fallen man: false witness. What we also need to realize is that to bear false witness means that the righteousness of God is not within our hearts.

A prisoner I was visiting once told me that at his trial what he found the most difficult thing to accept was the lies some of his previous friends had told on oath from the witness box. Such people will not *have any share in the kingdom of God.*

Tenth Commandment

'You shall not covet anything that belongs to your neighbour' – Paul writing to the Philippians confessed that he had learned to be content regardless of his circumstances. It is that self-sufficiency through Christ where we are satisfied with what we have to the point where we are undisturbed and at peace within our hearts with whatever situation we find ourselves in.

What point is there in looking at the things of the earth when our future is with God? I have personally found that throughout my life God has provided my every need, time and time again.

Moses told the people that throughout their forty years of wanderings in the wilderness neither their clothes or sandals wore out (Deut. 29:5). In which case why covet something that you think you need but could well do without just because someone else has it? Think what happened to Achan when he stole from God at Jericho! (Josh. 7:16 – 26).

It is noticeable that the desire for a neighbour's wife is separate from his other possessional cravings by the different use of words.

In the first case the word used is **covet** — which means to wrongfully long to possess something inordinately, or without due regard for the rights of others. It is a state of mind that can drive a man to do something he would not normally do.

In the second case the word used is **desire** which is a fundamental distinction with far-reaching moral consequences. To desire is to have a strong feeling of wanting to have something, particularly if it is not yours or available to you. In this commandment the word field is included which is appropriate for a people about to go in and possess land.

Both feelings are to be held in check.

Moses' summing up

> "These are the words the Lord spoke to all your assembly, from the mountain in the midst of the fire, the cloud, and the thick darkness, with a loud voice; and He added no more. And He wrote them on two tablets of stone which He gave to me.

This is a remarkable statement. *These are the words the Lord spoke to all your assembly.*

The Almighty God who created all things and had snatched His people from the might of Pharaoh and his army, demonstrating so clearly His control of the environmental elements, even to using the sea to destroy Pharaoh and his army in one foul swoop. And all because the Pharaoh was driven to hold onto that which God had asked him to release.

As they wandered through the wilderness, it was God who supplied them with food and water and dealt severely with the disruption of the rebels, whilst preserving those who were prepared to trust God for the future.

Battles were won because of God's intervention and, if it had not been for the distrust of ten of the twelve spies, they would have taken possession of the promised land thirty-eight years earlier.

4 MOSES THE GO-BETWEEN

Perhaps the saddest thing is that having experienced the loving care of God through the exodus and the initial stages of their journey in the wilderness, the people still could not allow themselves to fully trust God. The leaders of the people approached Moses and first admitted that,

> *5:24 Surely* **the Lord our God** *has shown us His glory and His greatness, and we have heard His voice from the midst of the fire. We have witnessed this day that God spoke with man; yet man still lives.*

As we discovered in the previous chapter, God gave them the basic rules for when they would be living in a settle environment. What on earth would have been the reason for God to promise them the land of Canaan that was flowing with milk and honey and give them the rules of living which, if adhered to, would enable them to live long in the land, and yet kill them before they were able to enjoy possessing the land?[6]

In saying to Moses with some amazement, *We have witnessed this day that God speaks with man; yet man still lives*, surely that proved that God had their best interest at heart. So why shouldn't they live? After all Moses had been up the mountain and far closer to God than they had for forty days and nights, and he was still alive.

---

[6] Matt. 7:1 – 12)

But these were the children of released, possibly paganized slaves, with the majority of them totally out of touch with the God of their forefathers. Fortunately, as was to be the case throughout the history of their nation, a remnant was still holding to the worship of the God of the Patriarchs, such as the parents of Moses because they taught him about their God during his years of being weaned.

There is no doubt that the lives of their parents would have been hard and coarse and the whole aspect of a loving God was a completely strange concept to them, and that coarseness will have in some measure rubbed off on the present adults. We have to realize that for so many this new life was very strange to them.

Having confessed that

> *We have witnessed this day that God spoke with man; yet man still lives.*

why should they quickly add:

> *5:25 Now therefore, why should we die?*

By now Moses had great confidence in God through personal experience, but for some reason he could not transfer that trust to the people.

> *For this great fire will consume us; if we hear the voice of the Lord our God anymore, then we shall die.*

This has all the hallmarks of irrational fear with an undercurrent of panic, which led to them asking Moses to be their go-between

> *You, go near and listen to everything that the Lord our God says; then pass on to us everything that the Lord our God tells you, and we will listen and do it.*

Their reluctance to speak with God direct, as Moses had done when he met with God t the burning bush, would be an impediment both for them and the nation which would cause them much suffering, particularly after the death of Moses who had been such a loving and caring father figure to them.

God was saddened that they clearly did not have the mental capacity to understand Him or the way He wanted to lead them in the future. It is true that one of the plagues involved thunder and lightning and must have remembered the devastation that that had caused, and were possibly fearful by association.

God told Moses

> *I have heard the voice of the words of this people which they have spoken to you. They are right in all that they have spoken.*

What was particularly sad is that they had not understood from all that had happened since the arrival of Moses and particularly during their wilderness journey, the way God had lavished so much love and care upon them, that providing they gained a respectful fear of God and kept His commandments then their lives and the lives of their children would be transformed.

> *Oh, that they had such a heart in them that they would fear Me and always keep all My commandments, that it might be well with them and with their children forever!*

You can see the love and commitment of God towards the people. This is not just any person speaking these words to Moses, but words of great and searching love from the heart of the glorious Divine creator, giving voice to the core reason for Him not only creating the heavens and the earth, but choosing them to be His special people.

Having already asked Moses, with his face bright with reflected glory after he had been with God, to cover his face once he had told them what God wanted them to know, the question that needs to be asked is why? What was there in their minds and hearts that caused them to want to keep God at arms-length? God would always be there, but Moses would go the way of all flesh.

To the Corinthians (2 Cor. 3:13 – 15) Paul wrote:

> *Moses put a veil over his face so that the children of Israel could not look steadily at the end of what was fading. For their minds were blinded through fear. Even now that same veil remains in their*

hearts when the First Testament is read, until the veil is taken away in Christ.

When the sun shines on a building, the building heats up, but as soon as the sun stops shining the heat dissipates. When Moses met with God, the glory of God shining on his face caused it to glow so that when he met with the people they were able to see his face shine with God's reflected glory, but gradually that glow faded. This tells us just how bright is the glory of God, even from His back view which Moses was permitted to see (Ex. 33:23).

For some reason the brightness of Moses face had an impact on the people. Perhaps it had the effect of amplifying their sense of sinfulness, or that it was so out-of-this-world look that it just frightened them. Whatever the reason, they could not handle it. Their remedy was to ask Moses to veil his face as soon as he had finished passing on to the people what God wanted them to know, which meant that they were unaware that that received glory faded the longer he was away from God.

Sadly this action caused the truth to be hidden from the people so that when they were away from the Lord, the glory He imparts fades and they were back to themselves, but it also prevented them from understanding that the first covenant was only a temporary measure that would one day be replaced by another.

The problem for the Jews at the time of Paul, which has been perpetuated even to those of today, was that the covenant of the law had already faded and a new covenant and a new relationship with God had come into effect but was now hidden from them.

After his spiritual transformation he saw the veil over the face of Moses as a symbol of the lack of understanding that he himself had had before God took him aside in Damascus to explain to him the truth of His complete plan of salvation.

First came the law and the animal sacrifices until the moment in time when the training in God's mercy and forgiveness received by the Israelites had come to an end. The Messiah arrived to trigger the transformation from Law to Grace, when the Aaronic high priesthood was ended and the throne of David was occupied by Jesus along with His appointment as the Melchizedek type high priesthood.

It was the ultimate combining of king and priesthood that could only be established in the Son of God.

It therefore becomes very clear that right from the start the Jews were not receiving the whole truth because the veil they wanted Moses to wear hid the fact that the covenant of the law under which they were then living would fade away and God would introduce a new covenant.

Paul explained this matter (2 Cor. 3:7 – 11):

> *Now if the ministry of death engraved in letters on stones, the covenant of the Law, which led to death because it identified sin in man, was announced with such glory and splendour that the Israelites were not able to look steadily at the face of Moses because of the brilliance of its fading glory, how more will the new covenant, the ministry of the Spirit which allows us to be Spirit-filled, fail to be even more glorious and splendid?*

Let us be very clear about this comparison between the covenant of the Law passed on to the people by Moses after he had been in the presence of God, which defined the Divine standard by which the people would live and be judged, and the covenant of grace sealed by God with the blood of the Messiah.

In the first instance the covenant of the law was delivered to the people by Moses whose faced glowed with reflected glory. Whereas in the second instance, the new covenant of grace was born out of the grim reality of the cross and the grave, but was established through the eternal brightness of the risen Son.

> *For if the ministry of the old covenant, the law, that brings condemnation (ref. Ro. 7:19 – 25) has glory, how much more does glory overflow in the ministry of the new covenant which declares believers free of guilt and sets them apart for God's special purpose that brings righteousness! (ref. Heb. 9:13 – 15).*

This clearly brings to the fore the salvation of mankind was planned by God in two stages. First came the covenant that established that sin was endemic within man. The law by which men were to compare their lives was impossible to fulfil, hence the animal sacrifices, thereby confirming that there was inherited sin in their lives. Whereas the second was revealed not by that voice from the mountain top, but by the grace of God as shown by the sacrificial actions of the Son of God.

The first may have been announced in the glory of the Divine presence as captured on the face of Moses, but the second provided the basis for a new and greater intimacy between the repentant sinner and the only one who could enable the sinner to achieve a life of love and service in the presence of God.

> *Indeed, the Law had glory at one time, but now the glory of the gospel [the good news of Jesus Christ] surpasses it. For if the Law, which fades away came with glory, how much more must the gospel of our Lord and Saviour Jesus Christ, which is permanent, abide in glory and splendour!*

Now it is very important that we do not merely pass over this historic event as being in the past without challenging ourselves, because that is what Paul pointed out to those Jews and Gentiles living in Corinth.

We must be ever mindful of the highly respectful way in which we must approach Him, given the divine purity of His person and with the knowledge that He is our creator and sustainer, supported also by the knowledge of His all-embracing love for us.

Paul also lamented to the Roman (Ro. 11:25 - 27) believers regarding the Jews rejection of Jesus:

> *I do not want you to be unaware, brethren, of the mystery of God's previously hidden plan for Israel, lest you should be wise in your own opinion concerning the partial blindness that has temporarily happened to Israel which will last only until the full number of the Gentiles has come in.*

Gentiles beware! We must accept the people of Israel as God's eldest son, for Abraham, Isaac and Jacob/Israel were each one chosen of God and it has been through Israel that all the oracles of God have been passed down to mankind. That was a decision of God and must be respected as such.

All that we are studying in Deuteronomy floods us with understanding of the particulars of God's loving relationship with Israel. That Israel did not respond in the way that they should have done must not detract from the revelation of all that God had wanted the people of Israel to know and for us to learn.

We too, being saved by the blood of the cross must be very conscious of the way in which the apostles and believers reacted to the commission given to them by the Lord Jesus to go out into the world and proclaim the new covenant in His blood. It was not an easy task in those days with many surrendering their lives as living sacrifices in the service of the God that had called them.

Finally all Israel will be saved, that is true Israel, those Jews who finally believe in their Messiah.

> *At that time all those of Israel*
> *that have a personal faith in Jesus as Messiah*
> *will be saved; just as it is written:*
> *"The Deliverer (Messiah) will come out from Zion,*
> *He will remove ungodliness from Jacob."*
> *"This is My covenant with them,*
> *When I take away their sins."*

As we continue to study this time of Moses' final discourses we cannot neglect the fact that right to the end of His life Moses was a listener, every ready to hear the voice of God. Even now, as the people returned to their tents, Moses remained to listen to all that God wanted him to know in order for him to teach the people.

So here is God's command to Moses about what he had to pass on to the people?

> *5:33 pay attention and be careful to do just as the Lord your God has commanded you by not deviate from His commandments either to the right or to the left. You shall, live each and every day in all the ways which the Lord your God has commanded you, so that you may live and so that it may be well with you, and that you may live long in the land which you will possess.*

This equates to the meeting Jesus had with the disciples when He gave them instructions as to their future role (Matt. 28:16 – 20):

Now the disciples went to the mountain in Galilee, Jesus had designated. And when they saw Him, they worshiped Him; although some doubted whether or not it was really Him.

Jesus approached them and said, "All authority in heaven and on earth has been given to Me. So I command you therefore to go and make disciples of all the nations, helping the people to learn of Me, believe in Me, and obey My words, baptizing them in the name of the Father and of the Son and of the Holy Spirit. Teach them to observe everything that I have commanded you; and lo, I am with you perpetually in all and every circumstance, even to the end of the age."

The Commandment (Chapter 6)

1 "Now this is the commandment, and these are the statutes and judgments which the Lord your God has commanded me to teach you, that you may observe them in the land you are crossing over to possess,

So Moses, in response to God's instructions, reveals God's commandment, that is the statutes and judgements of God, to the people for them to obey as they take possession of the new land of promise.

The God/nation relationship had to be founded on Israel's total respect for, and commitment to God, and by obeying His instructions they would receive His protection and blessing:

*2 that you may **fear** the Lord your God, to keep all His statutes and His commandments which I command you, your son and your grandson, all the days of your life.*

The **fear** expressed here is not being terrified, more for them to show awesome respect to almighty God who had chosen and called them to be His people.

To illustrate this we read in Leviticus (10:1 – 3)

Then Nadab and Abihu, the sons of Aaron, each took his censer and put fire in it, then incense on it, and offered profane fire before the Lord, that He had not commanded them. So fire went out

from the Lord and devoured them, and they died before the Lord.
And Moses said to Aaron, "This is what the Lord spoke, saying:

'By those who come near Me
I must be regarded as holy;
And before all the people
I must be glorified.' "

As sons of Aaron the high priest, Nadab and Abihu should have realized the awesomeness of God and shown Him due deference, particularly for the reasons we will see below. Certainly they had been witnesses to His majesty and the awesomeness of His presence on the mountain, therefore to insult God in the way they did was reprehensible, for which transgression they paid with their lives.

Let us take stock of where the nation was at this stage.

It had spent 400 years in Egypt with much of it in hard slave conditions and had been crying out to God for release. Then came Moses, called of God to lead His people out of that harsh environment, and towards a land God promised them and that the spies had discovered really was a land flowing with milk and honey.

God took them by a devious route because he knew their rebellious, ungrateful and demanding nature and did not want such unruly and rebellious people taking possession of His land until after they had been purged.

The people seemed to find it hard in their hearts to be thankful for anything that God had done for them. They were never satisfied with the freedom they now had, possibly because they could not give up their slave mentality and wanting everything done for them.

Having been so used to taking orders and toiling in a punishing daily round, even though they had called upon God to rescue them, the transformation from the shouted commands of the taskmaster and crack of the whip, to the peace and freedom in their new state as a sovereign nation in the wilderness seemed too much of a dramatic change for them to cope with.

Under the continuing slave conditions there must have been a sense of permanence, of security, however harsh that regime appeared to be; whereas now in the wilderness life no longer seemed so regimented and contained, creating within them a sense of uncertainty about what each new day would bring. So many of the people were lost. Suddenly they were responsible for their own daily tasks.

I knew some prisoners, during my days as an official prison visitor, that had got so institutionalized that they did not want to face the outside world, because they had gained comfort and security in the virtual monastic surroundings of the prison and they had nothing outside of the prison that attracted them.

Also, the people, certainly those without a faith in the God of Abraham, been surrounded by religious structures and effigies and religious worship along with much superstition, they could well have found the worship of this unseen God unnerving.

Yes they could see Moses and hear what God had to say to them through him, but for them to properly understand the whole aspect of a mighty unseen God with whom Moses met and who caused his face to unnaturally shine, was a different matter.

We cannot possibly ignore the effect on the minds of these, for the most part, simple people, the transformation from the oppressive fear of the Egyptians right up to the moment they saw the sea drown their oppressors as they looked on from the other shore of the sea, to the life of wandering as a nomadic people.

You will inevitably have the rebellious in any society. Jesus spoke about the tares and the wheat (Matt. 13:26). Although a man sowed good seed in his field, an enemy (notice that word *enemy* because the Lord was clearly identifying Satan) came and sowed tares amongst the wheat (like the wolves that would come in and not spare the flock mentioned by Paul to the Ephesian elders). The owner of the field would not allow his servant to remove the tares in case they disturbed the roots of any of the wheat. No, the tares would be dealt with in the final days.

During the nation's wandering in the wilderness, however, the rebels were dealt with promptly in order to purify the people that would eventually go in to possess the land.

> *3 Therefore Israel, listen and be careful to do them (the statutes and the judgments), that it may go well with you and that you may increase greatly, as the Lord, the God of your fathers, has promised you, in a land flowing with milk and honey.*

The whole point of creating the nation of Israel from the embryo of the Patriarchs was that they should become a people of God, distinguished by their respectful fear of God. By being willing to obey the commands of God, they would be entering into the type of relationship He had desired to have with man from the start.

They would also, from a purely selfish point of view, enjoy spiritual growth that would definitely single them out from all the surrounding nations and allow them to be an example to all mankind.

What is also clear, given the experiences of those leaders devoted to God such as king David, is their singleness of purpose and moral high standing that would attract many to emulate their lifestyle.

The next verse exemplifies the singleness of their faith as opposed to the multitudinous nature of that of the pagan nations:

4 Hear, O Israel!
The Lord our God,
the Lord is one!

This declaration of the oneness of God, is *the* basis of the Judeo/Christian faith, the foundation stone on which all the commandments and judgements are based. It declares God's sole, supreme and unassailable authority over everything on, in and all around the earth. Nothing whatsoever can happen without His knowledge and approval. Indeed there can be no greater declaration than this. *The Lord is our God; the Lord is one!*

And notice how it was phrased by first identifying the ultimate supremacy of *The Lord* as **our** *God,* and then acknowledging and accepting His choice of them as a nation and their need to absorb and integrate that knowledge into all their thinking and make it the basis of their daily lives.

But that is quickly followed by the qualifying declaration of the uniqueness of God being singular, *the Lord is one*, as opposed to the multitudinous gods worshipped by the other nations, and therefore it is imperative that the worship of no other god is contemplated.

With the multitude of gods worshipped amongst the surrounding nations, and even in Egypt, it was necessary to establish that their God was not one of many, but *the* God to whom they owed their complete and sustained allegiance.

Speaking through Isaiah God says regarding His empowering of Cyrus the great (Is. 45:5): *I am the Lord, and there is no other; "There is no God besides Me. I will gird,* or embrace, *you, though you have not known Me"* This message out of the mouth of God declared that everything was in His power to do because there were no gods equal to Him that could oppose Him.

It harps back to the first verse of scripture *In the beginning God* and this declaration of the unity and oneness of God to the newly moulded nation of Israel that was on the brink of wiping away the evil of the pagan tribes then inhabiting the land, established the true, supreme sovereignty of their God.

It was to be their insurance that nothing could prevent them from succeeding in the land providing they held the uniqueness and singularity of God in their hearts and minds at all times.

We now come to a unique verse because it is the first time in human history that having a love for God takes a prominent role. Indeed no other religion so emphatically and prominently puts such a requirement upon its adherents.

This is the first commandment from which all other commandments stem. Without understanding and observing this commandment, all the others are of no consequence.

> *5 You shall love the Lord your God*
> *with all your heart and mind*
> *and with all your soul*
> *and with all your strength,*
> *that is your entire being.*
> *(cf. Matt. 22:37)*

Love is of God. It is at the centre of His creation because in Him there is no darkness, or hatred, or deception at all. John in his first letter says this:

> *Dear friends, let us continue to love one another, for love comes from God. Anyone who loves is a child of God and knows God personally. Whoever does not love does not know God, because God is love (1 Jn. 4:7, 8).*

Love, along with all other essential people-bonding attributes, is at the core of human relationships, because being made in the image of God we initially had the love of God implanted in our hearts. It is, after all, a supreme unimaginable love that binds the Godhead.

Hate and suspicion, which was introduced by the rebellious angel Satan, divides, whereas love brings people together and unites them, and that is the basis of God's design because although love is just one of the many attributes of God, it is by far the most important.

Unless that love dominates our relationship with the God who gave us that love, then it is of that lower fickle human love that lacks the power and intensity necessary to love a God that cannot be seen with the naked eye, only experienced by our regenerated spirit.

Paul writing to the Corinthians spoke of the many gifts of the Spirit of God (12) and (14) and how prophecy, that is the forth telling part, the opening out of God's word to others just as these books of mine seek to achieve, was by far the most important gift. And sandwiched in between is the celebrated chapter 13 on the importance of love. Without love not one gift of God is of any value whatsoever.

If God did not have love, then love would not be a central theme amongst families, husbands and wives, parents and children. It is love, of which God is the source, that brings a man and woman together and cements their relationship in marriage in order to produce children, if they are physically able.

What is special about this commandment is that just as God is love and loves the man he created, He wants man to love Him in return and as we have already discovered, God's relationship with Israel, and now since Christ's sacrifice, for all who truly believe, was (and is) to be in the form of an engagement.

Notice that the love God expects from us is to be life absorbing, for it is to be *with **all** your heart and with **all** your mind and with **all** your soul and with **all** your strength,* **that is your entire being** as enhanced by God.

It is worth analyzing this very important commandment further:

The ***heart*** was considered at that time to be at the very core of a person

The **mind** was considered to be that inner part of the human being in which thought takes place along with perception and understanding resulting in decision making that result in the outward expression of a person to do good, or evil, and similar actions.

The **soul** (nephesh), was considered to be the living, breathing conscious person, rather than an immortal soul. The person themselves as distinguished by their personality. The immortality part is the spirit within a person.

Did ever a king require His subjects to love Him? Surely love, in its purest sense, can only be expressed between two people attracted to each other by a mutual attraction and with a deep desire to be together. It is that bonding in true love that provides a strong bonding.

In Exodus after God had revealed His might in the crossing of the Red Sea by Israel and the drowning of Pharaoh's army we read:

The Lord is my strength and my song, and he has become my salvation; this is my God, and I will praise him, my father's God, and I will exalt him. (Ex. 15:2)

When we consider the command *and with* **all** *your strength* it is interesting to be reminded of what Moses said concerning the Lord being *my strength*. In other words, it is possible for us to have the resolve to love the Lord our God. But even better if we are in such a loving relationship with Him that we can also call upon the strength of God to provide us with that added element of strength to stay the course that we can so often need.

Seek the Lord and his strength;
seek his presence continually!
(1 Chron. 16:11)

Love is such an essential ingredient in our relationship with God that without it not only can we not get that added support from Him, but our lives would be at the mercy of all the vagaries of life as the Israelites were ultimately to find out to their cost.

> *6 These words, which I am commanding you today,*
> *shall be inscribed on your heart and mind.*

What Moses was teaching the people had to be assimilated into their very being in order for it to take effect and become a natural part of their daily living.

It is interesting that it was essential that the words from God that Moses was passing on *shall be inscribed* on both their heart and mind. As we have already seen the ***heart*** was regarded as the very core of the person, that central part from which love and hate, good and evil originate. And the ***mind*** was that inner part of the human being in which thought takes place along with perception and understanding.

In other words the commandments of God had to become a core part of a person's very being. They had to become a central part of their lives to establish and enhance their relationship with God. How else could Moses and all the prophets that followed him enjoy such a strong faith that even in the most hostile of circumstances, when their lives were in very great danger and even when they were being tortured to death, they were able to be obedient to God and tell the people what God wanted them to know, even when God was reprimanding the people through them?

But the people's responsibility did not end with their own state of heart and mind. It was essential that they also taught their children, whether or not the children learned the lessons of their parents as in Jacob's case where only Joseph loved God as much as he did.

> *7 You shall teach them diligently to your children*
> *impressing upon their minds the importance of God's precepts*
> *and causing His truths to penetrating their hearts.*

What better way of learning and establishing God's word in our hearts and minds than to speak of them in conversations within the family so that it becomes part of the children's natural development.

Also one of the best ways for a person to establish information of a subject that they are learning about in their minds and hearts is to speak about it and discuss it. Even to mull it over in the mind.

For me to write these books it is necessary for me to turn the subject matter over and over in my mind, to think about it, meditate on it in order to grasp its meaning. Although I consult with commentaries and search the web I never copy what others have written word for word, preferring to allow God to sort the information out in my own mind and then write as He directs.

Therefore the advice Moses gave to the people for them to *speak of them when you sit in your house and when you walk on the road and when you lie down and when you get up* was most sensible.

For others there was the need for an object of some kind, a memory jogger, hence the suggestion of binding them *as a sign on your forearm, and as bands (such as a frontal or, frontlets) on your forehead* or even writing these commands *on the doorposts of your house and on your gates.*

The one problem with such physical things is that their true meaning can often vanish and the commandments can so easily become forgotten and the object itself become an object of worship.

The Peril of Forgetting

This need for every person to know the commandments, the rules that were to govern their life in the promised land, was for the relationship they had with God to be enhanced and become part of their natural way of life and thinking. Their 'religion' was not to be an add on but the essence of their life before God.

What is more it was important that they never forgot certain facts:

1. that it was God who had brought them to the land that He had sworn to give to the descendants of *Abraham, Isaac, and Jacob* because of the faithfulness of those men.

2. It was a land with great and splendid cities which they did not build.

3. The houses were full of all good things which they had not provided.

4. There were excavated cisterns (underground water reservoirs) which they had not dig out.

5. vineyards and olive trees which they did not plant.

6. they would eat and be full and satisfied. No further need of manna.

Having received the gift of so much of what they had not worked hard to build up, there was a very strong chance that they would not appreciate it and completely forget that it was *the Lord who brought you out of the land of Egypt, out of the house of slavery* and had provided all that there was for them to enjoy.

This brings to mind the thought that as sinners saved by the blood of the Lamb of God, we could well not appreciated all that God through Christ has done for us!

This is especially true of those who, having been told about salvation, have been led to understand all about it from scripture and accepted Christ as their Lord and Saviour, but then have not pursued the study of scripture, as the Israelites were being instructed to do, in order to gain a deeper and more solid understanding of all that the Lord had to go through in order to provide them with that salvation.

As the writer to the Hebrews (5:12 – 14) wrote:

> *For though by this time you ought to be teachers because of the time you have had to learn these truths, you still require someone to teach you again the elementary principles of God's word from the beginning, needing to be continually fed with milk like spiritual infants still at the breast, not solid food like spiritual adults who have studied the scriptures to fully understand what salvation is all about.*
>
> *Every believer who lives on milk is inexperienced on matters of doctrine and unskilled in the word of righteousness, since he is a spiritual infant. Solid food is for the spiritually mature, whose senses are trained by practice through the knowledge of the word of God to distinguish between what is morally good and what is evil.*

How many of those who go to church, who regularly worship with other believers, really understand what being a member of spiritual Israel really means, if they even know what spiritual Israel is.

A relative, who had been brought up in the church with parents that both had lay positions in the church, had gone to Sunday School and was confirmed as a church member, bought a copy of my book The Tent of the Meeting and had to admit to me that she did not understand a word of it, yet is solid scripture from Genesis through to Revelation. After over seventy odd years in the church she did not know scripture. Still just a babe needing to be bottle fed with milk.

Do such people really know what the Christian faith is all about or what they have to do to remain in that fold and not wander off like an errant sheep? After all there is always the chance that, like so many Israelites, they may be met with God rejecting them on the day of judgement with the words, *begone from me, I never knew you!*

Moving on we read about what they had to do to remain close to God.

> *13 You shall fear the Lord your God alone; and you shall serve Him with awe-filled reverence, profound respect and swear oaths by His name and His name only.*

You shall be fearful of not fully appreciating the power and ability of God to love and protect you. Although the charge of rebelliousness against God is always there over our heads because of Adam and the resulting DNA of sin that seeks to destroy us, God is constantly providing the antidote all the while we seek after Him *with awe-filled reverence,* and *with profound respect* worship Him only.

It is our focusing upon God who alone is able to block out the debilitating distractions of the world, thus enabling us to become united spiritually with God.

The gods worshipped by the nations surrounding Israel that had proved so disastrous for them at Baal-Poer, must be avoided because God is rightly jealous of such activities. And let us not be confused by that word *jealous* because it has nothing to do with being envious of the achievement of other gods because they have no power at all.

The creator God who had aligned Himself with Israel is supreme and because of the spiritual battle that has been going on in the world since Adam sinned, He is intent on protecting His great name because it is the ensign, the flag of salvation to which desperate people are attracted when they become tired of the spiritual emptiness of what the world has to offer.

God, having chosen the nation of Israel to be His channel of communication to the rest of mankind, was rightly aggrieved by the spiritual adultery[7] committed by Israel that corrupted the engagement between Him and His people and caused it to become ineffectual. In fact we can now learn more about how our relationship with God

---

[7] See my book on Hosea

should be from their errors than from their obedience to the commandments of God.

We have to see the relationship between God and His people in the light of God's plan for the eternal salvation of the whole of mankind through the death of His Son. It is clear that in order for that to be achieved, particularly through such capricious people, God had to use considerable skill and cunning, threats, and a carrot and stick approach, and be considerably long suffering in mercy throughout their history.

Even now with Jewish and Gentile believers and a 'church' that has been every bit as capricious as Israel, as illustrated by the letters to the churches in Revelation[8], God has had to use those who have pursued a dedicated path that has honoured the bride to bridegroom love relationship so central to what God planned for man from the beginning.

God had already more than proved Himself to them by His provision during their wandering in the wilderness.

"You shall not put the Lord your God to the test,
as you tested Him at Massah.

What was wrong at Rephadim (renamed by Moses as Massah)?

By contending against Moses, the people were in effect complaining against God. In fact they were continually complaining if anything did not go as they expected it to go.

There was no water at Rephadim, so they challenged Moses to provide them with water because in Egypt it had been provided for them by those detailed to provide it. Now they had to rely on God to provide it and because they could not actually see God with their physical eyes, and they did not have the ability to perceive God in all that had happened to them, the only one to whom they could voice their complaints was Moses.

However it was not the fact that they approached Moses to voice their concerns, rather it was the way in which they did so.

The difference between the people and Moses was that he immediately had a word with the God who had first reached down to him at the burning bush and who told him what to do. Moses relied

---

[8] See my book Letters to the Seven Churches of Revelation

on God to provide the answer to what seemed, as far as he was concerned, to be an impossible situation. Moses did not know where to find water, but he knew God knew.

> *17 You shall be diligent in keeping foremost in your thoughts the commandments of the Lord your God, and His testimonies and His statutes which He has commanded you and be active in living them out in your daily lives.*

It is only by taking the commandments seriously with an inner desire to be faithful in carrying them out, that the people could demonstrate their commitment to God. What is particularly concerning is how prepared modern believers are in being *diligent in keeping foremost in* their *thoughts the commandments* and teaching *of the Lord* Jesus Christ their Saviour?

The Methodist covenant prayer is repeated annually in January:

> *I am no longer my own but yours.*
> *Put me to what you will,*
> *rank me with whom you will;*
> *put me to doing,*
> *put me to suffering;*
> *let me be employed for you,*
> *or laid aside for you,*
> *exalted for you,*
> *or brought low for you;*
> *let me be full,*
> *let me be empty,*
> *let me have all things,*
> *let me have nothing:*
> *I freely and wholeheartedly yield all things*
> *to your pleasure and disposal.*
> *And now, glorious and blessed God,*
> *Father, Son and Holy Spirit,*
> *you are mine and I am yours. So be it.*
> *And the covenant now made on earth, let it be ratified in heaven.'*

But how many of those who have repeated that covenant prayer year by year actually meant what they were reciting? Saying *And the covenant now made on earth, let it be ratified in heaven* is of no use whatsoever if it is not heart felt, and with diligence, acted out in their daily lives. Just reading words in the service book is meaningless unless the heart and mind are engaged.

How can God influence the lives of anyone who does not fully surrender their lives into His control. Repeating the words, *I am no longer my own but yours,* and by that means allow Him work with them and in them through a daily, hourly or even minute by minute relationship if empty of that deep heartfelt desire and determination to follow up those words with action is of absolutely no value whatsoever.

What then of the Israelites as they listened to Moses repeating what God had told him to pass on to them? Sadly the lack of faith is clearly recorded in scripture for us to read and to hopefully learn by.

This is where it is so important, essential even, for all believers to read the whole Bible through from cover to cover, as they would any other book, at least once in order for them to come to an understanding of the history of man in relation to their service under God, and God's many attempts to attract man back to Himself.

It will certainly put things into perspective and be a lesson on how essential it is to be true to their word in their heavenly ratified covenant made every January, and all those who in some other way commit their lives to God.

If they do it out of duty or routine with no intention of ever carrying it out, then they should not be surprised if God does not ratify it and at the end tells them:

> *And then I will declare to them publicly, 'I never knew you; so be gone from My presence, you who act wickedly by completely disregarding My commands and teaching. (Matt. 7:23)'*

It is only by doing *what is right and good in the sight of the Lord* that He is able to do His part in blessing them and looking after them *so that it may be well with you and that you may go in and possess the good land which the Lord swore to give to your fathers.*

The whole purpose of their very existence was for the Israelites to go in and possess the land in the name of the One eternal God, their God, driving out all the evil that had been built up amongst the pagan tribes over the centuries and establish a new country filled by a nation of God focused people so that God could demonstrate to the world how He was able to bless them and ensure they had a life of peace and prosperity.

As it was however, throughout their history that we see a pattern of alternatively enjoying the blessing of God and experiencing the wrath of God. Through it all, however came this clear evidence of God's determination to pursue His plan for the salvation of all mankind.

Sadly *driving out all your enemies from before you, as the Lord has spoken,* was to be only partially achieved by them because of their faithlessness and lack of resolve.

It is most important to keep abreast of history and in the remaining verses of chapter 6, Moses impressed upon the Israelites the importance of teaching their offspring the nation's history from the time God brought them out of the land of Egypt and all that happened to bring them to the land promised to the patriarchs.

Finally the repeat of the command:

> *to do all these statutes, to fear and worship the Lord our God with reverential awe and profound respect for our good always and so that He might preserve us alive, as it is today.*

5 WARNINGS

Chapter 7

1 When the Lord your God brings you into the land which you are entering to possess, and has cast out many nations before you, the Hittite and the Girgashite and the Amorite and the Canaanite and the Perizzite and the Hivite and the Jebusite, which are seven nations greater and mightier than you,

2 and when the Lord your God gives them over to you and you defeat them, then you shall utterly destroy them.

You shall not make a covenantal treaty with them nor show mercy and compassion to them.

One of the problems people have today regarding the First Testament is the seeming slaughter of innocents, as recorded in this chapter suggested by the verses above. But we must be mindful of two things.

The first is that Satan made his claim to govern the world through mankind by deceiving Eve, causing Adam to rebel against God in support of his wife without realizing the consequences. Ever since that moment Satan has been a powerful player in the world and is the author of chaos and hatred, conflict and destruction.

Second, the reason why God wanted the Israelites to ensure that there was no one left of the tribes then inhabiting the land, was that as disciples of Satan every single person was a threat to the Israelites future relationship with God. As is made clear in scripture at the time of Christ, with demonic possession being a real problem.

It is essential for us to remember that God created the world and mankind and Satan has tried his level best to take over the world and everything in it by deception. What this means is that all those led away from God whilst on earth will have to endure a lifetime in hell, which is that place God has created in which He never goes.

As God is the source of both light and love, the environment of hell has neither of those things, in fact the Messiah was quoted as stating that in hell there will be weeping and wailing and a gnashing of teeth, suggesting that it is the last place anyone would want to go for a never ending existence.

It is worth a thought that as Satan is himself a created being, to think that he could ever be on a par with God is ridiculous. On the other hand heaven, the place of God's rest, is full of light, love and laughter

One thing is certain and that is it is impossible to apply the current sense of skewed morality, which in far too many cases is a superficial thing, to the time of tribal conflict and the depths of crude, sexual and barbarous paganism to which the pagan nations had sunk.

In fact God had waited patiently until the land had become so defiled that he decided it was time for His chosen people to go in and purge the land of all its depraved moral corruption and as a centre of Satanic power.

Leave one person to whom this was normal, even a child, and there was every chance that that person would infect the weaker members of the house of Israel and then it would spread throughout the nation like a rampant disease.

It is said that one bad apple can infect a basket full of them, making the whole contents of the basket only fit to be thrown away.

Only those who have experienced the enormity of the love and presence of God know the difference between living according to God's laws and those of Satan.

> *3 You shall not intermarry with them. You shall not give your daughter to his son, nor take his daughter for your son; because being part of their family they will turn your sons away from following Me to serve other gods; then the anger of the Lord will be aroused and burn against you and He will quickly destroy you.*

A good illustration of this is Solomon who, against the commandments of God, married pagan wives with hundreds of pagan concubines and it was those wives and concubines who corrupted that once great man of God. Solomon's successor, Rehoboam was the most likely to be the son of a pagan mother.

Spiritual warfare is no less cruel than physical warfare, and is often hidden, like terrorism, being full of subterfuge.

It is also important to compare life in those parts of the world today under the dominance of barbarism, with bizarre killings, severe oppression through a police state and unelected leaders in the Middle East especially, with those living in peace and reasonable harmony within in other more stable countries in the west.

The seven nations identified as being greater and mightier than the Israelites that God was going to help them conquer, had to be utterly destroyed. What we have to remember, not only in respect to the Israelites but also in respect to us as believers in the Lord Jesus Christ, is that God is the final judge and it is incumbent upon us to be pure before Him, because it is possible that even people we know as friends, could well be amongst those whom the Lord rejects when He sits in judgement on the great white throne at the end of time.

5 But this is how you shall deal with them: you shall utterly destroy their altars and completely demolish their sacred pillars, and cut down their wooden images (such as the Asherim which were symbols of the goddess Asherah), and burn their carved or sculpted images in the fire.

Like a cancer, one minute it will suddenly explode into life through the efforts of Satan and his demonic spirits to cause mayhem.

All those nations the Israelites were commanded to slaughter were people already bound for that place referred to as hell, and could do untold spiritual damage not only to the people of God but could even seek to destroy His plan of salvation, therefore the people of Israel were ridding the world of those who served Satan and his fallen angels and dragging others down to their level.

Sadly, as we are well aware, the nation did not fully carry out God's instructions and therefore suffered all that God through Moses had warned them about, and they still do to this day.

However, there is every sign that the time is very near of their realization that the Jesus of Nazareth, they have so despised, is in fact their long awaited Messiah.

> *6 For you are a holy people that have been set apart from the world to the Lord your God; indeed the Lord your God has chosen you out of all the peoples on the face of the earth to be a people for His own possession, His very own special treasure.*

Let us be in no doubt concerning the place of Israel, even today, in the heart and affections of God. After all it is to the land of Israel, to the mount of Olives, that the Lord Jesus will return in glory.

God has not finished with Israel, which is why they won the 1967 war when no one expected them to do, and why the fiery rhetoric of the leaders of some of the surrounding countries will never be anything but fiery rhetoric.

Think about what God said to Israel through Moses

> *Now therefore, **if** you will indeed obey My voice and keep My covenantal agreement made between us, **then you shall** be My very own special possession and treasure from among all peoples, for all the earth is Mine; and you shall be to Me a kingdom of priests and a holy nation, that have been set apart for My purpose.' (Ex. 19:5, 6)*

This is the clearest statement in scripture to support the special status of the nation of Israel even in the 21st century. It was not only the Levites who were commissioned to serve God, although they had a special place in the nation to minister to God, but the whole nation had a part to play in letting the world know about the creator God that had selected them as His showcase people.

What is more that special place of his people now includes those Gentiles that truly love Him and have vowed to serve Him (1 Pet. 2:9).

As creator of the world, God could have chosen any number of nations already established, but He wanted a nation that had its origin in one dedicated man, Abram (Is. 51:2 *for I called him alone*), because God wanted to emphasize that it was not the nation's size that mattered, but personal relationships.

What singles out the God of Israel from all other gods is Love, but God's love, as can be discovered by reading scripture, is far, far greater than any love of men. First God's love is not there for the benefit of large numbers, because throughout scripture God deals with individuals, as we have already mentioned.

> *7 The Lord did not love you and choose you because you were greater in number than any of the other peoples, for you were in fact the least of all peoples.*

God's love is not fickle like the love of men because it is long suffering. Consider that the love God had for Israel started with one man, Abram. It was his willingness to respond to the call of God that started the process. Abram did not have anyone else he could turn to and ask if they knew God, or have a mentor nearby to help him understand who this God was who was calling him, because he was the only one who both heard and responded. Neither did he have any holy book from which to learn as we have.

By the time of the maturing of the nation of Israel, the people were told by Moses that *the Lord loves you,* and the reason for that love was because He was determined to keep true to *the oath which He swore to your fathers,* Abraham, Isaac and Jacob (Israel).

The spiritual fight in which God has been engaged was seen in the plagues that were intended to overwhelm all the gods and goddesses worshipped by the Egyptians. And as the Pharaoh considered himself a living god, by killing his firstborn son, who would have been his pride and joy, God again demonstrated that he was no god at all, because he could not protect his son and heir[9]. Not only that but the Pharaoh himself died opposing God's desire for His people to be release to pursue His plan for them.

> *The Lord has brought you out with a mighty hand, redeemed you from the house of slavery, from the hand of Pharaoh, king of Egypt.*

Abraham gained confidence in the God who had called him. The same applied to Isaac and Jacob who both had a rock solid faith in

---

[9] See God Rescues His People to read why it was necessary for the Pharaoh himself to die.

God. Moses was now seeking to impress upon the people of Israel not to doubt but *rather understand that the Lord your God, He is God, the faithful God, who is keeping His covenant and His steadfast, unchanging lovingkindness,* not just towards them in their present situation but *to a thousand generations [a time with no end] with those who love Him and keep His commandments.*

It is essential that those two conditions are met to, *love Him and keep His commandments,* because, as is very clear, the covenant, the agreement between God and man, shall be honoured by both parties to that agreement otherwise He *repays those who hate Him to their faces, by destroying them; indeed He will not hesitate to deal with him who hates Him, He will repay him to his face* because in so doing they become as the Pharaoh, who wants to destroy what He was then seeking to achieve in this world (and still is), that no one should face the second death, a place in hell.

Let there be no doubt that God shall wreak vengeance on all those that oppose Him and His will for mankind.

Moses sought to encourage the people to *keep obeying the commandments and the statutes and judgments which I am commanding you today* by making them part of their daily living.

Promises of God

> *Then it shall come about, because you have listened to these judgments and kept and did them, that the Lord your God will maintain the covenant and the steadfast lovingkindness He swore to your fathers.*

It is vitally important that believers of today realize, as the nation of Israel had to realize, that the covenant was two way and they were responsible for carrying out their side of the agreement to enable God to carry out His. It is by listening to God and keeping faith with Him and being obedient to Him that God would be able to bless them (and us). It must be very clear by now that God works with and through His willing human servants. It is part of His self-imposed method of working in the world.

But the question has to be asked, how many believers in churches today *have listened to these judgments and kept and done them?* How many in fact even know what the commandments are, let alone have been able to keep them and obey them in their daily life.

Yes Jesus died and offers us salvation, but that is not the be all and end all of our faith, merely the start when our focus is on God and there is a willingness to listen to Him and live according to His will and purposes for us, just as Abraham had done.

It is as time goes by after our acceptance of the Lord Jesus Christ as Saviour that the initial excitement has the potential to fade and we lose that willingness to put our worship and service of Him in first place behind the daily practicalities of living, and yet it is His desire to be there all the time and encourage and bless us.

What then were the promises of God to the people of Israel if they *listened to these judgments and kept and did them?*

13 He will love, bless and multiply you; He will also bless the fruit of your womb, the fruit of your land, your grain and your new wine and your olive oil, the offspring of your cattle and the young of your flock, in the land which He swore to your fathers to give you.

God desperately wanted to show both His people, and through them the nations all around them, what He was able to do for all those that loved and obeyed Him.

1. *the fruit of your womb and the fruit of your land, your grain and your new wine and your olive oil,*

2. *the offspring of your cattle and the young of your flock, in the land which He swore to your fathers to give you.*

3. *there will be no infertile male or female among you or among your cattle.*

4. *The Lord will take away from you all sickness; and He will not subject you to any of the harmful diseases of Egypt which you have known, but He will impose them on all [those] who hate you.*

5. *And you shall consume all the peoples whom the Lord your God will give over to you; your eye shall not pity them, nor shall you serve their gods, for that would be a deadly trap to you.*

What a remarkable list. It would have been the envy of all the other tribes in that area, and be a witness to God.

117

As they had now at last reached the border to the promised land, it was important for their morale that they remembered not only the way in which the Lord their God had demonstrated His mighty power in Egypt, but also how he had looked after them in all their wanderings over the last forty years.

It was that more recent experience of God for them and their parents that must be behind their resolve as they went into the land flowing with milk and honey. It was essential that they were not to be phased by the apparent strength and weaponry of the people they would have to face, but have their faith in the fact that the invincible God was on their side and would assist them to win the battles.

Is that not the place where we should be? To have faith in the fact that the invincible God is on our side and will assist us to win the battles that face us now and in the future?

The one thing they had to do in return was to cleanse the land by destroying all that was offensive to God, and not even covet the precious metal that covered them. After all God was more than capable of creating more precious metal.

Blessings follow Believing Faith

The land had to be cleansed of Satanic corruption in order for the Lord to demonstrate the beauty of life as He originally designed it.

> *16 And you shall destroy all the peoples whom the Lord your God will give over to you; your eye shall not pity them, nor shall you serve their gods, for that would be the trap of death to you.*

The heartlessness that might be seen in this action must be considered in the light of evil. Let us be in no doubt that the Canaanites had been given plenty of time to repent and change their ways but, because they were under the dominating regime of Satan, they only knew his Godless ways. Did they not throw their children alive into the fire? And practice human sacrifice? As well as much more corrupt and corrupting practices.

Remember how Balaam gave Balak the king the clue as to how to defeat God's chosen people Israel and remove the threat they posed to his country? Get the women to entice the men to come and worship your gods with all the sensual pleasure that involved (Num.

25). And God was right because for many thousands - *it became the trap of death to you.*

The other matter was their belief and faith in the power of God to overcome the nations that lived there. It was obvious those nations would put up a fight to defend themselves but, as with Jericho, the fear not of them but of God went before them causing the bravery of the fighters to melt. It was this factor, the fear of God, of which the ten spies were ignorant.

The question had already been asked when the ten spies gave their verdict concerning the ability of those nations to fight. *"If you say in your heart, 'These nations are greater than I am; how can I dispossess them?'* Then the men of Israel would be as frightened as the men of Jericho were.

But what does the God of Israel tell them? *You shall not be afraid of them; you shall remember with much confidence what the Lord your God did to Pharaoh and to all Egypt.* It is that experiential knowledge that is so important. The revelatory signature of God.

The importance of that battle of God against the establishment of Satan in Egypt can never be ignored, even today, because God demonstrated that Satan had no power against Him.

The news of *the great trials which you saw with your own eyes,* (those that had not then been born would have been told by their parents all about) *the signs, the wonders, the mighty hand and the outstretched arm by which the Lord your God brought you out,* would not only not go away, but were firmly fixed in the memories of the people they were going to wipe out, and have been indelibly included in recorded history for our benefit.

Again we must have fixed in our minds that this was not needless slaughter, Those of us who have been saved to the uttermost and are assured of a place in God's glorious rest, would not have that joy had the Israelites not gone in and wiped out those nations that were in the service of Satan and established themselves in that land even to today, albeit in a much reduced form.

God was their security if they were prepared to trust *the Lord your God to do to all the peoples of whom you are afraid.* But there is far more to this than their faith in God to do what He was instructing them to do.

There will be times when God instructs us to do something that is of a similar nature when it is only through our faith in Him that will get us through.

We are reading about something that happened thousands of years ago, but the God of Israel, who has become our God, has not lost any of His power and therefore why should we be afraid of others with whom we will have to do battle?

Many an enemy has played mind games in order to weaken the opposition. God is able to influence the minds of those that oppose Him and his people.

> *Moreover, the Lord your God will send the hornet (that is His terror) against them, until those who are left, who hide themselves from you, are destroyed.*

The most important lesson for the fighting men of Israel was that they should not be *terrified of them, for the Lord your God is in your midst, a great and awesome God.*

The awesome power of their creator God was such that those that believed could have complete faith in Him.

The wisdom of God prevailed because it was no use God clearing away all these nations from before them in one phase, because there is always the matter of maintenance both of buildings and land, and particularly of crops.

So it was a case of *little by little; you will not be able to put an end to them quickly, otherwise the wild animals would become too numerous for you.*

It must be realised that the land was then not so heavily populated as it is today and therefore there were large tracts of uncultivated land where the wild animals prowled.

What is clear from the message Moses was commanded to give them was the certainty, *The Lord your God **will** clear away these nations before you.* Confusing the enemy is as much part of the art of warfare as fighting and that is what God did to the Amorite hordes with Gideon's three hundred men, none of whom were harmed.

> *23 But the Lord your God will hand them over to you, and will rout them in a crushing defeat.*

24 And He will hand over their kings to you, and you will make their name perish from under heaven; no man will be able to stand before you until you have destroyed them.

The whole purpose of the Israelites going into the land was for them to purifying it from all the demonic artefacts and way of life. To achieve that they were commanded to *burn the carved and sculpted images of their gods in the fire. You shall not covet the silver or gold that is on them* (as Achan did in Jericho), *nor take it for yourselves, so that you will not be ensnared by it* because God had forbidden them to do so.

The reason for that was it was contaminated by demonic activity and those that took it would be under great pressure from demonic spiritual activity, *for it is an abomination, and repulsive to the Lord your God so that anyone taking it would not enjoy God's protection.*[10]

Just as Rachel suffered for hanging on to her family's earth gods by not only giving birth to just two sons to Leah's six, but also by dying in childbirth and not being buried in the family's burial cave but by an oak tree.

The commands of God were clear. They were not in any way to allow spiritual demonic contamination of physical things entering their homes.

The Israelites were not to know of the implicit danger of holding on to anything that had been dedicated to gods[11]. Thus it was essential for them to be obedient to the commands of God who knew very well that even the gold covering of the images was dangerous.

You shall not bring an idol or anything that was used in the worship of gods into your house, lest you like it and become doomed to destruction.

There was always that danger of being led into the worship of the demonic.

---

[10] Read Law & Grace in which certain kings of Judah tried to destroy such artefacts which the Israelites themselves had made during times when the leadership lost sight of God.
[11] 1 Cor. 10:28

Remember and Obey (Chapter 8)

You shall be careful to do every commandment that I am commanding you today so that you may live and multiply, and go in and possess the land which the Lord swore to your fathers that He would give them.

There are two very important points here that we need to consider.

The first is remembering who has authority over us. As far as the Israelites were concerned, and the whole purpose of them being a chosen nations, was that the creator God had authority over them because it was He who had not only called their founder Abram, but had also called them to be His chose people.

The second is that it was incumbent upon them to be obedient to every commandment He gave them in order for them, like Abram, to be blessed by Him, *so that you may live and multiply.*

Not only that but just as God's promise of land to Abraham was the result of his commitment and loyalty without the law being in place, it was now a requirement on the people, His descendants, to be equally committed and loyal to God through their obedience to His commandments in order for His original promise to Abraham to be fulfilled.

Unless the Israelites *were careful to observe every commandment that I am commanding you today,* not only would they not *live and multiply* but neither would they *go in and* fully *possess the land.* It is probably a verse that does not come to the mind of many believers very easily, but in saying to the people that not everyone who calls Him Lord would enter into the kingdom of heaven, the Lord was giving fair warning to people that they had to obey the rules He set down as to who would be saved and who would ultimately be rejected. The neglect of the commandments in the First Testament is very dangerous for believers in Messiah.

Hindsight is the believers most important asset, because it has the potential to encourage and help build up our store of experiences of God's bounty *if so be that the Holy Spirit lives in us.* In fact it has the potential to be a good temperature gauge of our relationship with God.

2 And you shall always remember the ways in which the Lord your God has led you these forty years in the wilderness, in order that He might humble you and test you, to know what was in your heart and mind, whether or not you would keep His commandments.

Remembering the way in which God had looked after them in the past was crucial to not just the Israelites but also to us today. Whenever they were faced with difficulties or seemingly insurmountable problems, all they had to do was to remember what God had done for them in the past and the future did not look so disastrous after all. There are a multitude of examples of the way in which God gave them victory even in the most dangerous of times.

Remember, says God, what I have done for you in the past and believe that I can do the same and even greater things in the future. That is why the prophets were willing to put their lives on the line, because they knew the certainty of the promises of God. Even if they were killed they knew that God would take care of them in the next life.

The emphasis on the teaching of God is that it is personal. Be *careful*, says the Lord, *to observe every commandment that I am commanding you today*. Why? Because there would be many distractions in the years ahead that had the potential to interrupt that relationship, and the observance of His instructions for life would enable them to overcome.

Although they had successfully negotiated the wilderness, it was clearly not achieved in their own strength and ability but through the love, care, protection and guidance of God.

When Aaron created the golden calf and the people announced, *"This is your god, O Israel, that brought you out of the land of Egypt"*, the people were reverting to type. The Egyptian sun-god was represented as a bull, so it seemed only natural to some to represent God as a golden calf. And we know what happened to those that accepted that god as being real.

But what about passing through the Red Sea? The miracle of the waters of Marah when God showed Moses a tree that, when cast into the water, made it drinkable? What about the problem of food? When they suffered hunger with no means of collecting food and were then at the mercy of God who, out of nothing but dew provided manna, a substance that none within the families knew what it was. But, remarkably, it had all the nutrients and elements their bodies needed and it sustained them for many years.

What is particularly interesting about the gathering of the manna was that however much the families collected, the greedy or the timid, they all had just enough and no more. Those that tried to keep it for the next day, against God's instructions, found it unusable.

What this was supposed to teach them, and should teach us too, is that God is able to supply all that we need and no more. We need to trust God every step of the way. But more than that God's word is not just instructions for us to follow, but food for our souls.

What these examples demonstrate is that from nothing God was able to feed their physical needs, but more importantly, that man not only needs physical food, but spiritual food also, which he can only receive from the mouth of God and through His written word.

3 that He might make you understand by personal experience that man does not live by bread alone, but by every word that proceeds out of the mouth of the Lord.

Recognize that statement? It is what our Lord repeated to Satan (Matt. 4:4). Everything that was happening to them was teaching them about God and how He was able to supply not just their physical needs but bring them into dependence upon Him from a spiritual point of view if only they were prepared to think about it and understand all that God was doing with them and in them.

Could the multitude in the wilderness have fed themselves where there was insufficient food? No. But God could and did.

One interesting fact, remembering that by this time they had been living a nomadic life for forty years, is that *their clothing did not wear out, nor did their feet swell.* Also it was important for them to realized that *the Lord your God disciplines and instructs you just as a man disciplines and instructs his son,* just as they had experienced during the rebellions.

Having proved His ability to sustain the people, it was only right that He should attract from them nothing but respect. As we have seen the commandments were provided for them to assist them in living a life that was worthy of His continued care and attention.

6 Therefore you shall keep the commandments of the Lord your God, to walk in His ways and to fear Him.

Providing they obeyed His rules of life they would remain in step with Him because those rules of life were designed to keep them away from worshipping created things and therefore anger Him and attract His wrath.

What follows now is a description of utopia that the Lord their loving and bountiful God was leading them into. It is a land of:

- *brooks of water,*
- *fountains and springs, that flow out of valleys and hills; (including underground springs)*
- *wheat and barley,*
- *vines and fig trees and pomegranates,*
- *olive oil and honey;*

It was a land in which bread would never be scarce. Whereas amongst desert tribes there was bread once a month, they would lack nothing, with even stones (possibly black basalt) yielding iron and where copper could be mined.

There is a danger in living in a land where there is plenty. Unless they blessed *the Lord your God for the good land which He has given you* there was a very great danger that they would *forget the Lord your God by not keeping His commandments, His judgments, and His statutes which I command you today.*

Moses' warning to *Beware that you do not forget* echoes out over the centuries to the present day because it has been proven time and again that when believers are comfortable with abundance.

> *10 When you have eaten and are full, then you shall bless. the Lord your God lest when you have eaten and are full, and have built beautiful houses and dwell in them; your herds and your flocks multiply, and your silver and your gold are multiplied, and all that you have is multiplied; your heart is lifted up, and you forget the Lord your God who brought you out of the land of Egypt, from the house of bondage; who led you through that great and terrible wilderness, in which were fiery serpents and scorpions and thirsty land where there was no water; who provided water for you out of*

the flinty rock; who fed you in the wilderness with manna, which your fathers did not know, that He might humble you and that He might test you, to do you good in the end.

There was a time when, as a contractor I was out of work, and I had discovered over time that I was never able to find work for myself, but only got work that the Lord provided.

On one occasion when I was out of work I said to the Lord, "I would like another job because I do have bills to pay", immediately the Lord replied, "Have I ever let you down?" The answer was No, so I never asked that question again.

There is a very important phrase in the text above which we do well to remember for there is no doubt that we are God's children and continually learning during this time of earthly training in preparation for eternity with Him.

Indeed it is during this time that we learn about God and our relationship with Him prior to our being in His presence for eternity. And that phrase is, *that He might humble you and that He might test you, to do you good in the end.*

Self-confidence can be an asset or a problem. I was intrigued to learn about King Uzziah[12], Isaiah mentioned (Is. 6) when he was in the temple and met the Lord. It is very interesting to discover that all the while the young king had Zachariah, a God fearing priest, as his mentor all went well with him, but when he was older and became strong his heart was lifted up to his destruction (2 Chr. 26:16).

For the Israelites, in particular the wealthy ones (Lk. 12:16 – 21), there was always the danger that they would say in their heart, *'My power and the might of my hand have gained me this wealth'*. But the scriptures tell us that it is God who gives the increase.

As Moses says:

> *18 And you shall remember the Lord your God, for it is He who gives you power to get wealth, that He may establish His covenant which He swore to your fathers, as it is this day. Then it shall be, if you by any means forget the Lord your God, and follow other gods, and serve them and worship them, I testify against you this day that you shall surely perish. As the nations which the Lord*

---

[12] 2 Chronicles 26 and chapter 7 of Law & Grace

destroys before you, so you shall perish, because you would not be obedient to the voice of the Lord your God.

It seems almost inconceivable that the people that were to go into a land to clear out all those worshiping false gods should over time themselves do exactly the same thing as those that had been killed.

God was continually reminding them that the land they were going in to possess was His land, that He was giving it to them as a gift. It was a present to them and particularly when they had *eaten and are satisfied,* it was at that moment when it was imperative that they *shall bless the Lord your God for the good land which He has given you* that they failed to do so.

It is worth repeating that one of the greatest problems we in the western style nations have is wealth and comfort. It is true that there are many on or below the poverty line, but even with such people the welfare state is, or charitable organisations are, there in the majority of cases to provide support, which in many other countries is just not there at all.

The church has also got into a rut because our faith up to the present has not been challenged as it has in many other countries where the church is being persecuted.

When the missionaries were evicted from China at the time of the communists coming to power, indoctrination was the order of the day. Communists hate Christianity because communism is an alternative religion under the control of Satan.

The missionary societies were extremely concerned that the indigenous church would die, yet the reverse happened. It grew. True it had to go underground, but the Spirit of God moved amongst His people and even with the danger of being sent to prison where they could easily face torture and death, the people knew that there was a place for them for eternity with God even if they did die a physical death.

Similar things have happened in other parts of the world where the church has been persecuted.

The church in the Western countries has had it easy and therefore it has forgotten about God and replaced Him with some pseudo being that they worship on a Sunday using their own interpretation of the Bible. Errant doctrine is the order of the day. It is just the few, the remnant, who seek to learn from the true God through His Holy Spirit.

The proof of this state of affairs is the emptying churches. It is God's pure word that provides us with food for the spirit.

The truth is, why do believers need God when they have a steady income and a house, with the family well clothed and enjoying holidays every year? That was the problem the Israeli people had. It is only when hardship comes that people call upon the Lord because they cannot see a clear way out of the predicament.

It is very sad that Christians in the west do not observe God's instructions to maintain a dedicated life given over to God. And this is the warning contained in the remaining part of this chapter.

> *7 – 14 Beware that you do not forget the Lord your God by failing to keep His commandments and His judgments (precepts) and His statutes which I am commanding you today; otherwise, when you have eaten and are satisfied, and have built good houses and lived in them, and when your herds and flocks multiply, and your silver and gold multiply, and all that you have increases, then your heart will become lifted up through self-conceit and arrogance and complacency, and you will forget the Lord your God who brought you from the land of Egypt, out of the house of slavery.*

This is exactly what happened. The things of the world became more important to them than being focused on, and being obedient to, God, and that is what has happened to the western church where the majority of members today live lives that vary little from those of the world with the exception of attending worship in a prescribed building on a Sunday.

Just as God withdrew His help and support from the Israelites, so He has done it to the established churches in the West. They suffered, and so do we.

6 VICTORY THROUGH GRACE

Chapter 9

1 Hear, O Israel! You are crossing the Jordan today to dispossess greater and more powerful nations than you of the land in which they are living. The people are great, tall sons of Anakim, of whom you have heard it said, 'Who can stand before the sons of Anak?', living in great cities are fortified to heaven.

This picture the inhabitants of Canaan received through the 'news channels' of the people they were to fight could not have been clearer. It was enough to frighten the most courageous fighting men, but rumours can sometimes make things appear far worse than they are.

The faith of the leadership and remnant amongst the people in the power of almighty God had already demonstrated that no human army was a match for him. Faith, as all believers know, is not only dependent upon the trust of the individual according to their experiential knowledge of God, but their willingness to take action according to God's instructions.

Just think carefully about what Moses said next:

So with assured confidence, know …

What was the state of mind of these fickle Israelites who had not shown a great level of faith in their God up to now? Those who saw only what was before them without the ability to conceive a God for whom nothing was impossible, did not have the capacity to trust a God they could not see concerning the future.

Sadly, even though the majority of the objectors had died in the wilderness, some of their offspring could well have had the same trait as their parents and refused to trust their God and thus to become an unsettling influence on the rest of the people.

We must assume, however, that most had sufficient faith to move forward. So, why should they *know or have assured confidence?* Because of what God had already done for them.

> *2 So with assured confidence, know that the Lord your God is crossing the Jordan before you like a devouring fire. He will destroy them and He will subdue them before you, and you shall drive them out and destroy them quickly, just as the Lord has promised you.*

It is so important to always remember that the God we are dealing with here is the same one that created the world and universe and therefore not only is nothing impossible for Him, but also as there is no other like Him, no contender, no adversary of equal ability and power. Indeed, He can be seen as being a God of His word. Whatever He promises, He **will** fulfil.

For those willing to believe in God, this was a faith builder. He had already proved Himself time and again. Now, although it was necessary for them to actively *take* possession of the land, God will have made it easy for them because rumours of the power of their God would have already reached the inhabitants and brought terror to their hearts (Josh. 2:8 – 11).

Whilst writing this the thought of the future for all believers is unknown and unless we are willing to put doubt aside, focus our spiritual eyes on our experiential knowledge of God and fully trust God, then we will not succeed in the way God wants us to succeed in His service.

God uses His silence to test believers, which is why our experiential knowledge of God is so essential.

This is what I wrote in my book A Tale of Three men:

A New Direction

Towards the end of 2001 God challenged me with the words "Do you trust Me?" The question was not only very clear, but was also definitely of God. My answer was "Yes Lord, I trust you. It is me I do not trust because I make too many mistakes and wrong decisions". Sometime later the Lord again broke into my thoughts with the same question to which I gave the same answer. Then a third time God challenged me with the same question. With the Lord three is a significant number, it is God's number, a holy number. I suddenly realized I had to think carefully about the question before answering.

What I had actually been saying was, "Lord I do not trust You to overcome my mistakes and wrong decisions", so I had not in fact been prepared to trust Him at all. My new carefully considered answer was, "Yes Lord, I trust You implicitly", an answer I was required to repeat twice more so that I gave the same answer three consecutive times. Only then did the Lord stop asking me that question.

Personal experiences are very important to us and others and need to be shared. Now some may asked what has that to do with the Israelites and what Moses was passing on to the people as they waited at the border of the promised land. The whole purpose of the account of all that happened to the Israelites in the First Testament is to teach us about how we should relate to God and not repeat their mistakes. Their times bereft of trusting and lengthy times of doubt and rebelliousness.

If we do not consider the events recorded in the First Testament as being real events, and try to put ourselves in the position of the real people of that time and understand the circumstances they were in and how they handled it, then we will miss out on a considerable amount of teaching.

This is not fiction. This is history which provides us with an amazing opportunity to ask ourselves the question, "What would I have done in those circumstances?"

It has the potential for us in our own walk with God to challenge us about how we, having the advantage of knowing the almighty power of God through the scriptures, react to our own challenges in life, for we, like the Israelites of old, have our own moments of decision making regarding the future that is completely unknown to us but known to God, if we are willing to trust Him.

Within this text and that of my other books is a window into my faith that has been built up over my eighty odd years, to the established state it is today.

Some of the Biblical text is included in this book so that we, writer and reader, look at the same information.

Those of us who have been believers in the Lord Jesus Christ, the Father and the Holy Spirit, for a long time, know for a certainty that we have not succeeded in serving God through our own abilities and efforts (please read Luke 17:10 which clearly declares my state before God). Even this book is the result of God's prompting and inspiration with me as His scribe.

These next few verses are the reason for the paragraph above:

4 Do not say in your heart when the Lord your God has driven them out before you, 'It is because of my righteousness that the Lord has brought me in to possess this land,'

The key to our relationship with God is truth. God is Truth. He can look deep into the heart of an individual and see what sort of person they are, truthful or liars. So personally we must be wary of the way we approach God because the saying, "Be sure your sins will find you out", has been well proven over the years.

What is for certain, therefore, is that we must be honest before God if we want our relationship with Him to prosper and for us one day to be with Him in glory. After all He is well aware of all that happens to us and what is in our mind and heart.

It was not because of the righteousness of the Israelites that the Lord allowed them to possess the land, rather it was :

because of the wickedness of these nations that the Lord is dispossessing them of that land before you.

So there were two reasons for *the Lord your God to drive them out before you* and thus allow the Israelites to go into possess the land, and none reflected well on them. His oath to the Patriarchs and the wickedness of the nations then inhabiting the land.

What is more the Lord made it very clear that by going into the land they were merely carrying out His instructions. *'Be of no doubt whatsoever, that the Lord your God is not giving you this good land to possess because of your righteousness'.*

Have you noticed the emphasis concerning their state of heart and mind where God was concerned by repeating His accusations about their lack of righteousness and uprightness of heart, and that they were *a stiff-necked, stubborn and obstinate people?* Sadly, many of their descendants would demonstrate just how obstreperous and true to type they were.

And even amongst the disciples and Jewish believers there was this element of arrogant pride that "God is ours," along with the gift of salvation so recently provided by the death of the Lord Jesus. Such arrogance! Let that arrogant pride not be perpetuated in our minds.

Consider the time when Cornelius and his household not only became believers but also received the baptism of the Holy Spirit (Acts 10:44 – 48), just as the disciples had received on the day of Pentecost. Notice that it was not asked for; it was given.

> *When Peter went up to Jerusalem, those of the circumcision, that is those Jewish believers who followed the oral Law of ritual, challenged him saying, "You went to uncircumcised men and even ate with them!"*

Had they learned nothing from their time with their Messiah? Those who religiously followed the oral law of ritual became slaves to that law and the love of God was driven out of their observance of their Jewish faith, which transferred itself to their faith in Messiah. And who were they to demand that God belonged to them and to no one else?

The task of the nation of Israel was to be a channel of teaching and blessing to the rest of mankind. God was not theirs by right, they had been chosen because of Abraham, and it was because of their ancestry that the Messiah had come to them.

After Peter had explained all that had gone on from the vision he received in Joppa to the moment the Spirit fell upon the assembly of people, the objectors fell silent and ere forced to accept the will of God. The baptism in the Holy Spirit, which will manifest itself in different ways in different people, was God's gift to give to whom He will.

Peter remembered the word of the Lord Jesus, how He used to say, *'John baptized with water, but you will be baptized with the Holy Spirit.'*

This is the essence of the message God was giving them, *"if God gave Gentiles exactly the same gift as He gave us after we accepted and believed and trusted in the Lord Jesus Christ as Saviour and Lord, who was I to interfere or stand in God's way?"*

God did not belong to them, rather they were chosen by God to take up the role of priests in order to spread the Word of God to the Gentile nations, and be examples of God's love and compassion towards mankind. Why then were they so opposed to the salvation of the Gentiles?

Here we have a nation of people, not all of whom were prepared to fully trust God. He is telling them plainly that they will be going in to reclaim His ground for Him because of the intensity of the sin of others, which had nothing to do with their righteousness.

Sometimes Satan reminds us of our past mistakes to try and wear us down. But in this case at this critical preparation time for the Israelite nation, God was reminding them through Moses of certain issues that were pertinent to their present situation and the dangers that lay ahead:

> *7 Remember with great sadness and do not forget how you provoked the Lord your God to wrath in the wilderness. From the day you left the land of Egypt until now, you have been rebellious against the Lord.*
>
> *At Sinai you provoked the Lord to wrath, in regard to the golden calves, and the Lord was so angry with you that He would have destroyed you.*

That time was a very serious moment for Israel if they did bur realize it, and they were only saved by a quick thinking Moses.

One thing the nation very easily forgot was the power of almighty God and His ability to look into and search their hearts. There were certain instances where the people went too far and really angered the Lord their God.

Remembering

Whilst Moses was on the mountain meeting with God, God saw what was happening back at camp. He was so angry after all that He had done for them, that they should abandon their loyalty to Him and worship the type of ineffectual gods that were so rife in Egypt and dishonoured by the plagues.

What was wrong with these people? Having been told that they must not worship any graven image, what were they doing but creating a golden calf that they accepted had brought them out of Egypt. But how could it have done that when it had only just been made by human hands?

This so angered the Lord that He said to Moses:

> *13 I have seen this people, and indeed, they are stiff-necked, stubborn and obstinate people. Let Me alone, so that I may destroy them and wipe out their name from under heaven; and I will make of you a nation mightier and greater than they.'"*

Whether or not the offspring of those rebels knew of God's intentions at the time or not, Moses was not informing them of the very grave danger they had been in at the time.

When learning what happened at this time, it is important that we think of what is happening in the church today with its focus on images and errant doctrine.

The men and women who twist the word of God, and women priests who focus on dressing up in fashionable clerical garb specially designed for the feminine look and refer to God the Father as Mother. Are they not doing the same as the Israelites back in the time of Moses?

The danger such perpetrators are in, which is obviously unknown to them, is made clear by what Moses is announcing. For this reason it is worth reading the letters to the seven churches as recorded for us in Revelation[13] for they tell us with great clarity that it is only he who has an ear and is prepared to listen to God, take notice and overcome that will enter into His rest.

I was asked by a lovely spiritual lady to take an evening service at a little country chapel where as a local preacher I had preached many

---

[13] Read my book Letter to the Seven Churches of Revelation for a factual analysis

times before I resigned from Methodism under God's instruction. Indeed I rejoiced in the fellowship of that small congregation. After the service the lady said to me, "that was of God". Curious I asked why.

Apparently the circuit superintendent minister had spoken to the members at the church earlier in the week on a similar subject and I had preached a totally different gospel. The dear lady was troubled that the people were getting confusing, contrary information fed to them. Shortly afterwards a group of the spiritually alive believers at that church set up a house church to focus on the true word.

What people today do not seem to understand is that leaders of the church today who preach and teach an alternative gospel could well find that they miss out on heaven because they have done a similar thing to that of the rebels by creating in their minds a benign god that did not demand much of them and teaching it to others.

It is vital that we do not study the scriptures in isolation, but seek to understand how we can learn from the mistakes of others and realize that although God seems silent today, He is watching us with a critical eye.

He is wanting to be part of our lives so that He could lead us into all truth that will enable us to be with Him in the new Jerusalem which He is right now preparing for us (Jn. 14:1 – 3), if we would allow Him to do just that.

He is also ready to judge those who are not His.

Moses realized that God's threat to *make of him a nation mightier and greater than they* was a very serious one, but he also realized that it was not a practical proposition when considering the timescale required and the psychological effect of God's change of tactics would have on Egypt and the surrounding nations, removing their abject fear of the replacement for Israel.

The character of Moses is here displayed, for in reply to what the Lord was saying to him, he dissuaded the Lord from carrying out that threat. Moses brother Aaron, who was clearly a very weak man, had bowed to the rebel leaders in their demand and organized the manufacture of a golden calf image for them to worship, whereas he should have stood firm and pointed out that it was a very grave sin they were intending to commit and refuse to take part in their activities.

What is so sad is that Aaron gave a very poor excuse for his actions, which clearly revealed that he did not have the same conviction of the power and ability of God as did his younger brother. Aaron was only saved by Moses pleading before the Lord for him.

Such was the fury of Moses when he came down the mountain and finally witnessed the revelry that he threw the tablets of stone on which God had inscribed the ten Hebrew words, or commandments, to the ground causing them to shatter. He then organized a purge of the rebels in order to save the nation and many thousand were killed to assuage the righteous anger of the Lord.

It is incumbent upon all believers to be fully aware that God has the authority to save or send a person's soul into hell. Jesus said,

> *Do not be afraid of those who kill the body but cannot kill the soul; but rather be afraid of Him who can destroy both soul and body in hell" (Matt. 10:28).*

The violent reaction of Moses against the rebels may seem barbaric to some today, but it was necessary to prevent the whole nation being contaminated by those godless rebels who got many others involved and could easily have destroyed God's plan for the nation had they been allowed to succeed.

Make no mistake, when God judges all men at the end of days He will only allow into the New Jerusalem those that are truly dedicated to Him, so that there will be many supposedly good Christian people who will not be allowed in and spend an eternity in that place where God never goes. Those that do not have within them the Spirit of the living God are not of Him, but of the Devil.

> *15 So I turned and came down from the mountain while the mountain was burning with fire, with the two tablets of the covenant in my hands. And I saw for myself that you had indeed sinned against the Lord your God by making for yourselves a molten calf (cf. Ex. 32)*

For the sake of their future and the future of us Gentiles it was essential that they became a nation of willing adherents, there was no other way. Be obedient to God and live a life blessed by Him, or live a troubled life in the grip of all that is evil and spend an eternity in a place in which the love and light of God never reaches.

But why had they *turned aside so quickly from the way which the Lord had commanded* them?

The terms of the covenant so recently inscribed on the stone tablets by God's hand that now lay shattered in full view of the people, because they had already broken those terms and the covenant had become meaningless.

Although God was willing to keep His side of the agreement, it was clear a large number of the people had decided that they were not.

But notice what Moses did.

> *18 I fell down before the Lord for forty days and forty nights as previously; I eat neither food or drink water, because of all the sin you had committed by doing what was evil in the sight of the Lord to provoke Him to anger. For I was afraid of the divine anger and absolute fury which the Lord held against you, that would cause Him to destroy you, but the Lord listened to me that time also.*

Moses pleaded their case before the Lord their God.

Aaron had been chosen by God to assist his brother, and had been in a responsible role during Moses meetings with the Pharaoh. Indeed he had been at the forefront of God's activities in Egypt and been given the lead role in ministering before God as the high priest. So how had he fallen so far? Fear of the people?

But Moses, knowing God as he did, had shown no fear, so why, having experienced the power and authority of God and the wrath of God, had Aaron not realized that God's authority and power was greater than that of the people?

> *20 The Lord was very angry with Aaron, and would have destroyed him, so I also prayed for Aaron at the same time.*

We are not considering here a normal breaking of the law of the land, but an action as serious as Adam's rebellion against God in the Garden. These were people defiantly defying their maker and creator.

> *21 I took your sinful thing, the calf which you had made, and burned it in the fire and thoroughly crushed it, grinding the metal thoroughly until it was as fine as dust; and I threw its dust into the brook that came down from the mountain.*

But that was not the only time many in Israel rebelled, so surely we can now see the wisdom of God in leading the people by a devious route to the promised land to weed out those that owned such a hardness of heart that they would have caused greater problems had they been allowed to enter the promised land.

The greatness of Moses leadership was not just in the way he reacted with the people as they continued their journey in the wilderness, but in his willingness to approach God on their behalf. For consider their rebellions, even after so many of their people had suffered the wrath of God and had died:

> *22 At Taberah, at Massah and at Kibroth-hattaavah you provoked the Lord to wrath. And when the Lord sent you from Kadesh-barnea, saying, 'Go up and take possession of the land which I have given you,' you rebelled against the command of the Lord your God, and you did not believe and rely on Him, nor did you obey His voice.*

There is no doubt that going into the land to take possession of it after ten of the spies had reported to the people that the opposition was too strong for them was challenging to say the least. But that was their personal assessment and did not consider the unlimited power God had made available to them.

Had those spies not remembered the advancing forces of the Pharaoh as they faced the barrier of the Red Sea? Did the Lord their God not demonstrate His power at that crucial moment by parting the waters and then drowning the Egyptian army?

Hindsight can be crucial to believers when faced with any seemingly insurmountable future difficulty, especially when we realize that our God is in a far better position than we are for two reasons.

The first is that He is all seeing and knows the strengths and weaknesses of the opposition, and second He has unlimited wisdom and power to overcome any and all people and obstacles. After all out of nothing He created and sustains all that we see.

Undoubtedly the key factor for all believers is, "Are we close enough to God to know what His will is for us?"

Moses declared that:

> *24 You have been rebellious against the Lord*
> *from the very first day that I knew you.*

How very sad that nothing Moses or the Lord could do was able to satisfy these complaining people. It was as though they had demonic possession. But consider what Moses did for them:

> *25 I prostrated myself before the Lord for forty days and nights*
> *because He had said He would destroy you.*

That was more than a month that Moses lay face down before the Lord in humble submission and all for this rebellious people the Lord threatened to destroy. Such dedication to the task God had given to him at the burning bush demonstrates God's incredible ability to choose the right person for a task

In pleading for the lives of these people before the Lord, Moses uses incredible diplomacy:

> *26 'O Lord God, do not destroy Your people, even Your*
> *inheritance, whom You have redeemed through Your greatness,*
> *whom You have brought from Egypt with a mighty hand.*

Moses first reminds the Lord that He chose these people and rescued them by performing many incredible miracles that displayed His mighty power that had put such fear into the hearts of those in Jericho that even the men of war were beside themselves with fear.

Moses pointed out that it was not just about these people He had rescued, but also the Patriarchs to whom He had made clear promises. So Lord,

> *do not look at the stubbornness of this people*
> *their wickedness or their sin,*

Surely God had dealt with those problems through the various and severe punishments He had inflicted upon them. The advantage of having a diplomat on the ground who was one of the people and could reason with God from a human point of view is made very clear in this action of Moses.

It also gives us confidence in having the Lord Jesus as our advocate because He has experienced life as a human being yet without sin.,

> *we have a High Priest who sympathizes and understands our weaknesses and temptations, because he has been tempted and knows exactly what it feels like to be human, in every respect as we are, yet without committing any sin.*
>
> *Therefore it is incumbent upon us to approach the throne of grace, the throne of God's gracious favour, with confidence and without fear, so that we may receive mercy for all our failures and find His amazing grace to help us in time of need.*
> *(see Heb. 4:15, 16).*

Moses was explaining to the Lord that it was not just about these stubborn people, but about those who had gone before and been found faithful, along with those amongst the people who had been faithful and served Him and those that would be born to them. As is often mentioned in the first testament there was always a remnant, which at this time, along with Moses, included Caleb and Joshua.

But now Moses makes a point that is truly telling. What about Egypt? When they hear of the destruction of the people God had rescued from slavery in Egypt, will they not say that it was:

> *Because the Lord was not capable of bringing them into the land which He had promised them and because He hated them He has brought them out to the wilderness in order to kill them.*

In fact that was the accusation of the rebels themselves, why have you brought us out of Egypt only to destroy us in one way or another? Whatever the rightness of his anger through frustration with the people corrupted with sin, it was essential that this wider picture was brought to God's attention.

Knowing that God is all knowing, one wonders about the tactics He was using here. This could easily have been a test of Moses loyalty to Him and for his concern for the people given that Moses became exhausted by the continual murmuring of the people.

Was it not also in preparation for this moment when the children of the rebels finally found out just how close they got to being wiped out by God had it not been for the intervention of Moses? Moses undoubtedly carried a mighty burden on his human shoulders.

What a mighty man of God was Moses. God's representative on the ground, seeing things from man's point of view and as an ambassador advising God from the front line. The people of Egypt and the surrounding nations would not see things from God's point of view because they did not know just who and what He really was, nor realize the unacceptability of the people's behaviour.

They would merely see the people having been rescued from Egypt and then being killed in the wilderness without knowing all the details.

It is essential that we accept that, yes He is *the* God of love, that is one side of the coin, but he is also total purity and cannot look upon sin, therefore on the other side of the coin He is the righteous judge of all men.

In creating all things the creator had every right to lay down rules and instructions for all His creation to obey; man included.

The people God had saved from slavery in Egypt were to be the foundation of the new nation of Israel that God wanted to mould into His people and bless them to the extent that people from other nations would want to become part of them.

Finally Moses told the Lord that the people were:

> *Your people and Your inheritance,*
> *whom You have brought out*
> *by Your great power and*
> *by Your outstretched arm.'*
> (Deut. 9:29)

It was because of His achievements that the nation was, to all practical purposes, now ready to enter the Promised land.

7 TABLETS REWRITTEN

Chapter 10

Interestingly God provided the first two stone tablets on which He had inscribed the ten Hebrew words that represented the ten commandments.

Those tablets having been shattered by Moses when in anger he witnessed the frivolity of the grave sinful act being perpetrated by those with no heart for God, had to be replaced. As man had shattered them because of sin, it was up to man to provide replacements which was not easy to do and very time consuming (many months) with just the very crude tools of that time (roughly 1273 BC). The ark would also have taken time considering they were in the wilderness and there was not a carpenter with his workshop available, so the ark is unlike to have been pristine like the beautifully fashioned antique furniture we see in fine houses.

It is easy to pass by such detail, but we have to consider the time, resources and facilities they had.

> *1 The Lord said to me, 'Cut out for yourself two tablets of stone like the first, and make an ark, or chest, of wood to contain the tablets. Then come up to Me on the mountain and I will write on the tablets the words that were on the first tablets you shattered, and you shall put them in the ark.*

Thus the new tablets represented cooperation between God and man. What was inscribed on the tablets was still by the hand of God. And it has been those words that have provided the basis of the covenant governing man's relationship with God ever since.

But what do we mean by covenant from a Biblical point of view?

The covenant represents the conditional promises made to humanity by God, as revealed in Scripture. In the agreement, which was between God and the ancient Israelites, God promised to protect them and bless them if they kept His law and were faithful to Him.

It is a matter of principle that we must never forget that God created all that we see and cannot see; the spiritual world that lives alongside the physical world, and man is affected and influenced by both. This thought is repeated because we need to be reminded of that fact because it is easily forgotten.

This agreement was not only about the ten commandments, but the willingness of mankind to be obedient to the guiding principles and regulations God put in place for man's benefit. Sadly the agreement was made necessary because the corrupting DNA of sin, caused by Adam's rebelliousness, had become part of man's make up.

All the rebellious acts of thousands of Israelites who perished during the forty years of wandering in the wilderness, were as a result of that DNA of sin and Satan's determination to prevent God's plan to save mankind being enacted.

As that DNA is still part of us, the requirements laid down in that covenant are still in place to govern the life of all believers, Jews and Gentiles alike, today. The blood of the Lord Jesus is, for us who believe, the cleansing balm that saves us from eternal destruction. When we fall short of those requirements it is necessary for us to call upon its cleansing power.

3 So I made an ark of acacia wood and cut out two tablets of stone like the first, and went up the mountain with the two tablets in my hand.

4 The Lord wrote on the tablets, just like the first time, the Ten Commandments which the Lord had spoken to you on the mountain from the midst of the fire on the day of the assembly; then the Lord gave them to me.

5 I then turned and came down from the mountain and put the tablets in the ark which I had made; and they are there, just as the Lord commanded me."

Although the tablets totally disappeared during their exile to Babylon, the covenant God made with ancient Israel is still relevant today, therefore we must be sure to know its requirements; after all it is an agreement between God and man with both having responsibility for carrying out their part of that agreement.

In the covenant God promised to protect those that were His, that is all those who were prepared to *keep His law and be faithful to Him.*

6 The Israelites travelled from the wells of Bene Jaakan to Mosera, where Aaron died and was buried and Eleazar his son became high priest in his place.

Notice that in the second sentence of verse 6 is the brief statement that *Aaron died and was buried and Eleazar his son ministered as priest in his place.* This was about the demise of a weak man who not only did not have the strength of character to support Moses, but from time to time caused him problems. Not only did he have no known resting place, but there seems to have been no time of national mourning for him either.

7 From there they travelled to Gudgodah, and then to Jotbathah, a land of brooks of water.

8 At that time the Lord set apart the tribe of Levi to carry the ark of the covenant of the Lord, to stand before the Lord to serve Him and to bless in His name until this day.

9 Therefore, Levi does not have a portion or inheritance of tribal land with his brothers; the Lord is his inheritance, as the Lord your God has promised him.

,

Those engaged in full time ministry needed an income because their work was in relation to people's access to and relationship with God. This required the support of the worshippers. What is interesting is that those who value the worship of God will always be willing to contribute well, but those that do not value the worship will contribute little. By making the statement, "will be willing to contribute well" does not refer to the amount, because of what the Lord Jesus observed:

> *Now Jesus sat opposite the treasury and saw how much money the people put into the treasury. Many who were rich put in much. Then one poor widow came and threw in two mites, which make a quadrans.*
>
> *So He called His disciples to Himself and said to them, "Assuredly, I say to you that this poor widow has put in more than all those who have given to the treasury; for they all put in out of their abundance, but she out of her poverty put in all that she had, her whole livelihood." (Mk 12:41 – 44)*

Because the sons of Levi had to dedicate themselves to the worship of God and looking after the services in the temple and its maintenance, no land was set aside for the tribe to use to farm or set up manufacturing facilities like carpentry to support them financially, therefore it became the responsibility of members of the other tribes to support them with offerings of food, which was part of the people's offerings to God offered on the altar. Finance was part of the annual giving to the temple treasury which also provided financial support for the work of the tabernacle and then the temple.

This arrangement was fine all the while the people's focus was on worshipping and glorifying God, and going to the temple on a regular basis. But there were times when their love of God went cold, in which case the Levites were forced to find other means of income.

Moses, having shown such dedication to protect the people of God, spent a second time on the mountain (see Deut. 9:18, 19) waiting for God to make His decision. Finally God spoke:

> *10 … like the first time, I stayed on the mountain forty days and nights, and the Lord listened to me at that time also. The Lord was not willing to destroy you saying to me, 'Arise, go on your journey ahead of the people, so that they may go in and take possession of the land which I swore to their fathers to give to them.'*

This was God and His chosen servant working in perfect harmony.

Tucked away in verses 8 & 9 there is a very important statement that we need to consider as it could well apply to some of us. Such was the importance of the covenant of the ten commandments contained in a wooden box called an ark that only dedicated people were allowed to carry it.

The Levites were being prepared to be the conduit through which the Lord God spoke to the people once Moses had died, and it was they who had the responsibility of carrying the ark of the covenant of the Lord when the people were travelling. They were,

> to stand before the Lord to serve Him and to bless in His name Therefore, Levi does not have a portion of tribal land for an inheritance along with his brothers; because the Lord is his inheritance, as the Lord your God has promised him.

Notice the importance of that statement. Because the Lord is the inheritance of the tribe of ministry, they would not inherit land. For those responsible for the handling of the Word of God, God was to be their all-in-all.

What is the modern equivalent?

Having the word, not on tablets of stone, but firmly in their hearts and minds, those commissioned were to be responsible for handling the Word of God to become ministers and missionaries. Which is what the ancient Israelites were supposed to be.

The equivalent today would be the ordained clergy and lay members that preach and teach the world of God. Their responsibility is not always taken as seriously as it aught, for they forget that all those in some form of leadership and teaching positions will ultimately be judged far more harshly than ordinary members of the church.

The command came from the highest authority when the risen Christ said to the disciples, *All authority in heaven and on earth has been given to Me,* which is in place of *Thus says the Lord God.*

> Go, therefore, into all the world and make disciples of people of all the nations, enabling them to learn of Me, believe in Me, understand and obey My words, baptizing them that believe in the

name of the Father and of the Son and of the Holy Spirit, teaching
them to observe everything that I have commanded you; and lo, I am
with you perpetually, in every circumstance, and on every occasion,
even to the end of the world. (Matt. 28:

… *the end of the world* is that time when the world will disappear and
no further outreach is possible.

For the ancient Israelites the challenge was:

12   And now, Israel, what does the Lord your God require from
you, but in holy fear to worship Him, approaching Him with awe-
filled reverence and profound respect, to walk in all His ways and to
love Him, to serve the Lord your God with all your heart and with
all your soul, and to keep the commandments of the Lord and His
statutes which I command you today for your good?

There is a very great danger today, especially when singing hymns
such as, "What a friend we have in Jesus" to bring the whole
Godhead of Father, Son and Holy Spirit down to a human level and
not treat Him as the awesome God He is. Let there be no doubt that
we also are required, *in holy fear to worship Him, approaching Him with*
awe-filled reverence and profound respect to walk in all His ways and to love
Him, to serve the Lord your God with all your heart and with all your soul, and
to keep the commandments of the Lord and His statutes

Indeed it is interesting that Moses adds:

14   Behold, the heavens and the highest of heavens belong to the
Lord your God, and the earth and all that is in it.

Therefore we have got to have it firmly fixed in our minds just
what a mighty God it is with whom we are allowed to converse.
Certainly the Israelites did not seem to be able to appreciate the
enormity of the greatness and wonder of God because of their
attitude towards Him. We must not make the same mistake!

It was essential that the people realized the scale of the calamity
from which Moses had saved them. Instead of being completely
destroyed, they had received new life and a future. But it was
incumbent upon them to be obedient by:

living each and every day in all His ways and to love Him,

and this love was not to be a fickle human type love, but a consistent and totally respectful love for such an awesome God who had chosen them as His own, above all the other nations.

They were His choice, however undeserving they may have been; and in a very privileged position, with all the possible blessings and protection with which He was able to provide them, and all they had to do was to be grateful and,

> *serve the Lord your God with all your heart and with all your soul, which includes your choices, thoughts, indeed your whole being, and to keep the commandments of the Lord and His statutes which I am commanding you today for your good.*

The whole point of the meeting between God and His chosen people was to enter into a spiritual engagement which was the precursor to marriage. We too, by accepting the Lordship of Christ over our lives, have entered into that same spiritual engagement in preparation for the wedding at the marriage supper of the Lamb in the new Jerusalem.

It may seem that there is a lot of repetition throughout this book of Deuteronomy, and there is, but it is all for a purpose, which is to ensure the people, along with all believers today, learned about God's desire to be the head of the national family in order that He could look after them; a sugar daddy perhaps, but much more than that. After all, think of the awesomeness of God:

> *Behold, the heavens and the highest of heavens belong to the Lord your God, the earth and all that is in it.*

It had to be pointed out to the people the awesomeness of God and their unworthiness. The reason they were where they were was not because of any virtue of their own, but they were benefiting from what had been promised to the patriarchs, who had been men of a far greater stature than themselves, being totally alone in serving God.

15 Yet the Lord had a delight in loving your fathers and set His affection on them, and He chose their descendants after them, you above all peoples, as it is this day.
So circumcise your heart, and be stiff-necked no longer.

Circumcision was the removal of the foreskin of a man's penis, carried out on the eighth day of life, which identified the man as a person of the covenant. So what does it mean to *circumcise your heart?*

As we have already discovered the heart was considered to be the centre of a person's life. So to circumcise the heart was to remove the outer hardness caused by sin that would prevent or impede the Spirit of God influencing their lives. It was imperative that the people softened their attitude towards God so that He could get close to them and allow them to get close to Him.

Whilst the people were exiled to Babylon, God through Ezekiel identified the people's problem since they had entered the promised land, which is evidenced throughout the scriptures

Son of man, when the house of Israel dwelt in their own land, they defiled it by the way they lived and acted; to Me their way was like the uncleanness of a woman in her customary impurity.

Therefore because of the blood they had shed on the land, and for defiling it by erecting and worshipping their idols, I poured out My fury on them.

How God must have despaired after all that He had done for them after rescuing them from Egypt and giving them a land flowing with milk and honey, a beautiful land that had all the potential to be blessed and give them a good life.

Instead of looking to their loving God and in appreciation for all that He had done for them by obeying the commandments, they ended up being constantly attacked, and subdued and sent into exile, squandering their substance just like the prodigal son because they kept looking to ineffective idols and gods with no power.

There is an interesting verse (Ez. 36:21) which is worth mentioning because it is very important for us to know and understand, and that is:

But I had concern for My holy name, which the house of Israel had profaned among the nations wherever they went.

It cannot be emphasized enough that God chose Abraham and his chosen descendants for the particular purpose of demonstrating to the world God's love for mankind and His desire to save them from their life of sin. Yet the descendants repaid their God through neglect, perverting the word and seeking to fit in with the people of other nations and persuasions, just as the church leaders are doing today.

No wonder God had concerns for His holy name which they and we have profaned. How many people outside the church see anything attractive in it that they should want to join a congregation? Where is the power of the word of God that changes lives? Where are the congregations where the Spirit of God had the freedom to move and do great things?

Imagine all those who might have been saved throughout all generations of human history that died in sin just because of the selfishness of generation after generation of the people of Israel who rebelled against almighty God. Indeed, instead of being faithful to their living God, they wanted to be like everyone else yet still hang on to the fact that they were Jews.

In spite of their unfaithfulness and defiling way of life, God was determined to continue with His plan to provide the world with eternal salvation through them. Having *concern for My holy name* God had to take a firm hold on the situation and prevent their rebelliousness to stop the salvation of souls.

The challenge to you the reader is how do you treat God and are you willing to surrender your life to Him and be used of Him?

"Therefore say to the house of Israel, 'Thus says the Lord God: "I do not do this for your sake, O house of Israel, but for My holy name's sake, which you have profaned among the nations wherever you went." (Ez. 36:22)

The nation of Judah was in exile because they had gone the way of the Canaanites, with even the priests worshipping creatures and various gods including the sun from the temple in Jerusalem (Ez. 8).

Horrendous! They could not have insulted the Lord anymore disastrously than they had done.

> *"And I will sanctify My great name, which has been profaned among the nations, which you have profaned in their midst; and the nations shall know that I am the Lord," says the Lord God, "when I am hallowed in you before their eyes". (Ez. 36:23)*

God was about to take charge of the nation of Israel[14] and purify them yet again, returning them to the land of Judah rebuilding the temple and the walls of Jerusalem in preparation for the arrival of the Messiah.

> *"For I will take you from among the nations, gather you out of all countries, and bring you into your own land."*

Let us be in no doubt about the power and ability of God to achieve all that He wants to achieve, something the people of Israel; were to learn the hard way. However, all that God does in the arena of man He does through individuals, even if they are but few in number.

Remember it was Nehemiah who oversaw the rebuilding of the Jerusalem city walls and hanging the city gates, and Zerubbabel who oversaw the rebuilding of the temple. It was Ezra who oversaw the cleansing of the priesthood and the people, and read to them the law (possibly Deuteronomy and Leviticus) which he had studied whilst in exile ready for the time when they would be able to worship at the temple once more.

> *Then I will sprinkle clean water on you, and you shall be clean; I will cleanse you from all your filthiness and idols. I will give you a new heart and put a new spirit within you; (Ez. 36:24, 25)*

We have been considering the message from God about the circumcision of the heart, which can apply to all the people, not just the men. But take note concerning the new pliable heart rather than the hard heart that rejected anything to do with God:

---

[14] See the end section of my book Law& Grace titled Exile

I will take the heart of stone out of your flesh and replace it with a heart of flesh. I will put My Spirit within you and cause you to walk in My statutes, and you will keep My judgments and do them. (Ez. 36:27)

God always places conditions on His gifts, for what is the point in Him giving us a gift only for us to go and do exactly what we want?

Then you shall dwell in the land that I gave to your fathers; you shall be My people, and I will be your God. I will deliver you from all your uncleanness. I will call for the grain and multiply it, and bring no famine upon you. (Ez. 36:28, 29)

Not all the people returned to Jerusalem but that was what was on offer to those Israelites who were prepared to return and re-establish themselves in the now drastically reduced area of the promised land and enter into a covenant relationship with God.

It is all very well hearing about the ups and downs of the Israelites in regard to their relationship with their God, but have we in the 21st century learned from their mistakes and the way they bent the rules of worship far too far? We must not think that we can do what we want, tampering with the way we worship the same God of Israel, including twisting the Divine message of the word of God to suit our current social sensitivities.

Although sadly that is precisely what far too many within the church have done for countless ages, instead of seeking a personal relationship with God and asking Him to guide us in regard to not just how we worship Him, but also our work in His service. Prayer and fasting are the most important means of us getting deeper into God.

God's gift of Salvation is free but with certain conditions, for what does the Lord Jesus say?

"Not everyone who says to Me, 'Lord, Lord,' shall enter the kingdom of heaven, **but he who does the will of My Father in heaven.**

Writing to the believers in Rome, Paul tells them that circumcision is only of value when those who have received the physical mark kept the law, but it is of no use for the law breaker because it is a sign of one who had been dedicated to God for the purpose of them having a spiritual relationship with Him, and those who break the law annulled that dedication. Just as baptism in the church is meaningless except the one baptized fulfil their duty to take God seriously and to love and serve Him according to His divine will.

What Paul is saying is that it is no use being a Jew outwardly, that is one who has merely received the physical mark of circumcision, because if he is living a life completely at odds with the God of Israel, the circumcision becomes merely a mark in the flesh with no real meaning.

Being of the circumcision is all about keeping the law of God, and living a life in tune with Him.

Paul then speculates that *if an uncircumcised man keeps the requirements of the Law, will not his uncircumcision be regarded by God as circumcision?* That is, he fulfils all the requirements of those that have been circumcised.

What is more, *he who is physically uncircumcised but keeps the spirit of the Law will have* every right to *judge those who, even though they, through their Jewish heritage, have the written code and circumcision, break the Law?*

The whole point of Paul's argument is this,

> *For he is not a real Jew who is only one outwardly, nor is the real meaning of circumcision something external and physical.*

No. The whole point of the phrase, *So circumcise your heart, and be stiff-necked no longer* is to emphasize that:

> *he is a only a true Jew who is one inwardly, that is within the heart; and true circumcision is that of the heart, operated on by the Spirit, and certainly not by the fulfilment of the letter of the Law. Thus the praise offered by the true Jew is not from men, but from God.*

The reason for this need of becoming a true member of the circumcision was to be able to open themselves up to the will and purposes of the God who is far above all other gods,

17 For the Lord your God is the God of gods and the Lord of lords, the great, the mighty, the awesome God who does not show partiality nor take a bribe.

Moses concludes this chapter by extoling the virtues of God and identifying the requirements God had put upon each and every one of them.

Indeed one of the most important aspects of their new life was that of caring, not only about those in need, but also about those that were not of true Israeli descent and God wanted to impress upon them their responsibility because God wants us to be concerned about the welfare of others that are non-believers without accepting their way of life.

If God cared so much about the people of the nation of Israel, did He not care also about the people of other nations? His patience in seeing the declining morality of the people living in the land of Canaan, and waiting for them to realize their way of life was incompatible with His created purpose for mankind, demonstrates that He would have all mankind to be saved and serve Him.

As Paul wrote to the believers in Rome:

> *How then shall they call on Him in whom they have not believed? And how shall they believe in Him of whom they have not heard? And how shall they hear without a preacher?*
>
> *15And how shall they preach unless they are sent? As it is written:*
>
> *"How beautiful are the feet of those who preach the gospel of peace, who bring glad tidings of good things!"*
>
> *16But they have not all obeyed the gospel. For Isaiah says, "Lord, who has believed our report?"*
>
> *17So then faith comes by hearing, and hearing by the word of God.*

But there comes a point where His justice must be enacted and now was the time for Israel to be His means of punishment, just as God was to use other nations to apply His judgements on Israel in the future[15].

---

[15] As explained in my books Law & Grace, and Hosea

Salvation was not to be the be all and end of the work of believers. God had demonstrated His holistic approach to dealing with the Israelites and so it is the same today.

What is the point in being confined to a building and be so involved in meetings within that building that it has no heart for those in need and those without God, out in the wider community? In fact it has been that insularity, that focus within themselves, that has been one cause of the church shrinking and becoming meaningless for the modern day young person in particular:

> *18 God executes justice for the orphan and the widow, and shows His love for the stranger, the resident alien, and foreigner, by giving him food and clothing. Therefore, show your love for the stranger, for you were strangers in the land of Egypt.*

This verse is so very important that it is immediately followed by a repeat of the importance of their attitude and relationship with God:

> *20 You shall worship God with a holy fear, and with awe-filled reverence and profoundly respect the Lord your God. You shall serve Him and cling tightly to Him, in order to be united with Him, and you shall swear oaths by His name.*

How can the reliance of the nation of Israel on God be fully and clearly expressed? In saying that God was their *praise and glory,* Moses was clearly making a statement of fact because God was their all in all. He was the whole reason for their being in such a privileged position as God's eldest son of all the nations of the earth. He was their portion. Indeed,

> *21 He is your praise and glory; He is your God, who has done these great and awesome things which you have seen with your own eyes. Your fathers went down to Egypt, seventy persons in all, and now, from that seventy, the Lord your God has made you as numerous as the stars of heaven.*

Surely a God such as their God, who is of such majesty and justice, way above the majesty and justice of any human monarch, should naturally command the reverence and selfless devotion of all those that truly believe in Him.

This teaching is just as important to those who have been baptized into the Christian faith. What is very clear from what we have just studied is that infant baptism is not true baptism because the infant has no understanding of what baptism is all about.

A note about adult baptism, performed either by the sprinkling of water or full immersion. It has no meaning except the individual not only truly believes in his heart that Jesus saves, but is also willing to validate that baptism by committing themselves completely to God even as the Israelites were required to do.

Baptism is not a ritual it is a sign of a repentant sinner's inner love of the Lord their God and their complete commitment to God and His service for the rest of their lives. That is some commitment.

There is no true salvation, no true experience of the filling of the Holy Spirit as the disciples experienced without an inner conviction and commitment to God that God Himself accepts. This knowledge must be viewed in the light of this next section.

Rewards of Obedience Chapter 11

1 Therefore you shall love the Lord your God, and accept your obligation to Him to always keep His charge, His statutes, precepts, and commandments.

Intimate relationships cannot be forced. God will not have barged in on Abram and called him to service, suddenly, out of nowhere. Rather God would have had Abram go through various experiences to prepare him for that important spiritual meeting.

We have to accept that God takes His time to ensure individuals are given time to be ready and that things happen exactly according to the time table He set at the beginning of time. We have only to think of the life of Moses to see how his life was organized before he was finally called to his ultimate position of service.

Isaac learned from his father and had that amazing experience of the ram saving his life when he laid bound on the wood preparing to be the sacrifice. With his father holding the knife above him that would end his life, the voice that stopped the slaughter and the appearance of the ram that saved his life had to be a dramatic time when the reality of God must have impacted his life. But then he seemed to have freewheeled his way through life.

It was his wife Rebekah who was more sensitive to the will of God, because the message from God about the twins in her womb and that the elder would serve the younger. I had been clear to her that God had rejected Esau from inheriting the tribe that He had chosen for the development and provision of His plan for the salvation of all mankind. So she ensured that Jacob received the blessing of his father.

Jacob learned from his father Isaac and was curious about God, finally having a personal experience of Him in that fight on the mountain.

David also and so many of the other leaders and prophets of Israel experienced God in their own individual and remarkable way that persuaded them that God was not just real but to be worshipped and become the focus of their lives.

After years of slavery the Israelites witnessed the mighty miracles of God first hand, in the sky and on the land. Then, with the death of the first born in Egypt, the taste of freedom until they were confronted by the impenetrable sea with the Egyptian army fast approaching; but God miraculously provided a path for them through the sea, and then allowed the sea to return and drown the Egyptians intent on recapturing them. God's planning and timing is without fault.

> 2 Know today that I do not speak with your children, who have not known and who have not seen the chastening of the Lord your God, His greatness and His mighty hand and His outstretched arm
> 3 His signs and His acts which He did in the midst of Egypt, to Pharaoh king of Egypt, and to all his land;
> 4 what He did to the army of Egypt, to their horses and their chariots: how He made the waters of the Red Sea overflow them as they pursued you, and how the Lord has destroyed them to this day;

Then there was the supply of provisions until the tests God used to see if they fully trusted Him. Tests sadly failed by far too many of the people.

Here Moses reminded them of those who met with rather spectacular ends because of their rebelliousness, such as Dathan and

Abiram who, along with their families and all their possessions, were literally swallowed up by the earth in full view of the people. A very frightening experience indeed.

> 5 Also remember *what He did for you in the wilderness until you came to this place; 6and what He did to Dathan and Abiram the sons of Eliab, the son of Reuben: how the earth opened its mouth and swallowed them up, their households, their tents, and all the substance that was in their possession, in the midst of all Israel, but your eyes have seen every great act of the Lord which He did.*

God's objective through the demonstration of His power was twofold. The first was to demonstrate that no one was a match for Him, thereby exerting a disciplinary influence over the nation in order to subdue the people's waywardness and reckless individual pride. The second was to promote humility and reverence and the desire to obey and serve Him.

From the plagues to that moment was a time of God getting to know the people He had rescued, and for them to get to know Him and all that He could do for them. Fortunately many did believe and it was they who, along with Moses, built up a relationship with God.

The forty years of their nomadic life was their pre-engagement, and engagement relationship with God which was kept in the memory of the people before being written down, hence the reference to comments such *as up to the present day*, which obviously meant the written record was made years later. But that does not detract from the immediacy of what Moses was telling the people there and then.

Having gone through those forty years of wandering they were now on the verge of entering the promised land and Moses was emphasizing their need to bond with God, not just through holy and reverential fear, but also through the bond of love and appreciation of all that God had done for them and was prepared to do for them in the future, because He was their ultimate guide and protector. The relationship needed to be strong, and the only way that could happen was with a bond of love and duty.

God save them and led them and in return they were to respond to His *statutes, precepts, and commandments.*

Moses makes it very clear that what he is telling them was for the adult population that knew something of all that had happened to the nation over the past forty years until now, from leaving Egypt, passing through the sea, hearing God on the mountain until the present time.

The Hebrews had very good memories and passed their experiences on to the next generation. Indeed the whole purpose of the feasts was to help them pass on that information for future generations. This is what happened at this or that time and the reason we are celebrating it is in order to thank God for all He has done for us.

Now it was time for them to take responsibility for their actions and become leaders of families and tribes and the nation as a whole. This was particularly pertinent because Moses would not be leading them any further.

The only way they would become strong in order to go in and possess the land and enjoy a long life in it was to be dutiful about keeping the commandments and feasts of God.

> *8 Therefore, you shall keep all the commandments which I am commanding you today, so that you may be strong and go in and take possession of the land which you are crossing over the Jordan to possess;*
>
> *9 so that you may live long on the land which the Lord solemnly promised to your fathers to give to them and to their descendants, a land of great abundance, that is flowing with milk and honey.*
>
> *10 For the land which you are entering to possess is not like the land of Egypt from which you have come, where you sowed your seed and watered it with your foot like a garden of vegetables.*

The land of Goshen was flat and very fertile, so even shepherds could hardly resist grasping the opportunity to at least grow richer feed for their livestock, but it had very little rain from heaven, so irrigation was essential, hence *and watered it with your foot* which is a reference to the irrigation wheel turned with the feet taking water from the river through irrigation channels to the fields.

This put a totally different complexion on the matter of their relationship with God as in future, instead of watering the land through arduous labour, they would be dependent upon God for the provision of the former and latter rains, as well as the dew watering the crops.

The new land was watered by God and the supply of rain could be cut off as it was in the time of Elijah who informed king Ahab that there would be no dew nor rain until he said so, and then God hid him.

Notice carefully that the land they were about to possess was a land of hills and valleys that *drink water from the rain of heaven*. It is also a land that God cared about because *the eyes of the Lord your God are always on it, from the beginning of the year to the end of the year*. It was a strategically important land connecting the continents of Asia and Africa.

It is easy to gloss over these verses by merely explaining them as God warning them that the topography was totally different to what they had been used to. But that would prevent us from learning the important spiritual implications of water on the people that would feature prominently in their future history.

There is so much that people in the West accept as their right, but as onetime President Julius Nyerere of Tanzania once said, "You people of the West are always going on about your rights, but never about your responsibilities."

What is particularly interesting about Israel is that by going into the promised land they were going to be totally dependent upon God for provisions as it had no natural rivers flowing through it such as the Nile through Egypt.

Rain was a blessing from God. No rain and there was drought. We have only to consider how Elijah, at God's command, called on the heavens to deny rain to Israel for two and one half years. Even Elijah had to leave Israel to stay safe away from Ahab and Jezebel. Only when he had proved that the God he served was the true God and had the prophets of Baal killed did rain fall again.

It is a salutary lesson that those that are truly willing to trust God must submit themselves in such a way that they are willing to commit all that they are and have to Him so that they willingly become totally dependent upon Him.

I have noticed in my own life, regarding the matter of money, that we have always had just enough to live on but when a large bill must be paid the amount of money we have available to us suddenly increases to cover the additional expense. Truly amazing.

For those with a good job and regular supply of enough income to cover not just daily expenses, but luxuries such as holidays and trips out and about, and new cars have no need of God. They can run their own lives without any input from Him.

I do not believe the only reason God had me become a contract technical author was to control my times of employment and therefore my money supply, although that was excellent training in itself, but because the training received in writing explanatory books on equipment and processes prepared me for writing these books on scripture.

> *13 – 17 the result of you listening obediently and paying attention to the commandments which I command you today, and learning to love the Lord your God and serve Him with all your heart and with all your soul, will be to ensure your choices, thoughts and actions, indeed your whole being is brought into line with His will, and that will allow Him to:*

> - *supply the rain for your land in its season, with the early rain in the autumn and the late rain in the spring,*
> - *enable you gather in your grain and your new wine and your olive oil.*
> - *give grass in your fields for your cattle, allowing you to eat and be satisfied.*

> *Beware that your hearts are not deceived, and that you do not turn away from the Lord your God and serve other gods and worship them, else the Lord's anger will be kindled and burn against you, causing Him to shut up the heavens so that there will be no rain preventing the land from yielding its fruit; and you will perish quickly from the good land which the Lord is giving you.*

This is a salutary lesson of which even we today must be very conscious, because God has not lost His power to control the elements. He might seem slow to anger, but when His anger is aroused, then His power to teach mankind a lesson that He is still in ultimate control remains considerable.

At the present time the whole world is suffering with Covid-19 (2020, 2021), and the financial markets are collapsing, people are dying in great numbers and mankind is in fear of this virus, which no one can seem to control.

Weather patterns have been disrupted, crops fail and flooding and earthquakes and fires are having such a devastating effect yet even the church seems frightened to tell the world that the creator God we worship is angry with the way man has totally ignored Him.

With all the deforestation that is going on along with vast areas being burned by horrendous forest fires, no one is considering what John writes of his experience in heaven, *The first angel sounded his trumpet, ….. and a third of the trees were burned up, and all the green grass was burned up.* (Rev. 8:7). Do we pay any attention to those parts of scripture that are more difficult to understand[16]?

It is, however, incumbent upon the church to set an example which it is not at present willing to do. Just as the Israelites failed from time to time to be loyal to God, so the church is doing exactly the same.

> *18 – 21 Therefore, you shall impress these words of mine on your heart and on your soul, and tie them as a sign on your hand, and they shall be as frontal / frontlets) on your forehead.*
> *You shall be diligent in teaching them to your children,*

What better way of teaching the children to know God and understand all that He had done for and meant to the people of Israel than to teach the children within the family situation and for the parents to demonstrate through the way they live their lives just how important God is to them. Children learn by watching their parents and emulating them and their behaviour whilst also developing a life of their own.

> *impressing God's precepts on their minds and ensuring His truths penetrate their hearts, speaking of them in your daily conversations and dealings with your family and friends.*
> *You shall write them on the doorposts of your house and on your gates, so that your days and the days of your children may be*

---

[16] See my book Seeing into the Future : Understanding the Revelation of John — written at the request of Rabbi Aaron

multiplied in the land which the Lord swore to your fathers to give them, as long as the heavens are above the earth.

This matter of making the Lord part of our daily activity is essential in making Him an intrinsic part of our daily lives. If we leave Him out of our work ethics and family conversation and activities, then there is a very big chance of us ignoring him more frequently.

Although God recommended them to *write them on the doorposts of your house and on your gates,* there was always the potential for them to become an automatic and meaningless gesture, as with them tying *them as a sign on your hand* except they get into the routine of consciously remembering the word of the Lord as they tied them on each day and whilst wearing them.

Remembering that the people are just about to enter into the promised land, the success of their campaign rested on their loyalty to God from that time forward.

22 For if you are careful to keep all these commandments (or perhaps: if you are prepared to commit yourselves wholeheartedly to living your lives according to my words of instruction), which I am commanding you to follow, it will enable you to love the Lord your God, and to live each and every day in all His ways and to hold tightly to Him …

Let us study this verse carefully as we must be conscious of what God was saying to those people, because although we are not going into a new land, there is much in our countries that are far from being beneficial, and the example of a holy life lived according to the instructions, will and purposes of God will have an incredible effect on the lives of those searching for something more worthwhile to order their lives.

'For if' is a very powerful introduction because it very clearly lays down the conditions for their success in ousting the current inhabitants in the land. Without God's help, as the original spies so rightly judged, the nation would not succeed, but with His help no foe would be of any real threat. And this can easily apply in our own lives.

My alternative for:

if you are careful to keep all these commandments

is

if you are prepared to commit yourselves wholeheartedly to living your lives according to my words of instruction.

Two different ways of saying the same thing but perhaps the second could easily be the focus of Christians today. The end result is all about the people's willingness to give due diligence to submitting themselves to the will and instructions of God that engender such bonding that they would have such a *love* for *the Lord their God,* that would allow them *to live each and every day in all His ways and to hold tightly to Him.*

Such a bonding of His people with their God would allow Him to work with them and through them to achieve what he wanted to achieve. Again the same could be applied to believers today and bring about a new and better world.

> 23   *then the Lord will drive out all these nations from before you, and you shall dispossess nations greater and mightier than you of the land.*
> 24   *Every place on which the sole of your foot treads shall become yours; your territory shall be from the wilderness to Lebanon, and from the river Euphrates, as far as the western (Mediterranean) sea.*

Now the land occupied by Israel is to the west of the Jordan and to the Mediterranean sea, nowhere near the Euphrates river

> 25 *No man will be able to stand before you; for the Lord your God will lay a great fear and dread of you on all the land on which you set foot, just as He has spoken to you.*

The church in the western nations is powerless to oppose or overcome the paganization of the countries in which it operates, for the very reason Israel did not succeed in irradicating paganism in the previous dwellers in Canaan. Few theological colleges teach the undiluted word of God, so is there any wonder that the churches are dying through the lack of the truth.

Success in the earthly life of any believer can only be achieved when that life is lived in spiritual union with God, and teaching the pure word of God that would enable them to grow into mature believers in the Lord. The whole history of Israel gives testament to that fact. Read my book Law & Grace about the separated Israel and Judah and you will see what happens when there is a disconnect between man and God.

26 Behold, today I am setting before you a blessing and a curse

Life with God is very simple. As designer and creator He knows us better than we know ourselves because He created us in such a way that we are not at our best except in a spiritual relationship with Him. He also designed the earth to be our place of physical and spiritual development in our relationship with Him to prepare us for our continued existence with Him in His place of rest.

Let us be of no doubt that God had all this planned before the big bang and the evolved creation of all that we see around us, which from the start had within it its own seed of destruction.

For example, in the beginning CO_2 was stored in trees to be released as man developed his skills and ability to use the resources of coal and oil and gas God had provided, not realizing that burning them would gradually destroy this planet. The book of Revelation, that so few have the nerve to study, reveals the end times when the world will gradually be destroyed.

The sin of man is just one reason why it is being destroyed, but what would have happened if sin had not entered the lives of men, we will never know. We can but speculate that it would have been a place of great joy an preparation for heaven.

27 **the blessing,** will be received:

if you listen to and obey the commandments of the Lord your God, which I am commanding you today;

This choice has everything to do with the people agreeing to honouring their part of the covenant, the agreement they both accepted on Mount Sinai, the people and God. Just as with Adam, God allowed them, both as individuals and as a nation, the freedom to choose the course of their lives. All Moses could do was to clearly define the two alternatives, of which they would be reminded throughout their history.

But it is also our choice today, even though Gentiles were not in on the covenantal agreement. Non-Israelis would only come under the terms of the covenant by becoming converts to Judaism in the first instance, or becoming a dedicated follower of the Lord Jesus Christ which would grant them membership of the church, which is spiritual Israel. That means Gentiles along with Jews come under God's covenant, which in our case is the Sinai covenant as modified by the new covenant of grace through the blood of Christ.

It is interesting that throughout the Bible there is not one threat about non-conformance; only a choice to be made by each and every individual. This way or that, which leads to this result:

the curse, will be applied

28 if you do not listen to and obey the commandments of the Lord your God, but turn aside from the way which I am commanding you today, by following, that is by acknowledging and worshipping, other gods which you have not known, thereby believing that they are greater than the Lord who chose you and rescued you from slavery and provided this land for you.

There is no middle way. We either listen to what God is saying through His word and obey His instructions for eternal life or we ignore it and suffer His curse. It is truly a case of God or the world.

The DNA of sin has led the human race for ever making the choice of going the way of the world, using their physical attributes of sight, hearing and touching. Throughout the world there are far more following gods of many shapes, sizes and types, including riches, and beautiful things that will not last after the death of the earth, than following our creator God.

29 Now it shall be, when the Lord your God has brought you into the land which you go to possess, that you shall put the blessing on Mount Gerizim and the curse on Mount Ebal.

These two mounts sit to the west of the Jordan river and in the middle of the land being possessed by Israel, with a deep valley between them. What better place to have two significant mounds with each representing one of the two principles of blessing and cursing given to them by Moses to remind the people of the wisdom of seeking the way of blessing.

With Mount Gerizim being fertile and lush it was so clear that it represented God's blessing, whereas Mount Ebal was rocky and barren, clearly representing the anger and cursing of God.

Theirs was the choice of seeking to be obedient and loyal to God which would inevitably attract His blessing, or rebellious which would only attract His curses, or rather not just the withdrawal of His blessings but punishment of one sort or another.

What was it better to do, choose the good path by cleaving to God and following in His ways, which leads to a rich, fruitful life, or embrace evil and negativity, which leads to an empty and barren life, devoid of all things good. As God is the provider of all things, surely it is better to live life in according to His rules to enjoy a rich and pleasant life?

The people would be forever reminded of these declarations of Moses throughout their pre-Messiah history.

Moses now deals with some positives:

- *For you will — cross over the Jordan and go in to possess the land which the Lord your God is giving you,*

- *and you will — possess it and dwell in it.*

- *And you shall — be careful to observe all the statutes and judgments which I set before you today.*

Moses was here trying to be positive.

8 REHEARSAL OF THE CODE

Deuteronomy 12

We have now dealt with the religious and historical preamble designed to prepare the people for the serious matter of the following statutes and judgements which provided them with the code of conduct that would keep them close to God in the new land, a supportive framework for everyday living, particularly in the beginning when they had removed all those who then lived in the land.

Up to now Moses had been speaking in general terms of the necessity to obey the laws of God by reminding them of the covenant so dramatically presented to them at Sinai that laid down the fundamentals of Israel's religious beliefs, and which was intended by God to be a way of life for them from birth to death.

In fact all God was doing was putting in place instructions for the people to conform to the way in which He had designed man to relate to Him, allowing easy spiritual communication. They were to be the prime example of how that relationship should work, except that man kept going the way of Cain, by ignoring/shunning the very one who had the power to make their lives a success.

Now come the detailed laws and precepts that were to govern their daily lives in the Land of Promise which are:

1. Religious institutions and manner of worship (Deut. 12:1 – 16:17)

2. Government of the people (Deut. 16:18 – 18)
3. Criminal law (Deut. 19 – 21:9)
4. Domestic life (Deut. 21:10 – 25)
5. Conclusion of code: First-fruits, tithes and accompanying prayers (Deut. 26:1 – 15)

Religious institutions and worship

Clearing the ground of all pagan contamination was essential to the future of the nation. Sin of any kind is anathema to God because it conflicts with His absolute purity. Taking possession of the land and purifying it by clearing out all symbols of paganism was to introduce a new beginning for the more matured nation of Israel as they established themselves in the land through which God had led His faithful servant Abraham and to whom He had originally promised it.

> *2 You shall utterly destroy all the places where the nations whom you shall dispossess serve their gods. Those on the high mountains and the hills and under every green tree.*
>
> *3 You shall tear down their altars and smash their idolatrous pillars and burn their Asherim in the fire; you shall cut down the carved and sculpted images of their gods and obliterate the name of all gods from that place.[17]*

The people, who were the beneficiaries of that promise were being sent into the land to purify it and make it a place where the worship of their glorious God was the norm.

Just one item or area or place name left alone that held the seeds of paganism would be enough to cause the cancer of sin to re-establish itself and then spread. Every vestige of paganism had to be eradicated.

An interesting phrase is:

> *4 You shall not contaminate the worship of the Lord your God with any pagan artifact or symbol or type of ceremony.*

---

[17] See 2 Chron. 30:14; 34:1 – 7 cf. 2 Chron. 33:1 -9; Hos. 8:11

This separation of the Divine from any semblance of the previous practice of the pagans was crucial. Much like those who have found Christ must give up all previous activities that led them down a path of evil. All such activities had to be sacrificed in order for them to receive the Holy Spirit and move on to a higher level of spiritual life.

It is all about a refocusing of mind and heart onto that which is well pleasing to God.

> *5 Instead you shall seek the Lord at the place which the Lord your God will choose out of all your tribes to establish His Name there for His dwelling place, and there you shall come to worship Him.*
>
> *6 There you shall take your burnt offerings, your sacrifices, your tithes, the heave offerings of your hand, your vowed offerings, your freewill offerings, and the firstborn of your herds and flocks.*
>
> *7 And there you shall eat before the Lord your God, and you shall rejoice in all to which you have put your hand, you and your households, in which the Lord your God has blessed you.*

Apart from eradicating paganism, the people had to be fully focused on entering into a loving, obedient relationship with their loving and caring God, a relationship that would fully support them in their new environment.

Setting up their worship in a place of God's choosing would emphasize the oneness of God and prevent not only the fragmentation of that worship, but also prevent worship being located in what had once been places of cultic worship.

They were going into a pagan country with a history of cultic worship throughout the land, therefore it was essential that the people of God did not fall into the trap of using the places and sites of cultic worship which had the potential of leading them into cultic practices.

The centralization of worship in the place of God's choosing would also ultimately establish the supremacy of Jerusalem as the city in which He would place His great and glorious name, and that is still true today even though the worship of another god is currently established on the temple mount.

The sacredness of and historical fact that Jerusalem was the place where God put His name and is the place to which the Messiah will come at His second visit to the earth in glory is very well known worldwide. Which is why Jerusalem will never be allowed to be commandeered by any other religious group.

There is one particular aspect of God's work that we need to consider.

It is once again brought to our notice that God does not do anything in a hurry? The people were [and still are] required to wait patiently for God's time because of all the undercurrent work God does to prepare the ground for the next event.

Now it is more than likely that those involved with God and who wanted to serve Him were completely unaware of all the preparatory work God had to do that was crucial to the success of His immediate plans, and more importantly His ultimate plan of providing eternal salvation and to welcoming the saved into his rest.

History can teach us much about the future and certainly studying scripture can teach us much about the enormity of the power and ability of the God of Israel, and because He is the same today as when the First Testament scriptures were written, even from the beginning of time, we know that by studying the Hebrew scriptures we will be enabled to better understand the work of God today.

Certainly there were countless prophecies about the coming of the Messiah and the fact that there would be two appearances; first as the suffering servant and then in glorious might coming out of the clouds of the sky through which He had ascended (Matt. 26:64), which is yet to happen.

But these were millennia away from the time Moses gave these discourses. Let us remind ourselves what Peter wrote: to God a year is like a thousand and a thousand like a year because He is outside of time yet involved in time as He works out His plans through the affairs of men.

Today we have the advantage of seeing the result of the evolution of God's plan for His people and the whole of mankind being here set in place. This means that we must not focus merely on what is happening as we study Deuteronomy, but understand it in the light of not just the history of Israel as recorded in the First Testament, but what is happening even in the present day world.

8 You shall not do as we are doing here today, which is every man living a life according to whatever is right in his own eyes.

This happened during the time of the Judges, *(17:6) In those days there was no king in Israel; everyone did what was right in his own eyes.*

But what was particularly interesting during that time is the apparent disappearance of the high priest and whoever succeeded Joshua as their civil leader. Indeed there seemed to be no civil or religious leadership. The nation was like a ship without a rudder drifting wherever the tide of events took them. This was to be a disastrous time when the tribe of Benjamin was almost wiped out.

9 for as yet you have not come to the rest and the inheritance which the Lord your God is giving you.

That was with regard to the promised land. But that statement is just as relevant to us today because we are preparing ourselves for that eternal place of rest that Jesus has gone away to prepare for us.

10 When you cross the Jordan and live in the land the Lord your God is giving you to inherit, and He gives you rest from all your enemies around you so that you will live in security,

This was the ideal scenario. It did happen when a dedicated king who loved God was on the throne. But for most of their history this did not happen.

11 then the place which the Lord your God will choose for His Name and Presence to dwell will be revealed;

This reveals the fact that nothing happens immediately, because the nation was not united and given peace from all their enemies so that *you will live in security* until the anointing and reign of David, God's chosen King. Neither was the place *God will choose for His Name and presence to dwell,* actually revealed until the capture of Jerusalem when it became the city of David.

God has a plan for mankind that was written before anything was created and He is following that plan that even today is slowly being revealed in the land of Israel and throughout the world.

The Ark of the Covenant was only located in Jerusalem when Jerusalem was captured and became the capital of Israel thus not only permanently establishing it as the city of the Lord and the location of the tabernacle without the ark and mercy seat, but also the centre for all sacrifices, offerings and family worship.

The reason for the disappearance of the ark and its contents at the time of the Babylonian exile was that its purpose as a focal point of the contract between God and man had ceased to be valid because God wanted to prepare the ground for the ultimate coming of the Holy Spirit to inhabit the temple that is the body of every believer.

After the disappearance of the ark, when the high priest entered the Holy of Holies in the new but far more basic temple, there was just an empty space which meant that his focus was not on the mercy seat above the ark, but on God who is Spirit.

Then, on the death of the Son of God, the temple curtain was torn in two from top to bottom making this last bastion of the Aaronic priesthood redundant. This was important because the Son brought in a new spiritual type of worship centred in the bodies of individual believes. We are the church (Eph. 2:19 – 22)

Objects and effigies do not represent God. He is a person [we are individual people made in His image therefore He too is an individual]. On the day of Pentecost the Holy Spirit filled those gathered in the upper room creating in each of them a holy of holies within the tabernacle of their body in which He could make a home. Is that not an amazing truth?

What is also made very clear by these instructions is the importance of conformity and structure to the worship. Whereas the pagan offered sacrifices to their gods in multitude locations, a sort of freestyle worship, the Israelites were to restrict their sacrificing to a prescribed location and a prescribed manner in order to ensure a uniformity and purity of worship.

It is interesting that king Josiah gathered the leaders of the people and read to them the book of the covenant and then proceeded to cleanse the temple and various places where incense and sacrifices were offered to Baal and other deities including those on the high ground (2 Kgs. 23)[18].

Although the man, as the head of the family, was directly responsible for presenting the sacrifice at the temple, it was important that the whole family was involved which not only gave

---

[18] See my book Law& Grace

the children a healthy attitude to worship, but also gave added meaning to it for the adults.

Watching a family member confessing their sin had the potential for bringing the family closer together. Although there are appropriate services for separate age groups, perhaps the most meaningful worship can best be experienced when shared by all family members, from the very old to the very young.

> *11 there you shall bring everything that I am commanding you: your burnt offerings, your sacrifices, your tithes and voluntary contribution of your hand such as a first gift from the fruits of the ground, and all your choice votive offerings which you vow to the Lord.*
>
> *12 And you shall rejoice before the Lord your God, you and your sons and your daughters, and your male and female servants, and the Levite who is within the gates your city, since he has no portion or inheritance with you.*

This provides wholesome, respectful worship.

One of the advantages of having the tribes camping on all sides of the tabernacle was that central worship was a natural function, there being no significant distance to travel.

It also meant that the killing of animals for family consumption, and disposal of the blood in the correct way, could also be centralized at the tabernacle.

However, once they had taken control of the promised land, such menial tasks could no longer be centralized at the tabernacle because of the distances involved for those living outside Jerusalem. Travel was very slow and time consuming in those days.

The main offerings would remain centralized at the tabernacle, wherever that was located, as it was imperative that Israel should focus on the building representing the presence of the one God.

In his dedicatory prayer after the completion of the first permanent temple structure, Solomon was most concerned that God would listen to all prayers seeking forgiveness prayed towards that temple building and answer them (1 Kgs. 8:22 – 53).

The danger was that some would try to offer their sacrifices in more convenient places rather than endure the long trek to

Jerusalem, but that was totally forbidden, because of the danger of 'innocent' paganism

> *13   Take heed to yourself that you do not offer your burnt offerings in every place that you see;*
>
> *14   but only in the place which the Lord chooses, in one of your tribes, there you shall offer your burnt offerings, and there you shall do all that I command you.*

This ruling was specific. They could worship their God wherever they lived but had to journey first to the tabernacle in Shiloh (Jdgs. 18:31) and then to the tent and finally the temple in Jerusalem for all their burnt and other offerings.

However, once the people were scattered throughout the land, it was obvious that when families needed their animals slaughtered for human consumption it was totally impractical to have to take them to the temple at Jerusalem for them to be slaughtered in the prescribed manner, because the meat would be inedible by the time is got back to the home, and the cost in time and finance would be prohibitive.

Therefore the slaughter of animals for human consumption was allowed to be carried out locally:

> *15   However you may laughter and eat meat within any of your city gates, as required, according to the blessing of the Lord your God which is His generous provision for your daily life. The ceremonially unclean and the clean may eat it, such as the gazelle and the deer.*

These would be the local licenced abattoirs allowed by God to ensure all animals were slaughtered in the prescribed manner. The main requirement concerned the blood within the animal which they were prevented from eating and the importance of ensuring the right animals were used for food:

> *16   ...you shall not eat the blood; you are to pour it out on the ground like water.*

What is particularly important about the Bible is that it is a history of the development and fulfilment of God's plan of salvation. It is essential that throughout the Bible we understand that in His dealings with Israel God had one agenda and that was to provide man with a way back to Himself.

Adam had sinned, which meant that he and all his descendants were condemned to spiritual death. Yes they had physical life, but no spiritual life which meant not only that they could never see God or communicate with Him, but that even after death they would never enter into His place of rest.

Throughout the First Testament animal sacrifices were made with the sacrificial animals being substitutes for believers, taking upon the sin of the worshipper. By the laying on of the worshipper's hands on the head of the animal sin was transferred from the worshipper to the animal. In a similar way, it was the death of the Messiah that ended that practice.

This was God's way of providing the means whereby a believer could maintain their relationship with Him. The key element was, by the shedding of blood the animal took away the believer's sin by dying in the place of the believer. Thus blood became a sacred and holy element in both humans and animals and was not to be consumed or shed needlessly.[19]

It was imperative that only animals for family consumption were slaughtered and eaten locally when the place God chose to put His name (Jerusalem) was too far away from them. With the proviso that

> *16 Only be sure that you do not eat the blood, for the blood is the life (soul), and you shall not eat the life with the meat, rather you shall pour it out on the ground like water; so that all may be well with you and with your children after you, because you will be doing what is right in the sight of the Lord.*

With regard to all sacred foods other than burnt offerings, they could be eaten only in the walls of the Holy City

> *17 You are forbidden to eat within your own city gates the tithe of your grain or new wine or oil, or the firstborn of your herd or flock, or any of your votive offerings, or your freewill offerings, or the contribution of your hand.*

---

[19] A full explanation can be found in A fresh Look At Easter

18   But you shall eat them before the Lord your God in the place which the Lord your God will choose, you, your son and daughter, and your male and female servants, and the Levite who is within your city gates; and you shall rejoice before the Lord your God in all that you undertake.

The inclusion of the Levite was critical because the whole population was responsible for ensuring that those dedicated to the service of God on their behalf were fed and supported financially. The service of God was their profession, for which they needed to be supported with food and finances and it is the same today with the ordained clergy and missionaries both in the home country and abroad.

19   Be careful that you do not neglect the Levite who is in the service of God as long as you live in your land.

These next verses are to do with domestic eating arrangements. It is important to remember that Noah was the first man to be allowed by God to eat meat. It is also the first time that blood is mentions and its importance as part of the sacrificial services as it represented life (Gen. 9:1 – 6; Lev. 17:11).

20   When the Lord your God extends your territory, as He promised you, and you say, 'I will eat meat,' because you want to eat meat, then you may eat meat, whatever you wish.
21   If the place which the Lord your God chooses to put His Name is too far away from you, then you may slaughter animals from your herd or flock which the Lord has given you, just as I have commanded you; and you may eat whatever you wish within the gates of your city.

Although the meat of the gazelle or deer was permitted, that is they were considered 'clean' for food, they were not to be used in any sacrificial services because they were not domesticated animals.

22   Just as the gazelle or the deer is eaten, so you may eat it, but you are not to include it or use it as an offering to God; although the ceremonially unclean and the clean alike may eat it.

Notice how frequently the prohibition on the consumption of blood is mentioned. This is for two particular reasons. Firstly to prevent any drift into cannibalism or pagan rite and secondly because it played a critical role in the sacrificial offerings. The critical verses are found in Leviticus 17:

> *10 Any man from the house of Israel, or any stranger living temporarily among you, who eats any blood, against that person I shall set My face and I will cut him off from his people and exclude him from the atonement made for them.*
> *11 For the life of the flesh is in the blood, and I have given it to you on the altar to make atonement for your souls; for it is the blood that makes atonement, by reason of the life it represents.'*

The seriousness of this point can be explained by what happened on the cross when the Messiah died, and the means of determining His death was that out of His side flowed blood and water (or rather plasma). Also, according to the writer to the Hebrews:

> *For if the ceremonial sprinkling of the blood of goats and bulls and the ashes of a burnt heifer on defiled persons is sufficient for the cleansing of the body, how much more will the blood of Christ, who through the eternal Holy Spirit willingly offered Himself as an unblemished sacrifice to God, cleanse your conscience from dead works and lifeless observances to serve the ever living God?*

The offering of the blood of animals cleansed the body of the sin that had been committed, but what about the inner man, the person withing the body? The sentence was placed on Adam the man.

The animal sacrifices could not fully cleanse the man. Only a perfect man could die for man, and the only perfect man that ever lived was the Messiah who was also the Son of God[20].

Because God Himself, in the form of the Son of God paid the price for man's sin, His blood does much more than merely cleanse the person from sin, but because the Holy Spirit is involved, that cleansing goes deep within a person and can cleanse their heart and conscience, bringing about a complete renewal of that person.

---

[20] This is explained in detail in my book: A Fresh Look At Easter

The freedom to kill certain wild animals as well as domestic stock for food was a boon to the people once they had settled land, especially when they were freed to use a local abattoir.

> *23   Only be sure that you do not eat the blood, for the blood is the soul, and you shall not eat the life with the meat.*
> *24   You shall not eat it; instead you shall pour it out on the ground like water.*
> *25   You shall not eat it, so that all may be well with you and with your children after you, because you will be doing what is right in the sight of the Lord.*

Jerusalem is where the umbilical cord from God is connected to the earth. It is in Israel that God influences the things of the earth. It was therefore in Jerusalem that all God focused and spiritually sensitive events took place to bring unity to the country and nation.

It was there that all offerings to the Lord were to be 'sacrificed' by fire or by other means such as with tithes, there were ones where only the priests were allowed to eat certain portions of the meat and others where the offeror was permitted to eat certain portions of the food on offer.

What was very clear is that no food went to waste by being presented to an idol and then removed because it went bad as the effigy obviously could do nothing but sit there.

> *26   However, you shall take your holy things which you have to offer and your pledged, or vowed offerings, to the place which the Lord will choose.*
> *27   And you shall offer your burnt offerings, the meat and the blood, on the altar of the Lord your God; and the blood of your sacrifices shall be poured out on the altar of the Lord your God, and you shall eat the meat.*

What is for sure is that these rules and regulations provided the worship of God with structure for they were all designed to focus the people's attention on the Lord their God and away from the cultish activities of the previous inhabitants, because God had a purpose for the people as individuals and as a nation that would affect the whole of mankind. In a perverse way they still achieved that honour but by default and the loyalty of the remnant.

> *28   Be careful to listen to all these words which I am commanding you, so that it may be well with you and with your children after you forever, because you will be doing what is good and right in the sight of the Lord your God.*

Our creator God knows what is good for us. The purpose of His instructions were to enable the people to live a good and purposeful life through His guiding and sustaining power. Love was to be at the centre of the people's relationship with God, with both working together as the people faced the unknowns of life.

They needed the rains in their seasons, the good land for growing crops for themselves, forage for the cattle and peace from potential enemies. It was not only king David who, by experience, knew that.

What they did not know at this time, but would ultimately learn the hard way, was that without God's presence with them, and every aspect of His loving care, they would experience a very troubled existence.

Their history following all that we have learned, and will learn, from our study of this foundational book, must be a lesson to us living in the 21st century, because God has not changed, nor the rules by which man must live his life in conjunction and communion with our creator God.

Hear what Jesus said about the law given to the people by Moses and all that was written by the prophets (Matt. 5:17 – 20)

> *Do not misunderstand why I have come. It is certainly not to abolish or annul the Law of Moses or what the Prophets wrote; rather I have come to fulfil all that was recorded by them.*

If the Lord came to fulfil all that was recorded by Moses and the prophets, surely it is by studying all that they wrote that we are better able to understand more about the One that came to provide us with eternal salvation.

> *For I assure you and most solemnly say to you, until heaven and earth pass away, not the smallest detail will pass from the Law until its purpose is achieved.*

This provides us with every reason for studying the far from redundant First Testament. It certainly gives us a far better understanding of where we stand with God and a deeper understanding of what we have to do to live according to His will and purpose for us.

The principles by which we must live our lives, even in these later centuries, are here provided in detail. Again let us read what our saviour taught:

> *Therefore, whoever breaks one of the least important of these commandments, and teaches others to do the same, will be called least important in the kingdom of heaven; but whoever practices and teaches them, he will be called great in the kingdom of heaven.*

This is also a salutary lesson for us because unless we know the commandments and the reason for God issuing them to man, there is always the possibility that unconsciously and in ignorance we might be falling short of what God requires of us, yes even today.

Paul is a prize example because all the Christian doctrine he provided was based upon his knowledge of the First Testament as God opened in up to him initially in the lodgings in Damascus, and just as God is revealing it to me. After all the Holy Spirit who is guiding me is the same as the one who guided Paul.

One other interesting point is that as a Gentile I was able to not only lead a Jew into a deeper understanding of his faith, but open up the First Testament teaching to a rabbi and lead him to meet with his Messiah. To hear from him that he had come to faith in Jesus as his Messiah and experience an epiphany moment that established an intimate spiritual relationship between him and the Lord was just so special.

The Lord promised to go before the people as they took over the land from the inhabitants and assist them to cut off and destroy the nations, thus the victory would not be theirs alone because they would be aided by God, therefore it was to be a joint effort. And such is the case for us today.

This was to be the start of a relationship, a bonding between God and the nation of Israel that had the potential to enable the people to prosper in the land in a new and progressive way in their new land-owning and established, settled life.

As we consider the last few verses, they bring to light the influence of superstitious fear that had been ingrained in the minds of the people during their time in Egypt that would not go away.

It clearly informs us that we must not allow the practices of the world that could well have had an unrealized influence on us, to have any credible influence on us once we have accepted Christ as our Lord and Saviour.

This is where the influence of the Holy Spirit must be allowed to take effect on the mind and heart of the believer by cleansing the believers conscience, that deep down part of the mind.

The Israelites are here being warned of something that would happen to them in the future and to hear these words repeated by other prophets in the future.

29 When the Lord your God cuts off and destroys before you the nations which you are going in to dispossess, and you dispossess them and settle in their land.

30 Beware that you are not lured into following their ways and practices, after they have been destroyed before you, and that you do not inquire about their gods, saying, 'How did these nations serve their gods, so that I too may do likewise?'

It may seem strange that having been sent into the land to clear out all those committing abominable and repulsive activities of every sort, that some of their number should want to do the same and bring about the wrath of God on themselves. But some people's minds and hearts seem so susceptible to being possessed by evil that they are led like sheep to the slaughter.

It is one thing reading about these events now and quite another being there at the time. Consider this time as newlyweds setting out on a life together having to make their own decisions and establish themselves as a fully functional, independent unit.

It is important to realize that paganism was endemic in the whole area and the nation of Israel was formed in one of the main centres of paganism in the area. Egypt. It was therefore a strong minded person who was able to resist the call of licentious pagan cultic worship.

That is where the priests were supposed to be most active, but that relied on their personal experience of and faith in their God and it quickly became clear that they needed to be led rather than taking the lead within the community in which they lived. After all, ten of Jacob's sons were far from God.

God had no time for human sacrifices which were rife in the land. Many children were thrown into the fire in the altar to the god Molech, but humans of other ages were also sacrificed including the old.

God did not create man for men to kill each other in ritual worship, which was a form of ritual murder. Indeed He clearly forbade it, as it is written in Genesis 9:6 *"Whoever sheds man's blood, By man his blood shall be shed; for in the image of God He made man."*

That is why the whole Canaanite way of life became so obnoxious to Him, and the reason He wanted the Israelites to go in and remove all those nations that worshipped pagan gods from the earth.

This was Satan at work, the same one that corrupted Adam and Eve. Although he wanted to be like God and usurp His throne, because, as a created being, he had no creative skills of his own, Satan could only corrupt and cause chaos through the worship of a multitude of gods.

After all, why would God so lovingly create man in His own image only for life to become so cheap that human sacrifices were the norm? The whole purpose of the creation of man into whom God breathed an eternal spirit, was for Him to have a spiritual love affair with each and every individual in order to bless man and enable him to have not only a joyous and blessed life on earth, but to join Him in His eternal abode at the end of his earthly life.

Killing is of the Devil/Satan and anathema to God's overwhelmingly pure love. He is a God who created rather than destroyed. He was, however, willing to destroy all that was corrupt and corrupting, such as all those who rebelled during the forty years of wandering. Being born in sin and persistent sinners bound for hell, God did not want them contaminating others through their life style.

Rather, God in Christ came to seek and to save those that were lost and looking to be changed and offer them eternal salvation.

Starting with animal sacrifices and God's teaching over time that it was not the sacrifices themselves that cleansed a person from their sin, but the real inner desire of the heart of the one offering the sacrifice to be forgiven.

This warning was in regard to both the place of sacrifice and the mode of worship because both were, as far as Israel was concerned, to significantly distinguish them from their pagan neighbours.

Consider what Isaiah wrote (Is. 1)

> *The ox instinctively recognizes its owner,*
> *And the donkey its master's feeding trough,*
> *But Israel does not know and accept Me as their God,*
> *My people just do not understand*
> *what their relationship with Me should be*
> *Oh, sinful nation,*
> *A people loaded down with the wickedness of sin,*
> *with injustice and with wrongdoing,*
>
> *"I have had enough of your burnt offerings of rams*
> *And the fat of well-fed cattle*
> *devoid of any sense of your willing obedience;*
> *And I take no pleasure in the blood of bulls or lambs or goats*
> *that you offer without heartfelt repentance for your sin.*

Pagan sacrifices were a ritual; no more than that, because as Elijah proved to the people on Mount Carmel, nothing happened even though the prophets of Baal made much noise. So he :

> *mocked them, saying, "Cry out with a loud voice, for he is a god;*
> *either he is occupied, or he is out for a moment, or he is on a*
> *journey. Perhaps he is asleep and must be awakened!" So they cried*
> *out with a loud voice to try to get Baal's attention.*

But nothing happened because their god was not real, existing only in the imagination of his adherents. Whereas as soon as Elijah called upon the God of Israel, the water saturated offering with its wood and even the stones of the altar were all consumed proving that He alone was truly the living God.

As we find in the history of the people of Israel, those that were truly faithful were few and far between. In spite of their father's remarkable relationship with God, both sons of the renown Samuel, who had been chosen of God to lead the nation, were far from having any personal knowledge of God and therefore did what comes naturally to fallen men and acted corruptly.

Today we have historical giants in the Christian faith who have left many works of literature which, alongside the Bible and a variety of commentaries, are available to those interested enough in learning about God to study and gain knowledge along with prayer and a heartfelt seeking to get to know God directly.

Yet the vast majority of believers seemed to be totally uninterested in learning about their faith, being perfectly happy to just continue to live their lives in ignorance of the true faith.

As a student of scripture and chosen of God, it was only when He led me into writing about His Word through my Jewish friend Derek, that my knowledge of God and His Word increased in width and depth without my having to go to theological college.

This is such an important lesson that it must be highlighted here:

> *"Study,"* Paul wrote to Timothy, *"to show yourself approved, a workman that is tested by trial, who has no reason to be ashamed of his faith in the Lord Jesus, but one who accurately handles and skilfully teaches the word of truth" (2 Tim. 2:15).*

That is my wholesome desire, and should be the desire of all those that have accepted God's eternal gift of salvation. No one calling themselves a Christian should allow themselves to be a passenger because they are then totally dependent on others telling them what to do.

Sadly, there are far too many false teachers and leaders, that will themselves not enter His rest, ready and willing to lead such casual believers astray. It is happening all over the world. This sad state of affairs will continue just as it continued with the people of Israel.

> *30 You must not even enquire about their gods by asking how they worshipped their gods so that you could follow their hateful practices, because that is the very reason for you going in to clear them from the land.*

When we have been to new places on holiday, it is always interesting to find out about the history of each place. But here Israel was urged by Moses not to do so because that could well encourage the weaker members of the nation to experiment and go the licentious way of the previous inhabitants God had called to be killed.

It would also lead to the seed of paganism being planted in the mind of those that are easily led. Sadly Solomon fell into that trap.

> *31 You shall not behave this way toward the Lord your God, for they have done for their gods every repulsive thing which the Lord hates; for they even burn their sons and their daughters in the fire [as sacrifices] to their gods.*

Blood was sacred to the Israelites, because God called for it to represent life itself (Gen. 9:4 – 6), and life was sacred because it was God given. The accusations of barbarism against the Jewish people over the centuries goes against all that the Torah stands for and is therefore an attack against the God of the Jews and is demonic.

God's desire was to purify the land by having His people take possession of the land and fill it with a people naturally inclined to praise the Lord God of Israel.

With the people living in tune with God he would be able to present them as an example to the other nations of the world as to how He was able to enable them to prosper and keep them safe from those that would do them harm.

> *32 You shall be careful to do everything I command you, not adding to it nor taking away from it.*

Compare this to verses at the end of Revelation:

> *I testify and warn everyone who hears the words of the prophecy of this book with all its predictions, consolations, and admonitions: if anyone adds anything whatsoever to them, God will add to him the plagues, afflictions and calamities which are written in this book;*
>
> *And if anyone takes away from or distorts the words of this prophetic book, God will take away from that person his share from*

the tree of life and from the holy city. the new Jerusalem, which are written in this book.

God's word must be held as being sacred because any distortion or change will attract the wrath of God, either in this life or in the next.

9 RELIGIOUS SEDUCERS & TITHES

Chapter 13

Satan wants nothing more than to dissuade individuals from worshipping God. He won with Adam in the beginning, and Paul warned the Ephesians about wolves that would come in and scatter the flock of God, which is exactly what happened because present day Turkey is an Islamic country.

Sadly the churches in the West are sleep walking into disaster with generation after generation watering down the truth of God, neglecting the teaching of the First Testament and the book of Revelation whilst allowing subtle changes to their doctrine, all of which is indicative of Satan's work within the nation of Israel.

In Paul's warning about wolves coming in to devour members in the Ephesian church (Acts 20:27 – 31), it is clear that it only takes a few dominant or dominating people, in a group of docile people for the sheep to be diverted from the true path of Christ.

It is not good to rely on others for spiritual teaching without knowing where they stand with God.

Consider the letters to the seven churches in Revelation[21]. The members of Ephesus had lost their love for the Lord that first persuaded them to believe, the members at Pergamon had allowed Nicolaitans who believed in sexual immorality and sacrificing to idols to work within the church. Then there was the church at Thyatira who allowed a self-confessed prophetess named Jezebel to teach and

---

[21] See my book, Letters to the Seven Churches of Revelation

seduce members. The people at Sardis were spiritually dead, the people at Philadelphia were doing well facing the Jews in the synagogue of Satan and finally the Laodiceans were only lukewarm about their faith, neither hot nor cold that were about to be rejected by God.

It is important to notice that in Acts 20:27, Paul declares that *"I did not shrink from declaring to you the whole purpose and plan of God."* Paul taught them the whole undiluted purpose and plan of God, but he did not do that in five or ten minute weekly sermons but through long sessions to those hungry for spiritual truth. A hunger that is clearly absent in many churches today.

Indeed it has been my experience amongst so called Christians that if I start to discuss the deep truths of the Christian gospel, far too many Christians either do not want to know or are embarrassed, or have no idea what you are talking about.

Deuteronomy is all about warnings, not only about the people's focus on the God that brought them out of slavery in Egypt, but also about the many dangers that they were to face when they went into inhabit the land and the dangers of departing from the word and way of God so clearly presented by Moses.

The subject matter in this chapter concerns seducers. Here the people were being warned about those who try to get the people to broaden their horizons and experiment with the worship of other gods, thus diluting, and even destroying God's word.

"Try it out," they might say, "there is no harm in it and you might like to experience the different ways of worship". The fact that such an 'experience' would automatically separate them from God was another matter, and therefore not mentioned.

> *1 If a prophet or a dreamer of dreams, arises among you and gives you a sign or a wonder, and the sign or the wonder which he spoke to you comes to pass, and if he suggests you follow after other gods you have not heard about to serve and worship them,*

Remember that we are dealing with God's preparation for the development of His plan of salvation within the nation of Israel designed to influence the whole of mankind. It is easy enough for believers in the twenty-first century to feel confident about the future, but in Deuteronomy we are dealing with the initial development of God's rescue plan of not just Israel but the whole of mankind.

Without these initial stages of the establishment of Israel as a land owning, God fearing nation, through which God wanted to reach out to the whole world, along with all the prophets and its physical and spiritual history, the Messiah could not have come and provide us with the eternal salvation that is now available to us.

It is essential that we, today, remember this is all about the *choice* made available to us to repent of our sins and be washed in the blood of the Lamb. This whole subject matter is literally a fact of life or death, from a spiritual perspective, and therefore not to be taken lightly. It means having the opportunity to rejoice in heaven with God, or to be consigned to hell without any means of escape (Lk. 16:26).

The fact that someone says something will happen and it happens does not confirm them to be someone you can trust. This is because Satan is able to foresee certain things and can use a person to try and convince you that they are knowledgeable about spiritual things when in truth they have no idea, rather it is what Satan is telling them, possibly through a demon. Alarm bells must ring if they suggest worshipping any god other that the Lord God of Israel.

God has always used dreams to pass on information to those that love Him (Num. 12:6). The Prophet Joel wrote this which Peter quoted on the day of Pentecost:

> *It shall come about after this*
> *That I shall pour out My Spirit on all mankind;*
> *your sons and daughters will prophesy,*
> *Your old men will dream dreams,*
> *Your young men will see visions.*
> *Even on the male and female servants*
> *I will pour out My Spirit in those days.*

Satan and all his spiritual and human followers are using the same tricks today along with many others to try and twist things in order to lure people away from God. That is what he did to Eve. Putting doubt into her mind whilst she focused her attention on the fruit of the forbidden tree.

"Did God say?" Asked Satan. Are you sure He said that? Surely what he meant was this. And he has been very successful within the church because many of those that attend Sunday by Sunday, especially those that teach the children, do not study the whole word of God for themselves to ensure they personally get to know God and His ways correctly and thus be able to teach others God's truth.

No, not all preachers (ordained and lay) study scripture as they should, given their responsibility for rightly dividing the word of truth.

One older (possibly by ten years) Methodist Local preacher asked me after I had presented a talk on the gifts of the Spirit (1 Cor. 12 & 14), what was all that about speaking in tongues? What with the old lady who had been to church since childhood knowing nothing about Genesis and the long standing preacher who had obviously not read much of Paul's letters, no wonder the church is in such a bad way.

Because of this many leaders within the church cannot be trusted to preach the truth or make right decisions for the day to day work of the church and guide members, therefore there is a responsibility on individual church members to carry out their own personal checks, to ensure they are not deflected from God or His word.

The key to the statement above,

> *If a prophet or a dreamer of dreams, arises among you and gives you a sign or a wonder, and the sign or the wonder which he spoke to you comes to pass,*

was not that someone dreamed a dream and it came true, but that they then suggests *you follow after other gods you have not heard about to serve and worship them.* That was the fatal flaw in their activity and the signal that they were a false prophet.

Therefore the question we must ask ourselves is, "does what the preacher or teacher say lead me to love and serve God?" If not then what they are saying must be discounted. We must be very selective in the preaching and teaching we are prepared to accept, and check what they say with scripture.

It is for this reason Moses kept repeating things to try and ensure the message got through to as many of the thinking people of the nation as possible. The problem was, would they then ensure the same message was accurately passed on to the next generation.

The warning from Moses was:

3 you shall not listen to, or take notice of, what that prophet or dreamer says; because the Lord your God is allowing you to be tested to find out whether or not you really love the Lord your God with all your heart and mind and all your soul, indeed with your entire being.

It has always been necessary for God to test people in order to ascertain whether or not they are prepared to serve Him, no matter what life throws at them. Which is why God challenged me with the question, "Do you trust me?" And ever since that challenge in 2001, he has, from time to time, challenged me to make good on my answer that I trust Him implicitly. It must be emphasized that that was not the only time God has challenged or tested me.

Consider Gideon and what God required him to do, especially when he ended up with just 300 men to fight against a vast Midianite army.

King Asa had a very big problem and this is how he handled it in an extract from Law & Grace:

Asa was not an ambitious king, preferring to fortify the land to protect it from being invaded and to live in peace. He did raise an army of 580,000 men, however when he heard that Zerah of Ethiopia was approaching with a vast army that outnumbered his army many times over, he called on the name of God and it is very interesting what he said to God.

"It is nothing for you to help us, the powerless against the mighty. Help us O Lord for we trust in you alone and it is in your name that we face this vast horde. Please do not let mere men prevail against you."

The Lord in answering the king's prayer, took action and destroyed the army of Ethiopia before there was any serious fighting.

The message Moses gave to the people was that they had to put their allegiance to God first and foremost:

4 You shall walk after the Lord your God, fearing and worshipping Him with awe-filled reverence and profound respect. You shall keep His commandments and listen to His voice, serving, and indeed clinging to Him.

I will always remember speaking to an old lady after the service I had led in a little country chapel. She said that she did not like the Old Testament because of all the violence it contained. The rural area in which she lived was very peaceful, so violence was foreign to her.

Yet we need to understand the volitivity of that time. Even in today's world, particularly in the Middle East, violence is endemic.

As the nation of Israel was still very young and immature, and going into a new land to take possession of it, it was essential that those that could lead others astray from their God had to be destroyed to save the majority:

5 But that prophet, or that dreamer of dreams shall be put to death, because he has counselled rebellion against the Lord your God who brought you out from the land of Egypt and redeemed you from the house of slavery, in order to deflect you from the way in which the Lord your God has commanded you to walk. So you shall remove the evil from among you.

This might be considered rough justice, but as always we must remember that it is all about living a life in this world that is in tune with the God that created it, for such a life leads to eternal life.

Satanic attacks on individuals and nations, which lead people down the path that leads not only away from God but to eternal spiritual death, will continue until the end of time and Satan and his minions must be fought against in every possible way as God encourages us to put on the whole armour of God.

The Western church's *laissez faire* attitude, that allows diverse and questionable teaching to take hold within it, has led many simple souls away from the true gospel of our Lord and Saviour Jesus Christ.

Unless we take the teaching of scripture seriously and assess the dangers of apparently innocuous subversive tactics of people such as the dreamer of dreams and those attacking scripture, then we are in danger of walking out of the will and purposes of Gods and we will not enter His rest (Heb. 4).

What we are studying may be in the First Testament, but Jesus stated that He had not come to abolish the law but to fulfil it. Also these are the scriptures Paul used to provide us with the basics of the Christian doctrine still in use today. It was the Hebrew scriptures that the Holy Spirit used to convince Paul about the authenticity of Jesus Christ as the Messiah, the Son of the Living God and the Saviour of mankind.

Therefore it is essential that we read and learn the basics of the way in which man must relate to God and learn by those basic teachings the wonderful knowledge that the blood of Christ alone can cleanse those that truly repent of their sins, making redundant the need to go to the temple to sacrifice an animal.

Isaiah chapter one is a prize example of how insincerity and merely going through the motions, is viewed by God who looks into the heart of man, whether it be at the time of Moses or today. It represents man's relationship with God in the raw.

Moses does not end with the false prophet or dreamer of dreams, instead he goes into the sensitive subject of family relationships and members of a loving group:

> 6 If your brother, the son of your mother, or your son or daughter, or the wife you cherish, or even your friend who is as precious to you as your own life, entices you secretly, saying, 'Let us go and serve other strange and unknown gods' that are worshipped by other nations around you, or even those far from you, you shall neither consent or listen to him; neither shall your eye take pity on him, spare him or conceal him.

As the nation prepared to enter its most serious time in its history and seek to establish itself in the new land, God's protection and support was critical to their success. Therefore anyone who puts their relationship with their Father God in jeopardy had to be removed.

The use of the phrase *If your brother, the son of your mother* was used because of polygamy, children of one mother were most likely to be far more intimate and supportive than the children of the father, as in the case of the sons of Jacob's wives.

In my book Law & Grace we see just how devastating was the upheaval experienced by the ten tribes of Israel because they rejected their God.

From the start of their separation from Judah under Jeroboam, the people of the ten tribes were encouraged to worship the golden calf idols produced by king Jeroboam and that inevitably led them away from the God who had rescued them of slavery in Egypt and had planned an amazing future for the whole nation if they had stayed loyal to Him.

In my book on Hosea we see just how hard God worked to entice the people of the ten tribes of Israel back to Himself, but with little success, although there is no record of those who might have sought the Lord and saved themselves from the impending disaster of exile and the disappearance of those ten tribes.

> 9 Instead, you shall definitely execute him; indeed your hand shall be first to be raised against him to put him to death, followed by the hand of all the people. So you shall stone him to death with stones, because he has tried to draw you away from the Lord your God who brought you from the land of Egypt, from the house of slavery.
>
> By doing this all Israel will hear and be afraid, and will never again do such a wicked thing among you.

The slaughter of this one person was all about saving the majority from the poison of the few. And in today's world, although such an action would get people into trouble with the law, God has not changed and therefore the perpetrator of such teaching will meet their reward at the judgement seat of Christ.

It is essential that we do not study this book of Deuteronomy in isolation, but in relation to the rest of the Bible, accepting the immediate and seemingly barbaric activities here being spoken of were not only necessary at such an early stage of the nation's development, but also as being of that time. These days in the church it is essential that anyone encouraging people to deviate from the true gospel must be expelled from the church.

Although such punishment for those opposed to, or seeking to twist, the Word of God in this day and age would be totally unacceptable by many so called 'fair' minded people, God's judgement of such people is merely delayed, not abandoned. Remember, the state of our personal relationship with God will decide whether we are accepted into heaven or consigned to hell, which is at His decision not ours.

There is always the problem of hearsay, but honest investigation is essential when protecting the nation from subversive individuals.

> *12 If you hear in one of the cities God has given you, some worthless and evil men going out from among you and tempting the inhabitants of their city to rebel against God saying, 'Let us go and serve other unknown gods', then you will investigate the matter, searching out witnesses.*

Throughout their travels there were those who caused trouble and led many into sin against God. Here worthless and evil men in Hebrew are identified as the sons of Belail, or those lacking worth; evil people who could be classified as criminals. *Base* in word, thought and action.

The key is *"If you hear"* then you can act, rather than going out to find trouble. Because rumour can be used for evil purposes and cause miscarriages of justice, an investigation to get to the truth was essential to maintain law and order and a sense of justice. What was at stake here was the sovereignty of God who was their king. Anyone who sought to worship other gods were committing treason against God their King and at such a sensitive time when the consolidation of His rule had to be secured in the minds and hearts of individuals, a severe penalty was essential. Not forgetting that the plan of salvation for the whole of mankind in the Messiah was at stake.

> *14 then you shall investigate and search out reliable witnesses and seek the truth thorough questions. If it is true and the matter is established that this loathsome thing has been done among you,*

There had to be a proper investigation and the evidence had to be proved before a judge before the lead convicting witness bore the initial responsibility in carrying out the execution.

15 you shall most certainly strike the inhabitants of that city with the edge of the sword, utterly destroying it and all that is in it, even its livestock with the edge of the sword.

The action God took over Sodom and Gomorrah was the result of God checking to see just how far reaching and endemic was the sin. The result was the complete destruction of both cities.

It was essential that the spoils left by those that had corrupted many people should not benefit anyone, but must also be destroyed to prevent vigilantes benefitting from the possessions of those executed. So by burning the possessions and the city itself to the ground, those that had carried out the executions were making representation to God that they had been obedient to His instructions.

16 Then you shall collect all the possessions of those executed into the middle of its open square and burn the city and possessions as a whole burnt offering to the Lord your God.

Destroying the city would leave a scar on the landscape and a reminder to all that passed by what happens to those that rebel against God or ignore God. Going on what happened during the nation's wandering in the wilderness it is very clear that such examples were very necessary.

It shall be a ruin forever. It shall not be built again.
17 Nothing from that which is designated for destruction shall you take, so that the Lord may turn away from His burning anger and
…

This is a very important point that was illustrated very clearly in the book of Joshua. The very first battle was against the city of Jericho. The fighting men were warned not to take booty from the city but it was to be all put into the temple treasury for God's use. After all it was God's victory.

Sadly Achan (Josh. 7:1, 19 – 26) saw a beautiful Babylonian garment, two hundred shekels of silver and a wedge of gold and admitted that he coveted them and took them.

In effect he had stolen from God, when God had enabled them to take the city of Jericho. He was punished most severely as an example to the others. Having burned everything within the city walls God's praise and promises would follow:

> *and show mercy to you, and have compassion on you and make you*
> *increase, just as He swore to your fathers,*
> *18 because you have listened to and obeyed the voice of the Lord*
> *your God, keeping all His commandments which I am commanding*
> *you today, and doing what is right in the eyes of the Lord your God.*

God could only reward those that followed His instructions, His rules, but those rewards would be well worth receiving.

It must be noted that such action might have been necessary in the early stages of their occupation of the land, but as the nation developed had this been done there would have been no city left intact. Israel's history in the land was one of turmoil from the start, particularly during the time of the Judges. Only under king David did the nation have any real sense of stability.

During the subsequent tribal split the ten tribes gave up on God and suffered the consequences because the majority of the population of the ten tribes were sent into exile in the Assyrian Empire and disappeared from sight.

The fact that God was able to sustain the nation until the arrival of the Messiah and for the nation to exist in its own land in the 21st century shows what a remarkable God He is.

Chapter 14

> *1 You are the sons of the Lord your God;*

It was important to establish the fact that the Israelites were the children of God, after all as He created man, the fatherhood of man is a fitting title for Him.

When Job lost all his children and possessions his response was:

> *"The Lord gave and the Lord has taken away,*
> *blessed be the name of the Lord."*

The Israelites were obviously able to mourn the death of a loved one but it was to be with the acceptance that life was in God's hands and they needed to accept death as part of life.

In pagan culture of the time the people believed they had descended from gods and demi-gods, although the relationship was conceived as being physical, which is a stretch of the imagination.

The cutting of flesh (1 Kgs. 18:28) was part of worship by priests and at times of mourning.

It was important that the chosen of God were more circumspect, and did not copy the practices of the heathen nations such as having their head shaved with the hair being buried with the corpse as an offering to the dead:

> *you shall not cut yourselves nor shave your forehead for the sake of the dead,*
> *2 because you are a holy people that have been set apart to the Lord your God; and the Lord has chosen you out of all the peoples who are on the earth to be a people for His own possession.*

Dietary Laws

These dietary laws are very important for one particular reason which is that Israel was to be a holy people, consecrated to Him as a light, supernaturally kindled in a very dark world lest the darkness of the world should become complete, which would suit the evil one very well. Initially they alone were to be a witness to God's sovereignty and purity lest he become utterly unacknowledged in the world He alone had created.

Amongst the voices in the world, seemingly of reason, but of worldly not of Divine knowledge or wisdom, and of violence and corruption, the very presence of Israel as a kingdom of priests to the most high God was a matter of great hatred. This was God setting up camp in the middle of what Satan considered his territory.

As a nation of people sanctified in themselves and sanctified for the sake of the rest of the world, it would cause them to be the only light in a spiritually very dark place and the only means of salvation for a world steeped in sin.

The commandments, and in particular these dietary laws, would be a daily reminder of their separateness from the world which, if taken to heart and treated as a means of acknowledging and worshipping God, could, furthermore, prevent any close and intimate association with the pagan nations that would inevitably result in complete absorption with the Satanic nations as finally happened with the ten tribes of Israel when they went into exile in the Assyrian Empire.

The ten tribes potentially disappeared with many of the people being assimilated with the other nations, which represented a partial victory for the evil one.

In fact the dietary laws have proved to be an important factor in preserving the uniqueness of the Jewish race during the time since the coming of their Messiah who they refuse to accept as such.

Furthermore, the dietary laws are an irreplaceable agency for maintaining Jewish identity in the present day until they are able to set them aside by accepting Jesus as their long awaited Messiah, as an increasing number of Jews are doing in this present age.

It is also important to remember that the dietary laws were originally brought in when the consideration of hygiene was not even in its infancy, and the forbidden meats were not prohibited arbitrarily, but were not suitable for human consumption, having parasites that are both disease-creating and spreading.

Also, as it is in the blood that germs or spores of infectious diseases are distributed around the body, the Jewish method of draining the blood from meat is the most effective method of reducing a potential source of sickness, and at a time when the sophisticated methods of cooking were thousands of years in the future, God's dietary statutes, which had to be obeyed, helped keep the people free of sickness.

> *3 You shall not eat anything that is detestable to the Lord and forbidden by Him.*
>
> *4 These are the animals that you may eat: the ox, the sheep, the goat, the deer, the gazelle, the roebuck, the wild goat, the ibex, the antelope and the mountain sheep.*
>
> *6 Among the animals, you may eat any animal that has the divided hoof, a hoof split into two parts especially at its distal extremity and that chews the cud.*
>
> *7 However, you are not to eat any animals among those which chew the cud, have a divide the hoof: the camel, the hare and the*

shaphan, for though they chew the cud, they do not split the hoof; they are unclean for you.

8 The swine, because it has a divided hoof but does not chew the cud; it is unclean for you. You shall not eat their meat nor touch their carcasses.

9 Of all creatures that are in the waters, you may eat those that have fins and scales, but not anything that does not have fins and scales; it is unclean for you.

11 You may eat any clean bird. But you shall not eat the eagle, the vulture, and the black buzzard, the red kite, the falcon, and birds of prey of any variety, and every raven of any variety, the ostrich, the owl, the seagull, the hawk of any variety, the little owl, the great owl, the long-eared owl, the pelican, the carrion vulture, the cormorant, the stork, and the heron of any variety, and the hoopoe, and the bat.

19 And all flying insects are unclean for you; they shall not be eaten. However you may eat any clean bird.

Apparently, a statistical investigation has demonstrated that Jews as a people are either immune from, or less susceptible to certain diseases. Also their life expectancy is frequently longer than that of their neighbours, which must logically be indicative of the dietary laws.

This should come as no surprise because the creator God knew more, right from the very beginning of the creation of man, about human welfare than any man, certainly before the sciences came into being and even in their infancy because they have had to develop spasmodically over hundreds or even thousands of years.

In the Middle Ages the Jews were far less affected by the epidemics that decimated many a country's population, an immunity that, through gross ignorance, gave rise to malicious accusations that the Jews were responsible for causing the plague by poisoning the wells, which is no surprise given that man has for a long time, separated himself from God and superstition has been Satan's ace card to try and eliminate the Jewish people. Greater study will inevitably reveal much that is unknown even today.

There is no doubt that the dietary laws were there to promote holiness, not as some abstract ethical idea, but as a regulatory principle governing the everyday lives of all members of the community. In particularly the laws provided a disciplinary aspect to dietary control over individual appetites thus allowing the body to become accustomed to a healthy lifestyle and mealtimes to be a time of social gathering encouraging family bonding.

Those eating forbidden foods would inevitably become convicted and cast out of the realm of Divine Holiness, except they reform and seek forgiveness.

These dietary laws were specifically for the people of God but the customs of others were to be respected. What the Israelites were not able to eat could be offered to those to whom it was perfectly admissible.

> *21 You shall not eat anything that dies on its own, however, you may give it to the stranger, the resident alien or foreigner who is within your city gates, so that he may eat it, or you may sell it to a foreigner since they are not under God's law.*

This could mean not only those animals that have died a natural death, but those that had been killed in other than the prescribed manner and certainly those that had been killed in accordance with the customs of others.

With regard to those referred to as *the stranger or the resident alien* they could well be people living with them after they had been well established in their land, that were not Israelites by birth, but proselytes or those that had abandoned idolatry but were not prepared to take on all the restrictions of the life and religious practices of the Israelites.

> *For you are a holy people, set apart from the rest of the world and dedicated to the Lord your God who is Holy.*

Tithes

To be able to understand the system of tithes it is necessary to understand the structure of the Priesthood and Levites.

Levi had three sons: Gershon, Kohath, and Merari (Genesis 46:11). Kohath's son Amram was the father of Miriam, Aaron and Moses. Of these:

- Miriam was a prophetess,

- Aaron was chosen as the first High Priest and his descendants became the priesthood dedicated to minister to God and oversee worship in the moveable tabernacle and finally the temple in Jerusalem

- Moses became the one God chose to lead the rescue of His chosen people and lead them out of Egypt to the promised land.

The remaining Levites were divided into three groups: Gershonites, Kohathites, and Merarites and served in peripheral roles:

- playing music,

- opening and closing the temple gates,

- standing guard.

In the case of the portable Tabernacle, each of the three tribe were individually responsible for packing up, transporting, and reconstructing designated parts of the Tabernacle whenever the Israelites travelled to a new camp. The most sacred tasks, including officiating at the sacrificial services, were reserved for the priests.

Once established in the Promised land the tribe of Levi was not allowed to own land or to have normal employment which meant that the other tribes had to provide for them, hence the need for tithes, from the laity.

22 you shall truly tithe all the increase of your seed, that the field brings forth year by year.

Note that it mentions the *increase of your seed* which also means other food and drink

But there were also a tithe within the tithe, that means that the Levites received tithes from the people and they in turn were to tithe to the priesthood who served God in the temple.

It was a holy tithe because the priests were dedicated to God therefore the Levites were in effect giving a tenth to God. Only after they had given that tithe, which was to be of the choicest of the tithes they had received, could they eat what they had received and not sin against God.

The tithe on the people was computed each year according to increase of the yield. Thus the people were encouraged to realize their dependence upon God for their harvests, for it was God who gave the increase.

Once they were established in the land, the people were to be taught many a hard lesson through drought and a shortage of grain and other commodities either because of a shortage of the former and latter rain, or when overrun by other nations that stole or destroyed their crops as at the time of Gideon (Judges 6:1 – 10).

The emphasis was always on *not neglecting the Levite who is within your city gates, because he does not have a share of land or an inheritance among you* that would enable them to grow their own crops and provide for themselves.

At the end of every third year the people were to give a tenth of their entire crop that year to be stored in their own city and made available in support of the Levite, the stranger, orphans and widows that live locally, *so that the Lord your God may bless you in all the work of your hands*

10 SEVENTH YEAR

Chapter 15

God's desire for Israel was that it would form itself into a self-sufficient nation that looked after its own.

Consider what the Psalmist said about God, which is particularly relevant to what we are about to study because, although it does not specifically mention debtors, it does refer to those dependent on the good will of others:

> *Sing to God, sing praises to His name;*
> *Lift up a song for Him who rides on the clouds*
> *By His name YAH [Jehovah], rejoice before Him.*
> *God in his holy dwelling,*
> *is a father to orphans and defender of widows.*
> *God makes a home for the lonely;*
> *He leads the prisoners into prosperity,*
> *Only the stubborn and rebellious dwell in a parched land.*

Everything we have is from God. Life, the ability to think and as far as the Israelites were concerned the land they inhabited along with the former and latter rains, all were a gift from God, therefore their relationship with God needed to be strong.

One other matter that is very important, and most often completely ignored, is their time and position in the history of the world. Except we seek to understand their lives in the context of their time in history, we will not understand scripture.

We must remember that Israel was coming to the end of a long period as a nomadic tribe of herdsmen and shepherds. Even in Egypt where they experienced 400 years of stability, albeit for many years as slaves. Their base was the land of Goshen and they were very conscious of being Hebrews, and members of an individual tribe. This stemmed from the rivalry amongst Jacob's sons as well as being part of the tribe of Jacob/Israel. Certainly today to be of Israel is a matter of pride, particularly for those that God is attracting back to the land of their forebears.

As the nation of Israel developed from the tribe of Israel (Jacob's God given name) the people would always be very conscious of the sub-tribe of their birth within the new nation, just as Paul referred to himself as being of the tribe of Benjamin. Just like in the UK people refer to themselves as being English, Welsh, Scottish or Northern Irish.

Year of Release

1 At the end of every seven years you shall grant a release, a pardon from debt. This is the regulation for the release: every creditor shall forgive what he has loaned to his neighbour; he shall not require repayment from his neighbour and his brother, because the Lord's release has been proclaimed.

In any rural community misfortune can cause families to fall on hard times and therefore be in need of a loan from their neighbours and friends to remain solvent. Such an agreement would be with the purpose of repaying the money at some point in the future.

The loan was contracted only in the case of misfortune and was therefore an act of charity by others, rather than a business transaction on behalf of those who could afford to loan to those in need. It also acknowledged a sense of community and solidarity with their fellow citizens by supporting other members of the tribe and nation that were in difficult circumstances. Something approaching a voluntary welfare state.

If after seven years (that is at the end of the seventh year), where full payment of the debt was not possible without them returning to destitution, the debt was not to be cancelled, rather the debtor would not be pressed for payment and the debt set aside.

What the Israelites needed to remember was that God was the ultimate source of wealth, for the Lord had promised to bless them.

> *3 You may require repayment from a foreigner, but whatever you have lent to your brother Israelite, your hand shall release it. However, there will be no poor among you,*

This is a very important principle the people had to learn. There had to be a willingness to support each other so that within the nation there would be *no poor among you*. There was always bound to be varying levels of wealth, but no destitution. And the reason for this was:

> *4 since the Lord will most certainly bless you in the land which the* <u>*Lord your God is giving you as an inheritance to possess,*</u>

The land was not theirs by right, it was theirs as a gift from God for their lifetime. True there would always be the leaders and the led, but there needed to be a cohesion within the tribal and national community that would strengthen the community bond and make the whole nation much stronger.

It is worth interjecting here that the whole purpose of laying good foundations for the future structure and solidarity of the nation of Israel was because God had chosen Israel to be *a light to the nations, that My salvation may reach to the end of the earth*. That was their particular mission for God to the world. Yes they were to be blessed, but for a very good reason, and that was to benefit the rest of humanity.

This was a remarkable commission that Israel never really understood, until this present age when so many are waking up to the fact that, way behind times, Gentiles are enjoying the eternal salvation they rejected when they rejected Jesus as their Messiah. Paul was very conscious about this failure of his own nation for his brethren to whom were given remarkable gifts.

Before we consider what Paul wrote to the believers in Rome that were at that time mostly Jews, we need to understand the position of what Paul refers to as the adoption of Israel. For compared to the state of all the pagan nations around at that time, God's choice of Abraham and then through the chosen seed of Abraham and the other patriarchs, the resulting individuals there progressed a real separation of them out of the normal worldly environment to become a *Family of God*.

We have only to consider the following passages of scripture to see that family of God identity being declared:

> *Then you shall say to Pharaoh, 'Thus says the Lord: "Israel is My son, My firstborn. So I say to you, let My son go that he may serve Me. But if you refuse to let him go, indeed I will kill your son, your firstborn (Ex.4:22)*

Considering all that God had done for them it seems incredible that the chosen nation could be so ungrateful:

> *Do you thus deal with the Lord, O foolish and unwise people?*
> *Is He not your Father, who bought you? Has He not made you and established you? (Deut. 32:6)*

> *Hear, O heavens, and give ear, O earth!*
> *For the Lord has spoken:*
> *"I have nourished and brought up children,*
> *And they have rebelled against Me; (Is. 1:2)*

So we can say with certainty that Paul is perfectly correct when he refers to Israel as being adopted through Divine choice:

> *4 for my brethren, my countrymen according to the flesh, are Israelites, that received the adoption, the glory, the covenants, the giving of the law, the service of God, and the promises; 5 of whom are the fathers and from whom, according to the flesh, Christ came, who is over all, the eternally blessed God. Amen.*
>
> *6 But it is not that the word of God has not taken effect. For they are not all Israel who are of Israel, nor are they all children because they are the seed of Abraham; but, "In Isaac your seed shall be called." (Ro. 9)*

The one aspect of all this is choice. Not man's choice but God's choice. Abraham, Isaac and Jacob were all God's choice, whereas Ishmael and Esau were not, for very good reason as is described in my book The Origin of Life. Ishmael was the product of human flesh being the result of Sarah's impatience, and Esau being the rebel against God.

The chosen of God were all believers in God, therefore only those that have believed and are prepared to follow and serve Him can be called true believers and therefore be part of the *Family of God*.

Therefore those that are of Israel through birth but in their hearts have rejected God through unbelief resulting in rebellion, have been replaced by those who have no right to be called Israel because they are not descended through the flesh, yet they, like Abraham have become part of Israel through belief, particularly in the sacrifice of God's Son Jesus Christ.

> 25 *As God also says in Hosea:*
> *"I will call them My people, who were not My people, and her beloved, who was not beloved."*
> 26 *"And it shall come to pass in the place where it was said to them, 'You are not My people,' there they shall be called sons of the living God." (Ro. 9)*

God Himself had given them the laws, statutes and instructions regarding how they should live and do business in order to establish a structure that could, should they follow it, enable them to weather all the storms life might throw at them. But through disbelief and hardness of heart, God rejected them and opened the way through the persecution of believers, in which Saul initially held an important position, to spread the gospel to the nations, releasing Israel's long term hold on all those particular blessings the people of Israel originally enjoyed. However Israel has and will always be God's first born son, just not including the unbelievers and rebels.

This idea of making the community robust and self-supporting so that God could bless them was so that the nation could demonstrate to the world that in God alone all the power of life was concentrated.

It was to be that the demonstration of God's power in the life of the nation of Israel was to be the light to the nations. Rather like an advertisement: "Look mankind, this is what the love and care of God can do for your nation if you are prepared to love and serve Him."

For this to happen the Israelites were given the Divine secrets of the means of salvation that God wanted to be made available to all men even to *the end of the earth.*[22]

That is something all the other people living on the earth should have witnessed, but in that mission Israel undoubtedly failed because rather than being an example, they spent much time and effort in trying to align themselves with the surrounding pagan nations causing God to frequently step in and redirect them back to Himself; something the Christian Church has sadly emulated.

There was a condition of course, because God was giving them not just the land but the promise to bless them in it, therefore it was essential that they realized that when they went in to take possession of the land it was on His terms, therefore it was imperative that they:

5 listened to and obeyed the voice of the Lord your God, to observe carefully all these commandments which I am commanding you today.

With regard to the application of the law of the seventh year of release, circumstances were bound to change dramatically when economic life became more complex and people engaged in commerce. Debts caused by errors in trading could not legitimately invoke this law.

This seventh year release was also a time when the soil was given a rest. Instead of sowing, what grew from the previous year's harvest, the gleanings (Ruth 2:8) that were left on the soil, was to provide food for that seventh year.

This law of release did not apply to foreigners, that is those that visited for the purposes of trade. The chosen people could lend money to others but could not borrow, putting themselves at a disadvantage.

6 When the Lord your God blesses you as He has promised to do, then you will lend to many nations, but you will not borrow; and you will rule over many nations, but they will not rule over you.

The purpose of that instruction was that the chosen nation was never to be in debt to other nations, because God was superior to the gods of all other nations, and as God held the real estate of the whole world, He would not allow His chosen nation to in effect be

---

[22] In my book The Tent of the Meeting : Illustrating God's Plan of Salvation I show how the very design of the tabernacle lays out that plan for all to see.

subservient to other nations. Had they truly believed and trusted in Him they would never have needed help from anyone else on earth.

Continuing on the theme of charity, no one should be so hard-hearted that they ignored anyone in dire straits.

> 7 If there is a poor man among you, one of your fellow Israelites, in any of your cities in the land that the Lord your God is giving you, you shall not be heartless, nor close-fisted with your poor brother; but you shall freely open your hand to him, and shall generously lend to him whatever he needs.

It is very interesting that the inner thoughts of a lender is also brought into question here because God wanted to challenge all those whose desire for money and riches set aside their humanity and God like love for their fellow man.

> 9 Beware that there is no wicked thought in your heart, saying, 'The seventh year, the year of release is approaching,' and your observation is hostile and unsympathetic toward your poor brother, and you give him nothing since he would not have to repay you;

Such hardheartedness was very clearly displayed after the return of the Jews from exile when things were very tough in Jerusalem and the surrounding land, particularly for those with very little.

The Jews that had returned from exile were surrounded by hostile forces, and yet the wealthy were guilty of usury towards their fellow Jews. This is from Nehemiah 5:

> Now there was a great outcry of the poorer people against their Jewish brothers to whom they were deeply in debt. 2For there were some who were saying, "We, along with our sons and our daughters, are many; therefore allow us to get grain, so that we may eat and survive." Others were saying, "We are mortgaging our fields, our vineyards, and our houses to buy grain because of the famine." Yet others were saying, "We have borrowed money on our fields and vineyards for the Persian king's heavy tax.
> We are the same as our brothers, our relatives, and our children are like their children, yet here we are being forced to sell our sons and daughters to be slaves; and some of our daughters are forced into

bondage already, and we are powerless to redeem them because our fields and vineyards belong to others."

Then I [Nehemiah] was very angry when I heard their outcry and these words of accusation. Thinking it over I challenged the nobles and the rulers. I said to them, "You are exacting usury from your own brethren, your own people." So I held a great assembly to confront them. I said to them,

"According to our own ability we have redeemed (purchased back) our Jewish brothers who were sold to the Gentile nations; now would you even sell your brothers, that they might be sold to us?"

Those guilty of such appalling conduct were silent and could not find a single word to say. So I challenged them, "What you are doing is not good. Should you not walk in the fear of our God to prevent the taunting by the pagan nations, our enemies?"

"As far as I, my brothers, and my servants are concerned we are lending them money and grain. Please, let us stop charging this high interest."

It seems incredible that some wealthy leaders were so wealth orientated that even though they were surrounded by hostile Gentile nations, they were willing to put money before the welfare of their fellow Jews and bleed them dry, even to the extent of putting themselves at risk of being overwhelmed by the surrounding Gentile nations just so they could build up their property portfolio and wealth. It is possible that this still continues today.

This greed had nothing to do with being a member of God's chosen people as God had intended, according to His instructions through Moses. Had they learned nothing from the exile and the destruction of the security wall and gates of the city, or the destruction of the Temple?

These were truly men of the world and not of God. Nehemiah, who was an honest man, said to these cruel individuals,

"Please, give back to those you have so cruelly treated this very day; their fields, their vineyards, their olive groves, and their houses, and also a hundredth part of the money, the grain, the new wine, and the oil that you are lending them."

Then they said, "We will give it back and not require anything from them. We will do exactly as you say." Then I called the priests

and took an oath from them that they would act in accordance with this promise.

This was what was behind the laws God was giving to them even before they had set foot in the land. They needed hearts of flesh not of stone because if they were so concerned with the accumulation of wealth and property, which they could not take with them when they died, then they would have no heart for God.

for he, the poor man, may cry out to the Lord against you, and it will become a sin for you.

All the instructions God was giving to the people in laws and ordinances were for the purpose of making the people like himself. God was/is and ever will be the source of all love, because love is not something He created because it cannot be created and as God is the creator He must be its source.

Also God wanted to bless the people as a whole and individually, but how could He do that when the people, particularly the leaders of the nation, were uncaring and heartless.

They have closed their unfeeling heart to kindness and compassion; With their mouths they speak proudly and make presumptuous claims. (Ps. 17:10)

Man without God is man without the true, pure love of God, more interested in self than others. Paul illustrates this in his letter to the Ephesians:

And the ungodly in their spiritual apathy, having become callous and unfeeling, have given themselves over as prey to unbridled sensuality, eagerly craving the practice of every kind of impurity that their desires may demand.

Such ungodliness may start out in wanting to ger rich or influential, but it soon develops into other areas of sinfulness, because Satan encourages such people to go all the way with their Godlessness. But as far as God is concerned He has no desire to see anyone lose out on the salvation that is available to all men.

10 Instead you shall freely and generously give to him, and your heart shall not be resentful when you give to him, because for this generosity the Lord your God will bless you in all your work and in all your undertakings.

In Proverbs 19:17 we read:

He who is gracious and lends a hand to the poor lends to the Lord, and the Lord will repay him for his good deed.

Because he will be a man after God's heart

11 For the poor will never cease to be in the land; therefore I command you, saying, 'You shall freely open your hand to your brother, to your needy, and to your poor in your land.'

This instruction is a salutary lesson to all of us, even in the 21st century. Jesus said that we will always have the poor with us (Matt. 26:11) for many reasons, not all because of their own stupidity or inabilities. Misfortunes through events outside their control such as wars and famine and drought, floods, fire and illness have impacted on many tens of thousands. Such situations can and do reduce even a once wealthy person to the level of destitution.

What this also exposed over time was the effect of the DNA of sin in everyone born of Adam, because the instruction to effectively love others as God loved them was very soon forgotten. Indeed in the book of Judges, so soon after the nation went into the land of Canaan, there was chaos, with everyone looking out for themselves.

In fact the hardness of heart was clearly exposed in the years leading up to the exile with the ten tribes disappearing into the vast Assyrian empire and Judah with Benjamin ending up in Babylon where Ezekiel[23] penned these words:

Thus says the Lord God, "Though I had removed Israel far away among the nations scattering them among the nations, yet I

---

[23] For a greater understanding of just how far the priests had gone in their move to pagan worship that finally caused God to send them into exile, see Law & Grace chapter 13, page 109 and read Ezekiel 8.

have been a sanctuary for them for a little while in the countries to which they had gone." '

Therefore "I will gather you from the peoples and assemble you out of the countries where you have been scattered, and I will return to you the land of Israel." '

When they return there, they will remove from it all traces of the detestable and repulsive remnants of paganism. And I will give them one heart, a new heart, and put a new spirit within them. I remove the heart of stone, and give them a heart of flesh, a heart responsive to My touch, that they may walk in My statutes and keep My ordinances and do them.

Then they shall be My people, and I will be their God.

But as for those whose heart longs for and follows after their detestable and repulsive things associated with idolatry, on their own head I will repay them in full for their vile conduct," says the Lord God.

The nation was supposed to reflect the love of God and His caring nature, but the rottenness of those like Rachel[24], who could not give up the family earth gods, even influenced the temple priests.

Servants

A man's misfortune may not be the person's fault but, via a series of unfortunate circumstances, end up in a position where a loan would not help him. In which case he seeks for employment as a servant, a bondman, in someone's household, thus earning his food and shelter through his labour.

To purchase a bride, Jacob did this in Laban's household, first for Leah and then for Rachel.

What is interesting is that in Hebrew society the bond master had certain obligations towards the bondman and any violence towards him would immediately secure his release. In the seventh year of service the bondman goes free with the master supplying him with sufficient support that would allow him to begin again with some confidence for the future.

---

[24] The relationship of Rachel with Jacob and his God are explained in detail in The Origin of Life.

This demonstrates the importance God, through the Torah, put upon those that could to look after those within the community that needed help. Philanthropy was God's idea.

So far we have been concerned with men, but as far as God is concerned men and women are to be treated in the same way.

> *12 If your fellow Israelite, a Hebrew man or woman, is sold to you, and serves you for six years, then in the seventh year you shall set them free from your service. But, you shall not let them go away empty-handed.*
>
> *You shall give him generous provisions from your flock, from your threshing floor and from your wine press; you shall give to him as the Lord your God has blessed you.*

It is important to remember that although times change, God doesn't. Therefore, although this was originally spoken just before the people took possession of the land of Canaan, the principle of philanthropic care of their fellow Hebrews, was to remain a guiding principle, for the simple reason they would not have been the nation they were with a long history if God had not chosen them and released them from slavery in Egypt, with them leaving Egypt with much wealth. Indeed, if they had remained it was most likely Israel as a nation would never have survived that hardship or Pharaoh's efforts to prevent their sons surviving after birth.

Today, believers in the Lord Jesus Christ must never forget the cross on which Christ died for their sins, nor the last supper Jesus had with his disciples. We are washed clean from our sins by the blood of the Lamb of God.

Unless we keep the reason for our salvation in our minds and hearts, knowing that we are saved not of ourselves but of God and therefore we belong to Him and have an obligation to love and serve Him as the Israelites were required to do, then there is a grave danger that we will get blasé about our state before God and unwittingly walk out of the will of God. A state to which many have succumbed.

In exactly the same way, and the nation was continually reminded of just how thankful to God they had to be, just how vital the exodus was and the blood that was shed at that first Passover meal to save their firstborn in Egypt, making the position of the firstborn, of both humans and domesticated animals, very important in the eyes of God. They were bought with the price of the blood of the lamb.

Previously it was the firstborn who inherited the father's property and took over the leadership of father's estate. Isaac took over from Abraham, then there was the interesting events surrounding Jacob taking over from Isaac by taking Esau's birth-right.

For many of those about to enter the promised land, the exodus was not a distant memory but recent. The record contained in this book of Deuteronomy was therefore essential for future generations, including the current citizens of that nation in this 21st century.

For all believers in the Saviour, Jesus Christ, it is also necessary to know these things. After all had it not been for the exodus, the following would not have happened:

- Israel established as an independent sovereign nation.

- the tabernacle/temple established as the centre of the worship of, and the place where God's great name resided.

- the altar of sacrifice on which sin and other offerings of fire were made that kept the people in the right attitude of mind before their mighty God.

- Jerusalem to become the centre of the worship of almighty God,

- the Christ would not have come and died as prophesied outside the city wall, for the sins of all mankind, not just the Jews

- the tearing of the temple curtain which signalled the end of the importance of the manmade temple and the Aaronic priesthood.

- Christ, on His ascension being elevated to the spiritual throne of David and becoming the new and eternal high priest after the order of Melchizedek[25] to be our advocate before the Father.

- the body of a believer becoming a temple of the Holy Spirit.

---

[25] This new high priesthood is fully explained in "The Origin of Life" chapter three.

This is just a sample of all that resulted from God, through His grace, rescuing His people from slavery in Egypt, and Gentiles from world bondage.

Surely, this exhibition of God's grace to His chosen people, and to Gentile believers who have benefitted from the expression of that same grace through the sacrifice of our Saviour, must surely make us be keen to remember that God's plan of salvation was activated immediately Adam rebelled against God in the Garden of Eden.

History is essential in enabling the seeker after truth to fully understand God's relationship to man and His desire to be intimately involved in the life of every individual.

What is the satisfaction in merely believing in the salvation through the shed blood of our Saviour without understanding the full character of God and the overflowing love that He has for mankind? Surely such detailed knowledge enables us to more intimately bond with the God who loves us so very much.

Certainly, as far as Israel was, and is still concerned, their history of being God's chosen people is forever relevant.

15 For you shall remember and consider carefully that you were once slaves in the land of Egypt, and the Lord your God, by His own power, redeemed you; therefore, I am commanding you to do these things today.

In relation to God, from a vertical perspective, men and women have the same status, it is only in the horizontal perspective, the person to person relationship, especially in a marriage, that the man is senior to the woman, not forgetting that this is according to God's own design for us.

What is made very clear is that it is the failure of men to take their responsibility of leadership seriously, as in the case of Deborah and Barak (Jdgs. 4:8, 9), that women have had to step into the breech. It must also not be forgotten the essential service women provided in support of our Lord Jesus Christ, and in many other ways throughout the centuries before and since.

The principle of the relationship between a man and woman came about because God saw that Adam was alone and needed someone like himself to comfort him, so out of Adam, God created Eve to be a helpmeet to him. Thus woman came from man, but all future males come from the woman through natural childbirth.

We must never forget that this is the way God designed the relationship to be and it is carried on in the believer's relationship to Christ within His church.

Consider what Paul wrote to the Ephesian church (read Eph. 5:22 – 33):

> *Wives, be subject to your own husbands, as a service to the Lord. For the husband is head of the wife, as Christ is head of the church, Himself being the Saviour of the body.*
>
> *As the church is subject to Christ, so also wives should be subject to their husbands in everything [respecting both their position as protector and their responsibility to God as head of the house].*

Here is where the relationship becomes interesting because this put great responsibility onto all men:

> *Husbands, love your wives, seeking the highest good for them and surround them with a caring, unselfish love, just as Christ also loved the church and gave Himself up for her, in order that He might sanctify the church, having cleansed her by the washing of water with the word of God,*

Husbands, therefore have the moral obligation to love their wives because in marriage according to God's design the two become one flesh through natural sexual intercourse, thus the two become one flesh both physically and spiritually, and who in his right mind hates himself.

This comparison to the way God loved the children of Israel in spite of their waywardness, and Christ loved the church (a church is its members not the building or organization), must be the principle of the husband as being the senior partner.

The role of the woman, although somewhat distorted in this present age, is still that of the child bearer and home maker and supporter of the husband. Remembering that the Lord Jesus was crucially supported by women, and the way women are brilliant at nursing and social care. A woman's influence in the home is critical to its success.

Here is a slight twist to the master/bond servant relationship referred to above. There are many who do not like the responsibility of going it alone, preferring to be under authority. God catered for such people:

> *16 Now if the servant says to you, 'I will not leave you,' because he loves you and your household, since he is doing well with you; then take an awl and pierce it through his ear into the door, and he shall willingly be your servant always. Also you shall do the same for your maidservant.*

Going back to the releasing of the bondservant at the end of year seven the Lord says:

> *18 It shall not seem hard to you when you set him free, for he has served you six years with double the service of a hired man; so the Lord your God will bless you in everything you do.*

That means the master has not had to pay the bondservant during his time of service as he would have had to do with a hired servant, Plus he had the benefit of the service of bondservant throughout the twenty-four hours (obviously taking out the time needed for sleep along with meal times), rather than just during the day, thus he got double the work out of him.

The importance of the firstborn in Hebrew culture referred to above is also reflected in relation to animals.

> *19 You shall consecrate all the firstborn males that are born of your herd and flock by setting them apart to the Lord your God. You shall not work with them, nor shear those in your flock.*

The instructions regarding the first born of the flock or herd was intended to be a constant reminder of that life changing moment when the angel of death passed over those dwellings where the blood of the sacrificial lamb was daubed on the door posts and lintel. It was for the safety of the first born, no one else. It was that night that Pharaoh lost his firstborn son.

Although the Passover was celebrated annually, the arrival of new lambs and calves was also a time of great anticipation, and because, in the new land the people were dependent upon God for the increase, by dedicating the first offspring of the flock and herd to the Lord the people were not only reminded of the salvation of the firstborn sons, but also of their dependence upon God for the increase to their livestock.

> 20 *You and your household shall eat it every year before the Lord your God in the place which the Lord chooses for worship.*

Although the owners of the new born offered it to God, as soon as it had been given to the priests, it was they who ate it in accordance with the instructions God had given to the priests as being their portion, which enabled the priest to have food to eat albeit it had to be eaten in the temple.

The next instruction is very important because nothing that in anyway was defective could be presented to the Lord, who was perfect.

> 21 *But if it has any defect or injury, such as lameness or blindness, or any serious defect, you shall not sacrifice it to the Lord your God.*

Consider what the prophet Malachi had to pass onto the priests:

> *A son honours his father, and a servant his master. If then I am a Father, where is My honour? And if I am a Master, where is the reverent fear and respect due Me?' says the Lord of hosts to you, O priests, who despise My name.*
>
> *But you say, 'How and in what way have we despised Your name?'*
>
> *You are presenting defiled food upon My altar, thinking that the table of the Lord is contemptible and may be despised.*
>
> *When you priests present blind animals for sacrifice, is it not evil? And when you present the lame and the sick, is it not evil?*
>
> *If you offered a blind, lame or sick animal to your governor as a gift or as payment for your taxes do you think he would he be pleased with you? Or receive you graciously? says the Lord of hosts.*

The people at the time of Moses giving the instructions we are now considering, had experienced God doing mighty things. It was through obeying God's instructions that would allow them to convert those experiences into trust and bring about a deeper and more intimate relationship with their God.

Faith is all about trusting God. Even though He might not 'feel' close and things seem to be going wrong, the fact that He has over time constantly and consistently proved that He exists and is interested in the individual and wants to bless them must be sufficient. After all a person's more obvious experiences of the love and care of God must be converted into faith building so that when nothing seems to be happening, that person still knows that God is always there supporting them.

God never makes Himself obvious in all that happens to us, which is why, certainly to me, hindsight can be so encouraging. Certainly it has dramatically increased my faith. We also have the advantage of the accounts of many outstanding First and Second Testament characters such as Samuel, king David and Paul where they have benefitted greatly from their strong faith.

Those animals that might have a defect but were alright for human consumption, that is they did not suffer from any disease, may be eaten by anyone in the population.

> *But if it has any defect or injury, such as lameness or blindness, or any serious defect, you shall not sacrifice it to the Lord your God.*
> *22 However you shall eat it within the city gates; and all may eat it, that is the ceremonially unclean and the clean alike may eat it, as if it were a gazelle or a deer. Only you shall not eat its blood; you are to pour it out on the ground like water.*

God has a right to demand the very best because <u>everything</u> we have is from God.

11 THREE PILGRIM FESTIVALS

Chapter 16

These three festivals in particular, which marked the three seasons of the agricultural year, were to be celebrated annually because they not only represented three major events in the history of the nation of Israel, but they would also all lead to a significant major event in the future.

It is important not to forget that the events they commemorate were all within the living memory of those Moses was addressing, but Moses had no knowledge of what they would lead to, except for his announcement of the coming of a prophet to whom the people were to listen[26].

The law concerning the three annual pilgrim festivals to the temple is recorded in Exodus, Leviticus and Numbers; but in this declaration in Deuteronomy, Moses was identifying a central, but as yet unknown, place of worship where these festivals were to take place.

It is interesting that through the commemoration of these feasts, the people were celebrate just how much God loved them by reminding them:

1.   what He had done for them in enabling the exodus

---

[26] Explained in Truth & Doubt

2. His meeting with them on Mount Sinai to establish a marriage relationship with them and the commandment that regulated their daily lives.

3. His care for them during their over forty years journeying in the wilderness

Although they would not necessarily have understood it at the beginning of the battles to come, He was revealing to them the blueprint of His plan of salvation[27] and redemption for all sinful mankind.

The feasts of Passover (in Egypt) and Pentecost (on Mount Sinai) establish a call to leave slavery and bondage and enter into a unique relationship with the God that had not only freed them from slavery in a worldly environment dominated by Satan, but set them on a journey that led to the land He initially promised to Abraham.

Egypt and Israel were the principle players – the world of sin and a new life in God are the reality and Israel's rescue from Egypt was achieved by the powerful and loving God and the author of the true message of this part of Israel's history. This is worth thinking about in relation to the communion service.

Initially the nation of Israel was engaged in agriculture and shepherding, it was only as time progressed that the commercial side became a necessary addition.

God's intention behind His people celebrating these feasts was for the nation never to forget the exodus of their forebears from Egypt and particularly His role in it. Indeed the prophet Jeremiah describes how God refers to, *the day that I took them by the hand to lead them out of the land of Egypt…" (Jeremiah 31:32)*

Gradually the pieces are being put into place with these festivals with each one not only reminding the nation of a significant event in the past, but preparing it for a significant future event.

Passover — this festival looked back on the exodus from Egypt and forward to the ultimate Passover Sacrifice of the Messiah, the lamb of God, for it was in that chosen place, Jerusalem, where the

---

[27] This is fully explained in The Tent of the Meeting : Illustrating God's Plan of Salvation in which the design of the tabernacle built by Moses clearly does just that.

Passover was to be celebrated and where the crucifixion took place, a place and an event of which those listening to Moses would have had no knowledge.

God is here preparing the ground for the future development of His plan of salvation, starting with the animal sacrifices and ending with the sacrifice of His Son.

Pentecost — this festival not only looked back on the engagement of God and Israel, and the giving of the Torah, but looked forward from the moment this was included in Moses speech to the people in preparation for them going into the promised land and the baptism the disciples received in the Holy Spirit. It was the spiritual binding of those in that upper room with God so that they could take forward the message of salvation in power, not forgetting that that baptism in the Holy Spirit was for all believers, not just the Jews.

The annual celebration in between was initially for thanksgiving for the harvests they would enjoy in the new land, but more importantly in the then far distant future, the giving of the Holy Spirit after the Messiah had ascended.

Tabernacles — the seventh and final festival of the year, looked back on their travels in the wilderness during which the people had to provide shelters for themselves when they stayed in one place for any length of time.

Of the seven festivals to be celebrated this is the only one, in which Gentiles will take part in future. Passover has concluded with the sacrifice of the Messiah; Pentecost has also concluded because that was when the disciples were baptized in the Holy Spirit and is being perpetuated when new believers, whether Jew or Gentile, still experience the baptism of the Holy Spirit, although not necessarily in the same dramatic fashion as with the disciples.

The Festival of Passover (Pesach)[28]

> *Observe the month of Abib and celebrate the Passover to the Lord your God, for in the month of Abib the Lord your God brought you out of Egypt by night.*

---

[28] This festival is also explained in A Fresh Look At Easter

We must never consider God from a human perspective! If all the computers in the world were linked together to provide the greatest computer of all time, it would not go anywhere near matching God's intelligence or ability. If, as we firmly believe, He created all things and sustains the world and universe and everything in it through His mighty power, then, as Jeremiah observed, nothing is too hard for God.

The scroll the Lamb of God unsealed according the book of Revelation, was written before the beginning of the world. Before the big bang God used to start the universe with the world just one minor element, but at the centre of it.

The first Passover may have been used for a particular purpose, which was the protection of the Hebrew firstborn from the angel of death as it flew through Egypt causing the death of all the firstborn in households that did not have the sacrificial blood on the door surround. But it had other future ramifications, therefore it is important for us to consider the Jewish *Pesach* more deeply.

Moses was sent by God to lead the children of Israel out of the land of Egypt, the reason for their departure, along with all their goods and livestock, was to worship the Lord their God outside Egyptian territory.

After previously being so long in the wilderness leading flocks of sheep, Moses was very nervous about leading Israel, complaining about his lost ability to speak with any authority, causing God to enlist the services of his older brother Aaron. Together the brothers persuaded the Israeli leadership of Moses' credentials and on behalf of Israel Moses gained an audience with the Pharaoh.

As no single leader of the entire Hebrew people had previously emerged to champion their cause with the confidence God had given to Moses, it is understandable for the Pharaoh to be curious about where Moses, with his assistant Aaron, had come from.

When Moses through Aaron demanded the Pharaoh release the slaves, who were engaged on prestigious projects that would make his name great in the history of the country, Pharaoh was not inclined to agree, particularly when the request was for them to journey three days to offer sacrifices to their God as a means of worship, taking them outside Egyptian territory and beyond his authority.

Who is the Lord, that I should obey his voice to let Israel go?

I know not the Lord, neither will I let Israel go."

Pharaoh was soon to find out who this God was, and why he should obey His voice as He demonstrated His power over all the Egyptian gods and goddesses.

Let us therefore consider the ten plagues and their relation to the Egyptian gods and goddesses, because there is much that we can learn from them that will help us better understand the Passover that prepared the Hebrews for their momentous time in history and why it was imperative that they should not forget it.

What is more this detailed study will hopefully demonstrate to those unused to studying the Old - but by no means redundant – Testament, just how much useful information it contains.

1.   **Hapi - Egyptian god of the Nile** (was a water bearer)

The first plague the Egyptians experienced was that of turning the water to blood which was against Hapi, god of the Nile. As Aaron touched the Nile River with the *rod* of the Lord the water immediately turned to blood, killing all the fish, thus causing the river to stink.

Pharaoh's magicians were only partially able to replicate turning water into blood, but it left Pharaoh unimpressed with this 'great wonder' from God.

Throughout all the land of Egypt the water remained unsuitable for drinking for seven days. The perfect length of time to demonstrate that the Lord was superior to the gods of Egypt.

2.   **Heket - Egyptian goddess of Fertility, Water, Renewal** (had the head of a frog)

The second plague was that of frogs. coming up from the river and entering their houses, getting into their food stores, their clothing and every possible place. Not the greatest nor the least, in Egypt escaped the plague of frogs. Pharaoh's magicians were able to bring more frogs in their attempt to imitate the power of God, but only Moses was able to make the frogs go away.

Sometimes individuals that believe their authority was being challenged can become very stubborn, particularly those who enjoy unbridled power such as the Egyptian Pharaoh.

3.   **Geb - Egyptian god of the Earth** (was over the dust of the earth

> Third Plague- caused lice to appear from the dust of the earth which attacked both people and beasts, but Pharaoh was becoming obstinate and would not concede, even after this display of power from the Lord.
>
> The dust, referred to in the creation process of man, is now used to plague men, as a reminder of his mortality and sin, both of which lead to death.
>
> Pharaoh's magicians are finally humiliated, being unable to compete with this power that was so much greater than themselves and the powers that they had from their satanic, demon possessed Egyptian gods and goddesses. They had to profess, that this was the finger of God.
>
> What is particularly interesting is that this was the last plague initiated by Aaron using the rod of God.

Moses, who had by now found his old authority as a prince in Pharaoh's household that had been lost during his time looking after his father-in-law's sheep, took over from his brother in calling the shots.

4.   **Khepri- Egyptian god of creation, movement of the Sun, rebirth** (had the head of a fly)

> The fourth plague, consisting of flies, started the great miracle of separation or differentiation between the Egyptian spiritual leaders and the representative of the God of Israel.
>
> For the next demonstration of God's power, Moses met Pharaoh at the Nile River in the morning and made the demand on behalf of the Lord, *"Let My people go, that they may serve Me."*
>
> Again, Pharaoh hardened his heart and disregarded the request, resulting in a pronouncement of swarms of flies afflicting Egypt.

This was the first plague that only affected the Egyptians, the children of Israel remaining unscathed. Not only did this move the plagues to a higher level by adding destruction to discomfort, but it demonstrated that God had such control over nature that He could insulate His chosen people from its effects.

Plagued by flies, Pharaoh tried bargaining with the Lord through Moses, who, he must have assumed, was the priest of the Hebrew God and could make decisions on His behalf. He did this in order to demonstrate that he had the same level of authority and power as this, to him, unknown God.

He tried to dictate the terms and conditions of the offer, telling Moses that they may sacrifice to their God but only in Egypt where he could keep control of the situation.

Not only did this clearly not comply with the requested *"three days journey"* that the Lord required, but the Egyptian people would have been offended by their sacrifices.

Realizing Moses would not budge, the Pharaoh relented allowing them to leave, but telling them not to go very far.

This temporary allowance was a tactic to have Moses entreat the Lord to remove the swarms of flies, but God knew full well that Pharaoh would renege on that offer.

By now Pharaoh had in part learned who the God was that Moses represented, cleverly asking for His assistance whilst supposedly setting aside his belief in the Egyptian gods and goddesses. What the Pharaoh had yet to realize was that the God of the Hebrews had limitless power for it was He who created all things, and knew what the Pharaoh was thinking.

However, this Pharaoh was so belligerent that he was to die in his fight to keep the slaves, being no match for the God of Israel.

As soon as the flies had disappeared, Pharaoh immediately reneged on his promise and would not let them go, continuing to believe in the power of his gods, of which he was considered one.

In the case of each plague the God of Moses was seen to have complete control over both the appearance, departure and, more critically, the timing of each plague. Because the plagues were directly affecting the Egyptian people who had to sit and watch powerless and probably with great frustration as the dramatic action between their king and Moses played out. That did not mean that they did not privately take sides.

5. **Hathor - Egyptian goddess of Love and Protection** (usually depicted with the head of a cow).

Moses once again presented Pharaoh, with the demand to *'Let my people go, that they may serve me'*, whilst revealing the type of plague that would occur in the event of his continued resistance to God's request, providing the Pharaoh with a period of reflection before it was enacted.

Tomorrow the hand of the Lord would be upon all the cattle and livestock, with a very severe pestilence with such severe consequences as to cause many of them to die. It is important to remember that all livestock and farm land belonged to the Pharaoh after Joseph commandeered it for the Pharaoh during the seven lean years.

This next plague would be a huge economic disaster, in areas of food, transportation, military supplies, farming, and economic goods that were dependent on the welfare of this livestock.

The Bible says that the Lord hardened the heart of Pharaoh, but in reality this was shorthand for the fact that God chose the time of this Pharaoh to have His people released because He knew the type of man he was and his belligerent attitude.

Dealing with him also allowed God to demonstrate His absolute power over His creation that is still recognized today, and demonstrate the uselessness of the Egyptian gods and goddesses for the benefit of all the surrounding nations to see, because Egypt was a major power in the region.

This was also a lesson and warning for the Israelites themselves not to worship other gods before the Lord their God.

6. Isis- Egyptian goddess of Medicine and Peace

The plague of boils on the skin arrived unannounced, and for the first time, directly attacked the Egyptian people themselves causing them considerable personal discomfort. This was the start of a process that would bring about a division between the ruler and his people because in the end the people were only too pleased to see the Hebrews go.

As instructed by the Lord, Moses took ashes from the furnace of affliction, and threw them into the air. As the dust from the ash blew all over Egypt, it settled on man and beast alike causing boils and sores.

As with the previous two plagues, and throughout the remaining plagues, the division is drawn between the Egyptians and the children of Israel, as God gives protection to His (Abrahamic) covenant people.

The severity of the judgment of God had now become personal, as it was actually felt by the Egyptian people themselves.

As cleanliness was paramount in Egyptian society, this plague pronounced the people as *unclean*.

The magicians, seen throughout the previous plagues, were rendered powerless, unable to perform ceremonial rituals to their gods because they were in such an unclean and painful state, even preventing them from standing before Pharaoh.

With all their potions and magic that had enabled them to be a powerful voice in the land for many generations, suddenly a far greater power had taken over control and they retreated into obscurity.

This meant that Moses and Aaron became the only spiritual leaders left standing in front of Pharaoh, with the One True God having proved that He alone was God and their support.

7.   **Nut- Egyptian goddess of the Sky**

God instructed Moses to rise early and stand before Pharaoh and say to Him, *"Thus says the Lord God of the Hebrews, 'Let my people go so that they can serve me.'"*

Pharaoh is warned of more plagues being directed at him, his officials and people to prove beyond any doubt that the God of the Hebrews was supreme in the earth and the heavens and that there was no God like Him.

This obstinate and cruel Pharaoh was so impervious to God's warnings that God was able to demonstrated His mighty power through the plagues, that would be recorded for the sake of historical fact and as being beyond the worst natural disasters that had ever been experienced by the Egyptian nation, whilst in the process showing the complete powerlessness of the all the gods worshipped by them.

God clearly demonstrated that He could act with impunity and all that was happening in Egypt was being broadcast from country to country through the travelling camel trains. In fact as the children of Israel travelled through the wilderness after their release, the remembrance of these plagues went before them bringing fear into the hearts of many nations.

The people were warned to bring the cattle in from the fields where the grass was now suitable for grazing, but, possibly because of instructions from the king or unbelief, some left their cattle and servants outside.

Hail of unspeakable size and force with the ability to destroy in a way never before witnessed in the area, would rain down from the sky in defiance of the goddess of the sky.

As soon as Moses lifted his hands up to the sky, the heavens opened and with the hail came thunder and lightning such as had never previously been known.

Again there was clear division between the Egyptians, some of whom took notice of the threat to their livestock and saved them, and the Hebrews living in the land of Goshen who were not affected.

Interestingly enough, the crops that were also destroyed by the hail consisted of flax and barley, which were ripening in the fields.

These two particular crops were not the mainstay of their diet, being more specifically used for their clothing and libations. This destruction would make their life uncomfortable, but as far as effecting their food supply, the wheat still survived.

Seeing the destruction Pharaoh relented, confessing that he had sinned, and that the Lord is righteous whereas he and his people were wicked. But once again it was a false confession just to have the plague stopped.

8.   Seth- Egyptian god of War, Chaos and Storms

The Lord told Moses that there was a purpose behind these plagues because He wanted the children of Israel to pass on to their sons and grandsons and succeeding generations knowledge of all that God did in the Land of Egypt so that they would not only be comforted by His mighty power, but also realize that He was indeed the Lord of all.

Moses and Aaron approached Pharaoh with the same request, *'Let my people go so that they may serve me'*, and pronounced the judgment of locusts if not heeded.

This is the second wave of destruction to follow the hail, and whatever crops were left intact after that display, were now completely consumed by the swarms of locusts that were unleashed from the sky.

This wonder definitely affected their life source. By hitting them in their food supply, the Lord was crippling the nation, making them dependent on other nations for food rather than being self-sufficient.

Yet still, Pharaoh would not listen.

9.   Ra- The Sun god

We are now getting to the finally and most significant of all the plagues because it would hit the Pharaoh in particular in the one place where it hurt the most, the life of his son and heir.

For a land where the sun shone brightly during daylight hours, for such a darkness to come upon Egypt unannounced was a traumatic and very frightening experience for the whole nation, particularly as it was so severe that the people could not see anything at all. It meant total lockdown.

This was a wakeup call of momentous proportions, and only the severely obstinate would ignore it, but that is what the Pharaoh did.

There must be no doubt that the ordinary people, who were very superstitious through the prominence of necromancers and magicians who stirred up their imagination, were traumatised by this plague because it isolated everyone from family and friends and even strangers standing nearby.

The people were by now very frightened indeed by this latest twist in the saga between Moses and the Pharaoh, particularly as Moses seemed to have the upper hand.

To have no light at all when even at night with the moon and the stars there was dim light, this total absence of even the faintest amount of light would have completely encased individual people as though there was no one else around.

Three days of palpable darkness, that was so immense and intense it could be physically felt, covered the land of Egypt, but did not affect the children of Israel.

Where was the sun god in all this? What powerful force brought about this terrible situation? How did God cancel all light in Egypt?

This was the latest demonstration of God's total power over His creation, and we would do well to take notice of it because this is historical fact. God Himself was responsible for all the plagues.

What is even more tragic is that the people were not only totally unaware that this was a prelude to a more devastating plague that was to befall the Egyptian people, along with the servants and slaves brought in from other nations, but were totally powerless to stop it.

This is was all because Satan did not want the people released and he worked hard through his servant the Pharaoh to stop them, but he was powerless to stop God having them released.

The sun, the most worshipped god in Egypt other than Pharaoh himself, gave no light. The Lord showed that he had control over the sun as a witness that the God of Israel had ultimate power over life and death and the environment.

The psychological and religious impact on the individual Egyptian would have been profound. Darkness was a representation of death, judgment and hopelessness. Darkness is the complete absence of light.

10.   Pharaoh- The Ultimate Power in Egypt

Pharaoh, the king of Egypt, was worshipped by the Egyptians because he was considered to be the greatest Egyptian god of all. It was believed that he was actually the son of Ra himself, manifest in the flesh.

After the plague of darkness, that was so intense that it was felt throughout the land, was lifted, Pharaoh resumed his position of "bargaining with the Lord" and offered Moses another "deal".

Since virtually all of the Egyptian animals had been consumed by the judgments of the Lord, Pharaoh now consented to the request made, to let the people go, but they must leave their animals behind.

This was a totally unacceptable offer, as the animals were to be used as the actual sacrifice to the Lord. The Lord is uncompromising when He has set the terms.

Enraged by the refusal, Pharaoh pronounced the last deadly plague to be unleashed upon the land from his very own lips as he warns Moses, *"Go from me, take heed to yourself, you may see my face no more; for in that day you see my face you shalt die."*

And Moses said, *"Thus saith the Lord, About midnight will I go out into the midst of Egypt: And all the firstborn in the land of Egypt shall die, from the firstborn of Pharaoh that sits upon his throne, even unto the firstborn of the maidservant that is behind the mill; and all the firstborn of beasts. And there shall be a great cry throughout all the land of Egypt, such as there was never one like it, nor shall be like it anymore."*

How ironic that the threat of death issued by the Pharaoh should rebound on his own family.

At this point the passive obedience that the children of Israel had shown throughout the plagues is now moved to a level of active obedience.

They are given strict instructions to follow so that they did not also experience the judgment of this last plague sent by the Lord. These instructions are known as "The Feast of Passover", "The Feast of Unleavened Bread", and "The Law of the Firstborn."

In these rituals are displayed the law of sacrifice [Christ being our sacrifice], the law of the gospel [unleavened bread being symbolic of sinlessness], and the law of consecration [all those that are covered by the blood of the sin sacrifice are consecrated to God]. These are all necessary requirements to receive ultimate salvation from spiritual death.

Number 10 in the Bible is a symbol of perfection, harmony and creation. It is also a number of integration, discipline, laws and wholeness. The phrase "God said" is repeated 10 times through Genesis. His word is reflected in 10 Commandments that symbolize the ultimate law for any person to live by.

There were 10 generations of people who lived before the flood and who were sinners, and the flood wiped them away for their disobedience. Noah was of the 10th generation and the ark was created to lead to the new beginning.

Pagan Egypt experienced 10 plaques from God, in order to release his people, which was also the reaction to human disobedience.

Instruction and Preparation for the Passover

The people were given strict and detailed instructions regarding the first Passover sacrifice with clear knowledge of what it was all about. It was made very clear that the sacrifice of a lamb was to protect their first-born from the judgemental work of the angel of death whom God would send throughout the land and would finally lead to their release from captivity and oppression.

Previously God had targeted the plagues at the Egyptian areas of the land thus protecting the Israelites. This time it was their task to protect themselves by acting in obedience to God's instructions because no area of Egypt was exempt from the work of the angel of God. It is very interesting that finally the Israelites were to realize that in future they were required to directly participate in God's work and not have everything done for them.

- The time they were in was to be to them the first month of the Israeli religious year.

- On the 10th day of this month each family was to obtain a lamb that was to be consumed three days later in the evening with nothing of the animal left over and no bones of the animal broken. Small families that could not consume a lamb in one sitting were to join with another family, or other families, and share a lamb; larger families would need more than one lamb. It was to be repeated annually.

- The lamb, of the sheep or (kid) of the goats, was to be of one year old and a male (as for a burnt offering — Jesus when in human form was a male) without blemish, free from any defect (Malachi 1:6-8:). The emphasis was that the lamb was symbolically innocent and free from sin — Jesus was the only sinless male ever to have lived.

- As the Israeli day was counted from 1800 hrs to 1800 hrs, the lamb for the Passover sacrifice was to be obtained on the 10th day but sacrificed on the 14th day which was three days later (10/11 [selection]-11/12 [day one]-12/13[day two]- 13/14[day three].

- The lamb was to be killed by the head of the house at dusk between three and five and the blood painted on the lintel and doorposts of the houses in which the people ate the meal. It was called the Pascal, or Passover lamb because at the sight of its blood the angel of death would *pass over* that house leaving the first-born alive. It is this saving of the first-born that led to the instruction that all first-born must be dedicated to God, the first-born children being bought-back with an offering before God, just as Isaac was and Jesus.

- The lamb was to be roasted, not boiled, because fire represented purification and sacrifice. It had to be completely consumed with nothing left over for scavenging animals or birds.

  Thinking ahead, the sacrifice of this lamb was to be symbolic of Christ's death, for the Cross represented the consuming fire of sacrifice. Jesus was totally consumed on it because of His death.

  Not a bone of the Pascal Lamb was to be broken *for not a bone in the Messiah's body was broken, whereas the bones of both the criminals crucified with Him were broken to speed their death (Jn. 19:31 – 37).*

- The people were not to leave their house until the morning.

- These were the Lord's instructions through Moses at that time (Ex. 12:14 – 20):

  This day will be a memorial to you, and you shall keep it as a feast to the Lord; you are to celebrate this Passover as an ordinance forever throughout your generations. Each year for seven days you shall eat unleavened bread, but on the first day you shall remove the leaven [representing sin] from your houses; for whoever eats leavened bread on the first day through the seventh day, that person shall be cut off and excluded from the celebration of atonement made for Israel.

  On the first day of the feast you shall have a holy and solemn assembly, and on the seventh day there shall be another holy and solemn assembly; and no work of any kind shall be done on those days, except for the preparation of food which every person must eat, but only that may be done by you.

  You shall also observe the Feast of Unleavened Bread, because on this very day I brought the people of Israel out of the land of Egypt; therefore you shall observe this day throughout your generations as an ordinance forever.

  In the first month, on the fourteenth day of the month at evening, you shall eat unleavened bread, and continue until the twenty-first day of the month at evening.

For seven days no leaven shall be found in your houses; whoever eats what is leavened shall be cut off and excluded from the atonement made for the congregation of Israel, whether a stranger or native-born.

You shall eat nothing leavened; in all your dwellings you shall eat only unleavened bread.

Because God wanted to teach the Pharaoh a lesson that he would never forget, and spur him to release His people [break the deadlock] this Passover sacrifice became a sin offering for the first-born of every Israelite family and had to be repeated year on year. Christ was Mary's firstborn for very different reasons.[29]

Christ's sacrifice as the Passover Lamb, on the other hand was, and is, a non-repeatable sacrifice for all those who believe and accept that they are sinners in need of a saviour and want to be freed from the penalty of death, whether Jew or Gentile.

The relationship between the sacrificing of the Passover lamb and the sacrificing of Christ on the cross is that they happened at exactly the same time[30] in the year, the first was to free the Israelites from slavery in Egypt, the second was to free all those that believed in the God of Israel from slavery to sin and the world.

It also fulfilled John the baptizer's claim that Jesus Christ was the Lamb of God; but the blood He shed on the cross was an all-sufficient sacrifice for the cleansing of all the sins of those who would confess their sins and seek God for cleansing. None are turned away. Salvation is available to all.

At the annual Pesach meal bitter herbs were to be eaten representing the bitterness of the Egyptian bondage.

The people had to eat the first Passover meal fully dressed, with shoes on ready to start their journey at a moment's notice.

The Significance of the Passover

As Moses and Aaron began to instruct the congregation of the children of Israel, they became God's ambassadors to both Pharaoh and Israel. This change in their role signalled the end of one relationship and the beginning of a new one that would last until Moses' death.

---

[29] See Appendix A of The Tent of the Meeting
[30] See A Fresh Look At Easter

By setting this festival as the first festival to be celebrated at the start of each religious year, God was identifying the Passover experience:

1. as the birth pangs of a new nation; a time when God, by His mighty power, separated them from the world (represented by Egypt) and its oppression in the form of sin (slavery to the world).

   Israel would utter the cry of freedom on their release, but the Egyptians would utter the cry of despair.

   The Passover was the culmination of years of hardship and grinding oppression. This was God in action; and for those who have come to faith through the acceptance of the Son of man Jesus Christ as their Lord and Saviour, it is just as important to them symbolically as it was to the physical seed of those who finally left Egypt.

2. with death as the basis of their freedom from the world and the cleansing of personal sin, the blood on the doorpost and lintel was only made available through the death of a lamb without blemish that died in place of the first-born.

   As they journeyed through the wilderness, the people were required to continually sacrifice a lamb for an atonement of their personal sin; that was to restore their at-one-ment with God.

   This sacrifice for sin was to be repeated annually until Christ's death on the cross, which represents the moment of our total freedom from the oppression of the world (the wages of sin inherited from Adam and the personal sins of all individuals against God is death – Ro. 3:23, 6:23; cf. Gen. 2:17).

   At the last Passover meal in the upper room the Messiah inaugurated the first communion service.[31]

   His is the once for all sacrifice that does not need to be repeated; for as we accept Jesus as our Passover sacrifice the Father sees the blood in relation to our sins and God sees no sin in us.

---

[31] See A Fresh Look At Easter

What does need to be repeated is the remembrance of His death until He returns in glory.

3.   as the gateway to the path that leads to the promised land. All those who accept Jesus Christ as Lord, whether Jew or Gentile, become members of the redeemed, the remnant of the new spiritual Israel.

         We no longer look, as those who were released from Egypt did, to the land of Canaan, but to the New Jerusalem that God is preparing for us (Rev. 21:9 – 11).

4.   as the beginning of a nation that accepted Him as their King and God. All those who left Egypt were to celebrate this festival once a year without fail. But only those men who had been circumcised, and therefore identified as belonging to God, could take part.

         Men slaves and servants were to be circumcised and guests who wanted to join in the celebrations also had to voluntarily be circumcised. This celebration was only for those who were born into the nation of Israel and had been circumcised by believing parents or who wanted to be part of this worshipping nation.

Although the physical mark of circumcision in fulfilment of the Abrahamic covenant was most important, even more important was the attitude of the mind and heart of the individual Israelite. Abraham received the covenant of circumcision because of his complete trust and faith in God. All those that received the mark of circumcision the reverse had to be true, for that mark had to be validated by a strong Abrahamic style *heart based* belief, trust and faith in God as they grew into adulthood.

From being an idolater in the beginning, by believing in the God who had called him to a new life as a believer in Him, Abraham became the forerunner of all believers through faith, both Jew and Gentile. By turning to God and committing his life to Him, Abraham became the example we (Jews and Christians alike) are to follow.

Jeremiah called upon his fellow countrymen to cause the physical circumcision to be reflected in the attitude of their hearts by believing and turning over their lives in covenant giving to the Living God (Jer. 4:4, see also Deut. 10:16) as we have already discovered.

Israel was not just a nation. It was also a religion in its own right, the one true faith in the only living creator God. This is because they had been chosen by, and were to believe in, Elohim Adonay, the God of Abraham, Isaac and Jacob from whom they had descended.

Abraham is the father of all believers whether or not they are his physical descendant. This is because all those that believe in the Lord Jesus Christ as the Son of God and, that through His death on the Cross at calvary believe that they are saved from their sin, becomes a person of faith just like Abraham who was the first man to believe in the same creator God. The connection is therefore true faith which is a spiritual not a physical concept.

No other nation on earth can claim such a heritage; that is to have been chosen by the creator of all things seen and unseen, to be a discipleship nation to the world. It is unique.

Their whole way of life was to be bound up with the worship and service of God. And for those not born an Israelite, but who have come into the faith in this same God, He expects nothing less than for *their whole way of life* to become bound up in the worship and service of that same God. We should not live like those in Egypt who are of the world and slaves to it, but unto Him who has called us just as Abraham was.

This celebration, this Passover festival would further single them out as the Lord's people, as being unique, as though He had branded them with His mark on their forehead (Rev. 7:3; 22:4). It would also attract the attention of Satan and his spiritual and human followers.

Pharaoh was by no means the first and is certainly not the last leader of a nation working to try to bring down the nation of Israel and upset the plan of God, even to this very day.

The Passover celebrations that were to continue year after year were used to keep alive the memory of this event and how God had displayed His mighty power over Egypt (representing the World) and saved His people both from slavery in Egypt and from sin.

There is one other interesting factor that is worth mentioning here and that is the human support needed by gods. The account of the calling of Gideon is very interesting in that God required Gideon to sacrifice a bull using the wood from the altar to Baal for fuel. He did it at night and in the morning the people were furious and wanted to know who had done such a thing. Discovering it was Gideon they called on him to be killed, but Gideon's father said a very interesting thing:

> But Joash [Gideon's father] said to all who stood against him, "Would you plead for Baal? Would you save him? Let the one who would plead for him be put to death by morning! If he [Baal] is a god, let him plead for himself, because [it is] his altar [that] has been torn down!" (Jdgs. 6:31

The god of any religious group in the world that requires its followers to kill those humans responsible for any act of apparent sacrilege against their god is not a living god at all. What does the Lord God of Israel say to all those who believe in Him? *Vengeance is Mine, I will repay says the Lord.*

As believers we are not here to protect God, rather He is there to protect His servants. We are here, however, to publish abroad His wonderful name and His love for all mankind.

With the coming of the Lamb of God as the perfect sacrifice, which had been a matter of prophecy throughout the history of Israel as recorded in the First Testament, all those of Israel who accept the Son as their saviour and Lord have been released from the power of the world, and cleansed from their sin, providing they are willing to surrender their lives to God be as obedient to Him as Abraham was, for that is what scripture required us to do.

All followers of the Jewish Messiah, Jesus Christ, remember His death until He returns in glory because it is the shedding of blood as applied to a repentant sinner by the Holy Spirit that cleanses the conscience of that person.[32]

As God wrote the Passover celebration service, so he provided the ingredients for the communion service, in a similar manner. It was the Passover service re-written by the Son of the living God as He celebrated it during the last Passover before His death that very same day.

Israel's freedom, nationhood and indeed the promised land were all God given, therefore their connection with God was not just one of Him being their saviour, but also their provider and sustainer.

---

[32] This is fully explained in A Fresh Look At Easter

After all as the years steadily went by, and they suffered varying degrees of tragedy through their own failures and rebelliousness, their complete dependence on God's power had not only not gone away, but from the nation's transformation from the tribe led by Jacob to the nation of Israel in Egypt, His power had so clearly sustained and guided the nation throughout their ever increasing length of history.

This understanding of God's influence on the life of the nation of Israel and the individual members of it, should not be lost on those who have come to believe in the Messiah Jesus.

In A Fresh Look At Easter chapter 8 is a sub-heading **The Last Becomes the First.** In it we learn that the Messiah told His disciples that He was anxious to celebrate that Passover with them. The reason was made clear for He changed the meal from the need of the Israelites to remember the way in which God released His people from Egypt, to a remembrance service of His death until He returns.

The unleavened bread which had reminded the celebrants that there was no time to allow the bread to rise using yeast because they were suddenly thrust out of Egypt, came to represent the sinless body of Messiah that was tortured and broken for us that believe in Him.

There were four glasses of wine, the third of which represented their redemption with an outstretched arm. That came to symbolize the blood shed by the Messiah to redeem us from the slavery of sin

God never does anything without a purpose, and that definitely applies to the Passover

The Feast of Weeks (Shavuot) / Pentecost

Shavuot, one of the three main pilgrimage festivals of ancient Israel, combined two major religious observances.

1. The grain harvest of the early summer.
2. The giving of the Torah on Mount Sinai seven weeks after the nation left Egypt.

The first concerned the command for the men of Israel, along with their families and members of their household, to appear before God in Jerusalem, bringing freewill offerings of the first fruits of their harvest or whatever they were able to give if they were not a land owner. Remember Israel was originally a farming nation, but not everyone was a land owner. It celebrated God's goodness to them just like we in the West celebrate harvest festivals.

It was a time to rejoice because they were in their own country harvesting their own crops and all because God freed them from the tyranny of slavery in a foreign land and gave them the land they now occupied.

The second was particularly significant for what has become known as Judaism, after the dominant kingly tribe of Judah. This is because this festival has been eternally linked with the moment the nation entered into a covenant with God on Mount Sinai; which was undoubtedly a major Jewish religious historical event.

It meant them not only coming under the authority of Divine law, but entering into a pre-marriage[33] relationship with God which was related to time and again by some of the prophets, especially Hosea.

The "Feast of Weeks," is celebrated seven weeks after Passover (Pesach). Since the counting of this period begins on the second evening of Passover, Shavuot actually takes place exactly 50 days after the first seder. Hence, following the Greek word for "fifty," Shavuot is sometimes referred to as Pentecost. Although its origins are to be found in an ancient grain harvest festival, Shavuot has long been identified with the giving of the Torah [the law].

This again is interesting because in Jerusalem on the day of Pentecost, fifty (a significant number in scripture – the year of jubilee) days after the Lord Jesus celebrated the last Passover meal He was to have with His disciples, an even more significant event than the event on Sinai took place when those closest to Jesus during His earthly ministry experienced the Holy Spirit coming upon them to empower them, otherwise known as the baptism in the Spirit.

This event, when the Holy Spirit actually entered into these chosen people, introduced a new relationship between God and individual believers which was not only far more intimate than any previous relationship man had with God, but it also empowered them in a way never experienced before, even between God and the prophets.

---

[33] The full marriage of God with His church, which is the spiritual Israel of Jewish and Gentile believers, will be at the Marriage supper of the Lamb when all believers are united with Him in that place where he has gone to prepare a dwelling place for us (Jn. 14:1 – 3; Rev. 19:7 – 10; cf. Matt. 22:1 – 14).

It transformed the frightened disciples causing them to boldly stand up and be counted as His followers and it empowered Peter to preach as he had never preached before, encouraging three thousand to accept that Jesus was the Messiah against the teaching of the religious authorities.

This event not only caused those individuals affected to enter into a far more personal and deeply spiritual relationship with God than that experienced by a largely unbelieving nation on mount Sinai, but it also gave them the power and wisdom to pass the foundational teaching about the new way of salvation that leads to the intimacy and transformational experience on to others.

Peter went to the home of the Italian army officer Cornelius and witnessed that same Spirit of God falling on that household as had happened to the disciples.

This meant the Holy Spirit was finally let loose into the world and is at work today in those that truly believe in the God of Israel.

The Importance of Jerusalem

> *at the place that the LORD your God will choose for his name to dwell in it, there you shall offer the Passover sacrifice, in the evening at sunset, at the time set. (Deut. 16:6).*

The reason for considering the importance of Jerusalem, which up to and including the point of Moses making his speeches had not been mentioned, because it was not then known, is because even in the 21st century Jerusalem is still the focus of world attention.

Initially after the conquest of Canaan, Moses tabernacle (Hebrew: מִשְׁכָּן, mishkān, meaning *residence* or *dwelling place*) was sited at the ancient city of Shiloh until it was moved to Jerusalem where David had built another tent tabernacle to accommodate the Ark of the Covenant after the Philistines had returned it to Israel (2 Sam. 5 & 6).

All three of these festivals were to be celebrated at *the place that the Lord your God will choose,* initially at Shiloh until it was finally centred in Jerusalem and finally in Solomon's magnificent Temple.

But that city was not made the capital of Israel until it was captured and David was king. The stone built temple was not erected until the time of Solomon, sometime after David's death, when God filled the newly built magnificent Temple with His glory.

Now it happened that when the priests had come out of the Holy Place, the cloud of the glory of the Lord filled the Lord's house, so that the priests could not stand in their positions to minister because of the cloud, for the glory and brilliance of the Lord had filled the Lord's temple (1 Kgs. 8:10, 11).

What an incredible occasion that must have been, seeing the glory of God shining out of the temple so powerfully that the priests had to evacuate the building.

Sadly however, Jerusalem itself was to have a chequered career because of the waywardness of the kings that sat on David's throne, until Israel became a republic after some of the people returned from exile. Also God was not always present there because of the paganism that infiltrated the priesthood and kings polluted the outer area with symbols of their rebelliousness towards God.

The city remained because God had placed His Holy name in it and throughout the centuries allowed it to be destroyed and then rebuilt to ensure it was thriving at the time of the Messiah, even though it was occupied by the Romans who were the ones to execute the Messiah.

The temple remained the centre of the worship of God until it was made redundant by the crucifixion when the temple curtain, which separated the holy place from the most holy, was torn asunder from top to bottom.

The confirmation that it was Jerusalem in which He would place His name can be found in two verse of scripture. The first was when God decided to divide the nation in two because of the sins of Solomon:

However, I will not tear away all the kingdom from the house of David; I will give one tribe, Judah, to your son for the sake of My servant David, to continue his line, and for the sake of Jerusalem which I have chosen (1 Kgs. 11:13).

Also at the time of the evil king Manasseh it is said that:

he built pagan altars in the temple of the Lord, of which the Lord had said, "In Jerusalem I will put My Name and My Presence (2 Kgs. 21:4)

So we have confirmed that the place God said He would choose through Moses was Jerusalem.

But even now God has maintained His control over the city in which He placed His Great name, and caused it to remain central to the history of mankind, like an umbilical cord that can never be cut, connecting the Lord God of Israel with the earth and particularly His people. Remember that it is to the Mount of Olives that the Messiah will return, this time in glory

As we have already learned the two festivals above were to involve Jerusalem and the temple and were brought to their fulfilment in that city. But there is one more important festival which also involves Jerusalem, that has yet to be fulfilled.

The reason it is worth focusing on Jerusalem at this point is because it teaches us something about the timescale God uses.

Moses speaks about *the place where the Lord your God chooses to establish His Name and Presence*, which was not made clear until King David captured Jerusalem from the Jebusites (2 Sam. 5:7).

It was after that that David brought the Ark of the Covenant into the city (2 Sam. 6; 1Chron. 15, 16) where it was installed in a tent like the tabernacle (1 Chron. 16:1) built by Moses that David had had made.

What is particularly interesting is not only that the Temple Solomon was to build was to be sited on the threshing floor of Ornan the Jebusite that David bought, but the manner in which that site was chosen. Against God's wishes David ordered a census (1 Chron. 21) and David was appalled at the carnage that ensued because of that decision.

Pleading for his people, the Lord directed David to the threshing floor of Ornan (1 Chron. 21:21)

But consider the timescale from the end of Moses life in the 13th century B.C. to around 1000 B.C. when David was king[34], along with what Peter wrote in his second letter to the diaspora:

> *Nevertheless, do not let this one fact escape your notice, beloved, that with the Lord one day is like a thousand years, and a thousand years is like one day (2 Ptr. 3:8).*

---

[34] King David reigned from 1010 – 970 BC and Abraham died around 1271 BC so there could be possibly 270 years between Moses speaking about the place of God's choice and King David establishing it as Israel's capital city.

Remember that God was silent for over four hundred years before the sudden appearance of John the Baptist. Therefore all prophecy must be seen against God's timescale. This is because so much preparation has to be completed for each piece of His plan to come to pass.

Jerusalem has been the place God chose to place His name, and this was sealed after the building of the temple by Solomon and the Lord demonstrated His presence by displaying His glory within it so that the priests, those that were to minister to Him, had to speedily evacuate the building.

What we must never forget is that as the Holy Spirit is never confined to one place, but is everywhere at the same time, the pillar of cloud by day and fire by night was but a minute portion of His presence. But that was the seal of His approval, the sign that that was where God's glorious name would be centred.

Because of the topography of the area surrounding the city, it is interesting that it can only survive an attack with His help. Therefore not only with the city but also with the whole land of Israel, God was telling His people that He was central to their success and safety. It is His land and His city and they have always been very precious to Him.

Let there be no doubt that God is in charge and let no attacker believe that they overcome the land or the city in their own strength. It is purely what God allows.

When Zechariah records *For I will gather all nations against Jerusalem to do battle,* what he is saying is that the Lord has allowed all the bottled up anger and animosity towards Him and His people that Satan has been stimulating throughout history within the unbelieving community of nations to suddenly erupt against the one symbol of God's involvement in the human race: Jerusalem.

Then the Lord will go forth and fight against those nations, as when He fights on a day of battle.

What is so sad is unbelief. Those of us that have experienced the presence of God, and the power of God in our lives not only know His limitless love, but through our study of His word we also know about the unlimited power of God. As nothing is impossible to God, that means the mightiest army with the most powerful, sophisticated weapons are like ants against an anteater. They are like fodder to Him. The Messiah will return to Jerusalem, the scene of His crucifixion in His own good time.

There is no point in this book investigating the end times, except to focus on verses sixteen to nineteen of Zechariah's prophecy about the last days in chapter 14, which are relevant to the final fulfilment of the next feast, that of Tabernacles.

> *Then everyone who is left of all the nations that went against Jerusalem go up from year to year to worship the King, the Lord of hosts, and celebrate the Feast of Booths (Tabernacles). (Zech. 14:16)*

There has to come a time during the end days of the life of the world when the Lord God of Israel, who created all things, finally not only asserts His great and awesome power, but receives the glory and honour due to Him.

> *And it will be that whichever of the families of the earth does not go up to Jerusalem to worship the King, the Lord of hosts, there will be no rain on them. If the family of Egypt does not go up [to Jerusalem] and present themselves, then no rain will fall on them. It will be the plague with which the Lord will strike the nations who do not go up to celebrate the Feast of Booths (Tabernacles). This will be the [consequent] punishment [for the sin] of Egypt, and the [consequent] punishment [for the sin] of all the nations that do not go up to celebrate the Feast of Booths (Tabernacles). (Zech. 14:17 - 19)*

This will be the only major festival that will include Gentiles for God will require members from *all the nations* to attend and worship Him. It will also be celebrated during the closing years of the world, just as the Jews celebrated the festival towards the end of the year.

The Feast of Tabernacles or Booths

This is the third and final major festival of the religious year for the people of Israel, which was celebrated for seven days after *you have gathered in the grain from your threshing floor and the wine from your wine press.* For this reason it is also known as the feast of ingathering.

It was to celebrate the years of wandering in the wilderness before gaining a more permanent home when they entered the promised land and the people took over the homes that had been built by the people they replaced.

Their instructions for the booth (Lev. 23:39 – 43)

> *'On precisely the fifteenth day of the seventh month (nearly October), when you have harvested the fruits of the land, you shall celebrate the feast of the Lord for seven days, with a Sabbath rest on the first day and on the eighth day.*
>
> *On the first day you shall take the foliage of beautiful trees, branches of palm trees, and boughs of thick (leafy) trees, and willows of the brook to make booths; and you shall rejoice before the Lord your God for seven days.*
>
> *You shall celebrate it as a feast to the Lord for seven days. It shall be a permanent statute throughout your generations; you shall celebrate it in the seventh month.*
>
> *For seven days all native-born in Israel shall live in booths, so that your generations may know that I had the sons of Israel live in booths when I brought them out of the land of Egypt. I am the Lord your God.*

This festival, along with all the others, is still celebrated by Jews, but the fulfilment of the second part is still in the future.

Of all the feasts that the Lord had prescribed for Israel to celebrate in commemoration of His relationship with them, the only one we know that will be regularly celebrated in the future by ALL nations that are left after the tribulation is the Feast of Tabernacles.

It is interesting that it was celebrated in Jerusalem after the return from exile in Babylon, remembering of course that not all the people were willing to return to their homeland.

Ezra the scribe who had studied the scriptures during the exile, was the only Israelite that knew them very well. It happened that when they had gathered before Ezra the scribe that the matter of the Feast of Tabernacles was relevant at that time, so they celebrated the feast, living in booths and there was a very great gladness.

This festival had not been celebrated from the time of Joshua until the return from exile in Babylon, which gives us some idea of just how far from following the scriptures the people had got.

What is also interesting is that during the days of the festival Ezra read from the book of the law of God, so for the first time they were hearing what they should have been taught from infancy for centuries (Neh. 8:12 – 18).

This was the feast on which the Messiah made His triumphal entry into Jerusalem (Mk. 12:12 – 18).

In Conclusion

> *"Three times a year all your males shall appear before the Lord your God in the place which He chooses, at the Feast of Unleavened Bread (Passover), the Feast of Weeks (Pentecost) and the Feast of Booths (Tabernacles), and they shall not appear before the Lord empty-handed.*
>
> *Every man shall give as he is able, in accordance with the blessing which the Lord your God has given you.*

There is no free ride with God. When David bought the threshing floor of Ornan the Jebusite, under extremely sad circumstances, he insisted that he paid for it:

> *Ornan said to David, "Take it for yourself; and let my lord the king do what is good in his eyes. See, I will also give you the oxen for the burnt offering, the threshing sledges for firewood and the wheat for the grain offering. All this I give to you as a gift."*
>
> *But King David said to Ornan,* **"No, I will certainly pay the full price. I will not take what is yours for an offering to the Lord, nor offer a burnt offering which costs me nothing."** *So David gave Ornan 600 shekels of gold by weight for the site.*

Does this not teach us something about our approach to the Lord? We must ask ourselves the question: "Are we also willing to only give to the Lord something for which others have laboured, so that we are not required to expend so much as a moment of our time and effort to putting before the Lord an offering to His Holy Name from the blessings we have received from Him?"

Not, we must remember, like the offering Cain made to the Lord, which was the result of his hard work, that is the crop that he had grown (Gen. 4:2, 3), but to *give as* we are *able,* **in accordance with the blessing which the Lord** *your* **God has given** *you.*

In Pursuit of Justice and True Worship

> *"You shall appoint judges and officers within all your city gates [where the governance of the city was carried out] which the Lord your God is giving you, according to your tribes, and they shall judge the people with righteous judgment.*

It is essential for us to fully appreciate the righteousness of God. He is purity personified and requires that all His people live a life of justice and impartiality.

> *You shall not distort justice or be partial, but totally impartial by not accepting a bribe, for a bribe blinds the eyes of the wise and perverts the words of the righteous.*

To uphold justice in its purest sense is the responsible of all those that love God. Just one lie or injustice can lead to others and that is not God's way. The pursuit of justice is another condition of the people taking possession of the land because it was to be God's showcase nation which was living proof of the Spiritual God ruling a physical nation.

> *You shall singularly pursue uncompromisingly righteous judgement, so that you may live and take possession of the land which the Lord your God is giving you.*

And underlying it all was the need for the people to remain focused on the Godhead because any distraction from their love for Him would only cause them to regress to type and be no different to the other nations.

> *You shall not plant for yourself an Asherah of any kind of tree or wood in competition to the altar of the Lord your God. Nor shall you set up for yourself a sacred pillar which the Lord your God hates.*

12 OF KINGS AND PRIESTS

Chapter 17

Purity of Worship

The one thing the Bible makes very clear is the purity of God and the greatness of His name, which, understandably, is very precious to Him. At times God did things, not for the benefit of the nation of Israel, which throughout its history was hard-hearted and wayward, but to protect His name, although on many occasions Israel was a beneficiary.

Sin was introduced by man under the guidance of Satan and is defined as man rebelling against God his maker.

Man has a problem. He was created by God to look after the world God had created, which is a very great responsibility that can only be carried out with God's empowerment. What is very clear is that man is not independent of God and never can be. In designing man God determined that He would create a person He could love, who would respond to that love, a person with whom He could enter into a deep and intimate spiritual relationship that was steeped in His love. That God is still working for that to happened is still the case.

With the introduction of the sin DNA into man, God had already designed a way for man to still enter into the loving relationship He had originally desired. However, it could never again be the type of intimate face to face relationship He had had with Adam at the beginning before the creation of woman.

At the time of Noah (Gen. 9), God established blood as being central to life, therefore the shedding of blood was symbolic of the removal of life from all living things. Hence the charge of murder followed the illegal shedding of blood. Obviously in today's sophisticated world there are other means of killing someone, but the principle of the shedding of blood was central to the understanding of sacrifices, and substitution.

The sentence against rebellious man is his eternal spiritual death, that is because of his rebellion man will never meet with God after his physical death. Obviously this was not what God had intended when He created man, therefore, using the symbolism of the shedding of blood representing the ending of a life, the idea of the sacrificing of prescribed animals in order to 'cover over' the sin of man was introduced as a temporary measure.

There is a very serious point here which it is essential to understand before considering the use of animals as substitutes for man. When an animal is sacrificed the man places his hands on the animal's head effectively transferring his sin to the animal; its blood is then shed in order for God to forgive the sin a man had committed.

If the animal is being sacrificed to pay the debt of sin owed by fallen man to a pure God, the introduction of an animal with a defect such as blindness, or lameness would surely automatically annul the effectiveness of the sacrifice.

This point cannot be easily brushed aside because the animal sacrifices were a precursor to the Son of the Living God sacrificing His own human life for the whole of mankind.

Being part of the Godhead, He was purity itself and completely sinless so for man to try to offer something that was not perfect they were insulting God and no forgiveness would be given[35].

God had to separate Himself from man's sinfulness. It is said that if a man saw God in all His glory, that man would die immediately. Purity and the filthiness of sin cannot co-habit because the comparison is just far too stark. Therefore, at all sacrificial services before God, the rightness of the worship and purity of the sacrificial offerings had to be in line with the purity of God.

---

[35] This matter of a perfect animal being offered for sacrifice is covered in detail in some of my other books.

You shall not sacrifice an ox or sheep to the Lord your God with a blemish or any defect, for that is a detestable thing to the Lord your God."

The best way of illustrating this is to go to the prophet Malachi who addressed the religious short comings of the post exilic community in what was Judah, but was renamed Israel.

'A son honours his father, and a servant his master. Then if I am a Father, where is My honour? And if I am a Master, where is the reverential fear and respect due Me?' says the Lord of hosts to you priests, who despise My name.

Here we have the crux of the matter. What do we think of God? Do we hold Him in the highest honour? Do we believe in Him at all? Or do we have doubts about Him? The answer to these questions will inevitably reflect in our attitude to Him and particularly in the way we worship Him.

It is undoubtedly true that in the Western church today the attitude of the church goers towards God is very casual, with worship focusing on us enjoying a good service, rather than thinking about the God we are worshipping, and how we can best tell Him that we love and respect Him and hold Him in the highest honour.

But you say, 'How and in what way have we despised Your name?'
By presenting defiled food on My altar.

The conversational way of presenting this message of the priest's corrupted worship of God is very forceful because it anticipates the response of the priests.

God is charging them with a contemptible attitude to the One who had released them from exile in Babylon and re-established them in Jerusalem. So why, after all that God had done for them, did they think that they could treat God so abominably? Had the priests not learned anything about the reasons for them going into exile in the first place, and the disgraceful actions of their forebears in the previous, glorious temple? Or the fact that after their return the whole priesthood had to go through a cleansing process before services in the rebuilt and less glamourous temple could restart?

Centuries earlier Moses had spoken to their forebears concerning this very thing:

> **"You shall not** *sacrifice an ox or sheep to the Lord your God with a blemish or any defect,* **for that is a detestable thing to the Lord your God."**

It seems incredible that they had learned nothing, because their view was very worldly, and their services had become a pretence.

> *By thinking that the table of the Lord is contemptible and may be despised. When you priests present blind animals for sacrifice, is it not evil?*
>
> *And when you present lame and sick animals, is it not evil?*

Then comes the challenge,

> *Try offering such a defective animal to your governor as a gift or as payment for your taxes. Would he be pleased with you, or receive you graciously?" says the Lord of hosts.*

It is very clear, especially with the sons of Jacob, that faith is an individual thing that is acquired by each and every individual member of every generation. Of Jacob's eleven sons, discounting young Benjamin, only Joseph had accepted and had faith in the God of Jacob, to the extent that he was prepared to suffer incredible reverses before God elevated him to the level of being second only to the Pharaoh.

The other ten sons were rebellious to the extent that they were prepared to do harm to Joseph. Except the Lord God saved him, he could well have died at their hands, which demonstrates so clearly the work of Satan amongst all those that do not fully love the Lord God of Israel, and was endlessly repeated throughout the history of Israel with the ultimate example being the death of their Messiah.

It is no wonder, therefore, that there were priests at either end of the spectrum. Those that loved and respected the Lord their God, and those that had little thought for Him.

Justice

The evil Satan seeks to sow amongst the population of countries throughout the world is best explained by a parable of Jesus:

> *The kingdom of heaven is like a man who sowed good seed in his field. But while his men were sleeping, his enemy came and sowed weeds that resembled wheat among the true wheat. When the plants sprouted and formed grain, the weeds also appeared.*
>
> *The owner's servants told him, 'Sir, did you not sow good seed in your field? Then how does it have weeds in it?' He replied to them, 'An enemy has done this.' The servants asked him, 'Then do you want us to go and pull them out?' But he said, 'No; because as you pull out the weeds, you may uproot the wheat with them.*
>
> *Let them grow together until the harvest; and at harvest time I will tell the reapers, "First gather the weeds and tie them in bundles to be burned; but gather the wheat into my barn." ' "*

Throughout the history of man Satan has caused chaos and disruption to the life of mankind. Those that have no time for God and in particular those that are so committed to evil deeds that God is anathema to them, will have hatred in their hearts towards those that do love Him. That is the whole objective of Satan which is still clearly evident in the world today with much antisemitism and antichristian activity in many countries.

Not only in the land of Canaan, but in all the surrounding area pagan nations were focused on worshipping and serving their nation's god or gods, even though they were completely ineffectual as the Philistines discovered when they captured the ark of the Lord.

Having been released from the pagan nation of Egypt, God wanted the people to snuff out any possibility of paganism being introduced to the new nation of Israel as it went in to possess and purify the land of Canaan. But it had to be done strictly to His type of justice.

> *"If you hear about anyone among you, within any of your cities, the Lord your God is giving you, who does evil in the sight of the Lord your God, by disobeying His covenant, by serving and worshipping other gods, the sun or the moon or any of the heavenly*

host, things I have commanded not to do, then you shall investigate all the charges thoroughly.

If it is confirmed beyond doubt that this detestable thing has been done in Israel, you shall bring that person to your city gates and stone the man or the woman to death. However, it must be on the evidence of two or three witnesses that he who is condemned shall be put to death; he shall not be put to death on the evidence of just one witness.

The witnesses shall be the first to carry out the execution, and afterward the hand of all the people. So you shall remove the evil from among you.

To ensure justice was done, God gave instructions that difficult cases should be taken to the Levitical Priests in what was to become the capital city of Jerusalem, or to a judge[36], and their verdict and sentence adhered to.

Those that try to circumvent the law, or ignore the verdict and sentence and carry out the sentence *they think* the person deserves should face the death penalty. Harsh words indeed, but necessary to maintain public order.

Rules for the king[37]

What is particularly interesting about this next statement is that God knew what the people would do in the time of Samuel.

When you enter the land which the Lord your God is giving you, and you take possession of it and live there, and you say, 'I will set a king over me like all the nations who are around me,' you shall most certainly set a king over you whom the Lord your God chooses.

However upset Samuel was that the people did not want God as their king any more, God allowed it to happen, choosing someone to whom the people would immediately respond, because of his good looks and stature. Although Saul was not a man of God's choosing because He knew Saul's faith was very weak, He allowed him to reign

---

[36] 2 Chronicles 19:8 – 11
[37] This has been covered at length in Law & Grace chapter 2 Solomon's Great Sin

in order to give time for His chosen king to mature and be ready for the task. It also gave David time to prove himself as fitting for the position of king (1 Sam. 18:5 – 8).

The time Saul tried to kill David was a time of quickly maturing the young shepherd boy and causing his character to shine demonstrating to the general population just how suitable he was for the role of king. Samuel had anointed him as king in secret.

Obviously the king had to be an Israelite because God wanted to maintain the purity of the nation. After all they were His chosen people with the purpose of illustrating to the world what being under the authority of God could mean for the ordinary citizen.

Israel was also the recipient and custodian of His statutes and regulations that were meant to regulate their personal and national life so that trough them God could bless them and demonstrate to the world His love and goodness.

Although that did not happen as it should have done, we Gentiles have the advantage of being able to study the history of Israel and God's involvement in it to provide us with a library of in-depth historical information that has the potential to enable us to get to understand God's relationship with man and His desire to become intimate with all men collectively and individually. But that can only be of value to those serious about discovering the truth.

Behind Israel's insistence in having a king was not just how they saw the way other nations were governed, but because of the corruption of the sons of Samuel. Through their complete lack of bonding with God, Samuel's sons had destroyed the faith of many Israelites because the priests were there to minister to God and in performing that duty lead the citizens into a closer relationship with God. Through their corrupt and insensitive relationship with worshippers they were effectively 'putting people off God'.

As we have already discussed the children of a devout father do not necessarily enter into a relationship with the God of their father. This was certainly the case of the sons of Eli and Samuel. Jacob's son Joseph seems to have been an exception and a type of Christ.

There were some rules for a future king to follow that would have kept him in tune with God:

1. *he shall not acquire many cavalry horses for himself, nor make the people return to Egypt in order to acquire horses in order to expand his*

military power, since the Lord said to you, 'You shall never return that way again.'

There are perhaps two points to be considered here. The first is that God was their defender. After all He had rescued them from Egypt and demonstrated His awesome power not only prior to the exodus, but in enabling the nation's volunteer army to win battles whilst travelling in the wilderness, and was fully competent to keep them safe. Just think of what God was able to accomplish through Gideon with just three hundred men against a vast army (Jdgs. 6 – 8).

The second is that God did not want them to become beholden to any other nation for their defensive forces. He alone wanted to be responsible for that, for the simple reason, if the king started to organize his defensive and attack forces it would be clear that he wanted to rely on purely human effort to defend the land of Israel or attack other belligerent nations that might be threatening them.

In this way God would be set aside, which was not part of His plan because the nation was His first born Son and at the centre of His plan of salvation for all mankind. The Messiah, the saviour of the world had to be murdered in Jerusalem as the capital of Israel even though they were occupied by the Romans.

2. *He shall not acquire many wives for himself, or else his heart will be turned away from God;*

This is exactly what happened to Solomon. His pagan wives turned him away from the faith in God.

3. *nor shall he acquire great amounts of silver and gold*

The same reason applies as for acquiring multiple wives. The visit of the Queen of Sheba shines some light on the sumptuousness and opulence of the court of King Solomon but that depended upon the servitude and suffering of the ordinary people. It was Solomon's complete lack of concern for his people, along with his departure into paganism that caused his son Rehoboam to make the decision he did which resulted in the nation being split, ten to two[38].

---

[38] This is fully explained in Law & Grace

4. *"Now it shall come about when he sits on the throne of his kingdom, he shall write for himself a copy of this law on a scroll in the presence of the Levitical priests. And the king shall keep it with him and read it all the days of his life, so that he may learn to fear and worship the Lord his God with awe-filled reverence, having profound respect for Him. Obeying the law, keeping it foremost in his thoughts and actively adhering to all the words of this law and these statutes,*

Note the king was to *he shall write for himself a copy of this law on a scroll in the presence of the Levitical priests* because by writing it out he would learn far more that he would just reading it. Just as I have learned far more by writing my books.

The law was fundamental to good order and for the nation to receive the blessings God had promised. What is more, as the incident of Solomon adjudicating in the case of the two prostitutes and the living child clearly demonstrated, the king was the final arbiter, therefore it was essential that he, above all others, knew the laws of God and understood what God expected of a man in that position. The key to this situation was that he should recognise that he was as much serving God in that position under the law as all the other Israelites:

Obeying the law, keeping it foremost in his thoughts and actively adhering to all the words of this law and these statutes, will prevent his heart from being lifted up above his countrymen with a false sense of self-importance and self-reliance so that he will not turn away or deviate in any way from the commandment, either to the right or to the left, so that he and his sons may continue to reign for a long time in in Israel.

It was not doing what God expected of all those serving the nation in that position that brought them down, particularly after the split when unbelieving, often self-appointed and self-serving kings ruled Israel.[39]

---

[39] This is fully explained in Law & Grace

Chapter 18

Regarding Priests

> "The Levitical priests, the entire tribe of Levi, shall not privately own any portion of land or inheritance with the rest of Israel; rather they shall eat the Lord's offerings by fire and His portion.

From the start God was insistent that the role of government and priestly ministry were never to be held by one man. This is because God Himself was to be the only one to hold both roles and this can be demonstrated first by the fact that king Uzziah tried to achieve that position and was struck by God with leprosy, and that the combined roles were reserved for the Messiah, who became both high priest and king of Israel after His resurrection.

Moses was chosen to be the leader of Israel and his brother Aaron was appointed to be the first high priest.

It is interesting that during the enslavement of Israel, the tribe of Levi was assign the privileges of the Egyptian priests, exempting them from the crushing labour tasks and permitting them to devote themselves to spiritual pursuits, thus providing the rest of Israel with much needed encouragement and a strong moral compass

At the time of the production of the golden calves in the wilderness it was the tribe of Levi that did not participate in the celebrations, and therefore were foremost in the execution of those that did, therefore it was clear that the tribe of Levi were better prepared to become priests, and ministers of God.

In Exodus 28 we read this:

> "Now from among the sons of Israel bring your brother Aaron near, along with his sons Nadab and Abihu, Eleazar and Ithamar, so that they may serve as priests to Me.

Aaron as the high or chief priest, and therefore in complete charge of the activities and services in the temple, had special dedicated ceremonial garments made that could only be worn whilst performing duties in the Tabernacle. Because they were holy garments, they could not be worn or used for any other activity.

His most sacred duty was to meet with God in the Most Holy Place, where the Ark of the Covenant was kept, once a year on the day of atonement.

His sons also had special, dedicated ceremonial clothes made for them, for use in the tabernacle.

It should be noted that not all that long after their dedication as priests ministering to God, the oldest two, *Nadab and Abihu* died for abusing their position (Lev. 10:1 – 3).

Levi had three sons Gershon, Kehot, and Merari. Moses, Aaron and Miriam were of the tribe of Kehot.

When transporting the Temple, during the wilderness years, each clan had different duties. Gershon was charged with transporting the Tabernacle curtains and veils of the enclosure; the clan of Merari was charged with the walls of the Tabernacle and the pillars of the enclosure; and the clan of Kehot carried the vessels used in the Tabernacle and the screen that separated the Holy and Most Holy place.

To emphasize how important it was to transport the ark according to the word of God, consider what happened when David wanted to move the ark from where it had been kept after it had been returned by the Philistines to Jerusalem.

> *From the house of Abinadab they transported the ark of God on a new cart with Uzza and Ahio driving the cart. David and all Israel celebrated with great joy before God with all their might, with songs, lyres, harps, tambourines, cymbals, and trumpets.*
>
> *When they came to the threshing floor of Chidon, Uzza put out his hand to hold and steady the ark, for the oxen pullng the cart nearly overturning it.*
>
> *The anger of the Lord burned against Uzza for touching the ark, so He struck him down and there he died before God.*

Just because God had allowed the Philistines to return the ark on a new cart pulled by cows did not mean His chosen people could do the same. It meant they had to research the word of God to find out how it should be transported and the ministering priests were employed to carry the ark, as God had instructed Moses.

What this tells us is the importance of serving God in the way He prescribes, not in the way we might find convenient.

Because they were dedicated to ministering to God, they were to depend on Him for their home, daily food and support. What might be referred to today as living by faith.

When the tabernacle / temple were operating normally the priest's food supply would come from the sacrificial offerings of the people. Specified parts of the burnt-offering, meal-offering, thank-offering and trespass-offering would belong to the priests. As servants of God, His priests were entitled to what was given to Him, and He prescribed as their due for their dedication to Him, along with heave-offerings, tithes and first-fruits.

> *"Now this shall be the priests' portion from the people, from those offering a sacrifice of either an ox or a sheep: they shall give to the priest the shoulder and the two cheeks and the stomach.*
>
> *You shall also give him the first fruits [first of the season] of your grain, your new wine, and your olive oil, and the first sheared fleece of your sheep.*
>
> *For the Lord your God has chosen the Levitical priest and his sons, to stand and serve in the name of the Lord forever.*

This puts the responsibility for the support of the ordained clergy, dedicated to ministering before the Lord upon the laity, which for the Israelites were the eleven other tribes. But this also emphasizes the responsibility of the ordained clergy to be completely God focused so that they could properly serve the people.

With our churches emptying and so many clergy doubting the Word of God, does this situation not tell us something about the state of our relationship with God?

There were further dues such as those accrued from the priests service in the slaughter of animals for ordinary consumption as opposed to those presented as an offering.

Obviously only a portion of the Levitical tribe would be stationed in Jerusalem at any time, their spiritual services being in demand throughout the country, so those living in other parts of the country would be required from time to time to journey to do duty in the temple in Jerusalem, in which case they would be included in the catering facilities as they served God in the sanctuary.

If a Levite comes from any of your cities throughout Israel where he resides, and comes to the sanctuary - the place which the Lord chooses - whenever he wishes ; then he shall serve in the name of the Lord his God, like all his fellow Levites who stand there before the Lord.

They shall have equal portions to eat, except what they receive from the sale of their fathers' estates.

Spiritism Forbidden

"When you enter the land the Lord your God is giving you, you shall not learn to practice the detestable and repulsive practices of those nations.

Not one among you shall sacrifice his son or daughter by fire, one who uses divination and fortune-telling. Nor shall anyone among you practice witchcraft, or interpret omens, or be a sorcerer, or be one of those who casts a charm or spell, or be a medium, or a spiritualist, or a necromancer [one who seeks to speak to the dead].

The realm of the spirit is an extremely dangerous area without God's protection. It is an area in which Satan and his angelic and human followers excel.

A lady caught up in witchcraft in Devon wrote a book after she had had seven evil spirits exorcized from her by a Baptist minister. On one occasion a Methodist Local Preacher, realising witches were operating in an area of Dartmoor, wanted to do something about getting rid of them. By this time the woman had become a queen of witches surrounded by a coven.

One night the man approached a little too close and she had to 'hide herself' from him. But although she tried to cast a spell on him, it had no effect because God was with him. That powerlessness over the preacher led to her seeking help and release from the power of Satan.

The danger for the people of Israel was the subtle way in which Satan enticed people into his ways, as demonstrated so clearly by his wooing of Eve and leading Adam into sin. Here God is seeking to warn the people, even before they put one foot into the land of Canaan, of the dangers that would face them

Because everyone who does these things is utterly repulsive to the Lord; and because of these detestable practices the Lord your God is driving out before you those that practice such arts.

Fortunately there was always a remnant that followed after God as that Devonian preacher who was so close to God that he was protected from the witches spells. That gives a practical demonstration of the power of God over the whole of creation both spiritual and physical.

The spiritual has no power before God and although it cannot be ignored, can only be overcome by the power of God, in His mighty and all powerful name, the name that is above every other name.

13 You shall be blameless before the Lord your God. For these nations, which you shall dispossess, listen to those who practice witchcraft and to diviners and fortune-tellers, but as for you, the Lord your God has not allowed you to do so.

Satan appears in a number of guises, especially in the form of many religions, in order to entice individuals away from the truth and thus prevent them from finding out about God and believing in Him. As a renegade spirit that sought to usurp the throne of God[40], Satan and those angels that followed him have caused multitudes of individuals and nations to experience immense suffering, hardship and chaos.

The plethora of religions even today, particularly in their opposition to Israel and Christians, provides evidence of Satan's work.

What is particularly interesting is that he hides in the background, preferring to work through individuals, organisations and governments, with many, particularly prominent leaders of governments and religious leaders accusing others of being him, but he is a spirit that cannot be seen except he reveals himself, often as an angel of light.

Even prominent scientists such as Richard Dawkins, who wrote a book called The God Delusion[41], tried to make out that even Christianity was a delusion. He was right about all other religions

---

[40] This has been dealt with in depth in The Tent of the Meeting
[41] I wrote a book in response called Assuredly God IS!

except Christianity, but by including it with all the others he was skilfully doing Satan's work.

I was told on one occasion by an Indian Hindu work colleague that Christians were hated because they believed theirs was the one true religion and therefore were devoid of religious tolerance. On an individual level we got on very well, but his thoughts about Christians was accurate up to a point.

I have never wanted to show religious intolerance because, as far as I am concerned, it is up to the individual to make the choice of what to believe. But with regard to our belief that Christianity is the only true faith; that is indisputable.

The Prophet that is to Come[42]

> *The Lord your God will raise up for you a prophet like me from among you, from your countrymen. You shall listen to him.*

It is interesting to read this prophecy of Moses, but it is even more interesting to be able to follow it up by seeing how it was fulfilled and the reaction of the Israelites, now called Jews because of the dominant tribe of Judah, when He appeared.

What is interesting is that Jews believe that this prophecy refers to other prophets, of which Moses was the spiritual father, on whom they purported to rely to hear what God wanted to say to them.

Although after the death of Moses there were many prophets called by God to pass on His message to the people, many of the descendants of those who heard what Moses had to say increasingly rebelled against and even killed those prophets (Matt. 23:27 – 39; Lk. 20:9 – 16).

But the direct defiance of those that were living when this message from Moses was fulfilled, is worth considering because, if for no other reason, it will alert all those who have committed their lives to God to be watchful for the fulfilment of other prophecies that are yet to come.

The prophet that was to come was like [not the same as] Moses. As this particular passage of Deuteronomy will have been read and studied throughout the history of Israel by many eminent rabbis, it is interesting that the association of the prophet Moses spoke about

---

[42] This subject has been dealt with in depth in Truth & Doubt.

and the prophecies concerning the arrival of the Messiah do not seem to have been linked up in the minds of the theologians of the time of Yeshua.

It is true that the prophecies concerning the coming of the Messiah are scattered throughout the First Testament from Genesis to Malachi, but the real Bible student who spent as much time in prayer as studying the text would have been led by God to correctly interpret the secret messages he had hidden in His word. Certainly Simeon and Anna did just that when the Messiah was still a baby of eight days old.

This is clarified by something the Messiah said to the religious scholars of the day:

> *You search the Scriptures, for in them you think you have eternal life; and these are they which testify of Me. But you are not willing to come to Me that you may have life.*

It seemed to have been the most inappropriate moment for the Son of God to make His appearance. The land was yet again under the yoke of an occupying foreign army, the Romans. The land was split up not in tribal territories but Roman designated regions and there were great divisions in the country.

So what was the problem with those that thought they were in tune with God but were far from Him? Here are a few possibly answers:

- They were not in a spiritual relationship with God. We know this because of what God had to do to Saul the Pharisee in the lodging house in Straight Street, Damascus for him to be transformed into the Apostle Paul.

    Blinded by the light of the risen Christ and His challenge about attacking Him, Saul was on his own in those lodgings when the Holy Spirit got to work on his mind and memory to reveal the secrets of the progressive prophetic announcements regarding the coming of the Messiah, from the moment man was evicted from God's garden to the moment of His arrival as a baby.

- They *assumed* He was born in Nazareth, not in Bethlehem without doing any investigation.

- They did not respond to the question raised by King Herod regarding where the Messiah was to be born on the arrival of the wise men. At a time when the Messiah was expected at any time, only King Herod was alerted to the possible threat to his position as king and dealt with the matter in his own murderous way. Where was the religious leaders curiousity?

  The clues were all there. The Messiah was expected anytime. Wisemen had travelled a very long way to worship a remarkable baby. They were asked by the king where the Messiah was to be born and gave the answer that He was to be born in Bethlehem and yet not once did they show any particular interest in the possibility that the Messiah had finally arrived.

- They were deaf to the report by the shepherds which was been widely broadcast by them in the area of Bethlehem.

- The miracles performed by the Messiah, even to the raising of the dead twice, when no miracles had been seen for over four hundred years?

- Not once were any of their religious elite able to outwit Him with regard to His knowledge of scripture.

- The evidence of when He was on the cross and gave up His Spirit. The skies darkening, the graves opening and the holy men of old witnessing, the temple curtain being torn from top to bottom, was all disregarded.

It was into this somewhat desperate scene that John the Baptizer suddenly appeared after four hundred years of no prophet preaching the message of God, and quoting a verse from the prophet Isaiah.

Remember there had been no prophet from God for over 400 years so the religious authorities were very curious when suddenly a priest's son, just like Jeremiah, started preaching a new gospel in the Judean wilderness. Remember that the visitation of the angel to

Elizabeth and Mary had happened over 30 years previously and the number of people who heard about those events and the birth of the two men six months apart was very limited.

> *"Repent of your sins and turn to God, for the kingdom of heaven is at hand!"*

It was Matthew who pointed out that this was the fulfilment of the prophecy of Isaiah where he said:

> *The voice of one crying in the wilderness: 'Prepare the way of the Lord Make His paths straight.*

What made this such a remarkable sight was that the prophecy of Isaiah was finally being fulfilled, because John was the voice of one crying in the wilderness. He wore clothing woven from camel hair, with a leather belt around his waist and his diet was locusts and wild honey, food that was available in the Judean wilderness where John lived.

Another feature of this story was the reaction of ordinary citizen, for they were immediately attracted to John and what he was saying. Such was the uniqueness of the man, the spiritual power of his message that the people were challenged to the extent that they were confessing their sins and being baptized by him and his disciples in the river Jordan (Matt. 3:1 – 6).

The religious elite, on the other hand, whose dull and uninspiring teaching had long had a negative effect on the ordinary citizen, were full of scepticism and criticism because their minds were blinded to the truth of God and completely unable, because of spiritual insensitivity, to appreciate the sign of the times.

John's boldness in his preaching was so out of the norm at that time that it was no wonder people were curious to find out more about him and his message. But this was John responding to the call of God and preaching God's word to the population as God gave him words to speak.

The authorities were also bound to be attracted to these events because of the huge commotion they were causing. They wanted to know what was going on, particularly when John's reaction to their presence was to denounce them in the most direct terms:

"Brood of snakes! Who warned you to flee from the wrath to come?"

Such a challenge to those who thought themselves superior to the ordinary citizens will have struck them hard, especially being demeaned so publicly in that way.

But then John added to that rebuke by announcing something rather strange that would totally confuse the very worldly religious leaders.

I baptize with water those who repent of their sins as an outward sign that they have turned to God, but He who is coming after me is so much mightier that I am not worthy even to carry His sandals (as would a slave). It is He who will baptize with the Holy Spirit and fire.

With the fiery language of John, and the fact that so many of the ordinary people were flooding to him to be baptized, the religious authorities were bound to be curious, so they sent messengers to question John, asking him if he was the Messiah, which he denied.

And they asked him, "What then? Are you Elijah?" He said, "I am not."

With John admitting that he was not Elijah the messengers brought up the other alternative:

"Are you the Prphet?"

This is the prophet spoken about by Moses in Deuteronomy 18:15 – 19. But to the frustration of the messengers from Jerusalem, John denied that he was any of those. In exasperation they then asked John the question:

"Who are you, so that we may give an answer to those who sent us? What do you say about yourself?"

In answer John repeated what Isaiah had said all those years ago, which should have satisfied them:

I am 'The voice of one crying in the wilderness: Make straight the way of the Lord,"

What this question and answer session clearly illustrates is that they did not know their scriptures very well and certainly could not realize that his answers pointed very clearly to the imminent arrival of the Messiah, who was the Prophet spoken about by Moses. So back to the prophecy of Moses.

The Lord your God will raise up for you a prophet like me from among you, from your countrymen. You shall listen to him.

Jesus said something significant and particularly relevant to our study. Consider carefully the verse above and then think about this:

... if you believe and rely on the Scriptures that were written by Moses, then you would believe Me, for he wrote about Me.

Surely that was a giveaway, but by then the religious leaders were looking at the man and not analysing what He was saying to them, bereft of any idea of His background such as where He was born and in what circumstances. Which meant that Moses warning for them to *listen to him* never happened.

False Prophets and True Prophets

In John's gospel we read that no one has seen God at any time, BUT the only begotten Son, who is in the bosom of the Father, that is He and the Father are inseparably linked, has declared Him [made Him known because He knows Him intimately]. But over time there were many bogus prophets (1 Kgs. 22:13 – 28), and for them there is this warning.

20 the prophet who presumes to speak a word in My name, which I have not commanded him to speak, or which he speaks in the name of other gods, that prophet shall die.'

21 If you say in your heart, 'How will we know and recognize the word which the Lord has not spoken?' When a prophet speaks in the name of the Lord and the thing does not happen or come true, that is the thing which the Lord has not spoken. The prophet has spoken it presumptuously; you shall not be afraid of him.

One problem with this is that sometimes the prophecy relates to something that will happen many years into the future, such as the Messianic prophecies. But the majority of false prophets would only deal with immediate concerns such as the one in 1 Kings above.

13 CRIMINAL LAW & WARFARE

Chapter 19

Criminal Law

The Lord God of Israel is a God of justice. Truth is essential to Him, therefore, even before they had put one foot into Canaan He ensured there was protection for the innocent.

Killing someone immediately causes a reaction within the family of the person killed. Life for a life. But what if the death was the result of an accident that no one could have foreseen? To prevent an injustice being done, God insisted that from thee start there had to be three safe places in central places, equidistant from each other so that they were within easy reach for such fugitives to go where angry relatives could not get at them.

Not only did God insist that there were initially three cities dedicated as safe cities, but as Israel expanded its borders, such as in the time of king David, three more cities were to be so designated.

In addition sign posts directing people to each of those cities were to be erected throughout the land making it easy for fugitives to find them.

However, those cities were not to be the hiding places for those definitely guilty of murder, especially premeditated murder. In such cases, the elders of the city in which the murder took place had the authority to send for the murderer to be extradited and returned to their city for trial and punishment.

Laws of Landmark and Testimony

*14 You shall not move your neighbour's boundary mark in the
land the Lord is giving to you, marks that were set up when the
territory was first portioned out by the forefathers.*

God was demanding honesty in everything even before they enter
the land of promise. The removal of a boundary marker by one
person in order to enlarge his own property was tantamount to theft.

The land was divided up by Joshua, Eleazar the priest and a prince
from each tribe, hence this law concerning land *portioned out by the
forefathers* was more for the generations that followed.

Because of the crude boundary marking it would not have been
easy to establish such exactness because it could well be one man's
word against another depending on how much land was taken.

This law would have extended into trespass or poaching, for
example.

*15 A single witness shall not attend a trial against a man for any
wrong or any sin which he has committed; instead only on the
testimony or evidence of two or three witnesses shall a charge be
confirmed.*

This is still a requirement in law today. Sadly there will always be
those prepared to give false witness and work in collusion. I have
already spoken about a prisoner I visited who was horrified at his trial
to hear onetime friends tell lies about him under oath. The lies will
weigh on the conscience on those witnesses who gave an oath before
the Lord to tell nothing but the truth.

*16 If a malicious witness rises up to falsely accuse another of
wrongdoing, then both parties to the controversy shall stand before
the Lord, before the priests and the judges in office at that time.*

Any intention to commit a crime is not a punishable offence
except it be followed through. To conspire to falsely accuse another
was an evil that needed to be dealt with severely but justly.

*The judges shall investigate the case thoroughly, and if the
witness is a false witness, and he has accused his brother falsely,*

then you shall do to him just as he had intended to do to his brother.
So you shall remove the evil from among you.

It must be emphasized that these proceedings were before the Lord who sees into the hearts of all men, thus it was incumbent upon the priests and judges to do their work with 'honesty of heart'. Only after very careful examination could the matter be resolved and where it became evident that the witness was indeed falsely accusing another, then the punishment had to be what the false witness had intended to happen to the accused.

With the judgement being announced to interested parties, or the general public, the intention was that such false accusations would be stopped.

> *20 Those who remain will hear and be afraid, and will never again do such an evil thing among you. You shall not show pity to the one found guilty: it shall be life for life, eye for eye, tooth for tooth, hand for hand, foot for foot.*

In sentencing the man found guilty of being a false witness to receive what they had wanted done to the one they had accused, came the principle of a *life for life, eye for eye, tooth for tooth, hand for hand, foot for foot.* However there is a vast difference between such a legitimate sentence being announced by a convened court of law and private revenge, which seemed to have become the norm even at the time of the Messiah.

This is something the Lord repudiated (Matt. 5:38-42)

> *"You have heard it said, An eye for an eye, and a tooth for a tooth: But I say unto you, That ye resist not evil: but whosoever shall smite thee on thy right cheek, turn to him the other also.*

What the Lord was doing here was to tell people that the cycle of retribution, still prevalent in the middle east today, was never ending and ultimately self-defeating and therefore needed to be stopped by not continuing the unending cycle. It was never God's intention in the first place.

Chapter 20

Laws covering warfare

Remember that these instructions were being given before the battles for possession of the land of Canaan began but were as much about future battles once they had established themselves in the land, because there had always to be an underlying sense of human kindness displayed.

There was a considerable difference between battles fought by the Israelites and the inhuman savagery promoted by the professional Assyrian army.

> *1 When you go out to battle against your enemies and see horses and chariots and people more numerous than you, do not be afraid of them; for the Lord your God, who brought you up from the land of Egypt, is with you.*

This will obviously only be legitimate when the battle is of God. Josiah, for instance, picked a fight with the Egyptian Pharaoh and lost because he should not have gone out to fight. Whereas king David always checked with the Lord not just about fighting but tactics.

> *2 When you approach the battle, the priest shall come forward and speak to the people, saying to them, 'Hear, O Israel: you are going into battle against your enemies. Do not lack courage. Do not be afraid, or panic, or tremble in fear] before them, for the Lord your God goes with you, to fight for you against your enemies, to save you.'*

Yes there was a priest appointed for war, who was there to encourage the men because fear of the battle would be as counterproductive as it was contagious.

> *5 The officers shall also speak to the soldiers, saying*

Now it was the officers turn to speak to the men. There are four specific situations where a man would not be able to give his all to the battle and was therefore told to go home:

- *'What man is there who has built a new house but not yet dedicated it?* [and lived in it] *Let him return to his house, otherwise he might die in the battle and another man would dedicate it.*

- *What man has planted a vineyard and not yet harvested its fruit? Let him return to his house, otherwise he might die in the battle and another man would begin to use its fruit.*

It is interesting that the fruit from any tree was not to be used for the first three years. An old man of the village where we once lived who helped us with the garden of our new house told us to allow the new fruit trees to 'make root not fruit' for the first few years. In Israel the crop in the fourth year was to be dedicated to God so that only on the fifth year could the fruit be harvested and used by the family.

- *who is engaged that is legally promised to a woman and has not married her? Let him return to his house, otherwise he might die in the battle and another man would marry her.'*

- *'what man is afraid and lacks courage? Let him go and return to his house, so that he does not cause his brother's courage to fail like his own.'*

Better to let them go rather than have them 'shot at dawn' for desertion.

And for those remaining:

9 And it shall be when the officers have finished speaking to the soldiers, they shall appoint commanders of armies over them.

It is important to remember that the Israeli army, also as it is today, was a part time, conscripted army with just a small proportion being professional. Until the time of the kings, particularly Solomon, it did not have a professional standing army although it did have professional mercenaries, or a king's guard.

Consider the situation Gideon was in when facing the might of the Midianite hoards (Jgs. 7:1 – 7). He started with thirty two thousand men and ended up with just 300.

> *"There are too many people with you for Me to hand over Midian to them, for with that number Israel will boast that by their own power they rescued themselves.*

The Midianites had brought Israel to its knees and caused the population to be fragmented so that most were in hiding. Already it had been God who had called the man He wanted to lead the fight to rid the country of these hoards, but knowing the vagaries of the people God wanted to ensure they could not boast about the miracle he was about to perform, because with those three hundred men and the tactics used by Gideon and what the Spirit of God did in the Midianite camp, the enemy was completely defeated

The battle had to be of God and the success attributed to Him alone. Thus it was not the number of men that mattered but their dedication.

Strategy to be used in the capture of heathen cities

This did not apply to the Canaanite cities they were going in to take over as we will see below, but to cities some distance from the land they were going in to possess.

> *10 When you advance to a city to attack it, first offer it terms of peace. If it accepts your terms of peace and opens its gates to you, then all the people who are found in it shall become your servants.*

This is the difference between the people of God and the people of Satan. War is to be the last resort so the offering of terms of peace was essential, better the people become servants than dead, because they will be able to see the way the Israelites served their God and perhaps be converted.

Whilst under Israeli suzerainty they were obliged to commit themselves to the seven commandments under which the descendants of Noah were required to live, which are: the establishments of courts of law, prohibition of blasphemy, idolatry, incest, murder, robbery and unnatural cruelty.

What this means is that the city would give tribute to Israel, as happened particularly during the reigns of king David and Solomon.

> *12 However, if the city is not willing to make peace with you, preferring to fight, then you shall lay siege to it. When the Lord your God gives it into your hand, you shall strike down all the men with the edge of the sword, saving only the women, children, the animals and everything that is in the city, all its spoil, you shall take as plunder for yourself; and you shall use the spoil of your enemies which the Lord your God has given you.*
>
> *That is what you shall do to all the cities very far away from you, which are not among the cities of these nations nearby you are to dispossess.*

This strategy was totally different to that require for clearing the land of the abhorrent practices of the nations that had corrupted the land to the extent that God wanted rid of them.

> *16 Only in the cities of the peoples that the Lord your God is giving you as an inheritance, you shall not leave alive anything that breathes, but utterly destroy them, the Hittite, the Amorite, the Canaanite, the Perizzite, the Hivite and the Jebusite, just as the Lord your God has commanded you,*
> *You will do this so that they will not teach you to act in accordance with all the detestable practices which they have done in worship and service for their gods, and thus cause you to sin against the Lord your God.*

It would be counterproductive to destroy productive fruit bearing trees, or any other tree producing harvestable produce. Therefore the Israelites were told not to follow the practices of nomadic warriors and devastate the land they were aiming to conquer.

> *19 When you besiege a city for a long time, making war against it in order to capture it, you shall not destroy its fruit-bearing trees by swinging an axe against them; for you may eat from them, and you shall not cut them down. For is the tree of the field a man, that it should be besieged (destroyed) by you?*

Only the trees which you know are not fruit trees shall you destroy and cut down, so that you may build siegeworks against the city that is making war with you until it falls.

14 SACREDNESS OF HUMAN LIFE

Chapter 21

Expiation of a Crime

> *1 If someone is found slain, lying in a field, in the land the Lord your God gives you to possess, and the killer is not known, then elders and judges shall discover the nearest city to the dead person.*

Obviously no city would want the responsibility to provide a heifer and go through the process of seeking forgiveness for this most unfortunate affair, so it was essential that judges be provided as arbiters and overseers to ascertain the nearest city to the dead man.

> *3 The elders of that city shall take a heifer of the herd, that has not been worked or pulled in a yoke, and take the heifer down to an uncultivated river valley with running water, and break the heifer's neck there in the valley.*

Sin requires forgiveness. But when approaching God for that forgiveness an animal not profaned by common use must be used.

The *uncultivated river valley with running water* was to be a rough, uncultivated, unfrequented area with a perennial brook because the running water was necessary to wash away the blood of the sacrifice.

This is an important lesson for believers today because if we are in anyway casual in our prayers and requests, then God will take no notice. Are we passionate about seeking after God, because He has no interest in those that are half-hearted or who are merely paying lip service to Him even though He is prepared to listen if we approach Him with the right attitude. Don't think that God is an easy go lucky human being type of person. He is not.

> *5 Then the priests from that city, the sons of Levi, shall come near because they have been chosen by the Lord your God to serve Him and to bless in the Name of God and settle every dispute and every violent crime.*

Everything had to be done correctly when seeking forgiveness of God. It is no good trying to cut corners, because God will not accept anything but the best, as we have already seen. Just as king David found out when transporting the ark without doing it as prescribed.

Where the people involve God, such as in this case, only those commissioned by God to serve Him as priests could officiate.

> *6 All the elders of the nearby city shall wash their hands over the heifer whose neck was broken; and they shall say,*
>
> > *'Our hands did not shed this blood,*
> > *nor did our eyes see it.*
> > *Forgive Your people Israel*
> > *whom You have redeemed, O Lord,*
> > *and do not put the guilt of innocent blood*
> > *among Your people Israel.'*
>
> *And the guilt of the blood of the murdered man shall be forgiven them. So shall you remove the guilt of innocent blood from among you, **when you do what is right in the sight of the Lord**.*

According to Hebrew law, murder is not only a crime against an individual created in the image of God, but also a sin against God Himself. We have only to consider the sacrifices and their accent on the shedding of blood and what God said to Noah:

Whoever unlawfully sheds man's blood,
By man, via judicial government, shall his blood be shed,
For in the image of God He made man.

Which means all life is sacred and must be respected. Where a murder takes place and the perpetrator flees without being seen, he would have been seen by God, but it was necessary for the people nearby to be released from any guilt of the man's death.

Domestic Relations

10 When you go out to battle against your enemies, and the Lord your God hands them over to you and you lead them away captive, and you see a beautiful woman among the captives, and desire her and would take her as your wife,

There is much to be wary about seeing things at face value. Here we have a situation where a captive woman, who is effectively defenceless and totally dependent upon the Israelis for her protection and wellbeing, is noticed and admired by an Israeli man who desires her and wants to marry her.

It is essential that we are not mercenary here, remembering that the woman has been captured and in the process has possibly lost members of her family, certainly the men folk. Therefore she must be allowed time to grieve.

Remember that in this situation she does not have a say in choosing a husband for herself, rather she has been chosen by someone she does not know, who is of a completely different culture, so she finds herself in a surreal situation and marriage is an intimate affair. This is a situation that God foresaw in a sinful and violent world, which is still the case today in many parts of the world.

Therefore, unlike with heathen tribes who rape and pillage with seeming impunity, God lays down instructions to bring order and respect to protect such vulnerable women.

12 then you shall take her to your house, and she shall shave her head and trim her nails in preparation for mourning. She shall take off the clothes of her captivity and remain in your house, and weep in mourning for her parents for a full month.

It is possible that this period of mourning and separation with her head shaved was to dissuade, or have the suitor think carefully about his intention to marry this women.

After all he was not marrying an inanimate object, but a unique living person created in the likeness of God who had had a completely different life to his and who was undoubtedly inwardly terrified of the future whilst full of sorrow for what had passed. It also gave her time to get acclimatized to her new surroundings.

She also has feelings and could well have been romantically attracted to a man of her own nation.

13b Only after that may you go in to her and be her husband and she shall be your wife.

Marriage gave the woman respectability and put responsibility firmly on the man to look after her. It also acted to prevent against the worse manifestations of the unbridled sexual passions of men.

But this is the problem with desire without first having time to get to know each other. In the excitement of the victory, passions could well have run high and lustful desire can so easily come to the fore:

14 But if you find that you have no delight or pleasure in her,

In other words if you find that the two of you are incompatible, which could easily have been the case because there would have bound to be some reluctance on the part of the woman whose emotions would have been a very difficult thing to control in a forced situation in a foreign land, especially in the intimacy of marriage.

It does not necessarily follow that they were incompatible, but this arrangement was written down as a worst case scenario.

then you shall let her go wherever she wishes. You certainly shall not sell her for money; you shall not deal with her as a slave or mistreat her, because you have humbled her by forced marriage.

Respect for others is central to God's requirement for His people. The man has forced himself on the woman by claiming her as his wife even though they had never previously met, and without her tacit approval and with the difference in cultures being a genuine problem.

Having humbled her through his selfish desire for her looks and body rather than love, to then reject her is contemptible. The woman still being at his mercy, God ensured that she was not further humiliated by being sold or use as a slave, but given her complete freedom.

> *15 If a man has two wives, one loved and the other unloved, and both have born him sons, and the firstborn son belongs to the unloved wife, then on the day when he wills his possessions to his sons, he cannot treat the son of his loved wife as firstborn in place of the son of the unloved wife who is the true firstborn.*

This is reminiscent of Jacob with Leah and Rachel with the loved and unloved being relative terms. It is more likely to be a matter of preference. Sarah's pride in Isaac and horror at the thought of Ishmael, as the true eldest son taking over from Abraham, gives us a flavour of the tension that can accumulate in a family situation.

Here is a law laid down that the father has to acknowledge the true firstborn as his heir.

> *17 Instead he shall acknowledge the son of the unloved as the firstborn, by giving him a double portion of all that he has, for he was the beginning of his strength; to him belongs the right of the firstborn.*

It is interesting how God anticipates problems within families as well as national situations. Just as God required respect so He also insisted on respect within families.

In Exodus 20:12 (cf. Deut. 5:16; Matt. 15:3 – 9; Eph. 6:1 – 4) we read this:

> *"Honour, that is respect, obey, and care for, your father and your mother, so that your days may be long in the land the Lord your God is giving to you.*

The whole basis of the Judeo/Christian faith is founded on respect starting with man's respect for God. Without that basic building block, human life on this earth will be a disaster. It is what Satan is trying to achieve with his mission to bring chaos to the whole world. It is therefore up to all God focused individuals to set a high standard.

'Honour (respect, obey, care for) your father and your mother, as the Lord your God has commanded you, so that your days [on the earth] may be prolonged and so that it may go well with you in the land which the Lord your God gives you.

A son, or a daughter, that is out of control is a threat to the life of a family and then society as a whole. It was important, therefore to ensure that any wayward juvenile was dealt with very firmly.

18 If any man has a stubborn and rebellious son who will not obey the voice of his father or mother, and when they reprimand and discipline him, he will not listen to them, then his father and mother shall take hold of him, and take him to the elders of his city at the gateway of his hometown.

The parents of an insubordinate son that is out of control and they are   unable to do anything more, were to take their son to the elders of the city who had greater corrective powers. The parents put their case to the city authorities in regard to their son:

20 They shall say to the elders of his city, 'This son of ours is stubborn and rebellious; he will not obey us, he is a glutton and a drunkard.'

It was within the powers of the city elders to order him to be stoned, because such a rebellious son had the potential to do great harm within the social fabric of the city

21 Then all the men of his city shall stone him to death; so you shall remove the evil from among you, and all Israel will hear of it and be afraid.

This next situation is very important because it has clear connotations for the death of the Messiah. The methods of execution in ancient Israel were stoning, burning, the sword or strangulation. Hanging was sometimes added after death as a further deterrent (Josh. 10:26)

Although crucifixion, nailing a person to a cross of wood in order to prolong the agony of death for days was a Roman invention, there are certain aspects of the killing of a sinful person and the subsequent treatment of the body described in these verses that so neatly fit the method and consequences of the death of the Lamb of God that it is well we study it more closely.

22 And if a man has committed a sin worthy of death,

Throughout the Torah there is this very clear instruction that all the animals offered up for sacrifice had to be pure. Because God is purity itself, nothing but pure offerings were to be made, indeed it was the offering of defective animals with the suspect attitude of the offeror that got the Israelites into a great deal of trouble (Is. 1; Mal. 1) as we have already discovered.

As we are dealing with sinful man, no man alive could become a pure sacrifice because, as Paul so eloquently put it, *For all have sinned and come short of the glory of God.*

Christ Jesus was the only perfect man that ever lived on this earth. Born of God, the Son was involved in the creation and entered the earth as a baby by way of a virgin, according to prophecy.

There is a twofold reason for the virgin birth. The first is that Adam was accused of sin when he ate of the fruit of the forbidden tree. He had no excuse because the warning of eternal death was given to him, not Eve.

Therefore had Joseph been involve the baby would have been contaminated by sin because inherent sin passes down through the male line. The second is that God first had to choose the mother of the body for His Son, and then cause her to become pregnant at the precise time necessary for the Christ to be born a man.

The Messiah was sent to pass onto the people the message the Father wanted them to hear. Inevitably those far from God objected to His teaching and wanted Him killed. This was the opposition prepared ready to build up the momentum that would lead to the accusations that eventually caused the death of the Lamb of God.

Although, as has already been pointed out, crucifixion was a Roman invention, a tree was used on which the unfortunate criminal was nailed, his body hanging on the nails. What is particularly interesting is that the text reads:

*and he is put to death, **and** you hang him on a tree*

which could easily mean that he is first put to death, and then you hang him on a tree to make an example of him.

However, it is important not to be pedantic and understand the spirit of what is being said, because without the ***and***, it follows that the Messiah was put to death ***by*** hanging Him on a tree with nails rather than rope.

What is also interesting is that it was the chief priests and elders (the members of the Sanhedrin) asking for the Lord to be crucified (Matt. 27:20 – 23), not the Roman governor, stirring up the crowd to get what they wanted.

So it would seem that this prophetic message, even though the Israeli method was to kill and then hang the criminal; at the time of Christ the Jewish leaders were more than happy for this imposter to be nailed to a tree by way of crucifixion.

23 his body shall not hang all night on the tree,
but you shall most certainly bury him on the same day

Remembering that the Hebrew day was from 18:00 hours to 1800 hours, which meant the day started with evening. We read that at the end of the day Joseph from Arimathea came to claim the body and put it in a newly dug tomb in which no one had previously been laid to rest.

The Hebrew day is divided into 12 hours from dawn to dusk. According to Acts 3:1 the nineth hour is the hour of prayer. Working on this understanding of dawn to dusk, daylight hours, which means the ninth hour is roughly 15:00 to 16:00 (3 to 4 pm). This means that the Lord's body hung on the cross until dusk which could have been another three hours.

because he who is hanged is cursed by God,
so that you do not defile your land

which the Lord your God gives you
as an inheritance.

This not only puts the seal of approval on this being prophetic of the type of death of the Messiah was to suffer, but with regard to ritual impurity the corpse, especially that of a man cursed of God, was a matter of grave concern.

It must not be left out for it to decompose and fall apart, which it would have done in that climate, but it should equally not become food for the birds. That would be a disgrace.

15 LAWS — VARIOUS

Chapter 22

1 You shall not witness your countryman's ox or sheep straying away or being stolen, without taking action to rescue them returning them to him.

2 If the owner is not around or you do not know him, you shall take it to your house, and look after it until he searches for it; then you shall return it to him.

3 You shall do this with his donkey or with his garment or with anything that your countryman has lost and you have found. You are not allowed to ignore your duty to help them.

Echoing Exodus 22:4, 5 these few verses make a bold statement that we are all responsible for helping our neighbour whether or not we know him and no matter whether he is a friend or foe. God is here emphasizing the need for absolute honesty.

4 You shall not be a witness to your countryman's donkey or his ox fall down along the road, and not help them; you shall certainly help him lift it up.

This establishes the need for neighbourliness because it brings about social cohesion and unity. Not to do so is theft.

*5 A woman shall not wear a man's clothing, nor shall a man put
on a woman's clothing; for whoever does these things is utterly
repulsive to the Lord your God.*

When God made man He made them very distinctly male and
female. As soon as we start messing around with this creational
arrangement then we are upsetting the balance of nature that God
established, and means that all those that try to promote sexual
deviation will discover all too late that they have been rebelling
against God and will reap the consequences.

For same sex couples who desire children, it is interesting that
they have to resort to members of the opposite sex to provide them
either with a female body in which the sperm of a man through
artificial means is united with a woman's egg and allowed to grow
and be born into the world. Or in the case of women for one of the
women to be artificially inseminated [no physical sexual contact] and
for the baby to grow and be born. That is not how God planned
families

We must never forget that this is God's world of which we are not
only custodians, but a created part and we are not entitled to make
changes, merely take care of it. He designed and created it because
He wanted to love it, but man has corrupted it beyond measure.

The creation was designed to be the antechamber to heaven, a
testing ground in which man (referring to both man and wo-man)
lived his life prior to entering into His eternal rest.

Over time in the world, dominated by Satan, the dividing lines
between the sexes has been blurred causing confusion and
psychological problems, particularly amongst the young.

There are now several laws that are interesting but not particularly
pertinent to this study so here they are listed.

o   Verse 7 - the care of nature and respect of motherhood.
     The sustainability of nature is here implied.

o   Verse 8 - Health and safety are not new. God produced
     the first Health and Safety instructions. Safety railings
     around a flat roof is not just sensible but obvious.

o   Verse 9 – purity of the grape is essential for all
     connoisseurs. Mixing of the produce, blending the wine,
     is allowed. Corrupting the seed is not allowed.

o   God wanted to instil into His people about those animals that are associated with sacrifice and those that were not.

Not only were they to be kept separate as far as sacrifices were concerned, but also in regard to working with them.

Besides the fact that the size, strength and temperaments of the two animals are so different. Scripture tells us that we must not be unequally yoked, a believer with an unbeliever, and this as emphasized in this law where *You shall not plow with an ox and a donkey together,* a clean with an unclean animal. This might seem rather pedantic, but what it tells us is that, as believers, we cannot separate our faith from our everyday life. Just as with the grape vine, there must be consistency.

o   What the pagans do you must not do. The Israelites must keep themselves separate both in worship and the way they lived their lives. The pagan's believed a fabric of a blend of wool and linen was magical. Satan is subtle and can easily draw a person into sin by playing on a person's conscience, so the lord is here warning them to be very careful what they wear to prevent putting themselves in any danger of Satanic attacks.

o   These cords were to be a reminder to the wearer of the uniqueness of Israel in the sight of God and his duty to withstand temptation.

The law of morality

It is very dangerous to view these laws against the morality of those of today. For a start there are many statutory laws today that are directly contrary to scripture such as abortion, same sex marriage and much more. Also in many ways the standard of public morality today is very low. It is a jungle out there.

Rather they need to be considered and assessed by the morality at the time.

Take for instance where a man takes a wife, has sex with her but is not 'satisfied' with her, probably because the man entered into the marriage to satisfy his sexual urge and not to love and respect her, so falsely accuses her of not being a virgin in order to get out of the marriage.

If her parents can provide evidence of her virginity and the case goes before the elders of the city and the man is proven guilty of false accusations, then he will be fined a large sum of money, possibly receive 39 lashes (being chastised) and be married to her for the rest of his life. Notice no divorce possible.

However if the charge is true, then the woman will be stoned outside her parent's home.

For those committing adultery both will be put to death, meaning that at the time of Moses there were no double standards. This is particularly interesting because of the account of the woman caught in the act of adultery (Jn. 8:1 – 11) and brought before Jesus by some scribes and Pharisees.

The critical point is, if she was caught in the act of committing adultery, then there had to be a man involved. But these religious men had focussed this accusation purely on the woman. Interesting to see how far the Jews had deviated from the laws of Moses.

For an engaged woman to be violated by a man in a city, except the woman cry out for help, both shall be stoned.

For an engaged woman to be violated by a man in the country, only the man shall be stoned, assuming that the woman cried out for help but no one was near to provide help. Such a law puts the responsibility on men to behave themselves and avoid contacting an engaged woman alone in the countryside.

In the case where a man violates a virgin in the countryside, and they are discovered, the man must pay the girl's father fifty shekels of silver and she will become his wife and he can never divorce her.

A son cannot marry his father's widow.

The sexual urge in both men and women can become intense in certain situations. These laws put the responsibility on the man to show constraint.

Chapter 23

Those excluded from the Assembly

In China during the time of the Emperors, men chosen to serve in the Royal Palaces had to have their sexual parts removed, becoming eunuchs to prevent any sexual activity with any of the Emperor's women. The Ethiopian treasurer to Candice the Ethiopian queen to whom Philip preached on the road from Jerusalem to Gaza was a eunuch. This was also prevalent amongst some heathen cults. They were excluded from the congregation of Israel.

Children from an adulterous of incestuous relationship as laid down in Leviticus 18 and 20 shall also be excluded for a long time, not just ten years. God's people had to be pure and any form of sexual deviancy had to be stamped out.

Moabites and Ammonites were the descendants of Lot's daughters, and born from an incestual relationship. Only Moabites sold bread to Israel during their journey to the promised land, but the people of Ammon did not even do that. Also it was Barak of Moab that hired Balaam to curse Israel

Therefore although a male of either of those tribes could not become a member of the congregation of Israel, there was not the same restriction on proselytized females from marrying into Israel. After all Ruth, who married Boaz, was a Moabitess becoming an ancestor of king David.

> *Nevertheless, the Lord your God was not willing to listen to Balaam, but turned the curse into a blessing because the Lord your God has loved you. You shall be indifferent to them all your days.*

Because Jacob and Esau were blood brothers it was important that there should be no animosity towards their descendants and they should not be excluded from the congregation of Israel. Neither should Egyptians be excluded because although Israel was oppressed in Egypt, it was entirely the responsibility of the Pharaoh, not the people, who also suffered particularly during the plagues.

Second group of miscellaneous laws

> *9 When you go out as an army to fight your enemies, you shall keep yourselves from every evil thing.*

God is pure, which requires all those serving God to be pure, keeping themselves from personal and moral pollution because the army was hallowed by the Divine Presence. God was fighting for them and with them.

Uncleanliness inevitably leads to ungodliness by way of decaying morals, religious purity and even the elementary rules of sanitation. For Israel, the strict observance of such things demonstrated that they were serving a higher power.

> *10 If there is any man among you becomes ceremonially unclean because of the emission of semen (Lev. 15:16), then he must go outside the camp; and shall not return until the evening when he shall bathe in water, and at sundown he may return to the camp.*

Good sanitation is essential for the prevention of disease, and here God is providing instruction in the form of laws to ensure all human excrement is buried so that contamination, particularly accidental contamination, is avoided.

There had to be a place selected outside the camp where holes could be dug to accommodate all human excrement which could then be filled in to ensure hygienic conditions were maintained.

> *14 Since the Lord your God walks in the midst of your camp to rescue you and defeat your enemies before you, your camp must be undefiled, unsullied for He must not see anything inside the camp that is indecent among you or He will turn away from you.*

It must be remembered that the Israelites were once slaves in Egypt. So to go from being a slave to owning slaves would be matter of deep regret, particularly as it was God that rescued them and it was He who was giving them a land filled with milk and honey and promising to bless them. So why deny freedom to other human beings created in the image of God just as they were? The victim becoming the oppressor.

It is not surprising that God sought to establish a law that undermined the keeping of slaves.

> *15 You shall not hand over an escaped slave to his master. You shall allow him to live among you, in the place he chooses in one of your cities where it pleases him; you shall neither mistreat or oppress him.*

Notice that freedom can be made to feel sweet for him, which was the reverse of the treatment of slaves in many of the other nations. What is also very interesting is the attitude of Roman and other slave owner who become believers in Christ. Having been freed from the slavery of sin and the world, they had to quickly adopt a complete change of attitude to their own slaves.

It is interesting how Paul handled the situation of the escaped slave Onesimus when he sent him back to his owner Philemon. Certainly there was no trade in slaves in Israel.

Temple virgins, male and female, were a common sight in certain pagan nations. As part of God's plan to clean up and purify the land of Canaan when Israel went in to possess the land and subdue it was the removal of all pagan practices Hence:

17 There shall be no cult of harlotry among the daughters of Israel, nor shall there be a similar cult of sodomy among the sons of Israel.

One of the key accusations God made against the ten tribes of Israel was that of spiritual harlotry, particularly through Hosea. If God did not want Israel to play the harlot, surely it was equally as bad for men to repeat the physical activities of Sodom and Gomorrah. It is a contradiction to believe that our personal physical lives can be completely separate from our spiritual relationship with God.

All the Laws God gave the people through Moses brought together the personal lives of men and their relationship with Him, because evil in life prevented any relationship with God.

Not only is the practice of an immoral life rejected by God, any earnings received from such activities could not be used in the temple sanctuary in the fulfilment of a vow or any other religious purpose.

The same applied to any money received for the immoral conduct of a male person engaged in sexual perversion as a religious rite. Such people were referred to as dogs. Both the gift and the giver are repulsive to God to whom the purity of every aspect of life is of paramount importance.

Israel was to be an exception in the way the people not only lived their lives, but the way they behaved in relation to each other within the nation. There will always be those whose business skills far exceeded those of others, thus accumulating riches.

In Israel God wanted mutual support to separate them from members of the surrounding nations. If a brother fell on hard times it was up to those that were able to give him support to do so in order for him, by his own industry, to get himself back on his feet without seeking to add to his burden by making money out of the situation.

It was permissible to loan money to a member of other nations in the course of their business and earn interest, but where the Gentile needed money for his subsistence then the same rules were to apply as if he was an Israelite.

It was essential that any dealings an individual had with God was honoured. No one needed to make a vow before God, but if one is made then prompt action was required to fulfil the vow. Because God could not be seen did not mean that He was not there, rather He even knows what you are thinking therefore any promise made before God must be fully fulfilled.

Hunger not greed may be satisfied when going through a neighbours vineyard, because it is not only his property but could well be his income.

> 24 *When you enter your neighbour's vineyard, you may eat your fill of grapes, as many as you please, but not put any in your basket to take with you.*
>
> 25 *When you come into the standing grain of your neighbour, you may pluck the ears of grain with your hand, but you shall not harvest your neighbour's standing grain.*

The second is reminiscent of the time when the Lord disciples began to pluck heads of grain to eat as they were passing through a grain field because they were hungry (Matt. 12:1).

Chapter 24

The law of Divorce

This is not a law instituting or commanding divorce. The Lord Jesus said:

> *Pharisees came to Jesus to test Him, and asked Him, "According to Scripture, is it lawful for a man to divorce his wife*

and send her away?" He asked to them, "What did Moses command you?" They replied, "Moses allowed a man to write a certificate of divorce and to send her away."

Jesus said to them, "Because of your hardness of hearts, your callous lack of concern for your wives and the provision of God Moses wrote this precept.

But from the beginning of creation God made them male and female. So for this reason a man shall leave his father and his mother in order to establish a home with his wife, and the two shall become one flesh; so that they are no longer two, but are united becoming one flesh.

Therefore, what God has united and joined together, man must not separate by divorce."

When a man marries and finds something indecent or unacceptable in his wife, anything that could cause embarrassment or a problem of chastity that causes him to lose interest in her and he writes her a certificate of divorce and she leaves his house, and if she then marries another man who either gives her a certificate of divorce or dies, the first husband cannot remarry her.

What this precept was seeking to do was to prevent the easy passage of a woman from one man to another. A woman is not a *thing* but a moral personality.

What is particularly interesting about this precept is that it appears to demonstrate a man's total lack of love and concern for the woman, who appears to be but a chattel.

Jesus points out to those hard-hearted, law focused religious bigots that the woman is as important to God as the man, and Paul writing to the Ephesian church, calls on the men to love their wives as Christ loved the church, putting a completely different emphasis on the uniqueness of the marriage relationship.

Bonding in marriage is essential, especially during the first year. Here God wanted the couple to be united as one flesh and have time to build up their relationship before the man was required to go into battle or be involved in any other public duty or responsibility for one year.

Depriving people of the means of earning a living, by using tools of the trade, such as a millstone, as security for a debt was tantamount to depriving him of life and was strictly forbidden.

For a man to kidnap another Israelite and treat him violently or sell him as a slave, then the kidnapper shall die.

During an outbreak of leprosy, be careful and observe the directives of the Levitical priests God had appointed. And remember all that God did to Miriam on the road after leaving Egypt.

Trust was essential within a community, and there were elaborate precautions to prevent excessive indebtedness. A lender was not allowed to enter the property of the borrower (v11), to prevent excessive pressure to repay and to particularly allow the borrower to retain some sense of respectability.

Just because he needed help at a difficult time there was no reason to be disrespectful, but honour his place in society. Therefore it was important for the lender to wait outside the property and for the borrower to bring to him the pledge (security deposit).

In the case of a poor man the lender shall not keep the pledge overnight (v12), because it could be a cloak or some other essential item, and such an act of consideration and kindness would earn the lender merit in the sight of God .

Payment of wages to a workman must be prompt (v15). Remember what the Lord said about wages being given at the end of the day before the sun set (Matt. 20:8):

> *When evening came, the owner of the vineyard said to his manager, 'Call the workers and pay them their wages, beginning with those hired last and ending with those hired first.'*

And in Leviticus 19:13b
,

> *You shall not withhold the wages of a hired man overnight until morning.*

The reason for this is that those available for hire will be poor and not always have work (Matt. 20:1 – 7):

> *The owner of a vineyard went out again about the sixth hour (noon) and the ninth hour (3:00 p.m.), to hire workmen for His vineyard, and did the same about the eleventh hour (5:00 p.m.) he went out and found others standing around, and he said to them, 'Why have*

you been standing here idle all day?' They answered him, 'Because no one hired us.' He told them, 'You go into the vineyard also.'

This parable was all about those that worked for the Lord. They must not expect to earn more than anyone else because working for God is sufficient reward, it is also about fairness in dealing with those working for you. I also mean that those who worked for God all their lives met with those who did so only in their later years should not be looked down on. No matter how long you have served the Lord the reward would be the same for all.

In a world where whole families could be punished for the actions of just one member (v16), or the child suffer for the father's error, or vice versa, this law was revolutionary and was in opposition to Babylonian law. Each family member must pay for their individual actions.

It is clear that many of the laws included in Deuteronomy have at the heart concern for the unfortunate, the impoverished and defenceless members of society. As the Lord said, *the poor you will always have with you.*

Because of sin it is everyone for themselves and those that are bright and in fortunate circumstances live like lords whilst for others disaster or unfortunate decisions or circumstances can cause them to drop to the level of the destitute with no friends to help them. Such were orphans, widows the poor and those with disabilities including the lack of the mental prowess to elevate themselves out of difficulties.

This is where the memory of the situation their ancestors found themselves in when God rescued them and then gifted them the land in which they were now living is so very important, which is why God kept reminding them of all that He had done for the nation since He rescued them from Egypt and why it was so important for them to worship and serve Him. After all, what He had done for their ancestors He could do for them and more.

17 You shall not pervert the justice due a stranger or an orphan, nor seize a widow's garment as loan security. But you shall remember that you were a slave in Egypt, from where the Lord your God redeemed you; therefore I am commanding you to be obedient to this law.

What makes the following three instructions so pertinent is the account of Ruth the Moabitess gleaning in the field of Boaz and then marrying him. It is a beautiful story about a young woman, descended from the elder daughter of Lot, the nephew of Abraham, and therefore a distant relative of Naomi and Boaz.

But God used this lovely and devoted young lady in the ancestral line of king David and the Messiah (Ruth 2, 3 : see Lev. 19:9, 10)

> *19 When you harvest your grain and have forgotten a sheaf in the field, you shall not go back to get it; leave it for the stranger, the orphan, and the widow, so that the Lord your God may bless you in all the work of your hands.*
>
> *When you beat olives off your trees, do not search through the branches again; leave whatever is left shall be for the stranger, for the orphan, and for the widow.*
>
> *When you gather the grapes of your vineyard, you shall not remove all the grapes but leave some be for the stranger, for the orphan, and for the widow.*
>
> *Think carefully about when your ancestors were slaves in the land of Egypt; therefore I am commanding you to consider carefully about the stranger, the orphan, and the widow.*

Such is God's concern for all people.

Chapter 25

Proportionate punishment

> *1 Any dispute between men that goes to court, when the judges decide the case between them, and they judge in favour of the innocent and condemn the guilty, if the sentence given to the guilty man is for him to be beaten, the judge shall make him lie down and be beaten in his presence with the number of lashes in proportion to his offense.*
>
> *He may have him beaten up to forty times, but no more. He is not to be beaten with more stripes than these and he is not to be treated like an animal in your sight.*

The trial had to be fair, without the use of torture to extract a confession, or evidence from witnesses. Once found guilty the punishment was to be carried out without delay, which would have caused less stress than having the punishment delayed, and whilst under the control of the Judges, the correct number of lashes would be metered out, using a leather belt which would have been readily available. Also the number of lashes was to be in accordance with the physical strength and state of the offender.

Paul confessed that he had received 40 lashes less one on several occasions.

The statement *he is not to be treated like an animal in your sight* is interesting because up to his punishment he is referred to as the wicked man, but immediately after the punishment it was important to let his past be forgotten and be received once again into the brotherhood of Israel.

What is very sad for all offenders in the UK, even after the punishment, particularly a term of imprisonment, has been served, as far as the public is concerned once a criminal, always a criminal making it nearly impossible for some men and women to start a new life and succeed except where there is someone willing to give them personal support.

It has been beneficial to give that support and experience all that released prisoners have had to suffer once back out in the big bad world where the chance to make a new life is severely limited by those that need to receive forgiveness.

The difficulty is those that really are of a criminal mind taking advantage of any kind soul willing to help, spoiling it for the many so that intuition is always required to identify the hardened criminal.

> 4 *You shall not muzzle the ox while he is threshing thus preventing it from eating any of the grain.*

What is particularly interesting about this sentence is the relationship of man with the animals.

> *Then God said, "Let the earth bring forth living creatures according to their kind: livestock, crawling things, and wild animals of the earth according to their kinds"; and it was so.*

But this did not happen in regard to mankind. It is important to note that God's decision to make man was a deliberate act. The Bible states that God said, *Let us make man*, which, in a special sense, means that mankind is the intentional creation of God, rather than *Let the earth bring forth*.

The additional statement,

in Our image, according to Our likeness

What we can derive from this is that man was to be given His characteristics, which were divine [Adam was spiritually as pure as God when he was first created], along with immortality [God having breathed a portion of His Spirit into Adam], so like his creator not only would he live after his physical death, but he was also given a spiritual personality with moral freedom and will, capable of knowing and loving God and having intimate spiritual communion with Him.

This was something not afforded to any other part of creation. It is man alone that can guide his actions according to reason.

As the psalmist wrote this assessment of man (Ps. 8):

You have made him a little lower than the angels.
You have crowned him with glory and honour.
You made him to have dominion
over the works of Your hands;
You have put all things under his feet

There is therefore a clear separation between man and the animal kingdom, which means that it is man's clear responsibility before God to look after His creation. Where it says:

"Be fruitful, multiply, and fill the earth, and subdue it putting it under your power; and rule over the fish of the sea, the birds of the air, and every living thing that moves upon the earth."

it is clear that man is being given dominion over all that God had created. But notice that it was restricted to all that lived on the earth, the control of the environment and much else remained under God's control.

What is also emphasized in that first chapter of the first book is the principle of the dominance of the spiritual over the physical. Notice that during the creation at each stage God said that it was good. We have only to see the amazing programmes on the television about the natural world to become aware of the incredible care in which God designed and created every aspect of every living thing on the earth.

We are told that it was the Spirit of God hovering over the surface of the earth that brought it all to pass; which is why when the Messiah was living on the earth, it was that same Spirit that caused the dead to come to life, the storm stilled, the darkness to come over the earth when the Messiah was suffering on the cross.

If God not only created the whole of the earth and the surrounding cosmos, but also loved man so much that He provided a saviour to save man, man, as the spirit in charge of looking after the earth, should have the same concern for all living creatures, and seek to ensure they do not suffer.

It is true Noah was the first person to be allowed to eat meat, and the slaughter of certain animals were singled out to be offered for sacrifice for sin, but killed in a non-cruel way by the severing of all major blood vessels with a very sharp knife by a skilled operator, nowhere in scripture is cruelty to animals permitted, and with the ox treading the corn and not being able to sustain itself, we have a prized example of how God wants us to care for His creation because it does not have a life after death as we do.

There is just one other lesson that we need to learn and that is, God made man dominant over the earth, not animals.

The problem of a brother dying without issue is complex, an understanding of which would not be of benefit to us today. Nor the one concerning the wife seeking to stop a fight that involves her husband.

However it is interesting that Sadducees who do not believe in the resurrection [life after death as described above] asked the Lord, If all seven brothers ended up marrying a woman but without issue, in the resurrection whose wife is she? (Matt. 22:22 – 33). His answer illustrates just how essential is our study of the First Testament.

First of all He accuses them of not studying the scriptures, which was their main occupation, because as we have seen above, it clearly teaches about the resurrection. Not only that but He had demonstrated to them the power of God to bring back life to the dead son of a widow (Lk. 7:12 – 15), Lazarus (Jn. 11:1 – 44) and the daughter of Jairus (Lk. 8:49 -56). Did not Elisha not bring a child back to life? (2 Kgs. 4:32 – 37)

Jesus tells them:

> *You are all wrong because you know neither the Scriptures which teach about the resurrection, nor about the power of God for He is able to raise the dead.*

This highlights the bigoted attitude of the religious elite. Surely they accepted the book of Genesis, after all the Torah [the first five books of Moses] from which they were quoting was their most sacred possession. If God is Spirit, and was powerful enough to create all that existed, and He was alive before the creation, there had to be a spiritual world outside of the physical world that they knew and in which they lived.

> *In the resurrection men do not marry nor are women given in marriage, but like angels in heaven they neither marry nor produce children.*
>
> *But as to the resurrection of the dead, have you not read what God said: 'I am the God of Abraham, and the God of Isaac, and the God of Jacob'? Therefore He is not the God of the dead, but of the living."*
>
> *When the crowds heard this, they were astonished at His teaching.*

The expression *so that your days may be long in the land which the Lord your God gives you* is significant in that the Israelites were require to obey God's laws with honesty, discretion, integrity and in the spirit in which they were given. As we have seen above, until Satan had a hand in man's relationship with God, man was pure (innocent) in his initially created state.

With the choosing of Israel, God wanted to encourage a nation of God focused people to live by rules that demonstrated His Divinity and authority over every aspect of His creation. Hence the need for honesty in using accurate weights and measures because those that are devious are *utterly repulsive to the Lord your God.* The prevailing practice in some nations was to use large weights for buying and small weights for selling.

This rule was about far more than honest dealing. It went to the heart of society because fair dealing in trade was central to the everyday life of every individual. It is said that a kingdom based on truth and justice will stand, because trust and social cohesion, as well as a sense of security, is the result.

> *17 "Remember what Amalek did to you along the road when you came from Egypt, 18how he met you along the road and attacked all the stragglers at your rear when you were tired and weary; and he did not fear God.*
>
> *19Therefore when the Lord your God has given you rest from all your surrounding enemies, in the land which the Lord your God gives you as an inheritance to possess, you shall wipe out the memory of Amalek from under heaven; you must not forget.*

What the tribe of Amalek did to the Israelite stragglers was an attack on God. Although the guiding principle for the nation was justice and brotherly love, in perpetrating a merciless and cowardly act on defenceless people, the people of Amalek's complete lack of natural justice in relation to their fellow man were abhorrent to God and had therefore forfeited all claim to mercy.

16 DIVINE PROVIDENCE

Chapter 26

First Fruits

> *The earth is the Lord's, and the fullness thereof,*
> *The world, and those who dwell in it.*

Because God created all things and is responsible for the increase of the produce of the womb, the crops of the field and new born of the herd, particularly of those that love Him, He deserves the best of the very first picking of the produce and birth of the livestock which were used for the support of His priests.

We have already considered the need to present the first born children to Him.

> *Also you shall observe the Feast of Harvest, [also known as Pentecost, or First Fruits], acknowledging the first fruits of your labour, the produce of what you had sown in the field. (Ex. 23:16, 19)*

The first fruits, particularly of grain, wine and oil, were to be for the support of the priests (Num. 18:11 – 13; Deut. 18:3, 4) although the amount is not mentioned, it is likely that there would be an abundance during times of revival and reform such as the reformation in the time of Hezekiah[43] (2 Chron. 31:5)

The Feast of FirstFruits

9Then the Lord spoke to Moses, saying, "Speak to the children of Israel and say to them, 'When you enter the land which I am giving you and reap its harvest, you shall bring the sheaf of the first fruits of your harvest to the priest.

This was to acknowledge on the 16th of Nissan (the first month and the day after the Feast of Unleavened Bread at the beginning of the barley harvest that everything came from God because of His creational ability and His goodness in providing the right conditions for the harvest to take place. In the years of drought, plague or conflict, harvests were either poor or none existent.

He shall wave the sheaf (an Omer - around five pints a sample of the Barley harvest) before the Lord on the day after the Sabbath to be accepted for you. On that day you shall offer a male lamb one year old without blemish as a burnt offering to the Lord.

Its grain offering shall be two-tenths of an ephah of fine flour mixed with olive oil, an offering by fire to the Lord for a sweet and soothing aroma, with its drink offering which is to be poured out, a fourth of a hin of wine.

14You shall not eat any bread or roasted grain or new growth, until this same day when you bring in the offering to your God; it is a permanent statute throughout your generations wherever you may be. (Lev. 23:9 – 14)

The barley was the first of the grains to be harvested and nothing from the harvest could be used for food until after this ceremony, as this was to thank God for the bountiful harvest that the people were expecting and it was their duty to thank God for His provision – in a way like giving thanks before meals.

This idea of firstfruits is also important for all believers in the Messiah because Christ is the firstfruits of those that had died because He was the first to die and receive a spiritual body whilst in the tomb. All believers must wait for the moment that God calls us to go to the place Jesus is preparing for us.

---

[43] See chapter 11 of Law & Grace

Tithes

In Deuteronomy tithes were required of those that produced food and those that gained financially from their work to be used to support the priests and Levites working in the Temple.

Paul writing to the Corinthians wrote:

> *Do you not know that those who officiate in the sacred services of the temple eat from the offerings of meat and bread brought to the temple as offering for the altar, of which those who regularly attend the altar have their share? So also the same principle applies to those the Lord has directed to preach the gospel, that they might get their living from the gospel. (1 Cor. 9:13, 14)*

The Israelites were required to offer sacrifices and offerings to God. The priests were appointed by God to accept the offerings from the people and officiate on behalf of the people. Part of those offerings were to be consumed by the priests of God as their share.

What was the point of making offerings to the gods when all that happened was that perishables perished and had to be removed. In Israel the offering of animals or perishable things such as grain were either burned or used as food for the priests so that nothing was wasted.

Three tithes were distributed every third year. The first was to provide for the landless Levites, those that served fulltime at the temple and were not blessed with land on which to grow food. It is for this reason that parts of various sacrificial offerings were given to the priests officiating in the Temple, along with tithes.

The third year was the time to ensure that all the tithes had been paid out. It was important that the Levites and the poor were always supported.

> *12 When you have finished paying all the tithe of your produce on the third year of tithing, then you shall give it to the Levite, to the stranger, to the orphan, and to the widow, so that they may eat within the gates of your cities and be satisfied.*
>
> *You shall say before the Lord your God, 'I have removed the sacred portion (the tithe) from my house and given it to the Levite, to the stranger, to the orphan, and to the widow, in accordance with*

all that You have commanded me. I have not transgressed or forgotten any of Your commandments.

I have not eaten from the tithe while mourning, nor have I removed any of it when I was ceremonially unclean thus making the tithe ceremonially unclean, nor offered any of it to the dead.

I have listened to the voice of the Lord my God; I have done everything in accordance with all that You have commanded me.

In other words *"I have been faithful in giving the tithes as is required of me."* Having fulfilled all the obligations the Lord required of them, they then called on the Lord to fulfil His promises to them. After all it was a two way agreement.

15 Therefore, look down from Your holy dwelling in heaven above, and bless Your people Israel, and the land which You have given us, as You have sworn to our fathers, a land of plenty that is flowing with milk and honey.'

Israel had entered into a covenant with God, therefore it was incumbent upon both parties to that covenant to each be loyal to the other. It is important to realize that it was not just a case of following the rules, but following them with due diligence and enthusiasm.

16 This day the Lord your God commands you to do these statutes and judgments. Therefore, you shall be careful to do them with all your heart and with all your soul, indeed your entire being.

It was that putting their whole selves into actively following the statutes of God willingly *with all your heart and with all your soul, indeed your entire being* that was so important because only in that way could serving God be a joy not drudgery.

17 Today you have declared openly the Lord to be your God, and that you will live each and every day in His ways and keep His statutes, His commandments, and His judgments, and listen to His voice.

It was important for them to willingly give themselves to God and focus on Him throughout their lives in order for the spirit of the covenant to be fulfilled. Only then could God acknowledge them as truly His people. It was a matter of the heart not the mind which it later became, particularly at the time of the Messiah.

> *18   Today the Lord has declared that you are His people, His treasured possession, just as He promised you, and that you are to keep all His commandments; also that He will set you high above all the nations which He has made, for praise, fame, and honour: and that you shall be a holy people, set apart and consecrated to the Lord your God, just as He has spoken.*

God loved them throughout their ups and downs, and at times sustained them purely to protect His great name and ensure that His plan for the salvation not just of Israel but of mankind in general was fulfilled.

MOSES THIRD DISCOURSE

17 ENFORCEMENT OF THE LAW

Chapter 27

Procedure on crossing the Jordan

It was essential for the Israelites on entering the land to declare the terms of their tenure. The dictionary definition being 'the conditions under which land or buildings are held or occupied'.

> *1 Then Moses and the elders of Israel commanded the people, saying, Remember and obey, [make them part of your daily life] all the commandments which I am commanding you today.*

The first monument built on the West side of the Jordan river was of twelve stones taken from the centre of the river, from the place where the feet of the priests carrying the Ark stood firm, and leave them at the place where they lodged for the first night in the promised land. This cairn told a story which in this case commemorated the second time God stopped the waters so that the Israelites could cross over on dry land (Josh. 4:1 – 9).

But there was to be a more important monument built of rough uncut stones on the top of Mount Ebal which was the mount of God's curse because of its bareness. On the other side of the valley created by the two mountains was Mount Gerizim which was far more fertile representing God's blessing.

> *2 So it shall be on the day [a period of time] when you cross the Jordan to enter the land which the Lord your God is giving you,*

that you shall set up for yourself large stones and coat them with plaster.

The plaster was a coating of lime or chalk on which the writing could be scribed with black 'paint' to highlight the inscription.

3 You shall write on the stones all the words of this law when you cross over, so that you may go into the land which the Lord your God gives you, to remind you of the terms of your tenure, for it is a land flowing with milk and honey, just as the Lord, the God of your fathers has promised you.

Because of the winter rains it is likely this was not to be a permanent monument. But that the words were before the people as they entered the land. Because there was no means of recording statements for everyone to read, the people developed excellent memories, so having passed the monument, the words would have been remembered.

First of course the people had to face the town of Jericho and then the disaster of the town of Ai where confidence in their own ability to conquer gave them the shock of losing the battle because God was not with them (Josh. 7, 8).

It was after the battle of Ai that the Israelites moved to the site of Mount Ebal and Gerizim and set about building the altar of local uncut stones on top of Mount Ebal.

4 Now when you cross the Jordan you shall set up these stones on Mount Ebal, just as I am commanding you today and coat them with plaster. There you shall build an altar to the Lord your God, an altar of stones; you shall not use an iron tool on them.

Why was it necessary to use uncut stone? Well there are two reasons. Firstly it was important that they had not been dressed up by sinful man. Because it was to be used for the sacrifice of offerings to the Lord it had to be holy, therefore the construction of the altar had to be with stone uncontaminated by the hand of man. Remember the sacrifice of Cain was unacceptable because he offered the product of his labour, not the perfect lamb offered by Abel, which was required to shed its blood for the forgiveness of sin.

Secondly, as a nomadic nation for the last forty years there would not have been any metal workers in Israel. In fact even at the time of King Saul we read this in the book of 1 Samuel 13:

> *Now no metal-workers could be found in all the land of Israel, for the Philistines said, "Otherwise the Hebrews will be able to make swords or spears."*
>
> *So the men of Israel went down to the Philistines, each to get his plowshare, pick, axe, or sickle sharpened. For the fee of a pim (two-thirds of a shekel) for the plowshares, picks, pitchforks, and axes, and also to straighten the goads (cattle prods).*
>
> *So it came about on the day of battle that neither sword nor spear was found in the hands of any of the people who were with Saul and Jonathan; although both Saul and his son Jonathan had them.*

Therefore they would have had to use the services of members of the very tribes/nations they were there to remove. It is also interesting that according to the Talmud an iron tool was, understandably, symbolic of division and destruction.

How Moses was able to supply tablets of stone to take up the mountain to the Lord for Him to inscribe the commandments is a mystery, unless there were some who had that skill from their time in Egypt in the initial years of their wanderings. We will never know.

> *5 You shall build the altar of the Lord your God with complete uncut stones, and offer burnt offerings on it to the Lord your God. You shall sacrifice peace offerings and shall eat there, and shall rejoice before the Lord your God.*
>
> *You shall write very clearly on the stones all the words of this law."*

There were times when Abraham, Isaac or Jacob moved to a different location they set up an altar and offered sacrifices to the Lord there. How much more important was it for the Israelites to offer sacrifices as they entered the promised land to establish themselves there.

Remember at the time of these discourses, as Moses was prevented from setting foot on the land of Canaan, the people were still on the eastern bank of the river Jordan ready to embark on their most important mission, so it was exceptionally important for Moses and the priests, who themselves would be taking on responsibility for the spiritual health of the nation, to emphasize the importance of obeying the commandments of God.

> *9 Then Moses and the Levitical priests said to all Israel, "Be silent and listen, O Israel! This day you have become a people for the Lord your God. So you shall obey the voice of the Lord your God, and do His commandments and statutes which I am commanding you today."*

In that statement Moses, with great clarity, announced with great clarity the uniqueness of the nation of Israel as the only nation on earth of which its life and faith were united under Divine governance.

> *11 Moses also commanded the people that day, saying:*
> *"These tribes shall stand on Mount Gerizim to bless the people when you have crossed the Jordan: Simeon, Levi, Judah, Issachar, Joseph, and Benjamin.*
> *These tribes shall stand on Mount Ebal to pronounce the curse for disobedience: Reuben, Gad, Asher, Zebulun, Dan, and Naphtali.*

It is interesting that the Levites, with the ark of God, would stand in the valley calling out the curses, facing Mount Ebal, and the blessings facing Mount Gerizim.

The Curses of Mount Ebal

> *The Levites shall speak with a loud voice to all the men of Israel:*
>
> *'Cursed is the man who makes a carved or cast image [an idol], which is a repulsive thing to the Lord, for it is the work of the hands of the artisan, who sets it up in secret, in opposition to the worship of the Lord your God.'* (This applies to any image set up in a church)
>
> *All the people shall answer and say, 'Amen.'*

'Cursed is he who dishonours his father or his mother, treating them with contempt' (cf. Matt. 15:1 – 9)

All the people shall say, 'Amen.'

'Cursed is he who moves the boundary mark of his neighbour's property.'

All the people shall say, 'Amen.'

'Cursed is he who misleads a blind person on the road.'

All the people shall say, 'Amen.'

'Cursed is he who perverts the course of justice due to a stranger, an orphan, and a widow.'

All the people shall say, 'Amen.'

'Cursed is he who is intimate with his father's wife, because he has violated what belongs to his father.'

All the people shall say, 'Amen.'

'Cursed is he who is intimate with any animal.'

All the people shall say, 'Amen.'

'Cursed is he who is intimate with his sister, whether she is his father's or his mother's daughter.'

All the people shall say, 'Amen.'

'Cursed is he who is intimate with his mother-in-law.' (The Persians married their nearest blood-relatives)

All the people shall say, 'Amen.'

'Cursed is he who strikes his neighbour in secret.'

All the people shall say, 'Amen.'

'Cursed is he who accepts a bribe to strike down an innocent person.'

All the people shall say, 'Amen.'

'Cursed is he who does not confirm the words of this law by doing them, that is keeping them, making them the rule of his life.'

All the people shall say, 'Amen.'

Chapter 28

Blessings at Gerizim

In contrast to the curses in the previous chapter, here we have the blessings afforded to those who set their minds to being obedient to the commands of God.

Moses has not just taught a higher law than man can ever fully attain without God's help, but throughout his long life he had been an example to the people, demonstrating the power and love and glory of God in his life. And all because he had surrendered all his human duty to both God, and through the commission God had given to him, also to the people God had appointed him to lead. In fact if ever there as a life devoted to both God and man this is it.

What a prospect for the future; what promises were theirs to receive and enjoy if only they were to fulfil the requirements God laid down for them.

> *1 It shall come to pass, if you diligently listen to and obey the voice of the Lord your God, being careful to live your life in accordance with all of His commandments which I am commanding you today, the Lord your God will set you high above all the nations of the earth.*

How awesome is that? But think dear reader, God has not changed even though we live no longer under the law as the Israelites were here required to do, but under grace. However, that does not mean that we can neglect the principle of what the law was trying to teach the people concerning the way they lived their lives, in order for God to be able to set them higher than the other nations.

Paul did not at any time say that we had to disregard the law. Let us look again at what he wrote to the Romans (7:14 – 25):

We know that the Law is spiritual

Although the law was given by God in order to structure the physical lives of the people, their purpose was spiritual because by living according to his commandments they would shun all the attractions of the earthly nations around them and live a life that He had designed for man to enjoy from the beginning.

If we are serious about having a relationship with God, it is imperative that we recognize what happened when Adam preferred to listen to Satan rather than God; for that is when the DNA of sin entered into the human chain.

As Paul then states:

> *but I am a creature of the flesh, physically married to the world and therefore self-reliant. Having become carnal — meaning focussing on the things of the flesh — it is by that means I have become unspiritual, sold into the slavery of sin and serving under its control, rather than under the control of God.*

Do you understand the importance of obeying the commandments of God written all those years ago?

God wanted the people to live as He originally designed man to live, not as Satan wanted him to live. It is only by focussing on the commandments of God, and spiritually getting as close to God as possible, that we resist allowing the world (dominated by Satan) to draw us down the slippery slope into sin.

The commandments were of God and therefore spiritually inspired. It is for this reason that the teachings of Paul are so important for our fuller understanding of the teaching of the First Testament.

> *So I find it to be the law followed by my inner self, that evil is present in me, the one who wants to do good. For I joyfully delight in the law of God in my inner self, that is with my new nature spiritually attuned nature,*

Paul complains about the inner confusion he experiences, that is the carnal[44]/spiritual fight within him concerning his desire to follow the commandments of God but still finding himself falling into sin such that he complains.

> *but I see a different law and rule of action in the members of my body, with its fleshly appetites and desires, waging war against the law of my mind and subduing me and making me a prisoner of the*

---

[44] Carnal meaning of the sinful flesh

law of sin which is within my members. O wretched and miserable man that I am! Who will rescue me and set me free from this corrupt, mortal body of death?

He recognizes the conflict within, between his inner nature, within which the DNA of sin operates, and his desire within his spirit to do good, to obey the commands of God.

What changed his life around was the transformational deliverance brought about by the death and resurrection of his Messiah, Jesus Christ, and the baptism of the Holy Spirit that wrought in his life a completely new perspective.

But all that was to come because at the time of Moses the Holy Spirit was not then generally available to the Israelites, apart from the selected few in God's service such as the prophets. There was much for man to learn before the coming of the Messiah.

But the choice before the Israelites was to enjoy great blessings by serving God, or experience disaster when seeking to emulate those of the world.

*2   You will experience all these blessings **if** you pay diligent attention to the voice of the Lord your God.*

And these are the seven (perfection and completeness) blessings they could expect, not forgetting that as creator and sustainer of all things, both physical and spiritual, God was more than capable of fulling His promises:

- *You will be blessed in the city, and in the field.*

- *The offspring of your body and the produce of your ground and the offspring of your animals, your herd and the young of your flock will be blessed.*

- *Your basket and your kneading bowl will be blessed.*

- *You will be blessed when you come in and when you go out.*

- *The Lord will cause enemies who rise up against you to be defeated before you; they will come out against you one way, but flee before you seven ways.*

- *The Lord will command the blessing upon you in your storehouses and in all that you undertake, and He will bless you in the land which the Lord your God gives you.*

- *The Lord will establish you as a holy people to Himself, just as He has sworn to you, if you keep the commandments of the Lord your God and live your life each and every day in His ways.*

The whole purpose of this arrangement where they were *established as a holy people, set apart unto Himself* was in order that *all the peoples of the earth will see that you are called by the name of the Lord, and they will be afraid of you.*

The people were to be His shop window display, illustrating just what He could do for all those that through their devotion to Him, in being enabled to live a prosperous and protected life. And there is more, for the proposal continues that the Lord:

- *will give you great prosperity, in the offspring of your body and in the offspring of your livestock and the produce of your ground, in the land which the Lord swore to your fathers to give you.*

- *will open for you His good treasure house, the heavens, to give rain to your land in its season and to bless all the work of your hand; and you will lend to many nations, but you will not borrow.*

- *will make you the leader of nations, not the follower; and you will be above only, and you will not be beneath, if you listen and pay attention to the commandments of the Lord your God, which I am commanding you today, to observe them carefully.*

Of course these promises are conditional - *if you listen and pay attention to the commandments of the Lord your God.*

We have referred to marriage already in this book and that is the key to all man's relationship with God, from the legal engagement on Mount Sinai to the marriage supper of the Lamb in Revelation.

Unless we realize that God wants a permanent, personal and marriage type intimate spiritual relationship with each and every one of us, then we are missing the whole point of scripture.

It is being able to comprehend that vitally necessary understanding and extent of the relationship God requires of every individual that is the stumbling block for many of those who call themselves believers.

For a couple to enter into a marriage that will last a lifetime, they need to know each other well, which is not achieved by one or even more casual meetings. Except the relationship gets to the point where the meetings become a necessary part of their daily lives, then they remain just friends or acquaintances.

The key for the Israelites was that they were not to *turn aside from any of the words which I am commanding you today, to the right or to the left.*

All these words would come to haunt them when they turned aside *to follow and serve other gods.*[45]

Consequences of Disobedience

So stark is this comparison between cursing and blessing that the people were inevitably drawn back to it after they had inevitably strayed yet again.

The people of Israel have always been very keen to point out their distinctive position in regard to other nations. The Second Testament is full of it, even after Peter witnessed the Holy Spirit fill those of Cornelius' household. All those of the circumcision were outraged that Peter should have gone into the house of a Gentile until Peter explained all that had happened.

But it was through their own failure that they went astray so often and so disastrously that caused God to focus His attention on the Gentiles.

The consequences of them not listening to and obeying the voice of the Lord, and not bothering to *being careful to do all His commandments and His statutes which I am commanding you today, then all these curses will come upon you and overtake you,* was at the time of

---

[45] See Law & Grace which deals with Israel after the 10/2 split and the exile both experienced.

Moses in the future. But the significance of the book of Deuteronomy is the way it was constantly referred to throughout the First Testament to remind the people that they had been warned and it was because they neglected the reading of the scriptures that so much disaster had befallen them.

The word of God is very clear, and with a few pointers from Paul, we today have even less excuse not to be careful to stay close to God.

These are words with awful power putting to the people the fact that the promises of God have a reverse as well as an obverse side. God is not playing games. The salvation of mankind is far greater than one nation. Just as the slaughter of many thousands of Israelis that died during the 40 years of wandering clearly shows, the choice God gives to all men is follow me or face the consequences.

Now for those sensitive souls that quickly say that this reveals a God without a heart, we need to spend a moment considering what is on offer here and who is putting forward the offer.

It seems astonishing that individuals even today fail to get it in their minds that the world and all that is in it is God's creation, which means that He, as the designer and creator, owns everything, including man.

Not only that but taking the Bible as a whole and not just considering it in bits and pieces, Revelation clearly tells us that throughout the Bible it is the same creator and sustainer God who is in control of where each individual goes once they leave this earth. Dust to dust etcetera. So we cannot ignore the role God inevitably plays in the life of each and every one of us.

In spite of man rebelling against God and trying to go his own way, God had prepared a plan even before the creation of the world and of man in particular. That plan, which has been most costly to God, was to provide those born in sin with a way back to Himself.

That plan is God's plan of salvation, initially involving the slaughter of animals but ultimately the murder of His only Son by men supposedly His ministers on earth who will all ultimately meet their reward because they had never had an intimate relation with Him.

The blessings offered by God were unique and beyond value, providing the people were prepared to enter into that intimacy that God so strongly desired to enjoy with all men.

Those so beholden to Satan that they cannot change would experience only the blessings Satan could provide, which in fact have always been hate and chaos and the total disruption of normal life.

In the book of Job (1), when God asked Satan where he had come from, his reply was that he had been going to and fro over the earth because man, in rebelling against God, had transferred the authority God had given him to Satan. In fact Satan is referred to as the Prince of the Power of the air.

Therefore what God was telling the Israelites through His servant Moses was, you either come under my authority which would allow me to bless you beyond your wildest dreams, or you come under Satan's authority in which case your lives will be a complete disaster because I hold the keys to life and only I can control all the environmental elements on which you will be dependent in the new land, and provide the protection you need from prospective enemies.

Hannah went to the temple barren and God enabled her to conceive and she gave birth to Samuel;. Sarah was the same before becoming pregnant with Isaac, as was Elizabeth who gave birth to John the Baptist. Satan has no such power over things but that power is limited by God.

So it is clear that the blessings and curses depended on who the people of Israel were prepared to serve. God or Satan. And what is just as important for us today is that God has not changed, for the offer of blessing or cursing is still on the table today.

Moses was hard hitting when he proclaimed:

> *15 all these curses will come on you and pursue and overtake you until you are destroyed, because you would not obey the voice of the Lord your God by keeping His commandments and His statutes which He has commanded you.*

Where it says *all these curses will come on you and pursue and overtake you until you are destroyed*, that actually happened to the ten tribes of Israel, when they finally went into exile into the Assyrian Empire and were never heard from again.

They will be a sign and a wonder to you and your descendants forever.

Let us consider what was in store for the people if they rejected the Lord their God and went their own way.

We must always be mindful of the reason these people, descendants of Abraham the faithful, were chose by God. They were at the centre of His plan to save mankind. We are not talking about ordinary people but people with a God appointed purpose and mission.

They were not given anything because of their goodness but because they were chosen. It was man that sinned and yet it was God who was seeking through man to heal and save the lost, therefore the attitude of the Israelites was not always helpful to God who was having to do all the work.

All the people had to do was to love Him and serve Him and He would do the rest. So with their rebellious attitude God, He had to use harsh methods to bring them back into line.

> 16 *You will be cursed in the city and cursed in the field.*
>
> 17 *Your basket and your kneading bowl will be cursed.*
>
> 18 *The offspring of your body and the produce of your land, the offspring of your herd and the young of your flock, all will be cursed.*
>
> 19 *You will be cursed when you come in and you will be cursed when you go out.*

The Israelites had to learn the very severe lesson that defying God was counterproductive with the list starting with "*The Lord will send upon you curses, confusion, and rebuke in everything that you undertake to do, until you are destroyed, perishing quickly because the evil of your deeds has caused you to turned away from Me.*" What a severe rebuke.

It is important to read the whole list <u>carefully</u> because it is possible to identify certain events here prophesied, including the words of Habakkuk. It will certainly clearly indicate the anger of God towards His recalcitrant people who could easily have been wiped off the map had it not been for His great name's sake, and the loyalty of the remnant and the need to maintain the nation in preparation for the arrival of the long promised Messiah.

They did suffer from those curse because of their unfaithfulness before God, with invading forces that stole their crops and animals, drought (Elijah), defeat *The Lord will bring you and your appointed king, to a nation which you and your fathers have never known; there you will be forced to serve other lifeless gods.* (Assyrians finally took the majority of the ten tribes into exile).[46]

In John 8:32, Jesus spoke about the truth setting them free. The Jews answered, *"We are Abraham's descendants, and have never been in bondage to anyone. How can You say, 'You will be made free'?"* How could they say they had *never been in bondage to anyone* when they were then under occupation from the Romans and were very restricted in what they could do?

As we are able to read about these things, it is to our benefit that we learn from their mistakes, else the study of the scriptures will be spiritually non-productive and reflect not only on the success of our lives but also affect our ultimate destination. We must take note of what God said to the people. Read carefully the following words:

> *47 Because you did not serve the Lord your God with a heart full of joy and gladness in response to the abundance of all things with which He has blessed you, you will therefore serve your enemies whom the Lord sends against you, in hunger and in thirst, in nakedness and in the lack of all things; and He will put an iron yoke of slavery on your neck until He has destroyed you.*
>
> *The Lord will bring a nation against you from far away, from the end of the earth, as swift as the eagle swoops down to attack its prey, a nation whose language you will not understand, a defiant nation that will have no respect for the old, nor show favour to the young, and that enemy was the highly trained, professional Assyrian army.*

---

[46] Much of this is explained in Law & Grace

Dear reader these things happened. These words were prophetic.

> *52 They will besiege you in all your cities until your high and fortified walls in which you trusted come down throughout your land; and they will besiege you in all your cities throughout your land which the Lord your God has given you.*
>
> *Then you will eat the offspring of your own body to avoid starvation, the flesh of your sons and daughters whom the Lord your God has given you, during the siege and the misery by which your enemy will oppress you.*

Again these things happened, particularly in Jerusalem when Nebuchadnezzar lay siege to Jerusalem after which his army destroyed the city wall and burned the gates. Why do you think Nehemiah wept when he heard about the state of the city and risked his life when he asked the king for leave go and rebuild the city?

God is not playing games, and we today must start taking God seriously. The church has meddled with His word, altering it to suit the thinking of the times, without any concern about what God had intended and therefore once again rebelling against Him.

They insult Him by twisting His word and thus putting out what today is called misinformation about God and His salvation. Such activity is having and will continue to have dire consequences until the church realizes that they have no authority to alter one jot or tittle. This is the act of enemies, not supposed servants of God.

Hear the further damaging news of what was to happen at some time in the future, which occurred purely because God took away His protection from them; events that can be read about in other parts of scripture.

> *58 If you are not careful to do all the words of this law that are written in this book, to fear and with reverence honour this glorious and awesome name, the Lord your God, then the Lord will bring extraordinary plagues on you and your descendants, even severe and lasting plagues, and miserable and chronic sicknesses.*

These warnings of curses that God would bring upon the house of Israel were for the nation as a whole, because instead of blessing Israel with His protection and ability to bring about good harvests and blessing the productivity of their livestock, He would turn His back on them and Satan and his forces will take great delight in attacking God's chosen people with the ultimate intention of destroying them. Even today countries in which Satan has all authority is still threatening to destroy Israel, and even church members are calling for Israeli goods to be boycotted, and investment to be stopped.

It is interesting how the fortunes of the people oscillated from good to bad throughout their history.

However, there were two things that ultimately saved Israel. The first was the faithful remnant that stayed loyal to their God, through every wave of rebellion, and the second was God's determination to fulfil His plan of salvation through them. It refers to this second as being not for the sake of the rebellious and hard hearted people, but *for His own name's sake*

We do well in this day and age to take seriously the power and far reaching effect of the judgement of God and allow Him to fulfil His plan for us through us.

18 COVENANTED ISRAEL

Chapter 29

1 These are the words of the covenant which the Lord commanded Moses to make with the sons of Israel in the land of Moab, in addition to the covenant which He made with them at Sinai.

Now is the time of summing up, of recapping what had gone before, for the time of the people entering into the promised land to take possession of it was close at hand.

The covenant God entered into with Israel was comprehensive and is contained in Exodus, Leviticus and Numbers, but, as has been discussed in this book, can be summed up in two sentences:

1.   God promises to bless Israel and its people by making it the nation through which all other nations could experience the love and power of God working with mankind.
2.   In return, the people of Israel promised to love and obey God in order to receive physical and spiritual blessings.

There are various aspects of the recapping that need to be considered because many of the people then alive had not actually been the ones that left Egypt at night after the first Passover meal. Because of rebellion and a complete lack of faith most of the adult population that left Egypt had died in the wilderness.

Along with Moses, Caleb and Joshua were the notable ones to have survived to see this day, so where it says:

2 Moses summoned all Israel and said to them, "You have seen all that the Lord did before your eyes in the land of Egypt to Pharaoh, to all his servants, and to all his land;

the information regarding all that happened in Egypt would have been passed down from parent to children, with just the faithful few being able to recall all the vivid details. We have the advantage of it being recorded for us so that we know what happened without having to suffer all the trials in the very basic conditions that existed at that time.

But let us not forget that these were real people, living real lives and experiencing momentous events of leaving the land of Goshen, passing through the waters of the Red Sea, and seeing the Egyptian army drawing near and then drowning as the sea returned to its place.

The children must have been spell bound as their parents recounted the events during an evening around the camp fire. Unfortunately, even though they had such good memories, there seemed to be within them a complete lack of an understanding of who God was, His reality and what He had done for them.

There was a complete disconnect between the historical and spiritual, hence Moses states:

Yet to this day the Lord has not given you a heart and mind to understand, nor eyes to see, nor ears to hear.

Focussing on the physical is a problem in all things relating to God who is spiritual. There seemed to have been a disconnect between what had happened to them in Egypt and during their nomadic existence in the wilderness and their ability to relate it to their relationship with their unseen God and His power and ability to provide for them.

All the amazing events that took place in Egypt that had the effect of filling the population of the surrounding nations with abject fear, seemed to have gone over the heads of those most involved; the people of Israel.

The nations were not fearful of Israel itself but, possibly because of their superstitious, pagan oriented nature, of the God of Israel.

Rahab in Jericho told the spies that the people were rigid with fear of them, having heard about the plagues in Egypt, what had happened to the Egyptian army and, during their travels in the wilderness, how they had overcome their enemies. To ensure that she and her family were saved from the disaster that was expected to befall the city, she entered into an agreement with the spies before she let them go.

But the understanding and appreciation of the Hebrews themselves concerning all that God had done for them in Egypt and during the wilderness years was sadly minimal.

Soon after the amazing events that took place when they crossed the Red Sea, they came to the undrinkable waters of Marah. All they could do was to complain. Did that not demonstrate how self-centred and insular they were?

Instead of thinking that if their God was able to perform such a miraculous event as the crossing of the Red Sea and then drowning the Egyptian army in one foul swoop, surely the purification of the bitter waters would be a simple matter to sort out.

But they were not on the right level. So many were still under the influence of slavery, where they were regimented almost becoming automatons. There was no positive thinking at all. Throughout Egypt there were images of the Egyptian gods so how could there be a God without an image?

They seemed not to have the capacity of understanding that the God of Moses could not be seen with the naked eye but was, nonetheless there with them with the sole intention of looking after them.

Hoshea had the same problem of having them understand that just because a statue was referred to as a god, it did not mean that it could do anything for them, however many sacrifices they put before it. It was just an inanimate object with a certain form created by a sculptor.

In fact they really did not understand who God was. Even with the spectacular environmental activity around the top of the mountain and the voice that came from the top at Horeb.

There was no doubt they were very frightened, but their many amazing experiences seemed not to impress upon them the overwhelming power and majesty and reality of God. It came down to just a very frightening experience.

Even today spiritual matters are beyond the ability of many to properly understand; that there is a God in heaven and an evil angel referred to as Satan, who also cannot be seen.

In Isaiah's day, after all the experiences of successes and failures during many generations, they seemed not to connect the successes with when they held God in high esteem, and their failures to when they had rejected God as their Lord and Saviour and focussed on the gods of the other nations.

Let us compare two characters of Genesis to get a better idea of what this is all about. Abram was receptive to the call of God. In his heart he was searching for the truth, and that truth came to him in Almighty God.

Because Abram's spiritual antenna was in reception mode and therefore in a position to hear God speak to him, he heard God speaking to him and over time was persuaded to give his heart and life to Him.

That was Abram's epiphany moment. The moment his life was turned around. Abram came to totally believe in this God that spoke to him out of the ether because he had never experienced anything like it with any of the gods and goddesses then being worshipped. Because of which the way he gave his life to God was set to make him righteous before God.

On the other hand His nephew Lot had no interest in God at all and looked to the abundance of the earth, and fitted into the local community in the Jordan valley and came to lose everything. From the abundance he had with his uncle, Lot ended up in a cave with his two daughters and two sons who were also without God.

Jacob was also wanting to understand about the God of his father, whereas Esau was more focussed on what was around him in a physical sense, and the excitement of physical activity.

In the Second Testament Martha was more interested in the practical matters of the home whereas Mary wanted to sit at the feet of Jesus to learn spiritual truth.

Isaiah was told to

"Go, and tell this people:
'Keep on listening, but do not understand;
Keep on looking, but do not comprehend.'

The people just could not, would not understand that God was not in the physical. Yes it was influence by Him. But God was far more than the physical. They had to search for Him using their minds and hearts. They had to want Him for Him to become real to them as did the characters mentioned above.

Surely with all that had happened to the people of Israel and their forebears, their history should have taught them that God was not something physical, something visual that they could worship, but far deeper that it needed their understanding.

The words of the prophets were heard but not understood, because they did not search for an understanding.

Solomon put it like this:

> *To know wisdom and instruction,*
> *To discern and comprehend the words of understanding,*
> *To receive instruction in wise behaviour and attitude*
> *And the discipline of wise thoughtfulness,*
> *Justice, judgment, and equity;*
> *4To give prudence to the simple and naive,*
> *And knowledge and discretion o the young*
> *5A wise man will hear and increase his learning,*
> *And a man of understanding will acquire wise counsel,*
> *6To understand a proverb and an enigma*
> *With its interpretation,*
> *The words of the wise and their riddles*
> *That stimulate reflection.*

The crucial verse is:

> *7The reverend fear of the Lord*
> *by worshipping Him in awe and respect*
> *is the beginning and preeminent requirement of knowledge,*
> *But fools despise wisdom and instruction.*

And the Psalmist wrote:

> *The fool says in his heart there is no God*

Sadly many of the Israelites could not relate what was happening to them to their relationship with the God of Moses. They had drifted far and had willingly embedded themselves into the human life that surrounded them.

Proverbs calls on the people to trust in the Lord with all their hearts, but that requires a knowledge of God which none of them, apart from the remnant, had, not even many of the priests who were supposed to be His ministers.

The sons of Eli were so corrupt that they were turning the people away from God when they should have been doing the opposite.

No matter what God said through the prophets, the people were not really listening or taking it to heart, they were not accepting Him as real, just the spouting of deranged men.

Sadly the religious elite reacted in the same way when they listened to their Messiah. Because they had different ideas on how to serve and worship God they were not prepared to take note of what He was saying to them, therefore it had no effect on them. They continued to ignore or oppose Him to the point where they finally had their way and had Him murdered on a cross.

Just as with Moses passing on to the people the commands and statutes of God which they heard but were not willing to apply their minds to in order to understand the full implications of what they were hearing.

Such an attitude is very much like someone today receiving some official notification and either ignoring it or not bothering to understand its implications for them and suffering the consequences.

God kept sending prophet after prophet to tell them important things but, as Jesus explained (Matt. 21:33 – 46), they either ignored them, abused them or killed them. Let us consider this more carefully,

> *Finally he sent his own son to them, saying, 'They will respect my son and have regard for him.' But when the tenants saw the son, they said to themselves, 'This man is the heir; come on, let us kill him and seize his inheritance.'*
>
> *So they took the son and threw him out of the vineyard, and killed him. Now when the owner of the vineyard comes back, what will he do to those tenants?"*

They said to Him, "He will put those despicable men to a miserable end, and rent out the vineyard to other tenants of good character who will pay him the proceeds at the proper seasons."

Consider carefully the ending of this story because it brings clarity to the matter we are here thinking about.

Therefore I tell you, the kingdom of God will be taken away from you and given to another people who will produce the fruit of it.

This was a threat that the religious authorities found difficult to stomach because the special place of Israel before God was their pride and joy and their livelihood.

But do you see, their religion had nothing to do with God. They were proud of their lineage and privileges and their way of life, but it was minus that one essential ingredient that would have made it legitimate. A personal spiritual intimacy with God.

They had a history of silencing or killing off the legitimate prophets of God, supplanting them with their own brand of religious fervour and understanding that, without them realizing it, had nothing to do with the real worship of the living God.

When the chief priests and the Pharisees heard His parables, they understood that He was talking about them.

They realized that this man, that they did not recognize as their Messiah, was criticizing them. It hurt their pride but did not affect their conscience, because they were the Lots and Esaus of their faith.

The one thing that clarified the fact that they were acting in their human capacity is the last verse, where it speaks of them wanting *to arrest Him* but because they did not have the control over the situation that the Lord as God had, *they feared the people, because the people regarded Jesus as a prophet* they were powerless to do anything bout it.

They did not have the authority from God to do what they wanted to do. It was just themselves acting out a life that was totally and utterly false. Corrupted by their own thinking and interpretation of the written word of God and use of the oral law which had over the centuries become more important than the word of God, the Torah, itself.

God was forever calling on His chosen people to return to Him and be healed, cleansed of their sin, but they would not.

> *Make [declare or foretell] that the heart*
> *of this people is totally insensitive*
> *to the message of God,*
> *Their spiritual ears are dull,*
> *their spiritual eyes are dim,*

A friend of mind has asked me many questions over several years including giving me books of total nonbelievers, and those opposed to religion in general and Christianity in particular. Even though I have discussed spiritual matters with him and he has read many of my books, he still remains obstinately unconvinced of the fact of God.

He has told me that he believes in some higher power, but that is as far as he will go. In the meantime he continues to put more faith in the likes of the anti-religion Richard Dawkins and those of like mind.

The Israelites, even in the days of Isaiah, had the same problem. In spite of all that God had done for them in blessings and curses, exactly in accordance with Moses' discourses in Deuteronomy, the majority seem incapable of properly hearing and taking to heart what they were being told.

Not only Isaiah, but Jeremiah and Ezekiel and many of the minor prophets faced the same resistance.

There seems to be a note of cynicism in the lines:

> *Otherwise they might see with their eyes,*
> *Hear with their ears,*
> *Understand with their hearts,*
> *And return and be healed."*
> *(Is. 6:9, 10)*

But those lines declare a truth which is that God cares enough to always keep the lines of communications between Him and man open through His prophets. Sadly Isaiah met a gory and very painful end but he is remembered for his faithfulness in serving God and will be rewarded in due time.

Paul also, having finally discovered that he was opposing the living Christ, found that just as he had been ignorant of just who the God he worshipped was, so too his countrymen were continuing to do the same thing.

There were three types of Israelis. The diehard unbeliever, those that thought they could find God by studying the scriptures and by trying to obey the laws of Moses, and those that realized that merely obeying the law was not enough; they realize that they had to use their minds, hearts and wills to seek after God.

As Isaiah said, *Seek the Lord while He may be found; Call on Him to receive salvation while He is near.* Not only will there be a time when He is not near, but it is too late when death comes calling.

Faith has nothing to do with our effort, but all to do with communicating with God with a willingness to listen to His instructions, surrender ourselves to Him and serve Him as he guides us. Our thoughts and speech can be continually heard by God and He willingly responds to those that call upon Him.

To the Romans Paul wrote:

> *What then? Israel failed to obtain what it was seeking, that is, God's favour by obedience to the Law, but the remnant obtained it, while the rest of them became hardened and callously indifferent; just as it is recorded in Scripture:*
>
> *"God gave them a spirit of stupor,*

But why would God do that? Surely, He wanted to draw them to Himself? The way we need to read this is not that He actually handed them the spirit of stupor, but that in separating Himself from them because of their obduracy [that is stubbornly refusing to change their minds and look unto their God to transform them into His people worshipping Him in spirit and in truth, as Paul did at first] the spirit within them entered into a stupor because without our spirit being regenerated by and communicating with His Spirit, it is deprived of its energy and spiritual oxygen.

Therefore, they lost their spiritual sight and hearing:

Eyes that do not see and ears that do not hear,

Which caused:

*a spiritual apathy that has continued
to this very day."*

In chapter 29 Moses seeks to explain the covenant oath that sealed their relationship with God.

*1 These are the words of the covenant which the Lord commanded
Moses to make with the sons of Israel in the land of Moab, in
addition to the covenant which He made with them at Sinai.*

Moses reminded the people their experiences of seeing the Lord in action in the land of Egypt and what happened to Pharaoh in the Red Sea. There were also their personal experiences of seeing what the Lord did during their time in the wilderness, even great and mighty wonders.

*4 Yet to this day the Lord has not given you a heart and mind
to understand, nor eyes to see, nor ears to hear.*

Even though they had seen so much there was still a complete disconnect between what they saw and their understanding of God. In spite of all the miracles they had witnessed they had no conception of what it meant, being strangers to the grace of wisdom that is liberally given to those that ask for it.

Their insensibility to the miraculous events to which they had a front seat view was all the more inexcusable. There seemed to be a complete lack of an enquiring mind that was mirrored by the Jews actually standing before their Messiah without any spiritual sensitivity that would have alerted them to His presence.

Remarkable facts

Moses recounted that during the forty years he led them through the wilderness:

- *your clothes have not worn out on you*

- *your sandals have not worn out on your feet*
- *you have not eaten bread*
- *you have drunk wine or strong drink*

The purpose of this reminder was *so that you might know that I am the Lord your God on whom you must depend.*

Moses did his best in his summing up to let the people know just what a big part God had to play in their successes:

> *7 When you reached this place, Sihon the king of Heshbon and Og the king of Bashan came out to meet us in battle, but we defeated them; and took their land, giving it as an inheritance to the tribes of Reuben, Gad, half-tribe of Manasseh. Therefore, keep the words of this covenant and obey them, so that you may prosper and be successful in everything that you do.*

So all Israel had gathered before Moses from the tribal leaders to the people themselves, even the resident foreigner, the women and children, so that together, as a nation:

> *12 you may enter into the covenant of the Lord your God, and into His oath and agreement which the Lord your God is making with you today, 13 so that He may establish you today as His people and that He may be your God, just as He spoke to you and as He swore to your fathers, to Abraham, Isaac, and Jacob.*

This was not a temporary covenant just for those present who stood before the Lord their God, but they were representatives of those that would come from their own bodies after them, their descendants who would also be bound by this covenant. Thus this was a great responsibility for each and every one of them.

The people had first-hand experience, or had heard from their parents, of all that had gone on in Egypt. How the Lord their God demonstrated His mighty over all the gods of Egypt through the plagues and how He had sustained them in the wilderness, and what they had experienced as they passed the nations in their path to where they were today, their contact with Edom, Ammon, Moab and Midian.

What Moses also wanted to stress to the people was the abundance of inanimate carved images, fetishes, and immoral acts of the people wearing costly ornaments that were an excuse for the worship of their deities that the Israelites had seen being enacted; things that were impediments to their relationship with the Lord their God and in fact had caused the deaths of many of their fellow Israelites.

The purpose of the covenant was to bind them to their God

18 so that there will not be among you a man or woman, or family or tribe, whose heart turns away today from the Lord our God, to go and serve the ineffective lifeless gods of these nations; so that there will not be among you the root, the merest hint of idolatry, which in itself bears poisonous fruit and the bitterness of wormwood that will potentially destroy the nation.

The unbelieving sinner is here depicted as a bitter root that bears deadly fruit that will cause many to lose faith and depart from God.

One of the problems of the relationship of a person with God is that it must be continually active. It is no use believing that we are alright with God just because we have, or think we have, been saved.

Just as in Israel there is the very great danger of becoming delusional enough to believe that just because God has provided us with the means of salvation, we can do what we like. God does not work like that.

To receive forgiveness for our sins is just the start of a process. Having been saved by the blood of the Lamb the believer then needs to seek after God to continue the process of salvation in order to gain wisdom and understanding. But most of all to enter into a personal, spiritual, direct one-to-one relationship with the saviour. Without that relationship becoming dynamic, daily, even a minute by minute active relationship by which a two way communion is entered into, then our Christian faith is a fake.

We cannot fully experience salvation from a distance; only by getting increasingly close to God. In that way alone are we able to enter into a spiritual, covenantal relationship with Him through the Holy Spirit. Only in this way will we even begin to gain spiritual knowledge and understand from Him what is required of us.

No one enters into a relationship with another without them both having first laid down some form of arrangement by which the two can live amicably together. What is different with man's relationship with God is that it is the legal engagement prior to marriage, therefore there are commitments to be made on both sides.

God established His credentials and expectations long ago, it is therefore up to the individual to willingly commit themselves to the relationship and allow God to draw them to Himself.

From that initial commitment there is a process of getting to know each other. For the new believer that means seeking after God through prayer and studying God's word, learning how to approach Him and understand Him. Which is why this study is so essential.

Here we have a case where a person could be part of Israel, or a member of a church. That does not mean they can do what they like believing they are safe as full blown Israelites or confirmed believers in the Lord Jesus.

Notice how the text below reads *It will happen*. Not that it might happen, but that *it will happen*.

> *It will happen that when one following the dictates of their heart hears the words of this curse, and he imagines himself as blessed, saying, 'I will have peace and safety even though I walk within the stubbornness of my heart by rejecting God and His law.*

There are those who do not fully believe in the power of God, and that unbelief leading to rebelliousness will act like the root of a poisonous fruit bearing plant that may have been cut down but is still active under the surface. That root will put new shoots that have the potential to cause others to stray.

The belligerent over-confident person who is prepared to defy God, believing they are invincible has the potential to drag others away from God.

> *when he hears the words of this curse, he blesses himself in his heart, saying, 'I shall have peace, even though I follow the dictates of my heart'—as though the drunkard could be included with the sober.*

Sadly he is disillusioned and will find himself rejected by God for:

20 the Lord will not be willing to forgive him, rather the anger of the Lord and His jealousy will burn against that man, and every curse which is written in this book will rest on him; in fact the Lord will blot out his name from under heaven.

Sadly the kings of the ten tribes of Israel all went astray. Jeroboam, the first king of the separatist tribes, was also the first to defy God and set the tone for all succeeding kings[47]

21 Then the Lord will single him out for disaster from all the tribes of Israel, making an example of him, according to all the curses of the covenant that are written in this Book of the Law (cf. Rev. 22:18, 19).

Personal responsibility was placed upon those that had heard Moses declare the blessings and curses and then ignored them believing, like Cain, they could make a life for themselves without God.

These people had experienced God first hand, from the way He dealt with the Egyptians to the way He dealt with those within Israel who thought they could thwart Him and paid with their lives.

The Korah rebellion (Num. 16) was a case in point. As Levites they had certain privileges because they served at the tabernacle, but they were not satisfied with that. They complained about the authority Moses had over the affairs of the nation, however, as it was God given they had no right to question it. But they did. So Korah and those following him were called to the tabernacle for God to decide whether or not they had a legitimate case.

Korah, Dathan and Abiram along with their families and all their chattels were consumed by the earth opening up, and the two hundred and fifty followers were consumed by fire from the Lord, to the horror of all the people.

One man brought a curse on the nation which brought death to those involved. If it had not been for Moses quick thinking many more would have died (vs. 44 – 50).

The responsibility to obey God and be faithful to the covenant was on each generation. Here Moses was warning them that in spite

---

[47] Law & Grace gives plenty pf information regarding the shameful activities of those kings.

of all the warnings they had received concerning the dangers of paganism there would be some who would not believe God could or would do anything.

> *It will happen, says God through Moses that when one following the dictates of their heart hears the words of this curse, and he imagines himself as blessed, saying, 'I will have peace and safety even though I walk within the stubbornness of my heart by rejecting God and His law.*

It was all down to those that would follow *the dictates of their heart.* But listen to what Moses is saying, because he was warning them that by defying the warnings they had received from God, there were consequences, not necessarily only for the perpetrators of the rebellion, but for future generations.

Just as Adam did not fully understand that when God said something, it really would happen until he found himself and his wife outside the comfort and security of God's garden, so future Adam types would discover that God was true to His word by the results of their rebellion.

> 22 *It will be the next generation, your children along with the foreigner who comes from a distant land, who, when they see the plagues of this land and the diseases with which the Lord has afflicted it, will say, 'The whole land is brimstone and salt, a burning waste, unsown and unproductive, with no grass able to grow in it; it is like the overthrow of Sodom and Gomorrah, Admah and Zeboiim, which the Lord overthrew in His anger and wrath.'*
>
> *The nations will say, 'Why has the Lord done this thing to this land? Why this great outburst of anger?'*
>
> *Then people will say, 'It is because they broke the covenant of the Lord, the God of their fathers, which He made with them when He brought them out of the land of Egypt. They defied Him by serving other gods and worshiped them, even though they were false gods they had not known and God had not told them about.*
>
> *It was because of this that the anger of the Lord burned against this land, bringing on it every curse that is written in this book; and the Lord even uprooted them from their land in anger and in wrath*

and in great indignation, and cast them into another land, as it is this day.'

Dear reader, just remember that God is the same yesterday, today and forever. He never changes. Do not be fooled into thinking that in this modern age you can experiment with other religions, because He is a jealous God insofar that He will not share His glory with another. It was He wo made us and not we ourselves.

29 The secret things belong to the Lord our God, but the things which are revealed and disclosed belong to us and to our children forever, so that we may do all of the words of this law.

There is much about God and this world and particularly the world of the spirit that we know very little about, although there are times when it impacts upon the physical, such as in the case of spiritual warfare that Daniel experienced (Daniel 10:13). God only reveals what He wants man to know. However He expects us to take notice of what He has revealed to us and obey it.

19 RESTORATION PROMISED

Chapter 30

What is made very clear is that from the beginning God gave the Israelites commandments by which they were to direct their daily lives in order that they might live a full and fruitful life. Had they done just that then all would have been well and God would have blessed them and protected them from potential enemies.

What is also made very clear is that man is fickle. Even though God gave Adam a beautiful garden in which he could enjoy his life in safety he listened to someone else.

Throughout the wilderness wanderings the people were fed and protected, they needed for nothing, yet there always seemed to be an excuse for someone to complain or cause unrest and for the weak to be led by the strong. But that is the DNA of sin erupting.

After the people had gone into the promised land and subdued it, after a fashion, there seemed to be no cohesion within the nation. After the death of Joshua, the book of Judges paints a sorry picture. But worst was to come.

For instance the exile of the ten northern tribes was terminal, and the exile of Judah brought about the end of the line of kings sitting on the throne of King David, so that the restored Israel became a republic with Zerubbabel becoming the first governor. However it is interesting that he was descended from the royal house of David.

In the first few verses of this chapter is seen the mercy and loving kindness of God, although there is a condition which is that they had to be prepared to:

obeyed His voice with all your heart and with all your soul, in accordance with everything that I am commanding you today.

In other words they had to make the laws of God part of their very being, part of their thinking and everyday way of life.

Through Moses God reveals that at some point they would rebel and go into exile because of it. Sadly, and it is as true today as it was then, instead of looking to a God that was above the earth, in the heavens, they had adopted a natural instinct to look at the world and see what was going on there.

They focused on worldly things rather than the word of God and on God Himself. Yet God had appeared to them, not on ground level with them, but high on a mountain top. He spoke to them out of the fire and smoke that erupted from the peak in their own language so that they could all hear what He was saying.

One of the commandments He issued was that they should make no carved image of him. After all they could not see Him. Only hear Him. So how could they make an accurate image of Him, but even if they had been able to make an image of Him, their attention would have become fixed on the image not on God Himself. That is the way of man, which God knew all about.

The Israelites lowered their gaze and saw what was going on all around them. They did not like being different, even though God was blessing them because of it. They had not opened their hearts and minds to Him and sought Him with all their being. And so they were easily distracted and started to assimilate with the ways of the surrounding nations. Not just the people but the priest also[48] (Ez. 8).

What is so wonderful about the mercy of God, and something many believers miss when they read the First Testament, is that God had prepared a plan for their return to the land should they realize their sin and want to start again obeying His commandments.

Moses was telling the people even before they had set foot on the promise land that when they found themselves exiled, if they recalled *the blessing and the curse which I have set before you* and there was a desire within them to return to the Lord and they were prepared to *return to the Lord your God and obey His voice, according to all that I command you today, with all your heart and with all your soul* then *the Lord your God will*

---

[48] See my book Law and Grace which deals with the events leading up to the exile and the return.

351

restore you back in the land from exile, and have compassion on you, and will gather you together again from all the peoples (nations) where He has scattered you.

For all believers reading this please understand, God never withdraws His offer of full salvation and blessing to those who are distracted for a time but then willingly return to Him. Be assured that He is there with open arms.

What other nation had that offer? What other nation ever recovered from being sent into exile? What other nation was restored to the land they had vacated?

It is worth considering Nehemiah's reaction to the problem of the remnant left in Jerusalem and the destruction of the city wall and gates at this point because his reaction illustrates exactly what Moses spoke about all those years previously.

> *In the month of Chislev, Hanani, one of my brothers, and some men from Judah came to see me in the capitol of Susa. I asked them about the surviving Jews who had escaped and survived the captivity, and about Jerusalem.*
>
> *They told me, "The remnant there in the province is in great distress and reproach; the wall of Jerusalem is broken down and its fortified gates have been destroyed by fire."*
>
> *When I heard these words, I sat down and wept and mourned for days; fasting and praying constantly before the God of heaven.*

Is this not the very situation that God was telling the people would happen through Moses, even before they entered the promised land? Read again the previous paragraph that starts, "When in exile if they recalled *the blessing and the curse which I have set before you …*", does this record of Nehemiah's not illustrate the very thing that God was telling the people about through Moses long before it happened and in effect prophesying that it would happen?

And consider how Nehemiah addressed the God of Moses,

> *"O Lord God of heaven, the great and awesome God, who keeps the covenant and lovingkindness for those who love Him and keep His commandments."*

What had Israel and Judah done but the very thing that God had warned them not to do. Go after other gods. With even the priests rebelling against God.

We read in Exodus:

> *you shall not worship any other god; for the Lord, whose name is Jealous, is a jealous [or impassioned] God rightly demanding what is uniquely His, that is the undivided and unadulterated worship of man who He elevated to the position of overlord of His creation. Not for them to worship what He had created or that demons had caused to be produced.*

This is the law by which they were to regulate their daily lives, *you shall not worship any other god*. Nehemiah amongst others such as Daniel, had to suffer the indignity of being exiled and had time to realize that their forebears had insulted God and rebelled against Him resulting in them having to live far from home. It was not that God had not warned the people even before they entered the land:

> *The nations will say, 'Why has the Lord done this thing to this land? Why this great outburst of anger?'*
> *Then people will say, 'It is because they broke the covenant of the Lord, the God of their fathers, which He made with them when He brought them out of the land of Egypt. They defied Him by serving other gods and worshiped them, even though they were false gods they had not known and God had not told them about.*

So we have Nehemiah in exile serving the king of Babylon pleading with God to help him persuade the king to allow him to go and put things right by rebuilding the wall and erecting new gates:

> *... please let Your ear be attentive and Your eyes open to hear the prayer of Your servant which I am praying before You, day and night, on behalf of Your servants, the descendants of Israel, confessing the sins of the sons of Israel which we have committed against You; I and my father's house have sinned.*

Notice how he includes himself,

We have acted very corruptly against You and have not kept the commandments, nor the statutes, nor the ordinances which You commanded Your servant Moses.

Please remember the word which You commanded Your servant Moses, saying, 'If you are unfaithful and violate your obligations to Me I will scatter you among the peoples; but if you return to Me and keep My commandments and do them, though those of you who have been scattered are in the most remote part of the heavens, I will gather them from there and will bring them to the place where I have chosen for My Name to dwell.'

This is what is recorded in Deuteronomy:

3   that the Lord your God will bring you back from captivity, and have compassion on you, and gather you again from all the nations where the Lord your God has scattered you. Even from the farthest parts under heaven. Then the Lord your God will bring you to the land which your fathers possessed, and you shall possess it. He will prosper you and multiply you more than your fathers.

It is clear is that God gives us second and third chances, and many more, (the Lord spoke about seventy times seven) but he would rather they had not reneged on the promises they gave on Sinai in the first place. But just as the Israelites reneged on their promises, so do Christians.

Over the years churches have made adjustments to the word of God and to the church legislation in small increments such that the teaching of the church to day is totally corrupted.

We have gone the way of Israel because congregations only give God lip service, singing hymns without really meaning what they are singing, and preachers delivering messages that they do not really understand or are so empty of the deep things of God that they are meaningless

Although we have not been scattered, as were the Israelites, we have assimilated ourselves into the way of the world to the extent that there is nothing to distinguish us from the people of the world.

We are no longer distinctive.

Going back to Nehemiah's prayer:

> *Now they are Your servants and Your people whom You have redeemed by Your great power and by Your strong hand. Please, O Lord, let Your ear be attentive to the prayer of Your servant and the prayer of Your servants who delight to reverently fear Your Name with awe; and make Your servant successful this day and grant him compassion in the sight of the king."*

As we know Nehemiah was successful and rebuilt the wall and rehung the gates even though there was fierce opposition from those that had infiltrated the land during Israel's absence.

But not all the Jews returned to Jerusalem and the kingdom of Judah. Many preferred to stay in Babylon where they had settled. Certainly the promised land had shrunk considerably and all because of their rebellious nature, and they were to have a troubled existence from then on.

> *4 Even if any of you are dispersed to the ends of the earth, the Lord your God will gather you together from there, and from there He will bring you back.*

What is also clear is that this promise has not yet been fulfilled because they had not been scattered to the ends of the earth as they are at this present time, so it could well be that the full return is yet to come especially when considering the next two verses

This is the promise God had made to them through Moses and the reason it has not yet been fulfilled:

> *5 The Lord your God will bring you into the land which your fathers possessed, and you will take possession of it;*

Sadly the land that their fathers originally possessed has shrunk over time because other nations had taken over parts of it. For example Ben-Hadad the king of Aram had acquired the town of Ramoth-Gilead from Israel and Ahab wanted to recover it with the help of troops from Judah under King Jehoshaphat. But because of Ahab's sin he was killed in the battle[49].

and He shall make you prosper and multiply — more than your fathers.

It is true that overtime the numbers of Jews has greatly increased and with the Aliyah the number of Jews returning to the land of Israel is increasing year on year.

Sadly from early on there were those who still persisted in their worship of the gods worshipped by other nations in defiance of God's commands, including leaders and kings.

*6 And the Lord your God will **circumcise your heart** and the hearts of your descendants removing the desire to sin from your heart,*

Jeremiah also spoke to the Jews in his day concerning circumcising the foreskins of their hearts,

Circumcise yourselves to the Lord, And take away the foreskins of your hearts, You men of Judah and inhabitants of Jerusalem, Lest My fury come forth like fire, And burn so that no one can quench it, Because of the evil of your doings." (Jer. 4:4)

From the time of Moses circumcision was practiced, but it was merely the outward mark that signified that they were Jews, not that they were dedicated to their God. True belief comes not from marking the body, but believing with the heart:

so that you will love the Lord your God with all your heart and all your soul, so that you may be a recipient of His blessing.

The Jewish religious leaders at the time of the Messiah prided themselves concerning their knowledge of scripture and the purity of their lives according to the oral law, not the written law that was the Torah. In doing so they had missed not one but two notable and essential facts.

---

[49] See Law & Grace chapter 5

They studied the laws of men which had taken away from the focus on God's law, and it was not the knowledge contained in the mind but the concerns of the heart that was most important for as the verse above tells us, it has got to be love for the law giver that emanates from the very centre of our being, that is the heart.

Unless the knowledge of the mind means so much to us that it is transferred to our hearts, then all that we learn and try to use that learning to live a good life by our own efforts, then all that learning is thoroughly wasted.

We have already discussed the importance of entering into an engagement leading to our spiritual marriage with God and it being a relationship founded on love centred in the heart which is what God wanted in the very beginning when He made man.

Having made man in His image, He then breathed into man the breath of His Spirit creating within man a spirit that could easily communicate with Him and which raised man above all other creatures and the whole of the animal kingdom.

The whole purpose of this was to bring man into an intimate relationship with God because God walked in the garden in the cool of the day wanting to meet with man and speak with him, but man hid from Him because he had disobeyed God in eating from the forbidden tree.

It is that desire to meet with man on his own level that illustrates not only the supreme love of God, but all that God has done after man had been ejected from the garden that God had so lovingly prepared for him.

It is because of God's love for man that He introduced the animal sacrifices to prepare mankind for the coming to the earth in human form of the Son of God, to bring the Word of God directly to man and then provide the eternal sacrifice for sin.[50]

It was not to be until the death, resurrection and ascension of the Messiah that a thorough cleansing of the heart could achieved.

For if the ceremonial sprinkling of the blood of goats and bulls and the ashes of a burnt heifer on an unclean person is sufficient for the cleansing of the body (under the law), how much more will the blood of Christ, who through the eternal Holy Spirit willingly offered

---

[50] This has been dealt with in depth in The Origin of Life and The Tent of the Meeting in which the reason for the virgin birth is fully explained.

Himself as an unblemished sacrifice to God[51], **cleanse your conscience from dead works and lifeless observances to serve the ever living God** *(under Grace)*? *(Heb. 9:13, 14)*

All the verses from Hebrews and other parts of the First and Second Testament that have been repeated throughout this book, have been repeated for emphasis. It is no good quoting scripture once so that it is forgotten by the end of the study, rather it is essential that the meaning of such verses is spread throughout because they are relevant and meaningful.

What God was saying through Moses was that there would come a time when sacrificial blood would be shed that was not merely symbolic with the one asking for forgiveness having themselves to believe that their sacrifice had been accepted by God and they were cleanse of their sin. But that the cleansing would be deep and more thorough.

However, it was not until after the time of the Messiah that the Jews and Gentiles could experience a spiritual transformation within themselves.

What is particularly interesting is that it was not the fact that other nations had been used of God to punish His people, but the degree of their treatment of them. Time and again the ones applying the punishment went too far and ended up being punished themselves. Therefore:

> 7 *The Lord your God will inflict all these curses on your enemies and on those who hate you, who have persecuted you.*

Throughout the First Testament there is this cyclical effect of belief and faith and then a with new generation arriving and applying new ideas to their belief and faith in God, rather than sticking to the original script issued by God through Moses, causing them to plummet to the depths. Bending God's instructions to suit themselves has never been the best way for a man to ingratiate themselves with God their creator.

---

[51] This is more fully explained in A Fresh Look At Easter

The book of Hosea is a prize example of the people having given up on God and no matter how consistently the prophet reminded the people about their marriage vows on Sinai, and demonstrating God's love through his own love for the loose living Gomer, he was ignored. And so exile awaited them.

There is one interesting aspect of the exile of the ten tribes compared to that of Judah that is worth mentioning here. Whereas Judah returned to Jerusalem, albeit only a fraction of those that had gone into exile to Babylon returned, the members of the ten tribes, except those that had moved into Judah, were assimilated into the nations to which they were exiled, thus there was no clear return recorded in holy scripture. In fact the Assyrians did a very good job in mixing all the people they took into exile in their empire meaning that many tribes completely lost their identity.[52]

Although God had promised:

> *that the Lord your God will bring you back from captivity, and have compassion on you, and gather you again from all the nations where the Lord your God has scattered you. Even from the farthest parts under heaven.*

it was not to be at this time although it was undoubtedly partially realized in that God had brought the remnant back from captivity. What is clear about scripture is that it is often meant for another time, and I think this is a case in point.

To illustrate the power and consistency of God, in many ways the Jews being gathered *from all the nations where the Lord your God has scattered you, even from the farthest parts under heaven* is happening now.

In the twenty-first century with not just the establishment of the Land of Israel as the dwelling place of the restored sovereign nation, but the *Aliyah* that has been happening particularly since the establishment of the land of Israel in 1948 has gained pace. The nation is again expanding, although restricted by the many hostile Gentile nations surrounding them and by the politicians of the Western world and those powerful nations under the influence of Satan that are, possibly inadvertently, trying to thwart God's plan.

---

[52] See my book Hosea

But what is Aliyah? It has two meanings. The word *aliyah* translates as *going up* or *elevation*, in relation to going up from the congregation to read the Torah or going up to Israel or Jerusalem.

The first Aliyah was when Joseph took the bones of Jacob to the cave in the field of Ephron the Hittite Abraham bought as a burial place in what is now Israel.

The whole of scripture has been played out in the land that God promised to Abraham, therefore the land is holy and although topographically it is not higher than any of the surrounding area, in a spiritual sense it is elevated, if for no other reason, it is where the Son of the Living God ministered in person.

What becomes very clear is that the whole of scripture points to the coming of the Messiah. The signposts are numerous, because it was according to God's eternal plan, that only after the Messiah paid the full price of the sentence of death served on mankind by God because of sin, that with the conscience of man cleansed, the Holy Spirit could once again bond with man so that all those who had a heart for God, as Abram did, could worship God in spirit and in truth.

It is that bonding, that baptism in the Holy Spirit that would bring about the circumcision of the heart, because it would allow the following to happen:

> *8 And you shall again listen to and obey the voice of the Lord, and fulfil all His commandments which I command you today.*

After the return from Babylon, Ezra took charge of the purification of the priesthood and the people before worship in the restored temple could begin. For the first time, possibly for generations, the word of the Torah was read out to the people so that they would be fed pure spiritual food.

However, after all that effort by the time of the Messiah the priests and people had again deviated from the truth and were back to square one. It was the coming of the Holy Spirit that allowed those that believed in the Lord Jesus to receive Him, enabling them to teach the people all about the Messiah's message and work.

Only by the spiritual transformation of an individual brought about by the Holy Spirit making alive the individual spirit within them were they able to become circumcised of heart .

As we have seen, much of what Moses was telling the people was for the far distant future, no less this next verse. Although the ten tribes prospered under Jeroboam II in regard to material wealth and the recapture of land lost to other nations[53], it was not to last long after his death.

It was not until after 1948 and the 1967 six day war, when God enabled Israel, against all the odds, to defeat the might of the surrounding Arab nations that wanted to destroy it that the real transformation of the nation of Israel took hold, and then only after a struggle.

Since independence, and the demonstration of its ability to defend itself, God has undoubtedly enabled the modern nation of Israel to prosper materially.

> *9 Then the Lord your God shall make you abundantly prosperous in everything that you do, in the offspring of your body and in the offspring of your cattle and in the produce of your land; for the Lord will again delight over you for good, just as He delighted over your fathers,*

But what is even more significant is that the prophecy of Zechariah is gradually being fulfilled (Zech. 12:10). There is a strong movement of Jews that believe Yeshua of Nazareth was the long awaited Messiah, a message that is reaching out to other Jews who are coming to faith in increasing numbers.

The Covid-19 lockdown is proving to be an excellent time for individuals to go on the world wide web and log on to One for Israel and read the testimonies of those that have accepted Jesus as their Messiah.

God is moving in modern day Israel so the following is also becoming true:

> *10 if you listen to and obey the voice of the Lord your God to keep His commandments and His statutes which are written in this Book of the Law, and if you turn to the Lord your God with all your heart and with all your soul (your entire being).*

---

[53] A more in depth account can be found in Law & Grace chapter 21

then God will be able to transform the individual and allow them to draw close to Him. God is transforming the seekers after the truth, and they are accepting Jesus as their Messiah and literally their spiritual lives are being transformed to the extent that they are new people in Christ.

It is the matter of an individual's willingness to turn *to the Lord your God with all your heart and with all your soul* that enables the transforming process to begin.

We now come to Moses comments about the commandment being readily available which we need to understand because they could be considered rather obscure.

> 11 *For this commandment which I am commanding you today*
> *is not too difficult for you, nor is it out of reach.*

The fundamental law that Moses had been teaching the people from their time at the mountain of the Lord was all about loving the Lord their God and obeying His instructions for their life. What it was not was instruction for worship as with pagan worship.

Because God was a living God, the fundamental law that Moses had taught the people over forty years was that God was a God of love; thus the most important commandment was that they should love Him in return. Not only that but as God had created in them a spirit, it was essential that they used that spirit to enter into a spirit based relationship with Him. Therefore:

> 12 *It is not a secret that is hidden and can only be found in*
> *heaven, making it necessary to ask, 'Who will go up to heaven for*
> *us and bring it to us, so that we may hear it and obey it?'*

So the commandment that Moses is here referring to is to love and obey God by living a life not only focused on Him and returning His love for them, but living a life in accordance with His instructions so that He would be able bless them and to guide and support them, particularly in difficult situations that they were bound to encounter.

God was not some distant being, rather being Spirit, God was able to be with them, not in heaven, but beside them. Unless they were willing to understand that, then they could not open themselves up to Him.

The problem to which they were oblivious was the reaction of other tribes that did not know about the creator God. Instead, by having Satan as their lord they would be bound to show hostility towards the Israelites. Indeed it is an attitude that has been demonstrated over the years to the present day.

Nor is it beyond the sea, so that you should ask, 'Who will cross the sea and bring it to us, so that we may hear it and obey it?'

Many an ancient sage would travel far and wide in a lifelong quest to gain knowledge. But the Israelites were in the remarkably privileged position to being given this fundamental truth of life from the creator Himself.

But the word is very near you, in your mouth and in your heart, so that you may obey it.

This is what Solomon says in Proverb:

When you walk about,
the godly teachings of your parents will guide you;
When you sleep, they will keep watch over you;
And when you awake, they will talk to you.

These are things that had been talked about by the adults and taught to their children throughout their time as a nomadic tribe in the wilderness. Not only did they know the commandments intimately, but had learned by way of many a painful lesson what would happen should they think that they could defy God.

Moses never said that it would be easy loving and obeying God, stressing the positive and negative effect of either doing being attuned to God or rebelling against Him.

It is a matter of the spiritual relationship that they needed to secure with God that would transform their lives and enable them to become united with God as the diagram shows.

BODY | SOUL | GOD SUSTAINED SPIRIT

We do not have to go anywhere to find God. Not to heaven or the extremities of the earth. Because He is all around us all we have to do is to call upon Him and He will enhance the spirit that He breathed into us.

Moses now brought the startling truth to them about their situation. God had chosen the descendants of Abraham to be His means of communicating with the rest of the world, which was a vital task if the message of the God of creation was to reach the rest of the world.

How sad that instead of being willing to be separated unto God for His purposes, which would benefit both them and mankind in general, they preferred to be focussed on themselves and their own desires, looking at how others live rather than trusting God. In that way they were denying the rest of mankind the essential information for them to be saved from sin and the Devil and live long and worthy lives in the sight of God. How many church members are doing exactly the same thing?

Let me relate this to you 9 from my book Christ IS King : A Guide for Doubters:

> Scotsman James Hudson Taylor was challenged by God to go to China as a missionary doctor in the mid 1800s to heal the sick and preach the gospel and in so doing started the China Inland Mission, which organization was used to send many missionaries out to that vast land which was so full of spiritual darkness. In his autobiography he tells this story:
>
> *"On one occasion I was preaching the glad tidings of salvation through the finished work of Christ, when a middle-aged man stood up and testified before his assembled countrymen to his faith in the power of the Gospel."*
>
> *"I have long sought for the Truth,"* said he earnestly, *"as my fathers did before me; but I have never found it. I have travelled far and near, but without obtaining it. I have found no rest in Confucianism, Buddhism, or Taoism; but I do find rest in what I have heard here tonight. Henceforth I am a believer in Jesus."*
>
> The man was one of the leading officers of a sect of reformed Buddhists in Ningpo (near Shanghai). A short time after his confession of faith in the Saviour, there was

a meeting of the sect over which he had previously presided. I accompanied him to that meeting, and there, to his former co-religionists, he testified to the peace he had obtained in believing in the Lord Jesus. Soon after, one of his former companions was converted and baptized. Both now sleep in Jesus. The first man long continued to preach to his countrymen the glad tidings of great joy. A few nights after his conversion he asked how long this gospel had been known in England. He was told that we had known it for hundreds of years."

"What!" said he, amazed, *"is it possible that for hundreds of years you have had the knowledge of these glad tidings in your possession, and yet you have only now come to preach it to us? My father sought after the Truth for more than twenty years, and died without finding it. Oh why did you not come sooner?"*

In conclusion Hudson Taylor wrote: *"A whole generation has passed away since that mournful inquiry was made; but how many, also, might repeat the same question today? More than two hundred million have been swept into eternity, without an offer of salvation. How long shall this continue, and the Master's words, "To every creature," remain unheeded?"*

That selfish attitude of bothering about themselves and rebelling against God was to take them to the depths of despair.

Paul brings a different perspective to this matter because he emphasizes Christ as the word of God. Firstly to Timothy Paul wrote:

> *All Scripture is given by divine inspiration and is profitable for instruction, for the conviction of sin, for the correction of error and restoration to obedience, for training in righteousness that is living in conformity to God's will and purpose, behaving honourably with personal integrity and moral courage; so that the man of God may be complete and proficient, outfitted and thoroughly equipped for every good work. (2 Tim. 3:16, 17)*

Linking in with the words of Moses Paul wrote to this to the believers in Rome

For Moses writes that the man who practices the righteousness which is based on all the intricate demands of the law shall live by it.

But the righteousness based on faith that produces a right relationship with God in Christ says the following:

"Do not say in your heart, 'Who will ascend into Heaven?' because that would be to bring Christ down again to the earth;

or,

'Who will descend into the abyss?' because that would be to bring Christ up from the dead and be as if we had to be saved by our own efforts, doing the impossible."

But what does it say? "The word is near you, in your mouth and in your heart"—that is, the word, which is the message, the very basis of the faith which we preach.

Just as Moses spoke to the people about being obedient to the commandments they had received from God on the Mountain, the Word that was tented amongst us tells us this:

"If you really love Me, you will keep and obey My commandments.

Is that not the same word that Moses gave to the people: *You shall love the Lord your with all your heart …?* But because of the Lord's sacrifice we are no longer under the Law but under Grace. Does that mean that the Commandments of God delivered on the mountain top no longer apply to us? Jesus said that He had not come to abolish the Law of God but to fulfil it, therefore it is imperative that we study the whole of scripture and allow the Holy Spirit to interpret its message to us.

Is it not true that not one jot or tittle will be removed from the Law? Therefore even though the Law still stands we are enabled to fulfil the Law not by our own efforts as previously required, but through the support and encouragement of the Holy Spirit through whom we are baptized into spiritual things.

Nicodemus could not understand the need to be born again, because he had no understanding of the things of the Spirit of God and the need to be born spiritually. But we who have been instructed through the coming of The Christ can enjoy a closer relationship with God through the offices of the Holy Spirit.

> *And I will ask the Father, and He will give you another One who will be to you a Helper, Comforter, Intercessor, Counsellor, Strengthener, Support, who will be with you forever. He is the Spirit of Truth, whom the world cannot receive and take to its heart because it does not see Him or know Him, but you know Him because He, the Holy Spirit of God remains with you continually and will be **in** you.*

We have the advantage of those who received the words of Moses, for through the indwelling Holy Spirit we are brought nearer to God and the things of God that are spiritual are opened up to us.

Choose life

Moses finally concludes this part of his discourse with a challenge that sums up all that he had been telling them. Jewish ethics has its roots embedded in the doctrine of human responsibility, which is the freedom of the human will. The rabbis' undisputed maxim is that 'all is in the hands of God except the fear of God.' Godly fear results in the awesome respect of God, and that must be central to our personal approach to Him. Without that respect for God, then a devious course will be certain to take us away from God with the inevitably results. But it is then our responsibility.

> *15 Listen closely to me. I have today set before you life and prosperity, death and adversity;*

Here are the stark choices:

> *16 to love the Lord your God, to walk, living each and every day, according to His ways and to keep His commandments and His statutes and His precepts, so that you will live and multiply, and that the Lord your God will bless you in the land which you are entering to possess.*

Or for their heart to turn away from God so that

17 you will not hear and obey, but are drawn away and worship other gods and serve them,

in which case:

18 I declare to you today that you will certainly perish. You will not live long in the land which you cross the Jordan to enter and possess.

What is very clear is that all Moses was telling them was being overseen by God in heaven.

19 I call heaven and earth as witnesses against you today, that I have set before you life and death, the blessing and the curse;

Moses had done his job in presenting the option to the people of Israel of enjoying a prosperous life in love and obedience to God, or rejecting Him and suffering the withdrawal of all His promises, which is what the curses are all about.

As much as darkness is the absence of light so the curses represented not only the absence of the blessings of God, but also attracting the visitation of the demonic (Lk. 11:24 – 26).

Moses recommendation was for the people to:

choose life in order that you, and your descendants may live, by loving the Lord your God, obeying His voice, and holding closely to Him; for He is your life, the key to a good life and abundant life, indeed He is your fulfilment and responsible for the length of your days, that you may live in the land which the Lord swore to give to your fathers, to Abraham, to Isaac, and to Jacob."

20 NEW LEADER APPOINTED

Chapter 31

Moses' Last Counsel

Being appointed by God as the leader of Israel at the burning bush sometime before his eightieth birthday, Moses now confesses to the people that he had finally reached his 120th birthday.

Remarkably, although neither his physical nor intellectual powers had diminished in any way, to him had been given the task of rescuing the people from the tyranny of Egypt and training them in the things of God throughout their pilgrimage to the promised land.

A land that was the gift of God to the descendants of Abraham to whom he first gave the promise of all the land his foot had touched.

It is true that Moses had erred when he struck the rock rather than ordering it to give up its water, but that was most likely through the frustration he felt with the constant obstreperousness of the people who had been a thorn in his side from the beginning, and would continue to cause problems to the present day with their lack of belief and faith and therefore their understanding and trust in the living God.

Moses had served the Lord his God with distinction which is why God spoke to him face to face, and why he appeared with Elijah during the transfiguration of Christ.

But now, knowing his time on earth was limited he announces both his departure as their spiritual and military leader, and his successor, with God's choice being no surprise.

Joshua is the one who will go across before you, to lead you, just as the Lord has said.

As Moses' servant for many years, he had experienced the leadership of his master, along with all its ups and downs. But he had also been introduced to Moses' spiritual side and had drawn close to God as a result. It was he who had led the army during the many skirmishes in which they were involved during their wanderings through the wilderness.

God is never one to leave His people alone to fend for themselves, rather He tells us that He will never leave us nor forsake us. Indeed David confessed that wherever he was, God was beside him (Ps. 139). Which is a very comforting fact, particularly when things seem to be going wrong.

So Moses exhorted the people not to be intimidated by the menacing opposition of those they were commissioned to destroy, assuring them that their covenant-God, who had overseen their safe journey thus far, would not only be going over the Jordan ahead of them, but would cause such fear and trembling within the hearts and minds of those living in the land that they would be able to overcome them.

4 The Lord will do to them just as He did to Sihon and Og, the kings of the Amorites, and to their land, when He destroyed them.
5 The Lord will hand them over to you, and you shall do to them in accordance with all the commandments which I have commanded you.

The problem is that even though God proves Himself to us in one or more instances there is within us a problem which is that of not being absolutely certain of what is going to happen in the future and therefore doubts crop up in the mind about the outcome even though we have received assurances from God.

Trusting God is easier said than done. It is this problem that has been with us since the time of Adam when Satan put the seeds of doubt into the mind of Eve before she ate of the fruit of the forbidden tree.

As we consider the promises the Lord Jesus gave to the disciples about the coming of the Holy Spirit, and we have the advantage of reading about the way the Holy Spirit empowered the disciples on the day of Pentecost. Even the impulsive Peter was given words and a boldness to speak for his first major public speaking engagement, we as individuals still have to make that move to trust God. This was the problem the Israelites had.

Moses did his best to encourage them:

> *6 Be strong and courageous, do not be afraid or tremble in dread before them, for it is the Lord your God who goes with you. He will not fail you or abandon you."*

Transfer of leadership

> *7 Moses then called to Joshua and said to him in the sight of all the people of Israel, "Be strong and courageous, for you will go with this people into the land which the Lord has sworn to their fathers to give them, and you will give it to them as an inheritance. It is the Lord who goes before you; He will be with you. He will not fail you or abandon you. Do not fear or be dismayed."*

To ensure Joshua's authority was not at some time questioned, Moses announces before the whole of Israel Joshua's official appointment as his successor. The encouragement Moses gave was as clear an instruction to the new leader and the people as it was possible to give concerning the promises of God to be there with them.

The law given to the priests

> *9 So Moses wrote this law and gave it to the priests, the sons of Levi who carried the ark of the covenant of the Lord, and to all the elders of Israel.*

With Moses having committed the Torah to a written document, he delivered it into the hands of the religious and secular heads of the nation for safe keeping, commanding them to have it read periodically to ensure all the people then living would be in no doubt about their responsibility towards their covenant-God.

The Torah was not the preserve of the religious and civil leadership, but was for all the people. However it was the responsibility of that leadership, as its guardians, to ensure it was periodically read out to the people, a responsibility that quickly fell into disuse.

It is interesting that after the Temple had been neglected, and when Josiah came to the throne he had the Temple of the Lord repaired and during the renovations Hilkiah the high priest found the book of the law Moses had written and presented to the leaders as described above.

How come the Torah had lain neglected in a decaying temple for many years? Surely that was a clear illustration of what the kings and leaders thought of God and the respect they had for His word (2 Kgs. 34:15).[54]

I wonder how many believers today have Bibles in their homes gathering dust, neglected as is their love and concern for the God that has provided salvation at great cost. They cannot rely on being welcomed into heaven.

Certainly during the exile in Babylon, Ezra the scribe had studied the Torah and by the end of the seventy years was the authority on it and was therefore made responsible for not only purifying the priesthood, but also the people and then reading the Torah to the people before legitimate worship could be started in the newly built Temple.

It is so easy not to bother, and yet God bothered to keep them from harm and bless them. By not bothering, God withdrew His hand from them so that the blessings and protection suddenly stopped.

> *10   Then Moses commanded them, saying, "At the end of every seven years, at the time of year when debts are forgiven, at the Feast of Tabernacles, when all Israel comes to appear before the Lord your God in the place which He chooses, you shall read this law before all the people of Israel so that they may hear.*

It is interesting that the sabbatical year was chosen because it was that year that there will have been no sowing or reaping and therefore

---

[54] See chapter 13 of Law & Grace

the people had had to depend on the goodness of God for their food.

According to the Talmud, the men were there to learn, the women to hear and the children for a reward to those that had spent time and energy in raising them in the faith. Although many of them would not necessarily understand all that was being read, the regular repetition over the years would instil a growing knowledge of what it was all about.

Part of their training was to be God focused (Ps. 8:2). The importance of the Torah for children is for them to hear, learn and observe as they watched their parents observe it and practice it. Merely hearing it once every five years would not have been sufficient, but it was a start when they were very young to understand its importance to the nation.

There would also be the need to study it and observe adults live a life in conformity to it.

If the adults were not bothering with it why should the children? So in society where children pick up a way of life practiced by their parents, it was essential for the future of the nation for the adults to realise their responsibility of observing the law so that the children followed the path of life provided by a loving God.

> *12 Assemble the people, the men and the women and children and the stranger, the resident alien, and foreigner hiding within your cities, so that they may hear and learn and fear the Lord your God, treating Him with awe-filled reverence and profound respect, and be careful to obey all the words of this law.*
> *13 Their children, who have not known the law, will hear and learn to fear and worship the Lord your God, as long as you live in the land which you are crossing the Jordan to possess."*

These instructions are very clear and yet, with the errant kings and leaders of Judah and their declining respect for God, they were very easily neglected. No wonder Judah also suffered going into exile.

Having presented Joshua to the nation as their new leader, it was necessary for both Moses and Joshua to present themselves to the Lord at the Tent of the Meeting for God to commission Joshua as the chosen successor to Moses.

With the cloud, the sign of His presence, beside the door of the tent to prevent any intrusion, Moses was once again told that his departure from this life was drawing near, prophesying that the people he had spent so much time and effort nurturing would *arise and commit apostasy with the foreign gods worshipped by the people of the land, where they go, in order to be among them,* abandoning Me, breaking My covenant with them.

What sadness that would have caused Moses by being appraised of the nation's future infidelity, their corruptions of the true personal and intimate faith in their God through intercourse with the gods of the inhabitants of Canaan that they should have destroyed but through weakness did not fulfil the complete task God had set them, and the chastisement incurred as a consequence of that failure and weakness of faith.

This revelation could well have made him realise that his time of leaving this life was very timely.

Mankind has this flaw in its character which was not as God designed and created man to be. Rather it was caused by the introduction of the DNA of sin by Adam's rebellion which was caused by him following the deceit of Satan.

It is surely this weakness from which the majority of the Israelites suffered and which caused God so many problems in ensuring they fulfilled their part in His plan of salvation for the whole of mankind.

And this flaw, which Paul complained about at the end of Romans 7, was also highlighted in the letters to the seven churches dictated to John and recorded in the book of Revelation.

For example the Ephesians had lost their first love; the church at Pergamos allowed errant teaching; Thyatira allowed a fake prophetess to corrupt the members; the believers in Sardis thought they were alive but many of them were spiritually dead; the Laodiceans thought they were rich but that was only in monitory terms, spiritually they were neither hot nor cold and therefore of no use to God as priests of the living God.

Only the people of Smyrna and Philadelphia were deemed fit for His service[55]. So how many churches in the West are deemed by God to be of any use to him?

---

[55] This is dealt with in depth in Letters to the Seven Churches of Revelation, which is an extract of Seeing Into the Future which is a study of Relation.

What the Israelites (or the churches in the Western world) would not have realized was that by abandoning God they themselves would be abandoned by Him, thus their protection would be removed and they would be open to any and all aggressors. As a nation they would be devoured, with many evils and troubles coming upon them so that there would come a point when:

> *they will say in that day, 'Is it not because our God is no longer among us that these evils have come on us?'*

It seems incredible that the people were so blind that they were not prepared to hang onto a good thing when they had it. After all they had experience good and evil and must surely have realized that it was only when they were God focused that everything worked well for them. But apparently not. Many times the people would realize their sin and waywardness and the justice of their punishment and cry out to God to save them. (2 Chron. 6:24, 25; consider 2 Chron. 6:16)

Having experienced the love and care of God myself, I know for sure that having God in my life is an asset beyond price, but one has to realize that that is not everyone's experience. To enter into a relationship with God it is essential to have a dedicated teacher who has an intimate knowledge of God themselves. Sadly that has not been the experience of either the Israelites or the church.

For consider King Uzziah who, in 2 Chronicles 26 we are told, *sought God in the days of Zechariah, who had understanding in the visions of God,* and as long as the king sought the Lord, God made him prosper. But at some point Zachariah had died and we read that without his mentor, *as soon as he was strong, in wealth and power, his heart was lifted up and transgressed against the Lord his God.*

From this time of Moses' discourses, the Israelites had to continually learn the hard way and even in Israel today, much of the land originally given to them by God is not occupied by them. The tribes that settled on the East side of the Jordan have long since disappeared. Many of the dedicated church buildings in the UK have since acquired other owners and been put to alternative use.

Songs have ever been important, none more than national anthems. If for no other reasons they are a means of bringing the citizens of a country together, uniting them and stimulating pride within them, particularly if far from home.

There are also the negro spirituals that brought a sense of self-worth in the days when human beings with a black skin were considered just chattels, something to be used, bought and sold.

Songs can, therefore, be a powerful influence stirring the deepest emotions in a people. They can also be a means of passing on information and history to the next generation.

So by Divine inspiration Moses composed, or had composed, this song which the Israelites would carry into the promised land with them, and be a witness for God against the children of Israel because when they sinned they would realize that by singing this song it was they themselves that had fallen into the trap of the attractions of the world, rather than focusing their attention on their God.

> *Now write this song for yourselves, and teach it to the sons of Israel; put it in their mouth, so that this song may be a witness for Me against the sons of Israel.*
>
> *For when I bring them into the land I promised to their fathers, which is a land of plenty, flowing with milk and honey, and they have eaten and are satisfied and become prosperous, then they will turn to other gods and serve them, and despise and reject Me and break My covenant.*
>
> *Then it shall come about, when many evils and troubles have come on them, that this sacred song will confront them as a witness. It will not be forgotten from the mouth of their descendants, because I am fully aware of their inclination which is developing even now, even before I bring them into the land which I have sworn to give them.*

God knew their hearts. He knew that they did not have hearts that were totally committed to Him and that as soon as they became established in the promise land their minds and hearts would become attracted to the fleshly lusts and decadent ways of the people they were going in to dispossess and reject Him. That was the message of Hosea[56].

Finally commissioning Joshua as his successor and commanding him to *"Be strong and courageous, for you will bring the sons of Israel into the land which I have sworn to give them, and I will be with you"*, Moses

---

[56] For more details please read my book Hosea.

completed the writing of the law and gave it to the Levites for safe keeping. It is not known if it was kept separate from the ark or in the ark. No matter where, but that it was kept for others to find (2 Kgs 22:8 – 17).

Moses had long experience of *your rebellion and contention and your stubbornness; even whilst I am still alive with you today, you have been rebellious against the Lord; how much more, then, will you be of the same mind after my death?*

Moses then called the tribal elders and officers to come before him where he would

> *28 speak these words in their hearing and call heaven and earth as witnesses against them. For I know that after my death you will behave corruptly and turn from the way which I have commanded you; and evil will come upon you in the latter days, because you will do evil in the sight of the Lord, provoking Him to anger through the work of your hands [by making and worshipping the very graven images God had forbidden them to make or worship].*

> *Then Moses spoke in the hearing of all the congregation of Israel the words of this song, until they were ended:*

21 THE SONG OF MOSES

Chapter 32

This is the second song of Moses. The first was one of rejoicing because the people had just been witnesses to a great deliverance:

> *"I will sing to the Lord,*
> *for He has triumphed gloriously;*
> *The horse and its rider He has thrown into the sea.*
> *The Lord is my strength and my song,*
> *And He has become my salvation;*
> *This is my God, and I will praise Him;*
> *My father's God, and I will exalt Him.*
> *The Lord is a man of war;*
> *The Lord is His name.*
> (Ex. 15:1-3)

This second song was far more sombre because after over forty years the people had shown their true potential which did not bode well for the future. But what the history of Israel proves is that the mighty God has the means whereby He is able to use even the rebellious to cause His plans to be established in the lives of men.

Whereas the first was spontaneous due to the enormity of the sudden dismissal of the impending and all too obvious threat to their safety and future wellbeing, this second is far more considered, initially calling upon heaven and earth to be eternal witnesses to the Divine truths he is about to declare.

Listen, O heavens, and I will speak;
And let the earth hear the words of my mouth.

These words immediately set the tone of the song which contains magnificence of language and grandeur of theme, leading to the sudden transitions from the personal, *I will speak*, to the enormity of God, *ascribe greatness and honour to our God.*

With the elevated ideas displaying sentiments that colour and fashion the underlying message,

2 Let my teaching drop as the rain,
My speech distil as the dew,
As the light rain upon the tender grass,
And as the spring showers upon the herb.

along with the skilful use of language, this song is entitled to be ranked amongst the most sublime specimens of poetry to be found in the whole of scripture.

Such gentleness of language, that describes the manner of the teaching of God through Moses, points both the hearer and the reader to the love and gentleness of God when the people were prepared to respond to His call to become His people.

God wanted to bless them, to protect them and show them a way of life that could be transformational in comparison to the lives of all other nations, but could not be forced upon them. It had to be willingly received.

Moses of all people knew about the love, sensitivity and overwhelming desire of God to develop this people to be His showcase to the world.

As the creator there was nothing God could not do through a willing and obedient people, but only obedient in the manner of a wife in a deeply loving relationship with her husband.

Sadly the people were unaware of the enormity and spiritual magnificence of God[57], but here Moses is stating his credentials for writing this remarkable song.

3 For I proclaim both the name

---

[57] Dan. 7:9, 11; Rev. 41 -11

and presence of the Lord;

The one thing that can be said of Moses is that he was called of God, and after his reluctant acquiescence to the task of leadership and initially relying on Aaron as his voice, he quickly got into the role and became a role model. A most humble man, he became God's servant and led the people in a way that was both impeccable and humbling.

Now we see him in his role as servant not only giving supreme honour to God, but describing the considerable greatness of the God with whom he had become very intimate.

4 Ascribe greatness and honour to our God!
The Rock! His work is perfect,

Just consider that line for a moment. The word *Rock* is expressive, describing not just the longevity of God, but also His consistency and unchangeableness. He had dealt with the errant Israelites with compassion, love and consistent firmness overseen by strong justice.

He was God and it was essential that the errant people were reminded that they could not take God for granted or abuse His person or His love.

Nothing He had promised had failed. If they believed their experience of God had been painfully chequered by severe and protracted trials and tribulations, notwithstanding the brightest promises, then the cause could be easily traceable to their own perverse and rebellious conduct.

For all His ways are just;
A God of faithfulness without injustice,
Just and upright is He.

God had freed them from slavery and provided for them in every possible way, even though at times through testing such as the waters of Marah, so why did they constantly complain that God wanted to kill them and they were better off in Egypt? Yet when they were under the whip of the slave master they had cried out for God to save them from slavery. How perverse is that?

5 They (Israel) have acted corruptly toward Him.
They are not His children, because of their blemish;
But are a perverse and crooked generation.

Their *blemish* alludes to the marks idolators inscribe on their foreheads and on their arms with paint or some other substance. Spiritual intercourse with idols, immediately negates any claim they might have on their Israelite heritage.

After all their time in Egypt, surrounded by countless gods and goddesses, to whom did they cry out? To any of the gods of Egypt? No. To the God of Jacob.

As Moses gained encouragement and trust in the God that had called him to lead His people, and be His visible human representative, Moses directed the display of the power of God through the plagues.

The first three also affected the Hebrews, but the other six avoided the land of Goshen. And from the tenth God enabled them to protected themselves with the sacrifice of a lamb that they had to eat.

So why did they hanker after ineffective gods, when the Lord their God had proved to them so conclusively that He alone was the only living God?

The question posed next is at the heart of their unstable character.

6 Do you repay the Lord in this way,
O foolish and unwise people?
Is not He your Father who has
acquired you as His own people?
He has made you and established you as a nation.

The people were so self-centred, so worldly oriented, so humiliated by the whip and repression that they were unable to see the bigger picture.

The establishment of the covenant on Sinai was in the past and did not affect them; or so they wanted to think. But that covenant bound them to God and particularly to living according to the laws of God. We will see below how God had not just made them as creator, but also established them as a nation.

Fortunately we are assured throughout scripture that there was always a remnant that was God focused and sought, often in very difficult circumstances, to be obedient to the Lord, and it was possibly their voice crying out for deliverance that God heard and responded at the right time in His plan.

> *7 Remember the days of old,*
> *Consider the years of many generations.*

When future Israelite generations had lost their way, the only possible means of finding out about who they were, where the nation had been born and who was their God, was to read again their history, and find out from where they had come.

Isaiah, at a crucial time in their history, called on the people to:

> *Listen to Me, you who pursue righteousness*
> *(that is the remnant seeking to be*
> *in right relationship with God),*
> *Who seek and inquire of the Lord:*
> *Look to the rock from which you were cut*
> *And to the quarry from which you were dug.*
> *(Is. 51:1)*

The foundational truths of their nation had no meaning except they went back to the very beginning of the nation's history, to its birth in the decision by Abram to put his trust in almighty God and follow Him, even to his willingness to sacrifice the son for whom he had waited so patiently.

Abraham is therefore the foundation rock of the nation *from which you were cut*, and the quarry is surely almighty God who had created all things and sustains all things and, moreover, had chosen Abraham as that foundation stone of the nation.

The Lord Jesus, after His incarnation, life, sacrificial death and resurrection, became the foundation stone of the church which is spiritual Israel that was born out of the nation for it includes those from all mankind who accept Jesus Christ as their Lord and Saviour.

It is important for all those that have been born again by the Spirit of God to remember their ancestry, for Gentile believers cannot divorce themselves from the struggles of the nation of Israel because just as those physically born of Israel are challenged to *Look to the rock from which you were cut,* so followers of Christ must go deeper and look *to the quarry from which you were dug,* and surely that quarry was God because Abraham was called of God and Gentiles are the spiritual descendants of Abraham.

After all the one thing that Christians seem to forget, or just ignore is that Jesus was a member of the Godhead, because they prefer to keep things simple and just understand their faith from Jesus the man. And yet by doing so they miss out on deepening their understanding of all things God and those deeper spiritual truths that would strengthen and empower their faith.

Abraham did not gain the righteousness that was awarded to him by follow instructions, but by instinctively having a personal trusting-faith in God and a willingness within his heart to be obedient to His call. After all if Abraham had not been willing to follow God's command to get out of the comfort of his country and travel to a land that God was going to show him, without any long experience of God or knowledge of where God was taking him, then they would not be the special people of God they were. It was all down to belief, trusting faith and faithfulness.

Except they went back to their founding father and considered how he had put his complete faith in the God that had called him, even though all he had previously known was pagan gods, they would not fully understand why their nation was unlike any other, or why God was so essential to their wellbeing and future prosperity.

Abraham's life changing decision was to give up the worship of pagan gods to serve the living God, because he realized that He was truly alive. Why then were many of His descendants so keen to do the reverse and give up worshipping the living God for the worship of ineffectual pagan gods?

After all it was God who led their birth father to the land in which they were about to live and it was through His belief and trusting faith in the God that had cause his offspring to proliferate and acquire the land.

Indeed the land in which they were to live was only theirs because of his faith and faithfulness, and because it was promised to Abraham and his descendants. They did not own the right to be there. He did. It was by them not following his example that was the cause of all their trials and tribulations and why they were exiled and much of the land lost to them, as it is to this day.

Look to Abraham your father

What was so special about Abraham? His righteousness that was awarded to him because of his faith and faithfulness to God. He was their example. This statement by Isaiah was to be an encouragement to the Jewish faithful remnant to continue to put their trust in God for their future deliverance from exile and bring them back from their present dispersion.

You are in a mess, therefore go back to the life of Abraham and see how he was prepared to love and serve God and do likewise.

And to Sarah who gave birth to you in pain;

It was Sarah who, even though she was old and had tried to force God to provide them with a son earlier through Hagar, finally gave birth to their forefather Isaac.

> *For I called him when he was but one,*
> *Then I blessed him and made him many.*
> *(Is. 51:1, 2)*

This verse emphasizes the fact that Abraham was singularly called of God, *For I called him when he was but one,* and it was that same God that caused him to have numerous descendants, *Then I blessed him and made him many.*

The Israelites were continually reminded that it was God who gave the increase be it of agriculture, or population and we only have to understand the situation of women such as Rachel, Sarah and Hannah, to realize just how dependent they were upon God for offspring.

Family story telling was a major feature of life that was used to pass the family history down the generations. That was why celebrating the Passover and recounting its meaning was essential.

During the Seder[58] the father explained to the children what it was all about. Hence Moses command to:

Ask your father, and he will inform you,
Your elders, and they will tell you.

Through his sons Noah became the ancestor of mankind after the flood, and they settled, according to Genesis 11, in the land of Shinar. However, God's command had been *to be fruitful and multiply; fill the earth and subdue it (Gen. 1:28).*

Families, especially in those early days of the human race, wanted to stick together and once again in so doing they neglected God believing they were supreme. The building of the tower of Babel was a step too far for God so in order that they would fulfil His command He brought about the confusion of language, thus causing the people to separate according to the language they had suddenly acquired.

8 When the Most High gave the nations their inheritance,
When He separated the sons of man,
He set the boundaries of the peoples

What is particularly interesting is that when God brought confusion to the sons of man, it was not random for God ensured that the area reserved for the future Israel was carefully chosen.

It was a strategic site being at the junction of the continents of Asia and Africa and almost in sight of Europe. Certainly it was central for news of the wonderful works of God to be transmitted to every part of the globe.

God foreknew the empirical changes which allowed Him to chastise those who were to be His people and broadcast the events in Egypt, the journey of the children of Israel through the wilderness, through to the Roman occupation and the rapid spread of the Gospel when believers were being persecuted.

More recent events have focused on both Israel and particularly on Jerusalem, His chosen city. The area was not large but:

According to the number of the sons of Israel.
For the Lord's portion and chosen share is His people;

---

[58] It is explained in A Fresh Look At Easter

Jacob (Israel) is the allotment of His inheritance.

Even before the choosing of Abraham God had already chosen the land in which His people would live within reach of both the Assyrians and Babylonians, and bordered by the sea and the river Jordan, although when the tribes were first allotted their land Reuben, Gad and the half tribe of Manasseh chose land to the East of the Jordan which has since long been Arab territory.

Israel as a nation was formed in the crucible of Egypt, and born immediately after the first Passover when they left the womb of Egypt, and went through the baptismal waters of the Red Sea.

It was in the wilderness that God *found him in a desert land, in the howling wasteland of a wilderness* where the wild beasts roamed. With fatherly love, He took care of the new born child, protecting him with the pillar of cloud by day and the pillar of fire by night *as the apple of His eye* and through instruction and guidance raised him to adulthood. Entering into an eternal covenant relationship with him.

This is a pictorial view of the fatherhood of God, who provided food and protection and learning through His commandments and instructions in that hostile environment. Most important of all was God feeding the spiritual needs of the people by providing the law by which they learned how to relate to their new Lord and protector.

There is much knowledge available to us about how the eagle cares for her young. Stirring up her nest when it is time for the young to try out their wings, she lures them out of the nest demonstrating how they need to spread their wings to fly for themselves. She hovers over them in case one is too weak or timid to fly, always ready to catch them on her wings should; they become exhausted.

This surely illustrates the care and concern God lavished on the people during their time travelling in the Wilderness School.

It could be said that they were protected from distractions afforded by the wilderness isolation for the text tells us, *so the Lord alone led him; for there was no foreign god with him.*

What becomes clear is that this is a progressive poem for we are now taken to the time when Israel inhabits the land.

13 He made him ride on the high places
of the earth (the promised land),

Or rather Israel was triumphant in becoming the undisputed possessors of the land, even of its high mountains, (the table lands of Gilead) which Moses foresees as an accomplished fact even though they had not yet set foot on the land.

> *And he ate the produce of the field;*
> *And He made him suck honey from the rock,*
> *And olive oil from the flinty rock,*
> *14 Butter and curds of cows, and milk of the flock,*
> *With fat of lambs,*
> *And rams, the breed of Bashan, and goats,*
> *With the finest of the wheat;*
> *And you drank wine, the blood of grapes.*

The Jordan valley was particularly fertile which gave produce and grazing for the domesticated animals. Even around Bethlehem there were flocks of sheep as when the Messiah was born.

Wild bees had hives in the crevices of the dry sandstone rock and in the caves, and olive trees grew singularly or in clumps in the flinty soil of the hills where very little else grew. The area was well known for vineyards and the quality of the wheat even as the fat of the kidneys is the choices of fat.

There is a very great danger of being self-sufficient. What man, who has everything that is required to live a comfortable life, has need of God? During their time in the wilderness the Israelites were dependent upon God for direction, for food and water, but as soon as they had conquered the land, they had an abundance of all they needed for a comfortable life, so what need did they have for God?

Yes God had brought them to the land and help them conquer it, but God was then dispensable.

Consider the name Jeshuran. It is formed from the Hebrew root meaning 'to be righteous', and is a title of honour afforded to Israel under its ideal character as being 'upright'. So it can be used as a complement or, as here, as a rebuke for Israel's future sense of ingratitude for all that God had done for them, and being deceitful and untrustworthy, believing God could not see the falseness of their hearts and actions.

There are many rebukes to Israel throughout scripture for paying lip service to the sacrifices, such as offering defective animals for sacrifice rather than the perfect ones required by God, when at the same time they were worshipping pagan gods. Their hearts were not at all right with God because they had wandered off from the way of righteousness.

Even today there are far too many carnal (of the flesh) Christians who are so divorced from God that their lives cannot be distinguished from those that have no interest in God. No matter that they had been baptised, probably as a baby, and then confirmed into the membership of a church organisation. Salvation is of God and God alone.

Therefore with no personal intimacy with God, no epiphany experience, no transformation by the Spirit of God to bring about the new birth in the Spirit, they have no legitimate claim on the title of Christian or of being true members of the spiritual church of Israel, the head of which is Christ Himself (Eph. 2:19 – 22).

In fact both Jews and Gentiles who, without the discernment provided by the Spirit of God, oppose those who are truly His, just as Paul (as Saul) did, not realizing that they are far from God. Such has been my experience over many years.

15 But Jeshurun grew fat and kicked out at God.
You became fat, thick, sleek, and obstinate!

That sense of being satisfied with your lot of living in peace and security with all your daily needs catered for, why should you bother with the regular process of worshipping God? Even though it was He who was totally responsible for their current situation, that was in the past and now they were comfortable and thought they had no more need of His help.

Tragically, they had become blind to the unknown dangers they faced such as diseases and crop blights, droughts (Elijah), floods and various enemies keen on extending their territories. They had forgotten that His protection was essential to them, along with His control of the environment.

Then he abandoned God who had made him,
And scorned the Rock of his salvation.

Because He cannot be seen with the human eye, it is so easy to forget all about God. Which is why our personal experiences of God are so crucial. If we have experienced the love and presence of God, and know the amazing transformation of our spirit when He touches us and speaks with us, then there is built up within us such a love for God that we do not want to be parted from Him. That has certainly been my experience.

These books of mine have been written purely by inspiration, because sensing His immediacy my thoughts seem to be prompted. True, sometimes large chunks of text have to be deleted, even to thousands of words, when it is evident I have been typing away on my own. But then comes the point where having deleted my work he then gives me further inspiration to write according to His inspiration.

No relationship can be maintained by just one person, rather it is the responsibility of all those in the relationship to be ever vigilant to maintain the value and wellbeing of that relationship.

Prayer is all about speaking with God and then being prepared to listen to God, which could well mean reading the word of God on a regular basis because He often speaks to us through His recorded word.

But the relationship we should be having with God is far more than just speaking to God, because during that moment of prayer there has to be included a part where we, as recipients of His love and goodness, give Him thanks and praise.

And it was in neglecting to afford that effort to regularly speak with God and tell Him that they loved Him and were grateful for all His goodness to Him that brought an end to that essential intimacy and acknowledgement of His covenantal involvement with them. So the importance of maintaining a relationship with their God was devalued and became ineffective.

What is so important to remember is that God never abandons us! Until, that is, we finally and permanently abandon Him. So through His prophets and the loyal remnant, that included people like Samuel, David, Isaiah, Jeremiah, Ezekiel and Daniel, God sought to constantly remind them that He had not gone away. He also found ways of securing His plan of salvation even through all the rebellious acts of the people. For that plan to succeed, the faithful remnant was crucial.

By the looseness of their obedience to His laws and their tendency to be drawn by their carnal senses to the sensuality and superstition involved in the worship of the gods of other nations *they provoked Him to jealousy.* For it was not just the *strange gods,* but *by denying Him the honour and loyalty that was rightfully and uniquely His.*

The whole purpose of them going into the land and destroying the other nations was to rid the land of *repulsive acts* that had *provoked Him to anger.* As creator the whole world belonged to Him, and still does. Therefore for any man to worship meaningless gods was abhorrent to Him, but for His chosen people to renege on their covenant promises and *sacrifice to demons, not to the God who had nurtured them* was particularly hurtful.

They worshipped:

> *17 gods whom they have not known,*
> *New gods who came lately,*
> *Whom your fathers never feared.*

They were effectively worshipping demons, angels of the Devil who was seeking to usurp the throne of God; an impossible task but relentless.

> *18 You were unmindful of the Rock who bore you,*
> *And you forgot the God who gave you birth.*

They were unmindful of the God who had brought about the birth of the nation in Egypt. In travail they had been transformed from a tribe with Jacob as their head to a nation in their own right; but only because of God. Consider all the other nations that had provided the Egyptians with slave labour, resulting in their nation dying out.

The Israelites were released from their slavery by God alone. Although the demonstration of His mighty power through the plagues was crucial to bringing about the exodus from the land of Egypt, it was the drowning of the Pharaoh that brought about their legal release from the authority of the Pharaoh.[59]

> *19 The Lord saw it, and rejected them,*
> *Out of indignation with His sons and His daughters.*

---

[59] This legal issue is explained in chapter 10 of God Rescues His People : Birth of a Nation According to Exodus.

This was the bleeding heart of God, seeing those to whom He had devoted so much love and care going their own way and rejecting Him. It is no wonder He was indignant concerning His sons and daughters.

As we continue to study this book of Deuteronomy, it is incumbent upon us who believe because of Christ, that we learn from their mistakes and ensure that we do not 'go and do likewise'.

The letters to the seven churches in Revelation[60] are a very useful guide as to what we, in the church should and should not be doing to maintain our personal relationship with God.

The problem is how many churches have wandered so far away from God through errant teaching and acceptance of the latest social 'norms' that they are living and worshipping totally contrary to His rules of life resulting in Him turning His face away from them without them realizing it?

Because of the nations rejection of Him it is no wonder that He should *'hide His face from them'*, and leave them to their own devices to *see what their end would be*. They were indeed *a perverse generation, with sons in whom there is no faithfulness*. With His blessings and protection removed, they quickly found out the hard way just how much He had done for them and still did, and after a while they would cry out to Him for deliverance just as they did in Egypt. This cyclical rejection and desperate reacceptance went on throughout their history.

> *21 They have made Me jealous with what is not God;*
> *They have provoked Me to anger with their idols.*
> *So I will make them jealous with those who are not a people;*
> *I will provoke them to anger with a foolish nation.*

Paul took up this theme in his letter to the believers in Rome, and what he said to his own people is relevant to believers today:

> *But they have not all obeyed the gospel.*

Or in the case of the Israelites, the words of God spoken through Moses.

---

[60] My book Letters to the Seven Churches of Revelation is a very valuable said for churches as to what they should be doing, and what they should avoid.

For Isaiah says, "Lord, who has believed our report?"

For sadly in the main the prophets were not believed because the people did not want to believe what they said, just as the Jewish leaders in the days of the Messiah did not want to believe Him!

> *So then faith comes by hearing,*
> *and hearing by the word of God.*
> *But I say, have they not heard? Yes indeed:*

For the creation speaks loudly of God, bearing His signature for the Palmist wrote:

> *The heavens declare the glory of God;*
> *And the firmament shows His handiwork.*
> *Day unto day utters speech,*
> *And night unto night reveals knowledge.*
> *There is no speech nor language*
> *Where their voice is not heard.*

Thus Paul echoes the word of the Psalmist when he wrote:

> *"Their sound has gone out to all the earth,*
> *And their words to the ends of the world."*

So from the start the Israelites had no excuse:

> *But I say, did Israel not know?*
> *First Moses says:*
> *"I will provoke you to jealousy*
> *by those who are not a nation,*
> *I will move you to anger*
> *by a nation devoid of understanding."*

Surely this came to pass when the word of God was opened up to the Gentiles, a word that Jews desperately tried to stifle. They were not a nation, being many nations, and we were devoid of understanding until the likes of Paul opened up the scriptures to us and then we, wanting to know more, studied the word for ourselves and through prayer asked God to open His word up to us. At least those that were interested enough to search for God as Jacob did.

But Isaiah is very bold and says:
"I was found by those who did not seek Me;
I was made manifest to those who did not inquire of Me."

What a contrast to those who from the beginning had been led and taught by God, for it was to them that God gave the commandments, the land and the promise of His blessing, with the only condition that they obeyed His word and served Him alone.

The Gentiles knew nothing about their God because with so many internal squabbles and problems and inward fighting, the Israelites had no time to act as a missionary nation. Once the Christ had come and many Gentiles heard Him they became interested.

Then with the Jewish authorities seeking to crush the spread of the news of eternal life, believing Jews refused to keep the good news to themselves and along with the disciples and later Paul, the Holy Spirit enables The Saviour to be *found by those who did not seek Me* and for Him to be *made manifest to those who did not inquire of Me.*

Suddenly the Gentiles, as individuals, learned about the Messiah and wanted to know more.

But to Israel he says:
"All day long I have stretched out My hands
To a disobedient and contrary people."

Throughout their time in the wilderness and their subsequent history God was there stretching out His hand to them. *"All day long I have stretched out My hands to a disobedient and contrary people."* They did not just reject Him when the Messiah was here on the earth, rather they had woven it into the rules and regulations that governed their worship and teaching such that the fabric of their very existence as a unique nation was anti-God.

It is that feature of the nation of Israel which rejects God, replacing that God focussing aspect of their faith with its own understanding of what and who God they believe He should be that we in the church must avoid emulating. Unless we open ourselves to the work of the Holy Spirit in child like faith, then we will never fully understand God and become intimate with Him.

Let us not be in anyway ignorant of the power and authority of God, nor His eternal right to our respectful love and obedience because, whether or not we believe it, God is our Father both bodily and spiritually. To put it bluntly we would not be alive today if God had not created Adam and then Eve; and we would not be able to communicate with Him except He gave us a spirit and through the work of the Holy Spirit made that spirit alive and responsive to Him. That is what being *born again* is all about.

God is Spirit, said out Lord, and they that worship Him are only able to do so when through their spirit and in truth of heart they communicate directly with Him. Which is a considerable privilege.

The Bible is a complete book and is eternally relevant from Genesis 1:1 to Revelation 22:21! Do you not realize that God is the origin and the source of all knowledge, understanding and wisdom?

There is nothing in this world, no not even science, that did not originate in God. After all before God created the heavens and the earth there was absolutely nothing except God: Father, Son and Holy Spirit.

Initially there was nothing on the earth except the Spirit hovering over the waters until that same Spirit started the final creational work that saw man in the garden of Eden on the sixth 'day'.

Therefore everything, bar none, had to be supplied and supported and sustained by God. Let us remind ourselves what Solomon wrote in Proverbs:

To know godly wisdom and instruction;
To discern and comprehend the words
of understanding and insight,
To receive instruction in wise behaviour
and the discipline of wise thoughtfulness,
righteousness, justice, and integrity;
To those that are of a simple mind
good judgment may be given,
And to the young knowledge and discretion,
The wise will hear and increase their learning,
And the person with understanding will acquire wise counsel
and with it the ability to lead others to eternal truth,

The reverential and obedient fear of the Lord
is the beginning and essential part of knowledge.
But arrogant fools despise Godly wisdom,
instruction and self-discipline.
(Prov. 1:2 – 5, 7)

If we are willing to gain knowledge, the contents of the Bible is a constant reminder that it was God who created all things and it is that very same God who will decide if we are to be gathered with the sheep or the goats; to be with Him in His rest (Heb. 4)[61] or separated with the goats.

How can that which was created tell the Creator that it has no need of Him?

When a person purchases a new item of equipment, the most obvious thing to do is to read the instructions to find out how to operate it and get the best performance out of the new acquisition. Something I did as a technical author in industry.

Unless the individual accepts that they were created by God and that only God can sustain them, not only in this life but also in the life to come, then they will not be able to enjoy what God has planned for those that love Him.

With the way the Israelites treated God and continued to do so in the promised land, it is no wonder that,

22 a fire is kindled by My anger,
And it burns to the depths of Sheol
(which refers to the place of the dead)
It consumes the earth with its increase,
And sets on fire the foundations of the mountains.

Because of their rejection of Him who had given the nation birth and blessed them with His covenant, God wanted to teach them a lesson they would never forget.

23 'I will heap disasters on them;
I will use My arrows on them.

---

[61] It is very important that you read the whole of Hebrews 4.

24 They will be wasted by hunger, and consumed by plague
And a bitter destruction;
And I will send the teeth of beasts against them,
With the venom of crawling things of the dust.
25 Outside the sword will bereave,
And terrors within
For both young man and virgin,
For the nursing child and the man of grey hair.

Moses had first mooted the problem of destroying the nation and starting again with him, now God publicizes the problem:

26 I would have said, "I will dash them in pieces,
I will make the memory of them to cease from among men,",
27 Had I not feared the provocation of the enemy,
That their adversaries would misjudge their victory,
By saying, "Our own hand has prevailed,
And the Lord has not done all this." '

Sennacherib boasted to King Hezekiah that His god was greater than the Lord God worshipped by Hezekiah, which led to his forced return home and his murder in the temple of his god[62]. The surrounding nations that attacked and gained victory over the Israelites at no time realized that their success was due entirely to God withdrawing His protection from them.

It is essential to understand that with Satan's success in gaining control of the earth from Adam, a battle started between God and Satan that continues even to this day. The book of Revelation gives details of Satan's ultimate demise.

Just as with the need to entice the Pharaoh to his death because of his refusal to legally release the Israelites from his control, so God is working according to the rules He set out in the beginning to bring the message of salvation to all men.

He would have honoured Adam had he remained living in loyal obedience to his creator, but because Satan took over the authority God had given to man, God is skilfully working through those that

---

[62] See Law & Grace chapter 11 – Sennacherib's Last Action

love and serve Him to bring salvation and justice to all mankind and ultimately the final demise of Satan.

Sadly the attitude of obstinacy and rebelliousness shown by such a large majority of the chosen nation made God's work that much harder, but not impossible.

Except He showed the extent of His authority to the nation of Israel, they would have been more of a problem than they were. They seemed to be completely ignorant of the special place they had in God's plan to bring salvation to the whole of mankind through them, and the religious leaders at war with the Messiah is a case in point.

How relevant is this book of Deuteronomy even today.

> *28 For they are a nation devoid of counsel,*
> *And there is no understanding in them.*
> *O that they were wise, that they understood this,*
> *That they could discern their future and ultimate fate!*

Sadly, because of their carnality, the Israelites completely lost sight of the commission God had given to them, which meant that they became spiritually blind. This is so very clearly illustrated in the case of Nicodemus, who alone of the religious leaders of Israel, realized that Jesus was more than just a man and was curious to find out more, which ultimately led him to believe in Jesus as the Messiah, yet privately because he liked his position within the nation.

Only after the death of the Messiah did he come out from hiding.

> *30 How could one chase a thousand,*
> *And two put ten thousand to flight,*
> *Unless their Rock had sold them,*
> *And the Lord had given them up?*

As in the case of Sennacherib who reached Jerusalem but was never able to conquer it, although he had captured most of the territory of Judah. He could only have done that by God removing His protection from the Jews, *Unless their Rock had sold them, had given them up.* It was the faith of Hezekiah that caused Sennacherib to lose out on Jerusalem.

It was very clear to other nations that God had initially established Israel in the land and it was not their gods that enabled them to win the victory but the God of Israel allowing them to do so.

> *31 For their rock is not like our Rock,*
> *Even our enemies themselves judge this.*

At no time did God approve of the deeds and spirits of the heathen nations, because they served Satan and not He who created all men. Rather they were corrupt in thought, word and deed. They were rooted in corruption with poisonous fruit.

> *32 For their vine is from the vine of Sodom,*
> *And from the fields of Gomorrah;*
> *Their grapes are grapes of poison,*
> *Their clusters, bitter.*

The root stock was derived from Sodom and Gomorrah. Rather than being righteous, they were spiritually of the Devil. The fruit of their labour and activities is poison, and their clusters give a bitter taste in the mouth because of their evilness.

> *33 Their wine is the venom of serpents,*
> *And the deadly poison of vipers.*
> *34 'Is it not laid up in store with Me,*
> *Sealed up in My treasuries?*

It is important to remember that God has always been long suffering towards errant man, but there comes a time when the moment of judgement comes to all those opposed to God, such as happened to Sodom and Gomorrah.

The final judgement of course is that place where God's presence is ever absent.

> *35 Vengeance (punishment) is Mine,*
> *and recompense (compensation),*
> *In due time their foot will slip;*
> *For the day of their disaster is at hand,*
> *And their doom hurries to meet them.'*

What is particularly interesting is that although it was necessary to use the pagan nations to chastise His chosen people, their barbarism, corruption and moral poison could not remain forever unpunished. The Divine punishment of the enemies of Israel, which were also enemies of God, had been written down from before the world came into being.

> *36 For the Lord will judge His people,*
> *And will have compassion on His servants,*
> *When He sees that their power is gone,*
> *And no one remains, whether bond or free.*

The demise of Israel was never part of God's plan, just their punishment for going astray, and then restitution, *have compassion on His servants,* although it was important that the punishment ran its course, *when He sees that their power is gone.* It is interesting that in the book of Judges, in a compressed timescale the cycles of punishment and restitution seemed to happen in quick succession.

The one thing that God will be able to do is to challenge His people about the power of the gods that they had left Him to worship.

> *37 And He will say, 'Where are their gods,*
> *The rock in which they took refuge?*

Where was their power to save you?

> *38 Who ate the fat of their sacrifices,*
> *And drank the wine of their drink offering?*

Of the offerings you put before them did they eat them? Or was it the birds and wild animals?

> *Let them rise up and help you,*
> *Let them be your hiding place!*

You have put your faith in these symbols of paganism, these gods, so let them help and protect you.

39 See now that I, even I am He,
And there is no god besides Me;
It is I who put to death and I who give life.
I wound and it is I who heal,
And there is no one who can deliver from
the power of My hand.

Finally a proclamation that there is no one like the God who has named Himself after Israel His chosen people. Indeed let all Israel realize that by going after useless, powerless idols along with their foreign followers, they have suffered calamity after calamity, which could so easily have been avoided if they had remained faithful to the almighty God who had called them to be His chosen, to be examples of all the blessings he could bestow on all mankind.

What is particularly amazing is that as true Gentile believers in, and servants of, the Lord Jesus Christ, Messiah to Israel, we are joined together with Israel to become spiritually aligned to God, because we *are no longer strangers and foreigners, but fellow citizens with the saints and members of the household of God* (Eph. 2:19).

The Saviour said, *there are other sheep that are not of this fold (of Israel), them also must I bring.* Is that not truly wonderful that we become *fellow citizens* with the remnant of Israel, because *not all Israel are of Israel, nor are they all children because they are of the seed of Abraham, that is those that are the children of the flesh, and therefore not of the Spirit, cannot claim to be the children of God. Only the children of the promise can claim to be the children of God* (see Ro. 9:6 – 9).

The whole purpose of studying the Torah and other books of the First (not the Old and redundant) Testament is to realize just what an amazing thing has happened such that we are able to be brought into communion with God the creator because of the blood shed by the Jewish Messiah Jesus Christ on the cross at Calvary, and both the why and how such a gift has been offered to all mankind.

40 Indeed, I lift up My hand to heaven,
And by so doing swear an oath that, as I live forever,
41 If I whet My sword,
And My hand takes hold of judgment,
I will render vengeance on My adversaries,
And repay those who hate Me.

We must never forget that as soon as the covenant between God and Israel agreed on the mountain became legal tender, those who hate Israel also have become haters of God.

Now this is significant, particularly in the present time when many within the established churches, particularly in the Western world, are against Israel with boycotts and other anti-Israel activities.

Who on earth is perfect? That is why we all need the forgiveness only God can give. So why do we who are sinners in need of salvation, and which we can only receive from the God of Israel, hate God's chosen people Israel?

Because just as amongst Gentile nations, within Israel there are both those that are citizens of the household of God *and* those that are not of Israel, for as quoted above, even though they were born of Israel, they are of the flesh, not of the Spirit of God and therefore not of the true Israel.

God's final vengeance on all those that oppose Him, and all that He is seeking to accomplish through both His people and the church will be remorseless and complete. There is no one of the flesh that can stand against Him who has the world in His hands.

We have only to read about the seals, trumpets and bowls in Revelation to begin to understand the effectiveness of the arrows and sword of the Almighty and the final outcome of the battle between Satan, along with all his followers, both angelic and human, and God.

Planet earth had a beginning, and it undoubtedly has an end when it will be consumed with fire.

> *42 I will make My arrows drunk with blood,*
> *And My sword will devour flesh,*
> *With the blood of the slain and the captives,*
> *From the heads of the leaders of the enemy.'*

There is a spiritual war that has been raging since Adam was ejected from the Garden, and will only end at God's appointed time.

Many of the spiritual battles that have been fought have spilled over into the physical creation. In the meantime we are to rejoice over all that God is doing in the world.

> *43 Rejoice, O Gentile nations, with His people;*
> *For He will avenge the blood of His servants,*

And will render vengeance on His adversaries,
And will atone for His land and His people."

As believers we too should rejoice in the power and authority of God and the stability that He alone can bring to the world.

> *44 Then Moses came and spoke all the words of this song in the hearing of the people, he and Joshua the son of Nun.*
>
> *When Moses had finished speaking to the whole congregation of the people of Israel, he said to them, "Take to heart all the words of warning which I am speaking to you today; and you shall instruct your children to observe them carefully and live by all the words of this law.*
>
> *For it is not a futile or trivial matter for you; in fact it affects the whole of your life. By honouring God by obeying this word you will live long in the land, which you are crossing the Jordan to possess.*

It was essential that not just the adults but the children also took to heart all that Moses was telling them, particularly because the warnings within the message being delivered concerning the necessity of observing and living their lives according to the words of the Torah because it would directly affect the lives of all succeeding generations. Which it in fact did, to a disastrous degree.

We also must realise that there is much of which we must be conscious because Jesus did not come to abolish the Torah and the law but to fulfil that part of it that related to His coming. For the Torah is not a book of empty words but reveals much to us about God and His desire for mankind.

> *48 And the Lord said to Moses that very same day, "Go up to this mountain of the Abarim, Mount Nebo, which is in the land of Moab opposite Jericho, and look at the land of Canaan, which I am giving to the sons of Israel as a possession.*
>
> *Then die on the mountain which you climb, and be gathered to your people, just as Aaron your brother died on Mount Hor and was gathered to his people,*
>
> *because you broke faith with Me among of the sons of Israel at the waters of Meribah-kadesh, in the Wilderness of Zin, and because you did not treat Me as holy among of the sons of Israel.*

Sadly for Moses, he showed just how much the people had worn him out because at Meribah Kadesh he did not carry out God's exact instructions.

In Numbers 20:8 God instructed him to, speak to the rock as they observe what was happening. But in 20:10 & 11 Moses in exasperation said, *"Hear now, you rebels! Must we bring water for you out of this rock?"* <u>*Then Moses lifted his hand and struck the rock twice with his rod;*</u> *and water came out abundantly, and the congregation and their animals drank.*

Here was an opportunity for the rebels to witness the power and authority of the word of God in action. For Moses to have spoken to the rock would have had a far greater impact on the people than in striking it for notice how the people, completely ignorant of the miracle that had just been performed, just got on and drank their fill. No grateful thanks, just fill themselves and their containers with water and allow their livestock to drink without any recognition of Moses or his God.

For Moses it meant that someone else would lead the people into the promised land, but one who was much younger and perhaps more resilient than he, although he too made mistakes.

At least Moses would be allowed to see the land in the distance before he died.

> *52For you shall see the land opposite you from a distance, but you shall not go there, into the land which I am giving to the children of Israel."*

22 FINAL BLESSING

Chapter 33

This is the final day and final oration delivered by Moses to the people he had led for over 40 years. From the plagues to their arrival at the river Jordan in preparation for them going over to take possession of the land of Canaan.

This blessing is just that. As a counterpart to the rather sombre tone of the song that filled the previous chapter with its admonition, depicting the calamities that were to befall the future wayward and disloyal Israel, this chapter is focused on blessing the people of Israel.

Like Jacob, when he was near to death, putting his hands on the sons of Joseph and prophesying over his other sons, so Moses was about to deliver ministerially a prophetic benediction to Israel before his death, not as a frail man like Jacob, but as a remarkably fit and healthy, renown and respected leader.

At the end he would walk the lonely ascent to the top of the mountain and depart from the human scene.

1 This is the blessing with which Moses the man of God blessed the sons of Israel before his death.

It is right that he should be referred to as *the man of God* because throughout his time as leader of the nation, it was his humility and unique closeness to God that identified both him and his outstanding style of leadership as the intermediary between God and the people.

It was His appointment by God in that unique experience in the wilderness at the burning bush and the longevity of his time as leader that undoubtedly promoted him to be head and shoulders above all other prophets and servants of God. It was why it was he of all past servants of God should appear before the Messiah on the mount of transfiguration.

His opening words of the blessing describe the awesome majesty of God, like the progressive splendour of the sun as it is revealed at the dawn of a new day, shining the light of His instructions for regulating everyday life amongst His people.

The Divine light of *the Lord came from Sinai, and* in all His Divine splendour *dawned on them from Seir,* (to the East of Sinai) scattering its beams on all adjoining regions as God directed Israel's onward march to Canaan. Led by the pillar of cloud by day and fire by night.

In shining *forth from Mount Paran,* which could be the mountain range forming the southern boundary of Canaan, demonstrates the Divine presence journeying with them, as He continually promised to do.

Moses told the people that God would go before them when they entered the land to put fear into the hearts of those that lived there allowing the Israelites to more easily overcome them.

Sinai, the moment when God and Israel were united in a covenantal relationship that would seal Israel's future as the chosen nation, through which God would manifest His divine glory; the moment of revelation, when the oracles of God were placed in their possession, to be used as a missionary tool in their role as the shop window of God, a role they neglected to properly fulfil.

Even though the majority of Israel would be ignorant of the full implication of the unique honour afforded them by God, in this present day a movement has been started for the realisation and acceptance that the Jesus of Nazareth, so despised for over two thousand years, really was the long awaited Messiah. Finally many have caught up with God's work with the church the Messiah set up through the disciples.

Many Jews have become furious that they have been fooled by the religious authorities over the generations that He was just an imposter and that the second testament was a book of lies and distortions, even though it was written mostly by Jews. The prophecy of Zechariah could soon be fulfilled:

"And I will pour on the house of David and on the inhabitants of Jerusalem the Spirit of grace and supplication; then they will look on Me whom they pierced. Yes, they will mourn for Him as one mourns for his only son, and grieve for Him as one grieves for a firstborn (Zech. 12:10)

It is interesting that before the battle of Jericho, Joshua was met by the commander of the armies of the Lord (Josh. 5:13 – 15). So when we read, *and He came from among ten thousand holy ones* it would imply the Lord coming forth from the angelic host that surrounds His throne (Ps. 68:17; 2 Chron. 18:18; Dan. 4:35; Lk. 2:3).

At His right hand was a flaming fire, a law, for them.

This could well be a reference to the giving of the law on Mount Sinai, and the penalties for disobedience, although the law was given in love in order for them to live a live worthy of Him.

3 Indeed, He loves the people;

There is no doubt that God has always loved the people He chose and with whom He entered into covenant relationship, indeed God showed that love by the way He continued to support and nurture them in spite of their waywardness.

However, it is important to remember that in creating Adam and Eve, God created all their descendants, not just the people of Israel, and therefore the salvation He offered and offers still, is for all mankind, not just for Israel.

Why would God send His only Son to die other than to allow all those, both Jews and Gentiles wanting to come back to Him, the opportunity to receive full salvation through the forgiveness of their sins, unless He was a God of love?

All those that have a heart for God
are in Your hand.
They sit at your feet
They accept and receive direction from You.

We cannot think of God other than we realize the whole purpose of choosing Israel was as a conduit through which He could reach out to the whole of mankind. In a way that is happening right now because of the study provided by this book which seeks to open up the scriptures to those new to the First Testament and to the Judaic/Christian faith. It could be said that All *those that have a heart for God,* sit down at His feet in order to learn of Him, as scholars at the feet of a renowned teacher in order to receive instruction and direction.

The law is crucial to that teaching, because it forms the basis of the way we live our lives.

> *4 Moses commanded us with a law,*
> *An inheritance for the assembly of Jacob.*

The law of Moses, the Torah, was an inheritance that could not be spent but was a resource from which much learning could be obtained, something that was passed down through the generations, even to us who have been granted access to the promises of God.

> *5 The Lord was King in Jeshurun (Israel),*
> *When the heads of the people were gathered,*
> *The tribes of Israel together.*

At that moment whilst at Sinai the supreme rule of God was established over Israel, and even when the people demanded a human king, ultimately God was never dethroned, only set aside until the Lord Jesus became both King and high priest.

Reuben

> *6 May the descendants Reuben live and not die out,*
> *But let his men be few."*

Living on the east side of the river Jordan, the tribe was exposed to constant attack by many enemies. At the first census at the time of Moses, the number of men able to bear arms was 46,500 (Num. 1:21). At the next census to decide land allocation that number had dropped to 43,730 (Num. 26:7).

According to the book of Numbers chapter 32, the people saw the land that it was good for grazing and requested land ownership right there. However it was not only exposed to other nations wanting to graze their cattle, but also to marauders. Memories of Lot and his choice of land.

In King David's time much of their territory was conquered by the Moabites, and by the nineth century BC, the tribe of Reuben had disappeared from the map. And as we know that area ultimately became Transjordan and dominated by Islam.

Judah

> 7 And Moses said this about Judah:
> "Hear, O Lord, the voice of Judah,
> And bring him to his people.
> With his hands he contended for them,
> And may You be a help against his enemies."

According to Jacob, Judah was to become the lead and kingly tribe. The tribe seems to have taken the lead role in taking possession of the unconquered areas of the land of Canaan, and at one point became isolated from the other tribes, surrounded by hostile Canaanites who were unlikely to have been pleased by what Israel was doing, hence the call for Divine intervention in order to *bring him to his people.*

Simeon

What is particularly interesting about Simeon is that his name is omitted here, and when Jacob prophesied over Simeon he was treated with Levi because, to the despair of Jacob the two men deceived and then brought about a great slaughter as Shechem (Gen. 36).

The two men were described by Jacob as instruments of cruelty, *let not my soul enter their council.* (Gen. 49:5 – 7).

This could well have been a prophetic announcement that both Simeon and Levi would not enjoy individual territory in the future. Simeon's descendants finally took possession of nineteen unconnected cities in the land allotted to Judah.

Levi

8 Of Levi he said,
"Your Thummim and Your Urim
belong to Your holy one, Aaron,
Whom You tested and proved at Massah,
With whom You contended at the waters of Meribah;
9 Who says of his father and mother,
'I did not consider them';
Nor did he acknowledge his brothers,
Nor did he regard his own sons,
For the priests have observed Your word,
And kept Your covenant.

There is no doubt that the Levitical priests had a difficult task because they were to separate themselves from the community in order to focus on their role as ministers of God.

As high priest, Aaron wore the breastplate in which were the *Thummim and Urim,* used to decide problems. This might be considered a lottery as to which the high priest took out of the pouch first, but God was able to direct the high priest to take out the right one. Little seems to be known about this matter, but it was pertinent at the time the stones were used.

At Massah and Meribah, Aaron was as much in the line of fire from the angry rebels as was Moses, and his responsibility in bearing the *Thummim and Urim* on his chest, must have been a heavy weight to bear especially after the death of his two older sons when he was not allowed to grieve. Be in no doubt that in his role as high priest he was on his own before God, Moses had other responsibilities.

The Levitical priests could show no favouritism towards family and friends, but with singlemindedness, and even-handedness carry out the will and purposes of God[63].

We need to put this into context because of the words of our Lord

Do not think that I have come to bring peace on the earth;
I have not come to bring peace, but a sword.

---

[63] See Exodus 32:26 – 29 to see just how focused on God they had to be.

Unless we accept that there is spiritual warfare going on constantly not only in the heavenlies but also here on earth, then we will never understand the position of the priests and believers today. For we have a choice of not just believing in God, but serving Him.

Belief is of no use whatsoever except we make a decision to leave the call of the world and give ourselves entirely to God.

It might seem barbaric that the Levites were called upon to put on their swords and kill even their nearest relatives, but a spiritual cancer had broken out. Those that preferred to do battle with God, driven on by the forces of Satan, wanted to stop God's plan of salvation that would ultimately allow God to provide and eternal antidote to sin, the blood of His Son.

This was a battle between God and Satan, and the realization of God's ultimate goal which was the provision of eternal life for believers or a life in hell for unbelievers. People cannot sit on the fence, everyone must make a decision to follow Christ or reject Him, there is no middle way.

The fight is on because Satan will use even members of our family to stop us being useful members of the church that Jesus Christ established by His death, having prepared the disciples to take on the role of attracting men, women and children to put their complete faith in Him. Therefore we must be resolute in rejecting anyone who opposes God's work in us and through us.

The priests under Aaron had to not just have a heart for God, but a determination to serve Him. Jeremiah, born into a priestly family, was spurned by his family and hated by his relatives just because He was sensitive to God and they were not.

So what did Jesus mean when He spoke of bringing conflict even into the family? He wanted all those who might want to believe in Him but still have a relationship with their family even though their family were active unbelievers or disbelievers, to know that conflict was bound to occur.

For the believer to progress and grow in the Lord they had to take a stand. There was no point in there being any animosity, if the family could live amicably together even though they had different beliefs.

It was only when the relationship with family or relatives became acrimonious, that the believer had to make a decision regarding their future accommodation and relationship with the family and friends. It is all about the division of belief and unbelief.

For instance if a son became a believer and the father told him to give up the whole idea, then the son has to stand his ground. Don't provoke, but respond to provocation.

> *For I have come to set a man against his father, and a daughter against her mother, and a daughter-in-law against her mother-in-law; and a man's enemies will be the members of his own household in the event where one believes and another does not.*

With regard to the incident in Exodus, there was an occasion where some were rebelling against God that could completely upset God's plan to establish Israel as His chosen people in accordance with His promises to Abraham and His desire to develop the situation where His Son could come to the earth and provide not only teaching from God but also new eternal life to the seeker.

The rebels were of the Devil and therefore needed to be silenced, so they would not destroy the remarkable work of God to change the lives of men and women then and even in the present age. They were rightly killed because of their rebellion, and would be rewarded by being assigned to hell.

What the priest were there to do was to:

> *10 Jacob Your judgments*
> *And Israel Your law.*
> *They shall put incense before You,*
> *And whole burnt offerings on Your altar.*
> *11 O Lord, bless Levi's ability to serve you,*
> *And accept and take pleasure in the work of his hands;*
> *Strike the loins of those who rise up against him,*
> *And of those who hate him, so that they do not rise again."*

The priests were there to explain the law of God to the people, and to officiate at the temple, dealing with the various sacrifices brought by the people.

Sadly their descendants, even up to the time of their Messiah, showed little regard for the importance of their role before either God or the people.

Benjamin

12 Of Benjamin he said,
"May the beloved of the Lord dwell in safety by Him;
He shields and covers him all the day long,
And he dwells between His shoulders."

Benjamin, was the second son of Rachel so loved by Jacob that when he was deceived into marrying Leah was prepared to serve another seven years for her. Sadly she died in childbirth which meant that Joseph and Benjamin became particularly precious to Jacob.

Jacobs attention was directed to Benjamin when he was deceived into thinking that Joseph, the only son that shared a similar dedicated love for God, had been killed by wild animals.

Jacob's love for the two sons of Rachel is reflected in God's love for the whole of Israel because God enabled the unloved Leah to bare six sons, with Judah being chosen as the tribe of kings and the Messiah.

Although, in the time of Judges the tribe of Benjamin was almost wiped out (Jdgs. 21), it is interesting that it was in the territory of Benjamin that the temple was built, and of course Jerusalem has forever been where God has placed His name.

Joseph[64]

13 And of Joseph he said[65],
"Blessed of the Lord be his land,
With the precious things of heaven,
with the dew (cf. Gen. 27:28),
And from the deep water
that crouches beneath and springs up,
With the precious fruits of the sun[66],

---

[64] See The Tent of the Meeting, particularly Appendix F and The Origin of Life chapter 7
[65] See what Jacob said of Joseph in Genesis 49:22 – 26)
[66] All produce is dependent upon the sun, particularly those that need the sun to

And with the precious produce of the months.
With the best things of the ancient mountains,
And with the precious things of the everlasting hills[67],
With the precious things of the earth and its fullness[68],
And the favour and goodwill of Him who dwelt in the bush[69].
Let these blessings come upon the head of Joseph (Gen. 49:26),
And upon the crown of the head of him
who was separated from his brothers
and was distinguished as a prince among his brothers.
His glory is like a firstborn bullock[70],
And his horns like the horns of the wild ox[71];
With them he will gore the peoples[72],
All of them together, to the ends of the earth.
And those are the ten thousands of Ephraim,
And those are the thousands of Manasseh."

Zebulun

18 Of Zebulun he said,
"Rejoice, Zebulun, in your going out,[73]

---

ripen them.

[67] The luxuriantly growth of vegetation on the peaks and slopes of the hills and mountains.

[68] Concerning the productive plains.

[69] In memory of the burning bush from which God spoke to and commissioned Moses.

[70] Refers to Ephraim to whom Jacob gave precedence over his brother Manasseh. In 1 Chron. 12:30, 31, it gives the number of men of valour of Ephraim as 20,800 and of Manasseh as 18,000.

[71] The horns of a bull are symbolic of strength and for wild ox see Num. 23:22

[72] Ephraim became the dominant tribe in Israel, particularly after the 10/2 split. Manasseh remained the smaller of the two tribes.

[73] The territory of Zebulun was between lake Galilee and the sea, hence the reference to *going out,* possibly over the sea. It is also interesting that the men of Zebulun were men of action (1 Chron. 12:33), whereas the men of Issachar were more studious and of a religious persuasion (1 Chron. 12:32), hence the reference to tents, possibly meaning a more homely life and implying the study of the law and being religious teachers, very similar to the differences between Esau and Jacob. Whilst in exile in Babylon Ezra studied the Torah to the extent that his role amongst the returnees was crucial in purifying both the priests and the people (see Law & Grace chapter 26)

Issachar

> *19 And, Issachar, in your tents [at home].*
> *They will call the peoples to the mountain (Mount Carmel);*
> *There they will offer sacrifices of righteousness;*
> *For they will draw out the abundance of the seas,*
> *And the hidden treasures of the sand."*

It is very interesting that the tribes of Zebulun, the merchant and man of action, and Issachar, the studious and man of the spirit, are linked to indicate how important the two types of tribe were to the overall whole, after all Israel was a composite nation of many different types, each one complimenting the skills of the others.

Israel needed the merchants and the men of war as well as those skilled in agriculture and other trades. With the men of Issachar, what they learned from their studies they were able to pass on to others, the *sacrifices of righteousness*. Also from their studies they were able to manufacture glass.

Whereas the men of Zebulun were able to *draw out the abundance of the seas*.

Gad

> *20 Of Gad he said,*
> *"Blessed is He who enlarges Gad;*
> *He dwells as a lion,*
> *And tears the arm and the crown of the head.*
> *He selected the best land for himself,*
> *Because a lawgivers portion was reserved there;[74]*
> *Yet he came with the leaders of the people;*
> *He carried out the righteous will of the Lord,*
> *And His ordinances with Israel."*

Gad was praised for his foresight in being the first tribe to be allocated the first portion of land and by Moses himself (Num. 32:1); although in the present day, as with the tribe of Reuben, it is no longer part of Israel.

---

[74] The meaning of this line is uncertain

It was the largest portion (*Blessed is He who enlarges Gad*) being the territory of Sihon, king of the Amorites (tearing *the arm and the crown off the head*), on the East bank of the river.

The men of Gad, crossed the river and helped the other tribes obtain their own territory, thus carrying *out the righteous will of the Lord, and His ordinances with Israel*

Dan

> 22 *Of Dan he said,*
> *"Dan is a lion's cub,*
> *That leaps forth from Bashan."*

In the blessings of Jacob, Dan was compared to a serpent because of his mischievous subtlety. Moses saw him, as represented by his descendants, as a lion cub for their agility [nimbleness and adventurous spirit for which the tribe of Dan was celebrated — as was Sampson], leaping forth from the crevices and caves in the rocks of Bashan, which was a land celebrated for the size and strengths of its livestock (Deut. 32:14)

Naphtali

> 23 *Of Naphtali he said,*
> *"O Naphtali, satisfied with favour,*
> *And full of the blessing of the Lord,*
> *Take possession of the sea of Galilee and the south."*

With their territory being to the West of the Sea of Galilee it had fruitful soil and a very good climate and the fruitfulness of the sea itself, one time known as Lake Tiberius.

Asher

> 24 *Of Asher he said,*
> *"More blessed than sons is Asher;*
> *May he be favoured by his brothers,*
> *Let him dip his foot in oil.*
> *Your strongholds will be iron and bronze,*
> *And as your days are, so will your strength, be.*

The name Asher means 'happy'. The allotted territory being by the sea in the North West, needed to be strongly fortified. But it was a good region for olive trees, hence the reference to oil.

God, Israel's sole security, prosperity & victory

In the final few verses following the blessing of the individual tribes, here Moses is using in more general terms that which was applicable to the whole nation.

Because God is Spirit, the author of all that exists, and having demonstrated to the nation all that He was capable of doing, it is no wonder that Moses, who was called God's friend because of the intimacy of their relationship, began this final part of his farewell discourse by not only acknowledging the supremacy of God, but also the fact that God had fully covenanted Himself with Jeshurun (Israel).

What is more Moses wanted to emphasize God's desire and ability to help and protect the nation, likening Him to a king on his chariot, riding upon the heavens to bring Israel victory.

> 26 There is none like the God of Jeshurun (Israel),
> Who rides the heavens to your help,
> And through the skies in His majestic glory.

With the nation having signed an eternal covenant with God, He alone had become their security and dwelling place for all generations.

> Lord, You have been our dwelling place in all generations.
> (Ps. 90:1)

Future generations were to find out just how true this was when they cried out to Him because of the tragedy that had befallen them, be it through invasion or exile.

> 27 The eternal God is your refuge and dwelling place,
>
> And underneath are the everlasting arms;

This told the people that God's strength never fails. Because God's is enthroned above the heavens, He cannot be considered in human terms, but He has demonstrated His presence throughout their wilderness wanderings by the pillar of cloud by day and fire by night.

My flesh and my heart fails: but God is the strength of my heart,
and my portion forever. Ps. 73:26

My flesh longs after you in a spiritually dry and thirsty land, where
there is no water (Spirit) (Ps. 63:1)

When you pass through the waters, I will be with you;
And through the rivers, they will not overwhelm you.

When you walk through fire, you will not be burned,
Nor will the flame scorch you. (Is. 43:2)

Although these verses express the experiences of those of future generations, there is no doubt that had the people in general been more aware of all that God had done for them, including passing through the waters of the Red Sea, and the constant supply of food and water, they would realize for themselves just how God dependent they had become, even to driving out the enemy from before them.

28 So Israel dwells in safety and security,
The fountain of Jacob alone and secluded,
In a land of grain and new wine;
His heavens also drop down dew.

In their preparation to go over the Jordan to begin to possess the land, there lay before them an incredible future all the while they placed themselves under His care, acknowledging Him as their God and protector.

Sadly as the book of Judges so clearly identifies, they did not last long in their ideal land before their propensity to wander away from God brought them into conflict amongst themselves and laid them open to the aggression of other nations.

The dwelling in safety and security became an imaginary goal that they could not seem to achieve.

29 Happy and blessed are you, O Israel;
for who is like you, a people saved by the Lord.

Such remarkable words should have made a deep impression on the people to go forward into the future with complete confidence. They were, not through anything they had done to deserve it, a unique people, living in the care of a unique God. They were saved by the Lord, not just physically but, had they attended to their duties responsibly, spiritually also. There was no other nation on earth so favoured as they were but it is the way of those that have received such treatment not to fully acknowledge or appreciate it.

The God of all creation. The only God with any power who was both willing and able to protect them from all other nations so that they could point to the Lord their God and explain to those other nations that their lives and future was in Him and Him alone. But they clearly did not, could not appreciate the full significance of it.

What a witness that would have been had they done so. As it was the other nations saw their ups and downs, realizing that it was their unstable and irresponsible behaviour that caused their many downfalls.

The Shield of your help,
And the Sword of your majesty!

How sad the earnest desire and dream of Moses was to become a nightmare of which he would fortunately be unaware, although it was most likely he suspected, knowing what they were like.

What believers of today need to consider is:

- How like the Israelites am I?

- Do I blow hot and cold?

- Do I fully trust God with my life and future, without reservation?

- Am I likely to go off on my own, rejecting God?

- Am I willing to commit my life fully and completely into His care, however uncertain and difficult the future might look at any particular time?

With the words of the Song of Moses still ringing in their ears, these words of blessing fell rather flat.

Your enemies will cringe before you,
And you will tread on their high places,
tramping down their idolatrous altars.

Although this was the original objective of them going into the land and was achieved from time to time, sadly they ended up putting up more altars and places of idol worship on high places than they trampled down.

23 MOSES' LAST JOURNEY

Chapter 34

We each appear on this earth as a single unit, and live before God throughout our lives as an individual, until finally we die alone, however many or few people there are with us when we leave our bodies. Married couples become one flesh, but spiritually they remain individuals before God, each with their own issues.

Then at some stage in the future as individuals we appear before the Great White Throne alone, to be separated with either the sheep or the goats.

Moses, knowing that he was due to leave this life, walked up the mountain, as he had done many times before, to present himself to the God who had called him to service to be taken into God's care, freed at last from all the stresses and strains of the leadership he had endured and so masterfully accomplished.

For the people, he was all they knew. He had become like a father figure providing a figurehead of security and firm leadership. He was the ultimate judge of family and intertribal affairs, who took firm control when required. The future for the nation seemed far more uncertain without him as leader.

He had been God's chosen from the start. The Levitical son of slaves, and left to the mercy of the Nile. Adopted by a royal princess and brought up as a prince of Egypt and trained by top Egyptian scholars, he became a man with royal authority. Yet his Hebrew roots never left him.

After murdering an Egyptian and scorned by those he tried to help, he was led into the wilderness where he learned to shepherd his father-in-law's flock of sheep, learning first hand all about the terrain through which he would lead the people of God.

Having trained him, at the appointed time, God attracted Moses to the area in which he would observe the bush that was burning but was not consumed.

Imagine the quietness and loneliness of the shepherd in that unpopulated expanse, with just the sound of bleating sheep, and the cry of lambs. The heat of the day and the cold of the night when temperatures could plunge to below zero.

He was his own man, with his own private thoughts, totally free from the problems of personal relationships and responsibilities, except when he returned to his father-in-law's tented encampment, to be with his wife and children.

However, with his training over, and the children of Israel crying out to be saved from their servitude, God called this man who had lost the sense of authority and power and become something of a recluse, unused to human contact and conversation, for a task from which he recoiled.

God refused to listen to his protestations causing Moses to finally concede and set off for Egypt, with his wife and two sons. What is particularly interesting is the way in which God almost killed him because he had not had his sons circumcised, but his wife saved the day by doing the job herself. From that point on his wife and children are no longer mentioned.

At first it was Aaron who was the mouthpiece for his younger brother, until the long forgotten disciplined authority of the young prince of Egypt once more came out and from then on Moses became the strong authoritative leader of the nation. However he never lost the humility and quietness of the shepherd along with the need to be on his own.

But it was the remarkable and intimate relationship that he had with God that brought about the greatest change in Moses. His times in the original tent pitched in an isolated area where he could be alone with God, to refresh his spirit which allowed him to cope with the punishing schedule of leading and judging the people, most of whom were not prepared to seek after God for themselves, but were prone to respond to those with a discontented and rebellious nature.

Finally, at the age of 120, although still incredibly fit, for *his eyesight was not dim, nor his natural strength abated*, and without any of the normal signs of a man of his age, yet he had been worn down mentally and spiritually by all the belligerent troublemakers, and was now being called home by his God, who he had met many times and with whom he had a special face to face relationship.

It was still a sad parting and the people grieved, over his disappearance, *So the sons of Israel wept for Moses in the plains of Moab for thirty days; then the days of weeping and mourning for Moses were ended.*

The time for mourning was over, and the future lay ahead with a new man in charge.

> *Now Moses went up from the plains of Moab to Mount Nebo, to the top of Pisgah, that is opposite Jericho. And the Lord showed him all the land, from Gilead to Dan, and all Naphtali and the land of Ephraim and Manasseh, and all the land of Judah to the western sea (Mediterranean Sea), and the Negev (south country) and the plain in the Valley of Jericho, the city of palm trees, as far as Zoar.*

And so Moses was able to see the promised land to which he had journeyed with such expectation and many frustrations. But he was not allowed to put a foot on it, that honour was left to his young lieutenant.

> *Then the Lord said to him, "This is the land which I swore to Abraham, Isaac, and Jacob, saying, 'I will give it to your descendants.' I have let you see it with your eyes, but you shall not go over there."*
>
> *So Moses, the servant of the Lord, died there in the land of Moab, according to the word of the Lord. And God buried him in the valley in the land of Moab, opposite Beth-peor; but no man knows where his burial place is to this day.*

The laying on of hands[75] is an important act that continues to this very day. When a sinner brought an animal sacrifice they laid hands on the head of the animal to symbolically transfer their sin to the animal. In this case Moses laid hands on Joshua to pass on to him the spirit of wisdom that God had given to him.

---

[75] 1 Tim. 4:14

Now Joshua the son of Nun was filled with the spirit of wisdom, for Moses had laid his hands on him; so the sons of Israel listened to him and did as the Lord commanded Moses.

Since that time no prophet has risen in Israel like Moses, whom the Lord knew face to face, there was none equal to him in all the signs and wonders which the Lord sent him to perform in the land of Egypt against Pharaoh, all his servants, and all his land, and in all the mighty power and all the great and terrible deeds which Moses performed in the sight of all Israel.

And so ended the remarkable life of a remarkable prophet, remembered throughout the First and Second Testaments.

ABOUT THE AUTHOR

After an electrical engineering apprenticeship in the Royal Navy, Peter served on ships in different parts of the world, finally being responsible for the weapons maintenance department of a frigate and lecturing to trainee officers on weapon control engineering. He also spent two years at the Royal Navy's training college in Fareham, Hampshire instructing on underwater weapon and defence systems.

Leaving the service at 30 in 1969, Peter worked as a quality engineer for the British Aircraft Corporation at Filton, Bristol on spacecraft and guided weapon systems before moving to R. A Lister (Diesels) where he became a technical author in 1984. He then worked as a contract author, mostly in the nuclear power generation before finally retiring in 2011.

A Methodist Local Preacher for 20+ years, he started to serve as an official prison visitor from 01.01.1990 and at the end of 1993 attending the prison chapel with his wife Joan in support of prisoners wanting to change their lives. Retiring from that work in 2016 he and his wife continued to worship at the prison until January 2020. He still supports a number of released prisoners.

At the prison Peter met a Jew named Derek who had become a Christian. On his release to the local community, Peter was able to help Derek adjust to a new life of going straight.

Derek first asked Peter to write on scripture in 2002, after which Derek's brother Aaron, a rabbi serving in the USA, came under the influence of Peter's writing and became a Christian. Aaron asked him to write first on the book of Revelation and then on the subject of Moses' Tent of the Meeting, which he self-published early 2011.

There are 21 books on Amazon as eBooks and paperback.

Peter was married 30th December 1961 and has three sons and six grandchildren.

The explanation of how he came to write his books is contained in "A Tale of Three Men."

Printed in Great Britain
by Amazon

58766028R00251